THE SPORTS RULES BOOK

SECOND EDITION

Human Kinetics

with Thomas Hanlon

HUMAN KINETICS

Library of Congress Cataloging-in-Publication Data

Human Kinetics (organization)

    The sports rules book / Human Kinetics with Thomas Hanlon.   2nd ed.

       p.   cm.

Includes bibliographical references (p.   ).

    ISBN 0-7360-4880-4

  1. Sports--Rules.   I. Hanlon, Thomas W.   II. Title.

    GV731.H85   2003

    796--dc21

                                   2003008871

ISBN-10: 0-7360-4880-4

ISBN-13: 978-0-7360-4880-4

The Web addresses cited in this text were current as of September 5, 2003, unless otherwise noted.

Developmental Editor: Wendy McLaughlin; **Assistant Editor:** Kim Thoren; **Copyeditor:** KLM Words; **Proofreader:** Coree Clark; **Permission Manager:** Toni Harte; **Graphic Designer:** Robert Reuther; **Graphic Artist:** Sandra Meier; **Art and Photo Manager:** Dan Wendt; **Photographer (interior):** Human Kinetics, unless otherwise noted; **Illustrators:** Sarah Wolfsmith, Tim Offenstein, Roberto Sabas; **Printer:** United Graphics

Human Kinetics books are available at special discounts for bulk purchase. Special editions or book excerpts can also be created to specification. For details, contact the Special Sales Manager at Human Kinetics.

Printed in the United States of America

10   9   8   7   6   5   4

Human Kinetics

Web site: www.HumanKinetics.com

United States: Human Kinetics
P.O. Box 5076, Champaign, IL 61825-5076
800-747-4457
e-mail: humank@hkusa.com

Canada: Human Kinetics
475 Devonshire Road Unit 100, Windsor, ON N8Y 2L5
800-465-7301 (in Canada only)
e-mail: orders@hkcanada.com

Europe: Human Kinetics
107 Bradford Road, Stanningley, Leeds LS28 6AT, United Kingdom
+44 (0) 113 255 5665
e-mail: hk@hkeurope.com

Australia: Human Kinetics
57A Price Avenue, Lower Mitcham, South Australia 5062
08 8277 1555
e-mail: liaw@hkaustralia.com

New Zealand: Human Kinetics
Division of Sports Distributors NZ Ltd.
P.O. Box 300 226 Albany
North Shore City
0064 9 448 1207
e-mail: info@humankinetics.co.nz

CONTENTS

CONTRIBUTORS

Alpine Skiing
John Yacenda
Ski and Snowboard Instructor

Archery
Catherine Spears
National Archery Association of the United States

Australian Football
Jack Halbert
South Australian National Football League

Badminton
Sergei Krasnyanski
Illini Badminton Intercollegiate Sports

Baseball
Emily McElheny
Little League Baseball

Basketball
Tony Oliver
Basketball Fundamentals

Bowling
Chris Cooper
American Bowling Congress

Boxing
Steve Ross
USA Boxing

Canoeing and Kayaking
Volker Bernardi
International Canoeing Federation

Cricket
Peter Hanlon
Australian Cricket Board

Cross-Country Skiing
Linda Johnson
U.S. Ski Team

Curling
Rick Patzke
United States Curling Association

Cycling
Asker Jeukendrup
High-Performance Cycling

Diving
Ron O'Brien
U.S. Diving National Technical Directory

Equestrian
Marie Murphy
USA Equestrian

Fencing
Chris Cuddy
U.S. Fencing Association

Field Hockey
Vern Stenlund
High-Performance Skating for Hockey

Figure Skating
Bob Dunlop
U.S. Figure Skating Association

Football
John Adams
American Football Coaches Association

Golf
Matthew Marcus
U.S. Golf Association

Gymnastics
Bo Morris
USA Gymnastics

Handball
Vern Roberts
U.S. Handball Association

Ice Hockey
Chuck Milky
USA Hockey

Judo
Katrina Davis
United States Judo Association

Karate
Pat Hickey
USA Karate Federation

Lacrosse
Brian Logue
U.S. Lacrosse

Netball
Chris Burton
Netball Australia

Racquetball
Jim Winterton
Racquetball Fundamentals

Roller Hockey
Jake Mersberger
USA Roller Sports

Rowing
Brett Johnson
U.S. Rowing

Rugby Union
Bruce Hale
Rugby Tough

Soccer
Douglas Wood
SAY Soccer

Softball
Kathy Veroni
Off the Bench

Speed Skating
Katie Marquard
U.S. Speed Skating

Squash
Faraz Hussain
Illinois Squash Racquet Association

Swimming
Mike Unger
USA Swimming

Synchronized Swimming
Jennie Harper
U.S. Synchronized Swimming

Table Tennis
Wendell Dillon
USA Table Tennis

Taekwondo
Tom Seaborne
Taekwondo Techniques & Tactics

Team Handball
Christian Latulippe
USA Team Handball

Tennis
Jim Brown
Sports Talent

Track and Field
Patrice Wilson
Illinois chapter USA Track & Field

Triathlon
BJ Hoepter Evans
USA Triathlon

Ultimate
Stephanie Kurth
Ultimate Players Association

Volleyball
Marjorie Mara
USA Volleyball

Water Polo
Terence Ma
USA Water Polo

Water Skiing
Ben Favret
Bennett's Water Ski School

Wrestling
Ted Witulski
USA Wrestling

INTRODUCTION

The Sports Rules Book, Second Edition, is designed for sport administrators, coaches, physical education teachers, players, and fans who want to know a sport's basic rules and procedures, penalties, scoring system, playing area dimensions, and officials' signals—providing a concise yet clear overview of how a sport is played.

The reader-friendly format helps you understand the fundamental rules without getting bogged down in every minute detail. Inside you'll find overviews and rule descriptions of 47 sports popular in the United States and around the world. You'll find historical descriptions of how each sport was started and interesting statistics about the popularity of the sport worldwide. To be accurate, the field dimensions and terminology individual to each sport were maintained (i.e., metric versus English measurements). You will also find a conversion chart to help you convert between metric and English measurements.

Here's what you'll find in each chapter of *The Sports Rules Book:*

- A brief introduction that touches on the sport's origin and provides an overview of the sport's main features (for example, number of players, length of game, scoring, and how the game is played)
- A diagram and description of the playing area
- Useful terms that will help you understand the sport
- Descriptions of the sport's equipment
- Rules that pertain to the players and to the various aspects of the sport (e.g., pitching, batting, and base running in baseball)
- Information on the sport's officials, often including drawings of their signals
- For many of the sports, rule modifications to help teachers and sport administrators adapt the sport to make it more appropriate for younger and less-skilled players
- Organizations to contact for more in-depth rules

You can find comprehensive officiating rules and information for most sports by writing to the National Association of Sports Officials, 2017 Lathrope Avenue, Racine, Wisconsin 53405, or by calling the association at 262-632-5448.

The Sports Rules Book is not meant to be complete in its coverage of any sport. It is meant to provide the basic rules and procedures of a sport and to be practical, understandable, and concise, without sacrificing the essentials. *The Sports Rules Book* provides you with the information necessary to teach and play everything from soccer and softball to curling and cricket through fundamental instruction of the basics.

MEASUREMENT CONVERSIONS

English to metric		Metric to English	
	Multiply by		**Multiply by**
Feet	.3048006 m/ft	Meters	3.280833 ft/m
Feet	30.48006 cm/ft	Centimeters	.032808 ft/cm
Inches	2.540005 cm/in	Centimeters	.39370 in/cm
Inches	25.4000 mm/in	Millimeters	.0394 in/mm
Miles	1.60935 km/mi	Kilometers	.62137 mi/km
Ounces	28.349527 g/oz	Grams	.0352740 oz/g
Pounds	453.5924 g/lb	Grams	.00220462 lb/g
Pounds	.453592 kg/lb	Kilograms	2.2046223 lb/kg
Yards	.91440183 m/yd	Meters	1.093611 yd/m

C.R.C. Standard Mathematical Tables, 12th Edition, Chemical Rubber Publishing Company, 1959.

Information Please Almanac Atlas & Yearbook, 50th Edition, Houghton Mifflin Company, 1997.

To convert: Start with the measurement with which you are dealing. Multiply by the appropriate conversion factor using all the decimal places. If there is more than one choice of conversion factor, use the one that is closest in comparison (i.e., pounds and kilograms rather than pounds and grams, or feet and meters rather than feet and centimeters). In general, round the answer to the same number of places after the decimal as you had in the original number. For example, to convert 99 pounds to kilograms, look under "Pounds" in the English-to-metric column where it specifies the conversion in "kg/lb." Multiply 99 lb by .453592 kg/lb and the result is 44.905608 kg. Since you started with a whole number, you may also want to round the result to a whole number: 45 kg.

Common conversions

10 meters = 32.8 feet

100 meters = 328 feet

500 meters = 1,641 feet

10 feet = 304.8 centimeters

100 feet = 30.5 meters

10 inches = 25.4 centimeters

10 centimeters = 4 inches

20 millimeters = .79 inches

50 millimeters = 2 inches

10 inches = 254 millimeters

10 kilometers = 6.2 miles

5 kilometers = 3.1 miles

5 miles = 8 kilometers

5 ounces = 142 grams

100 grams = 3.5 ounces

5 kilograms = 11 pounds

500 grams = 1.1 pounds

100 pounds = 220.5 kilograms

20 yards = 18.3 meters

10 yards = 9.1 meters

Alpine Skiing

© Empics

Accounts of Alpine ski competition date back to the 6th century. Skiing competition began on a broader scale in the early 1800s; the sport was introduced to the United States in the mid-1800s by Norwegian immigrants. Early skis were made of wood and were laminated. By the early 1900s, skis had become shorter, and during the 1940s Alpine skis took on a more versatile shape. Today's skis offer many shapes and lengths to accommodate different styles of skiing, racing, and snow conditions.

Today there are more than 40 million Alpine skiers taking to more than 300 slopes in alpine resorts in more than 40 countries. Alpine skiing is popular in the United States, Europe, and numerous countries around the world. It consists of several disciplines, including downhill, slalom, giant slalom, super-giant slalom (super-G), parallel, team, and speed competitions.

Overview: In downhill, giant slalom, and super-G competitions, skiers start at intervals of 60 seconds. Slalom competitors begin at irregular intervals at the starter's command. Competitors must pass across the gate line with ski tips and both feet. If a competitor loses a ski without committing a fault, the tip of the remaining ski and both feet must pass the gate line. Competitors must cross the finish line on both skis, one ski, or with both feet (in case of a fall at the line). The time stops once any part of the competitor's equipment or body crosses the line.

TERMS

A **blocking pole plant** is a forceful placement of the ski pole's tip in the snow to slow progress.

The **edge angle** is the degree of angle between a ski's edge and the snow; a greater angle creates greater resistance to the pull of gravity.

An **edge set** is the equal edging of both the inside (uphill) and outside (downhill) skis to create a momentary or permanent stopping of one's progress.

Edging is the combination of edge angle; ankle, knee, and hip angulation; pressure and weight distribution; and steering that influences the degree of skidding of the skis while turning.

A **flat ski** is one that is not edged.

The **gate line** is the imaginary shortest line between the gate poles. In parallel slalom, the gate passage is correct when both the ski tips and feet pass the outside gate markers in the direction of the turn. If a competitor misses a gate, he is disqualified.

The **inside ski** is the one that's inside the arc of the turn.

The **outside ski** is the one that's outside the arc of the turn.

A **pole swing** is the preparatory movement of the pole forward that precedes a pole plant or pole touch; it's often used as a timing device for turning in rhythm.

A **sideslip** occurs when the skis slide sideways, under control, down the fall line.

A **sidestep** occurs when a skier lifts one ski and moves it sideways away from the other ski, and then moves the other ski next to the first ski to re-form the original parallel position.

RACING

Each discipline in alpine skiing has various course measurements and obstacles. Specifics for each one follow.

Downhill

The vertical drop for men ranges from 500 to 1,100 meters; for women, from 500 to 800 meters. Men's courses are marked with red gates; women's courses have either red gates or alternating red and blue gates. The gate width is at least 8 meters. The course must be free of large stones, tree stumps, and similar debris. Courses through wooded terrain must be at least 30 meters wide. Competitors are required to take part in official training on the course, which takes place on three separate days before the event. A downhill event may consist of one run or two runs. If the event has two runs, those runs take place on the same day.

Slalom

The vertical drop for men's courses ranges from 140 to 220 meters; for women's courses, from 120 to 200 meters. The gates alternate in color. Each gate must be between 4 and 6 meters wide. Men's courses have 55 to 75 gates, with exceptions allowing for as few as 52 and as many as 78. Women's courses have 45 to 65 gates, with exceptions allowing for as few as 42 and as many as 68. Successive gates must have at least .75 meter and no more than 15 meters between them.

At major competitions the course has a gradient of 20 to 27 new degrees. It may reach 30 new degrees in brief portions of the course. The course includes a series of turns that the competitors should be able to complete rapidly. The course must be at least 40 meters wide if two runs are set on the same slope. It must contain both horizontal (open) and vertical (closed) gates, as well as one to three vertical combinations consisting of three or four gates and at least three hairpin combinations.

The slalom start takes place at irregular intervals; on the starter's command to go, the competitor must begin within 10 seconds. Competitors take two runs on two different courses; usually both runs are taken on the same day.

Giant Slalom

The vertical drop for men's courses is 250 to 450 meters; for women's courses, 250 to 400 meters. A giant slalom gate consists of four slalom poles and two flags. Gates are alternately red and blue and are between 4 and 8 meters wide. Successive gates must be no greater than 10 meters apart. The course must be at least 30 meters wide and should present a variety of turns. A giant slalom competition consists of two runs. The runs may be held on the same course, but the gates must be changed for the second run. Both runs are usually held on the same day.

Super-G

The vertical drop for men's courses is 500 to 650 meters; for women's courses, 350 to 600 meters. A gate consists of four slalom poles and two flags; gates are alternately red and blue. They must be between 6 and 8 meters wide from inner pole to inner pole for horizontal (open) gates, and between 8 and 12 meters wide for vertical (closed) gates.

Men's courses have a minimum of 35 gates; women's courses have at least 30. The distance between the turning poles of two successive gates must be at least 25 meters. A super-G course is undulating and hilly with a minimum width of 30 meters. The competition consists of one run for each competitor.

Parallel Events

A parallel event is a competition where two or more competitors race simultaneously side by side down two or more courses that are as identical as possible. Competitions typically consist of 32 competitors, paired off as follows: 1st and 32nd; 2nd and 31st; and so on. (These placings are based on previous races.)

Each match consists of two runs; the two competitors change courses on the second run. The competitor with the lowest total time on the two runs advances; the other is eliminated. The second round also consists of two runs. Eight skiers from this round advance to the quarterfinals; four advance to the semifinals; and two advance to the final.

The vertical drop is between 80 and 100 meters. Each course has between 20 and 30 gates; the run-time of each race should be between 20 and 25 seconds. The first gate is between 8 and 10 meters from the start. The difference between the competitors' times—not each competitor's total time—is recorded at the finish. Difference is recorded in thousandths of a second.

EQUIPMENT

Poles are either rigid or flex-poles. Rigid poles have a diameter of 20 to 32 millimeters and have no joints. They are made of a nonsplintering material, such as plastic, and when set they must project at least 1.8 meters out of the snow. Flex-poles have a spring-loaded hinge; they must be used for all competitions except downhills.

A turning pole is the pole that is closest to the skier's line of travel in the gate. Turning poles for slalom, giant slalom, and super-G must be flex-poles. Slalom poles are red or blue and carry a flag that matches in color. In giant slalom and super-G competitions, two slalom poles, with a banner between them, make up one half of the gate; a like pair of slalom poles makes up the other half of the gate.

OFFICIALS

The chief of race controls the event and the officials. The chief of course is responsible for course preparation. The chief of timing and calculations coordinates the start and finish officials. The chief gate judge supervises the gate judges. The chief steward is in charge of safety precautions and keeping spectators off the course. A jury oversees adherence to race rules.

MODIFICATIONS

Children 13 and 14 years old may take part in a downhill competition. The maximum vertical drop is 400 meters for both boys and girls. Courses may have no jumps, sharp curves, or other special difficulties. For maximum vertical drops and number of gates, see table 1.1.

Table 1.1 Children's Drops and Gates

Classification	Event	Vertical drop (max. meters)	Number of gates
Children I	Slalom	140	32 to 45
Children II	Slalom	180	38 to 60
Children I	Giant slalom	300	15% of vertical drop +/- 3 gates
Children II	Giant slalom	350	15% of vertical drop +/- 3 gates
Children I	Super-G	250 to 350	25 to 10% of vertical drop
Children II	Super-G	280 to 400	28 to 10% of vertical drop

Adapted from International Ski Federation 1995.

ORGANIZATIONS

American Ski Association
P.O. Box 480067
910 15th Street, Suite 500
Denver, CO 80202
303-629-7669

U.S. Skiing
P.O. Box 100
Park City, UT 84060
801-649-9090
www.usskiing.com

2

Archery

© Photo courtesy of the National Archery Association

Archery began as a method of defense and as a way to hunt game. It evolved into a sport by the mandates of English kings, as a competition among the men who defended the crown. By the 17th century, tournaments were commonplace. In the United States, the first archery club was formed in Philadelphia in 1826.

Archery made brief appearances in the Olympic Games in the early 1900s and was readmitted to the Games in 1972 after enough countries had adopted international rules. Since 1972, technology has greatly advanced the equipment. Archery has become wedded to skiing in the sport of ski-archery and to running in arcathlon.

Objective: To score the highest number of points by shooting arrows into a target marked with rings worth various points.

Scoring: Determined by where the shaft lands in the target; rings are valued from 1 to 10 points.

Number of Players: Individuals or teams of three.

Number of Arrows per Archer: 36.

Length of Range: From 15 to 90 meters, depending on the category.

Length of Contest: An agreed-on number of rounds, or *ends* (see "Terms").

Overview: For an end consisting of three arrows, an archer has two minutes to complete shooting. For an end of six, a maximum of four minutes is allowed. In case of equipment adjustment, such as changing a bow string, additional time may be granted. Archers shoot in rotation and can shoot either from the longest to the shortest target or vice versa. Scores are entered for each arrow; the score is called out by the archer and checked by competitors.

RANGE

The shooting range is divided into lanes and is laid out so that shooting is done from south to north. Each lane has lines at right angles between the shooting line and the target; a lane can contain up to three targets. Men and women are separated by a clear lane of at least five meters.

A waiting line is set at least five meters behind the shooting line. No more than four competitors may shoot at one target. Each buttress is numbered and set at an angle of about 15 degrees from vertical. The distance is measured from the ground directly below the gold of each target to the shooting line. The center of the gold is about 130 centimeters above ground.

TERMS

An **end** is a series of either three or six arrows for each archer.

A **gold** is an arrow that lands in the center of the target. The outer portion of the gold is worth 9 points; the inner portion, 10.

A **round** is a series of ends—the total number of arrows that each archer shoots in the competition.

ARCHERS

Archery is a sport for people of all ages. Men, women, and children compete. The distances that archers shoot vary by category:

- Men 18+: 90 and 70 meters
- Junior boys up to age 18: 70 meters
- Women 18+: 70 and 60 meters
- Junior girls up to age 18: 70 meters
- Cadet boys and girls up to age 16: 70 meters
- Cub boys and girls up to age 14: 50 meters
- Bowman boys and girls up to age 12: 30 meters

SHOOTING

Shooting takes place in one direction only. Archers shoot from a standing position, without support, either with their feet straddling the shooting line (one foot in front of, one foot behind the line), or with both feet on the line.

When a signal is given to begin the time limit, archers may raise their bows and shoot. If archers shoot either before the signal to start or after the signal to stop, they forfeit their highest scoring arrow for that particular end. (In team competition, the highest scoring arrow for any member of the team—regardless of who committed the foul—is forfeited.)

A spent arrow is not counted as a shot if the competitor can touch it with her bow without moving her feet from shooting position, or if the target face or buttress blows over. The judges may compensate for lost time in such cases.

Shooters can receive no advice or instruction while they are on the shooting line, except to correct faulty equipment. (In the Olympic team event, however, the three teammates and the coach may talk to each other while one is on the shooting line.)

SCORING

Scores are checked by competitors, and, if assigned, by scorers. The score is determined by where the shaft lands in the target (see figure 2.1). No arrows are touched until the archer completes the end. Scoring takes place after every end. Here are rules that cover specific occurrences:

- **Shaft touching line:** If the shaft of the arrow is touching two colors, or a dividing line between two scoring zones, the higher value is awarded.

- **Bouncing off target:** Unless all arrow holes are marked when scored, subsequent arrows bouncing off or passing through the target will not be scored. If an arrow does pass through the target or bounce off another arrow, however, and its mark can be identified, it scores however many points it would have had it stuck in the target.

- **Landing in another arrow:** An arrow that lands in another arrow receives the same points as the first arrow.

- **Deflecting off another arrow:** An arrow that deflects off another arrow and lands in the target receives the points awarded for that portion of the target face. An arrow that rebounds off another arrow scores the point value of the arrow it struck as long as the damaged arrow can be identified.

- **Hitting another target:** An arrow hitting another target does not score any points.

EQUIPMENT

The target is made of straw mat or other material and has a target face of canvas, paper, or cloth. The target face has five concentric, colored zones arranged from the center outward as follows: gold, red, light blue, black,

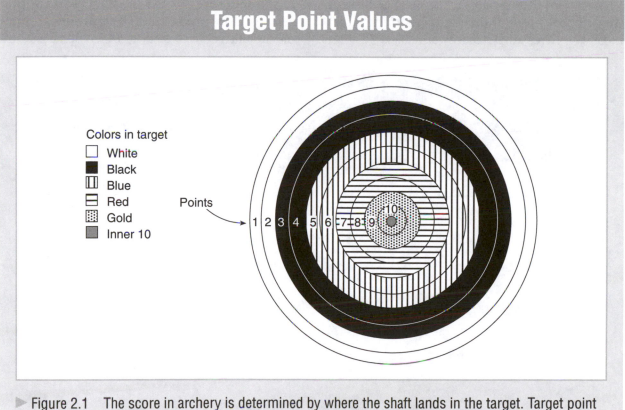

Target Point Values

Colors in target
- White
- Black
- Blue
- Red
- Gold
- Inner 10

Points

1 2 3 4 5 6 7 8 9 10

► Figure 2.1   The score in archery is determined by where the shaft lands in the target. Target point values are shown on the target.

Adapted from Fédération Internationale de Tir à l'Arc (FITA) 1994.

and white. Each color is divided by a thin line into two zones of equal width, resulting in 10 zones of equal width. Diameters for 122- and 80-centimeter target faces are shown in table 2.1.

The target face is supported on a buttress, which is at least two centimeters larger in diameter than the target face itself. Each buttress is numbered and set at an angle of about 15 degrees from vertical. The distance is measured from the ground directly below the gold of each target to the shooting line. Any portion of the buttress that can damage an arrow is covered.

A bow consists of a handle (grip), riser, and two flexible limbs ending in a tip with a string nock. A single bowstring is used; an adjustable arrowrest is also allowed. No crossbows are allowed. A bowsight or bowmark is permitted, but only one or the other may be used at one time. A bowsight may not incorporate any magnifying lens or electronic devices to aid in sighting.

Arrows of any type may be used as long as they do not cause undue damage to the target faces or buttresses. An arrow consists of a shaft with a head, a nock, fletching, and, if desired, cresting.

Finger protectors, such as tips, gloves, or tape, are permitted, but they cannot include any device that aids in holding, drawing, or releasing the string. Field glasses may be used to spot the arrows.

OFFICIALS

Officials include a competition director, director of shooting, and judges.

MODIFICATIONS

Archery can be modified in a number of ways. The following are among the most common.

Field Archery

In field archery the archer takes on the terrain as well as the target. A course is set up with 24 targets that are marked with the distance to the shooting line. The distances to another 24 targets are unmarked. Three arrows are shot on each target for a total of 144. The targets are

Table 2.1 Diameters for Target Faces		
Target zone	122-cm face (cm)	80-cm face (cm)
Inner 10	6.1	4
10	12.2	8
9	24.4	16
8	36.6	24
7	48.8	32
6	61.0	40
5	73.2	48
4	85.4	56
3	97.6	64
2	109.8	72
1	122.0	80

Adapted from Fédération Internationale de Tir à l'Arc (FITA) 1994.

placed with such difficulty that the shots do not resemble target archery. Many of the shots are made uphill or downhill and require consideration for obstacles. Field events are held for the recurve (Olympic) bow, compound bow, and barebow divisions.

Flight Archery

Shooting for distance is the objective of flight archery. Two types of arrows, regular flight and broadhead flight (arrows with cutting heads, suitable for hunting), are used and can be combined with many types of bows: standard recurve and compound bows, crossbows, flight bows that have an extended handle and a large overdraw, "primitive" bows, and the "footbow." In a flight tournament, each archer shoots four ends of six arrows. Each end can be in a different class. A different bow can be used for each class or the archer can shoot the same bow for all four classes. Note that the world record for the footbow is more than a mile!

Clout Archery

Clout archery is a rarely practiced discipline that most archers take part in only for fun. Basically, it is a test of trajectory skill. The target, which is 15 meters in diameter, consists of five concentric circular scoring zones that are outlined on the ground. The innermost circle is worth five points, and scores decrease to one point in the outermost circle. Each senior recurve archer shoots 36 arrows at the target at a range of 165 meters for men, 125 meters for women; male compound shooters shoot 185 meters, females 165 meters. Youth rounds are identical, except that the distance is 125 meters.

Crossbow Archery

Crossbow events are held in target (indoor and outdoor) and clout. Outdoor target events are shot at a 60-centimeter, 10-ring multicolored target face. Indoor rounds are shot at a 40-centimeter, 10-ring target face.

Ski-Archery (Ski-Arc)

A relatively new discipline, ski-archery combines archery with cross-country skiing. It is performed much like the Olympic biathlon, which features rifle shooting instead of archery. Each archer carries bows in a backpack while skiing. The course is 12 kilometers long for men and 8 for women. One end of four arrows is shot every four kilometers, and, in one of those ends, the archer shoots from a kneeling position. Targets are 16 centimeters in diameter and are positioned 18 meters from the shooter. Each shot is either a hit or a miss. For every target missed, the archer must ski a 350-meter penalty circuit before leaving the target site. The first athlete to complete the course is the winner.

Arcathlon

A summer arcathlon event is a combination of target archery shooting and running. The athlete is required to run a course and stop at prescribed points to shoot at fixed targets. The typical course is between 5 and 12 kilometers. Athletes make three shooting stops, shooting four arrows at each. The typical event consists of a one-mile run followed by four arrows shot from a standing position, then another one-mile run followed by four arrows shot from the kneeling position, then another one-mile run followed by four arrows shot from the standing position.

Bows are normally stored at the shooting range, but competitors have the option of carrying them. Targets are 16 centimeters in diameter and are positioned 18 meters from the shooter.

3-D Archery

Targets in 3-D events are life-size replicas of a variety of wildlife. These events combine the skills of determining distance to the target, determining what part of the target to hit, and shooting. Most archers who compete in these events use a compound bow. Archers competing in the typical 3-D tournament walk a course and shoot 40 arrows at 40 different targets.

ORGANIZATIONS

National Archery Association of the United States
1 Olympic Plaza
Colorado Springs, CO 80909-5778
719-866-4576
www.usarchery.org

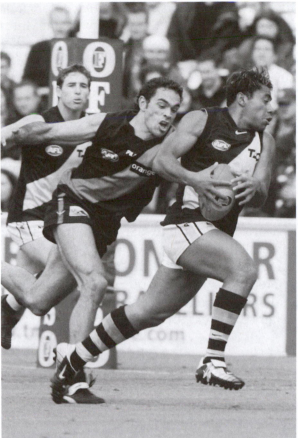

© Empics

3

Australian Football

Australian football was originally developed as a game unique to Australia, incorporating elements of rugby with some aspects of Gaelic (Irish) football. The game was initially devised as an off-season training regimen for Australian cricketers. It quickly evolved into a fast, rough, and free-flowing sport. The first official match was played in 1858 in Melbourne. Today, Australian football is played by more than 500,000 players at the senior, junior, amateur, and school levels. It was a demonstration sport at the Melbourne Olympic Games in 1956.

Objective: To score the most points.

Scoring: Goals are worth six points; behinds are worth one point (see "Scoring" on page 16).

Number of Players: 18 on each team, plus three interchange players each (four at the elite level).

Length of Game: Four 20-minute quarters of actual playing time; there are no timeouts. If a game is tied at the end of regulation, it is a draw; there is no over-time.

Overview: Play begins with the field umpire bouncing the ball in the center circle (see figure 3.1 on page 12); opposition players contest the ball. Until the ball has bounced, no player may enter the center circle, and only four players from each team are allowed in the center square.

Except for when a behind is scored or a ball goes out of bounds, possession of the ball is continually contested. Players advance the ball by kicking it, punching it, and running with it; throwing it is not allowed. Any player who runs with the ball must dribble it (bounce it or touch it to the ground) every 15 meters. Catching a kicked ball in the air after it has traveled at least 15 meters allows a player to take a free kick, without the risk of being tackled.

Players are freely interchangeable at any time. A runner conveys messages from the coach to the players in the game. This message bearer must stay away from the ball but can stay on the field as long as necessary.

FIELD

The field is oval shaped, usually between 110 and 135 meters wide and between 135 and 185 meters long (see figure 3.1; the smaller dimensions are common in football played at the junior level). Boundaries are marked with white lines. The center square is at midfield, measuring 45 meters square. The center circle is in the middle of this square; it measures 3 meters in diameter and is bisected by a lateral line extending 2 meters on either side of the diameter.

The goal square is 9 meters long and 6.4 meters wide. It is directly in front of the goal posts, which are set 6.4 meters apart on the boundary line and are at least 6 meters high. Two behind posts, each at least 3 meters high, are set 6.4 meters outside the goal posts. For the players' safety, the posts are padded up to 2 meters.

Many fields have two 50-meter lines drawn in semicircles 50 meters from the center of the goal line, to give the umpire a point of reference for marking off 50-meter penalties and to give spectators a means of assessing the distance of kicks for goal.

TERMS

The **backmen** are the six defenders across the full-back and half-back lines on a team's defensive half of the field.

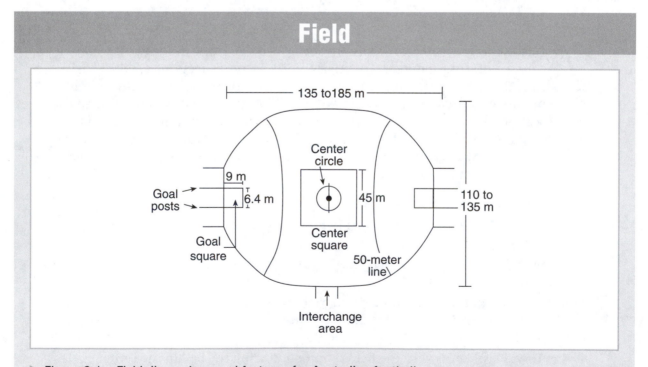

▶ Figure 3.1   Field dimensions and features for Australian football.
Adapted from Jacques 1994.

Ball up is the term that describes the moment when the umpire bounces the ball or tosses it up to restart the game after a stalemated scrimmage.

A **behind**, worth one point, is scored when the ball passes over the goal line after being touched or kicked by a defender, when it hits a goal post, or when it passes over the behind line without touching the behind post. A behind is sometimes called a *minor score*.

The **behind line** is the line drawn between a goal post and behind post.

The **behind posts** are the two smaller posts 6.4 meters outside the goal posts.

The **boundary line** marks the boundary of the playing field. The ball must go completely over the line to be out of bounds.

A **bump** occurs when a player uses his hip and shoulder to knock an opponent out of position. A bump is legal if it occurs within 5 meters of the ball and is not in the back or above the opponent's shoulders.

A **center bounce**, made by the field umpire, occurs in the center circle at the beginning of each quarter and after each goal.

The **center circle** is 3 meters in diameter; it is where the umpire bounces the ball. No player can be in the center circle until the umpire has bounced the ball (or tossed it up, if conditions are too wet to bounce it).

The **center square** is a 45-meter square in the center of the field. Only four players from each team can be in the center square for a center bounce.

When a player **drops** the ball, a free kick is given to the tackler, provided the tackle is legally executed.

A **drop punt** is the most common kick in Australian football. It travels end over end, spinning backward.

Followers are a team's ruckman, ruck rover, and rover.

A **foot pass** occurs when a player passes to a teammate by kicking.

A **free kick** is awarded for a variety of offenses (see "Free Kicks" on page 15).

A **goal**, worth six points, is scored when the ball is kicked over the goal line without the ball touching any player or a goal post.

The **goal line** is the line drawn between the goal posts.

The **goal mouth** is the area directly between the goal posts in front of the goal.

The two **goal posts** are 6.4 meters apart. A ball kicked between them scores six points.

The **goal square** is the rectangle measuring 6.4 meters by 9 meters in front of the goal posts from which the ball is kicked off after a behind is scored.

Handball is the term that describes the method of striking the ball with a clenched fist while holding it stationary with the other hand. This is also known as a *hand pass*.

When a player **holds** the ball after being tackled, without disposing of it legally in a reasonable amount of time, a free kick is awarded against him.

Interchange players are a team's substitutes. In senior football a team has three; at the elite level there are four interchange players.

A **mark** occurs when a player catches a kicked ball in the air, if the ball has traveled at least 15 meters and not been touched by another player.

The **oval** is the playing field, usually between 110 and 155 meters wide and between 135 and 185 meters long.

The **pockets** are the areas on the field close to the behind posts.

A **rocket handball** is a handball that spins end over end backward in flight.

A **runner** is a person who carries messages from the coach to the players during the game.

Shepherding occurs when a player uses his body to block an opponent from the ball or from a teammate in possession of the ball.

Shepherding farther than 5 meters from the ball is illegal.

A player **stands the mark** where his opponent has been given a free kick or marks (catches) the ball to ensure that the opponent does not play on and has to kick over the mark.

A player can **tackle** the player with the ball by grabbing him above the knees and below the shoulders.

A **throw-in** occurs when the ball has gone out of bounds. The umpire throws the ball in over his head toward the center of the ground.

A **torpedo punt**, or *screw punt*, is a kick that spirals the ball through the air.

A **tumble pass** is a handball that tumbles end over end forwards.

A **turnover** occurs when a team loses possession of the ball to the opposition.

PLAYERS

There are five general lines of play, with three players in each line. The remaining three players are the followers, who roam the whole ground, following the ball. These players are the ruck, rover, and ruck-rover.

The lines of play are shown in figure 3.2. Note, however, that players are free to move anywhere on the ground. There is no offside rule in Australian football.

PLAY

The basic rules of play include those for ball possession, restarting play, ball out of play, and free kicks.

Ball Possession

A player may hold the ball for an unlimited time if he is not held by an opponent. If the player with the ball is held by an opponent, he must immediately either kick the ball or handball it. The hand holding the ball must not move excessively; the motion is that of a quick punch. A player lying on the ball is considered to be in possession of it.

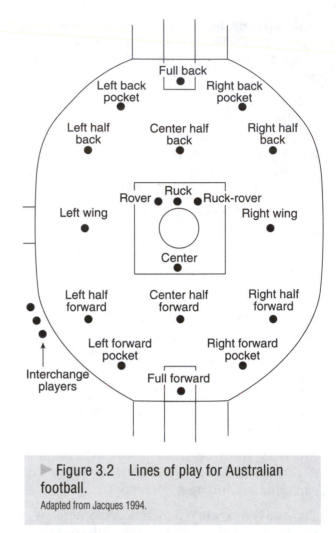

▶ Figure 3.2   Lines of play for Australian football.
Adapted from Jacques 1994.

A player running with the ball must bounce the ball or touch it to the ground every 15 meters. When a player catches a kicked ball that has traveled at least 15 meters in the air without being touched by another player, he has the choice of playing on immediately or kicking the ball from where he received it, without being impeded by any opponent.

Within 5 meters of the ball, a player may push an opponent in the chest or side or otherwise block the opponent's path to the ball (when he himself does not possess the ball). This technique is called "shepherding."

Restarting Play

After a goal is scored, the field umpire restarts play by bouncing the ball in the center circle, just as he did at the start of the game. Play is also restarted in these situations:

- When a team scores a behind, a player of the defending team kicks off from the kick-off square in front of the goal.

- When the ball bounces out of bounds, the umpire throws the ball over his head toward the center of the ground; if the ball is kicked out of bounds on the full (without first bouncing the ball in the field of play or being touched), the opposing team receives a free kick from the place where the ball went out.

- When no player in a pack can gain clear possession, the umpire bounces the ball where the scrimmage has occurred and play has stopped.

Ball Out of Play

The ball is out of play and the clock is stopped in these situations:

- When a team scores a goal; the clock starts when the ball is bounced in the center circle to restart play.

- When a team scores a behind; the clock starts when the ball is kicked in by a defender.

- When the ball goes out of bounds; the clock starts when the umpire throws the ball back into play, or when the team receiving a free kick returns it into play. Note: If any portion of the ball is on or over the boundary line in fair territory, it is still in play. A player can be out of bounds and in possession of the ball, but if the ball is not out of bounds, play is not stopped.

Free Kicks

An umpire may award a free kick against a player either with or without the ball. A player takes the kick (or hand passes) where the infringement occurred, unless the player is fouled after he has disposed of the ball. Then the kick is taken where the ball landed.

Infringements against a player with the ball may be called for

- not disposing of the ball within a reasonable time when correctly held (tackled) by an opponent,

- not disposing of the ball with a kick or a handball,

- kicking the ball out of bounds without it bouncing or being touched by another player,

- deliberately forcing or carrying the ball over the boundary line, or

- running farther than 15 meters without bouncing or touching the ball to the ground.

A free kick is also awarded when any player

- grabs or tackles an opponent above the shoulders or below the knees when the opponent has the ball;

- pushes an opponent in the back, charges an opponent, or trips or attempts to trip an opponent;

- bumps or punches an opponent trying to catch a kick in the air;

- shepherds an opponent farther than 5 meters from the ball; or

- enters the center square before the ball is bounced to restart play.

An infringement is also called if a ball that is kicked back into play after a behind is scored goes out of bounds without any player touching it. In this case the attacking team receives a free kick.

A 50-meter penalty is called against a player following a free kick if the player refuses to stand on the point indicated by the umpire, deliberately wastes time in returning the ball to the player who is to kick, holds the player who is to take the kick, or runs over the mark before or as the ball is kicked.

When a player has been infringed on, the umpire may choose not to award a free kick if the player or a teammate in possession of the ball has an advantageous position. In this case, the umpire immediately calls, "Play on," and play continues. If the player infringed on is injured, a teammate may take the free kick. This call is at the umpire's discretion.

SCORING

A ball kicked between the two larger goal posts is a goal worth six points if it does not touch a post or a player. A behind, worth one point, is scored when

- a ball passes between a goal post and a behind post;
- a ball hits a goal post, no matter whether it passes between the two larger posts or rebounds back onto the field; or
- a ball is carried over the scoring line between the goal posts.

To score, the ball must completely cross the goal line.

EQUIPMENT

The ball is made of leather—tan or reddish brown for day games, yellow for night games. Its length is 27 to 28 centimeters; diameter, 16.7 to 17.3 centimeters; and circumference, 72 to 73 centimeters by 54.5 to 55.5 centimeters. It weighs between 446.6 and 496.2 grams.

Uniforms consist of numbered guernseys (jumpers) with or without sleeves, socks, and boots with "sprigs," or stops. No padding is worn, but mouth guards and soft, protective headgear are allowed.

OFFICIALS

Three field umpires control the game. Each controls about a third of the ground. Two boundary umpires judge when the ball is out of the playing area. Two goal umpires, one at each end of the oval, judge the scoring of goals and behinds and record the progressive scores.

MODIFICATIONS

The following modifications are made by many junior leagues to encourage younger players' development:

- The number of interchange players is unlimited.
- Players may bounce a ball only once before disposing of it.
- Players may not soccer the ball off the ground (kick it while it's on the ground).
- After scrimmages the contest is restarted by throwing a ball up between two players of about equal size.
- Tackling is not permitted.
- The players who may score are limited, and scoring must take place within a certain zone.

ORGANIZATIONS

Australian Football League
GPO Box 1449N
Melbourne, Victoria 3001
Australia
61 (03) 9 643 1999
www.afl.com.au

4

Badminton

© Empics

A form of badminton, with players kicking a small, feathered shuttlecock, was first played in the 5th century B.C. in China. The game derives its name from its introduction in England in 1873 at a country estate called Badminton. By this time players were using rackets, and the shuttlecock was put into play after each point by servants (this is where the term "to serve" comes from). Badminton was introduced in America in the 1870s, grew in popularity in the 1920s and '30s, and became a full-medal Olympic sport in 1992.

Today badminton is enjoyed worldwide; international competitions are typically dominated by Indonesia, Malaysia, and China, as well as Korea and Denmark. In the United States, more than 7 million people play badminton each year, about 900,000 on a regular basis.

Objective: To score points by hitting a shuttlecock over the net and into the opponent's court so that the opponent cannot return it over the net and in bounds.

Scoring: One point for each successful hit that the opponent cannot return over the net and in bounds.

17

Number of Players: Either two players (singles) or four (doubles).

Game and Match Length: Games are to either 11 or 15 points, with the highest score winning. (Women's singles are played to 11 points; all other games are played to 15 points.) A match is the best two of three games.

Overview: Before a match, the winner of a coin or shuttle toss, or of a spin of the racket, chooses either the end of the court on which he will begin or else whether he will serve or receive first. Play is continuous from the first serve to the end of the match, except for a 90-second break between the first and second games, and up to a five-minute break between games two and three.

COURT

The court is 17 feet by 44 feet for singles matches and 20 feet by 44 feet for doubles

(see figure 4.1). The *short service line* is 6.5 feet from the net. The *long service line* for doubles is 12.75 feet behind the short service line. The long service line for singles is 2.4 feet behind the long service line for doubles. This is also the back boundary line. The *singles sideline* is 1.4 feet inside the sideline for doubles play. The cord net stretches across the center of the court, 5 feet high at center court and 5.08 feet high at the posts. The net is 2.5 feet in depth.

TERMS

A **fault** occurs in a number of situations (see "Faults and Lets"). A fault committed by the serving side gives the serve to the opponents; a fault by the receiving side gives a point to the serving side.

A **let** occurs when a point must be replayed. See "Faults and Lets" for such situations.

The **serve** is the hit that begins each play.

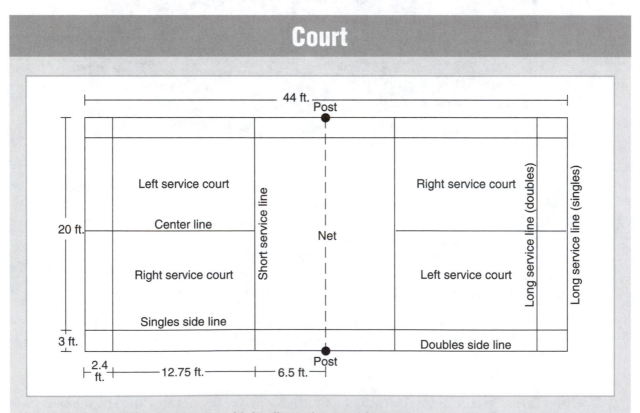

► Figure 4.1   A badminton court with its dimensions and features.
Adapted from White 1990.

The **shuttlecock**, also called the shuttle or the birdie, is the feathered object the players hit with their rackets.

PLAYERS

A singles match consists of one player on each side; a doubles match is contested by two teams of two players each. Players may not have play suspended to catch their breath or recover from an injury, nor may they receive coaching or instruction from anyone else during a match (except during the five-minute break between games two and three).

PLAY

The fundamental rules of play include those for serving, changing ends, and faults and lets.

Serving

The server faces the net and stands inside the service court on her right. The receiver stands inside the service court on his right side (diagonal from the server). Partners may stand anywhere as long as the receiver's view of the serve is not blocked. In doubles, only the receiver can return the serve. If the serve hits, or is hit by, the receiver's partner, the serving team scores a point. Once a serve is returned in doubles, either player may return a hit; partners do not have to take turns in hitting the shuttle.

When the server's score is even (0, 2, 4, and so on), she stands on the right side. When her score is odd (1, 3, 5, and so on), she stands on the left side. In doubles, when the serving team's score is even, the players are in their starting positions; when their score is odd, they switch positions.

The receiver may not move until the server hits the shuttle. A server commits a fault and loses her serve if she misses the shuttle, if the shuttle becomes stuck in the net on the serve, or if she serves incorrectly. The server must

- keep part of both feet stationary on the court while serving (as must the receiver, while receiving the serve);

- be totally within the boundaries of the service court, touching no lines;

- hit the base of the shuttle first;

- make initial contact with the shuttle below waist level;

- have all of the racket's head clearly below the hand that holds the racket at the moment of contact with the shuttle; and

- serve in a continuous motion (i.e., no faking).

Only the serving side can score a point. In singles play, if the server scores, she moves to the other service court side and serves again. If the server does not score, the opponent gets to serve. In doubles, if the serving team scores, the server switches service court side and serves again. If the serving team loses the rally, the partner serves from the other side. If the serving team loses that rally, the opponents gain the serve. If they win the rally, the server switches service court sides and continues to serve.

At the beginning of a game in doubles play, the team that serves first gets only one turn at serving. From then on each team serves as previously stated. In doubles, each time a side gains the serve, the first serve is made from the right service court.

A service court error is made by a player who serves out of turn or serves from the wrong side of the court, or by a receiver who is standing on the wrong side of the court when the serve is delivered. If a server or receiver is on the wrong side and a rally is played, the play stands if the person who made the mistake loses the rally, in which case the players will not correct their positioning. If the player who made the mistake wins the rally and the error is discovered before the next serve, the play is a let (it doesn't count) and the positioning is corrected. It is not a fault if the serve hits the net, as long as it crosses the net and lands within the receiver's service court.

The shuttle is put into play by the server and remains in play until it

- hits the floor,

- hits the ceiling or any side walls,

- hits a player or a player's clothing,
- hits the net or post and drops on the hitter's side, or
- gets stuck in the net or suspended on top of the net.

The shuttle is not in play when a fault or let occurs.

Changing Ends

Players change ends at the end of each game and in the middle of the third game. This occurs when the leading scorer reaches 6 points in an 11-point game or 8 points in a 15-point game. If players forget to change ends, they will do so as soon as the mistake is discovered, but all points will remain.

Faults and Lets

Service faults were covered in "Serving." Faults also occur in play, when the shuttle hits outside the court; passes through or under the net; does not pass the net; or touches the roof, ceiling, or any side walls.

In addition, a fault occurs when the shuttle touches a player or player's clothing; touches any person or object out of bounds; is caught, held, and slung on the racket; or is hit twice in a row by the same player on the same play. A fault also occurs when both partners hit the shuttle before it is returned to the other side.

A player also commits a fault when the shuttle is in play and he

- hits a shuttle when it is on the opponent's side of the net;
- touches the net or posts with his racket, clothing, or any part of his body;
- has his racket or any part of his body over or under the net (exception: a racket can cross the net, without touching it, on a follow-through, as long as the shuttle contact was on the hitter's side of the net); or
- obstructs an opponent's stroke (e.g., obstructing a follow-through as described in the above situation).

A let is a situation that calls for a halt in play. A let occurs when a shuttle remains suspended on top of the net, or passes the net and then becomes caught on the other side of the net (except on a serve; this is a fault on a serve). Lets are also called when the server and receiver commit faults at the same time; the server serves before the receiver is ready; and when the shuttle comes apart.

When a let is called, no score counts for that play, and the server who began the play serves again.

SCORING

In 2003 the official badminton scoring system was set as follows: women's singles are played to 11 points; men's singles, men's doubles, women's doubles, and mixed doubles are played to 15 points, with the best two games out of three. If the score is 10-10 in women's singles, or 14-14 in any other play, the side that reaches that score first can choose to *set* or *not set* the game. If the game is not set, the winner of the next point wins the game. If the game is set, the score goes to 0-0 and the first side who scores three more points wins. The side that wins the game serves first in the next game. Either player on the serving team can serve first in a new game, and either player on the receiving team can receive first.

EQUIPMENT

The shuttlecock either contains 16 feathers or is made of a synthetic mesh. It has a cork base covered by a thin layer of leather; the base is 1 to 1.13 inches in diameter. If feathers are used, they can be from 2.5 to 2.75 inches long (the same length must be used in any one shuttle). The shuttle weighs from .17 to .19 ounce. The racket frame may not be longer than 27.2 inches or wider than 9.2 inches. The stringed portion may not be over 11.2 inches long and 8.8 inches wide.

OFFICIALS

An umpire is in charge of the match. Other officials may include a service judge to call service faults and a line judge to indicate whether a shuttle is in or out of bounds.

ORGANIZATIONS

USA Badminton
One Olympic Plaza
Colorado Springs, CO 80909
(719) 866-4808
www.usabadminton.org

Baseball

Abner Doubleday is reputed to have invented baseball in Cooperstown, New York, in 1839, though some insist the game evolved from the British games of cricket and rounders. Alexander Cartwright, a former player, is credited with formulating the first set of rules, and the first game of record was between the New York Knickerbockers and another New York team, played on June 19, 1846, at the Elysian Field in Hoboken, New Jersey.

Baseball has long been popular in the United States and in Latin American countries, and it is a major sport in Japan and many other countries as well. The sport is played at the youth level in more than 90 countries; it ranks behind only soccer and basketball in youth participation in the United States.

Objective: To score the most runs.

Scoring: A player scores a run when he safely touches first, second, third, and home before his team makes three outs.

Number of Players: 9 per team (10 if a designated hitter is used, though only 9 are on the field).

Number of Innings: Nine (five to seven for younger players).

Number of Outs per Inning: Three outs for each team.

Overview: The defense fields nine players. Each team has a batting order it must adhere to, though substitutions can be made. Once a player is removed from the game, he cannot return. The pitcher pitches, and attempts to get the batter out; the batter attempts to get on base and eventually score. The most common ways to record outs are by strikeout, force out, tag out, and fly out.

FIELD

Figure 5.1 shows the dimensions of a major league field. Distance to outfield fences vary, but distances of 320 feet or more down the lines, and 400 feet or more to center field, are preferable. The figure also shows player positions.

TERMS

An **assist** is credited to a fielder when his throw leads to the putout of a runner. Two or more fielders can receive an assist on the same play.

Field and Player Positions

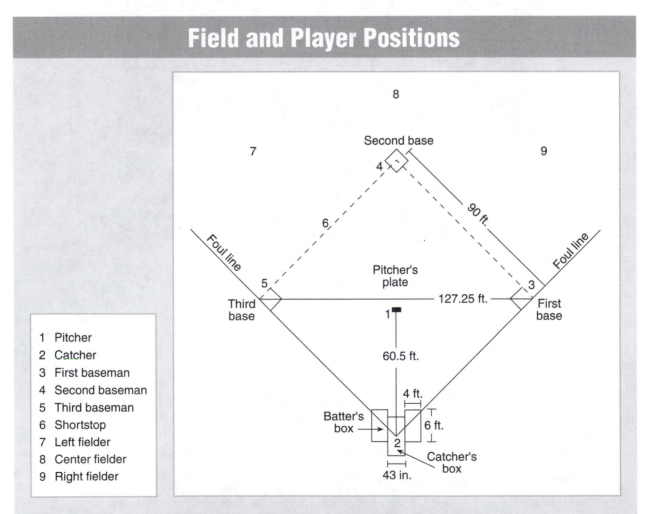

1 Pitcher
2 Catcher
3 First baseman
4 Second baseman
5 Third baseman
6 Shortstop
7 Left fielder
8 Center fielder
9 Right fielder

▶ Figure 5.1   A baseball field and its dimensions, features, and player positions.
Adapted from White 1990.

A **balk** is an illegal move (usually toward home plate) by the pitcher with a runner or runners on base. All runners automatically advance one base when a balk is called.

The **ball** is cork or rubber wrapped in yarn and covered by cowhide or horsehide. It weighs 5 to 5.25 ounces and is 9 to 9.25 inches in circumference. A pitch that the batter doesn't swing at and that is outside of the strike zone is also called a ball.

First, second, and third **base** are made of white canvas, 15 inches square, between 3 inches and 5 inches thick, and secured in the ground. Home plate is five-sided, 17 inches wide, 8.5 inches long on three sides, and 12 inches long on the sides that meet to form the point at the rear of the plate.

A batter is credited with a **base hit** when he reaches base safely on a hit, without aid of an error.

The **baseline** extends three feet on either side of a direct line between bases. A runner is out when he runs outside the baseline, except to avoid interfering with a fielder fielding a batted ball.

A batter receives a **base on balls** (is awarded first base) when he takes four balls during a time at-bat. This is also called a *walk*.

The **bat** is a smooth, round stick not more than 2.75 inches in diameter at its thickest, and no longer than 42 inches. The bat handle can be treated with a sticky substance to improve the batter's grip, but this substance may not extend beyond 18 inches from the bottom of the bat.

Batter's boxes are four feet by six feet on either side of home plate.

Batter's circles, or *on-deck circles,* are in foul territory between home plate and each team's bench.

The **battery** refers to the pitcher and the catcher.

Batters must wear **batting helmets** with at least one ear flap (facing the pitcher as the batter is in his stance).

A batter **bunts** the ball by letting the ball meet the bat to drop a soft ground ball on the infield. A bunt can be an attempt to beat out a base hit or a sacrifice to move a runner or runners up a base.

A **catch** means a fielder has secured the ball in his hand or glove. A fly ball is not caught if the fielder simultaneously falls or collides with the fence or another player and the ball is dislodged. A fly ball that is dropped may still be ruled a catch if the fielder had control of the ball long enough before he dropped it.

A **catcher's box**, 43 inches wide and 8 feet long, is directly behind home plate.

Catcher's interference occurs when the catcher hinders the batter from hitting the ball.

Coaches' boxes are set near first and third base, in foul territory, for the offensive team.

A pitcher is credited with a **complete game** when he starts and finishes a regulation game.

A **cutoff throw** is one that is received by a fielder who is not the final target of the throw. For example, a right fielder may throw to the second baseman, who then relays the throw to the third baseman in an attempt to put out a runner.

A **designated hitter** takes the place of the pitcher in the batting order but does not play defense.

A **double** is a hit in which the batter safely reaches second base.

A **double play** is recorded by the defense when two outs are made on the same play.

An **earned run** is charged against a pitcher every time a run scores on a hit, sacrifice, bunt, sacrifice fly, wild pitch, stolen base, putout, fielder's choice, base on balls, batter hit by pitch, or balk. A run is *unearned* if that runner scores by benefit of an error, a passed ball, or defensive interference or obstruction. A relief pitcher who enters a game is not charged with any run, either earned or unearned, scored by any runners already on base.

An **error** is charged to a fielder who misplays a ball (e.g., a dropped fly ball or throw, or a fumbled ground ball) and consequently prolongs an at-bat for a batter or the life of a base runner, or permits a runner to advance one or more bases. An error can be charged even if the fielder does not touch the ball (e.g., a ground ball that goes through the legs).

A game goes into **extra innings** when it is tied at the end of nine innings.

Fair territory and foul territory are marked by two foul lines. Each line extends from home plate. One line creates a third baseline and left field line, stopping at the left field fence; the other creates a first baseline and right field line, stopping at the right field fence. Anything on or in between the foul lines is considered fair territory. Foul poles rise above the fence in left field and right field. A ball striking a foul pole is a home run.

A **fielder's choice** occurs when an infielder fields a ground ball and elects to throw to another base, rather than to first base to put out the batter-runner.

A **fly ball** is a ball batted high in the air.

A **fly out** is a fly ball caught before it touches the ground or the fence.

A **force play** occurs when a runner is forced to advance to the next base because the batter becomes a runner. When a batter hits a ground ball with a runner on first, the runner is forced to run to second. If a fielder touches second base with the ball in his possession before the runner reaches second, the runner is "forced out" at second. If a runner is on second when a ground ball is hit, he is not forced to advance if first base is unoccupied.

A **foul ball** is any ball hit into foul territory.

Foul territory is all territory outside the foul lines. A ball striking a foul line is a fair ball.

A **ground out** refers to a batter being thrown out at first base after hitting a ground ball.

A **ground rule double** is awarded a batter when his fair ball bounces into the stands, passes through or under the fence, or is caught in vines or shrubbery in the fence.

When a batter is **hit** by a pitch that is not in the strike zone and that he attempts to elude, he is awarded first base.

A **home run** is recorded when a batter hits a fair ball over the fence, or circles the bases on an inside-the-park hit without being thrown out.

The **infield** refers to the portion of the field that contains the four bases. In terms of players, the infield is made up of the first, second, and third basemen and the shortstop. The pitcher and the catcher are also positioned in the infield.

The **infield fly rule** prohibits an infielder from intentionally dropping a fair fly ball that can be caught with normal effort. This rule is in effect with first and second, or first, second, and third bases occupied before two are out. When an umpire calls an infield fly rule, the batter is automatically out and runners may advance at their own risk.

The **losing pitcher** is the pitcher charged with the runs that give the opposing team a lead that is not relinquished.

A **no-hitter** is credited to a pitcher who pitches a complete game and allows no hits.

A fielder can be called for **obstruction** if he impedes the progress of a runner if the fielder does not have the ball or is not fielding the ball.

An **out** can be recorded in a variety of ways, including strikeout, force out, tag out, and fly out.

The **outfield** is that portion of fair territory between the infield and the fence. In terms of players, the outfield consists of the left fielder, the center fielder, and the right fielder.

A **passed ball** is charged to the catcher when he fails to control a catchable pitch and allows a runner or runners to advance.

A **perfect game** occurs when a pitcher pitches a no-hitter and allows no base runners at all (e.g., by walks, hit batters, or errors).

A **pinch hitter** is a player who bats for another player. The player replaced cannot return to the game.

A **pinch runner** is a player who runs for another player. The player replaced cannot return to the game.

The **pitcher's mound** is a circular mound of dirt 18 feet in diameter and 59 feet from its center to the back of home plate. The mound has a rectangular rubber plate, called the **pitcher's rubber**, set perpendicular to home plate. The pitcher's rubber is set in the ground, and its front edge is 60.5 feet from the back of home plate. The rubber is 6 inches by 24 inches and is set 10 inches higher than home plate.

A **putout** occurs when a batter-runner or base runner is called out (e.g., force out, tag out, caught stealing, and so on).

A **relief pitcher** is any pitcher who enters a game after the starting pitcher has thrown at least one pitch.

A batter is credited with the appropriate number of **runs batted in (RBIs)** when his hit is responsible for one or more runners scoring. RBIs are not tallied for runs scored as a result of errors, or if a run is scored as the batter grounds into a double play.

A **sacrifice bunt** is placed by a batter to advance a runner or runners. A successful sacrifice bunt does not count as a time at bat; an unsuccessful attempt does.

A **sacrifice fly** is credited to a batter whose caught fly ball results in a runner on third base tagging up and scoring. A sacrifice fly does not count as a time at bat. A run must score for a sacrifice fly to be recorded.

A pitcher may be credited with a **save** when he finishes a game his team wins and he is not the winning pitcher—if he meets one of these criteria:

- He enters the game with a lead of no more than three runs and pitches for at least one inning.
- He enters the game, regardless of the count, with the potential tying run either on base, or at bat, or on deck.
- He pitches effectively for at least three innings.

The **set position** is one of two positions from which a pitcher can deliver a pitch. In the set position, a pitcher comes set (halts his motion) just before pitching. This is also known as the *stretch position.*

A **shutout** occurs when a team is held scoreless. A pitcher must pitch a complete game to receive credit for a shutout.

A **single** is a one-base hit credited to the batter.

The **starting pitcher** is the pitcher who begins the game for his team.

A runner is credited with a **stolen base** when he advances one base without aid of a hit, putout, error, force out, fielder's choice, passed ball, wild pitch, or balk.

A **strike** is a pitch that the batter takes (doesn't swing at) in the strike zone; that the batter swings at and misses; or that the batter hits into foul territory.

A **strikeout** is recorded after a batter has three strikes. Exceptions to this are if the third strike is a foul ball that is not caught in the air, or a strike that the catcher does not catch. In the latter case, if first base is unoccupied, or if it is occupied with two out, the defensive team must put out the batter by either throwing the ball to first base before the batter reaches it, or by tagging him with the ball before he reaches first. Batters attempting to bunt on the third strike are out if the ball is picked up in foul territory. This play is considered a strikeout.

The batter's **strike zone** is over home plate, between the top of the knees and the midpoint between the top of the shoulders and the top of the pants.

Substitutions can be made when play is dead. Once a player leaves the game he cannot return.

A **suspended game** is one that is halted, to be completed at a later date. The game is resumed at the exact point of suspension, with the same lineups intact.

A **tag out** is one way a fielder can record a putout. When a force play is not in order, such as with a runner on second, the runner must be tagged out (touched with the ball, which can be in a fielder's glove or bare hand) when the runner is not touching a base.

On a caught fly ball, a runner must **tag up** (be in contact with his base) after the catch before advancing.

A **three-foot line** to guide the runners is parallel to the first baseline, beginning halfway between home plate and first base and ending beyond first base.

A batter is credited with a **triple** when he reaches third base on his hit.

A **triple play** occurs when the defense records three outs on the same play.

The outfield has a dirt **warning track** that alerts outfielders that they are approaching the fence.

A **wild pitch** occurs when a pitch eludes the catcher, allowing one or more runners to advance one base. A wild pitch is judged to be the pitcher's fault, not the catcher's. A ball that bounces in the dirt and allows any base runners to advance is automatically a wild pitch.

The **windup position** is one of two positions from which a pitcher can deliver a pitch. The windup is normally used with no runners on base.

The **winning pitcher** is the starting pitcher if he pitches five or more innings and leaves the game with the lead, and the lead is never relinquished. If a pitcher leaves a game with the lead, but the game is later tied or the opponent takes the lead with runs not charged to that pitcher, that pitcher cannot be either the winner or loser. In most cases, if the winning pitcher is a relief pitcher, he is the pitcher of record when his team has taken a lead that it does not relinquish.

PLAY

The basic play of baseball can be understood through its rules for pitching, batting, and base running.

Pitching

Following are specific pitching rules that have not been previously stated.

1. Once a pitcher begins his motion to home, he must throw home or be called for a balk.

2. When the bases are empty, the pitcher has 20 seconds to pitch, or the umpire will automatically call a ball.

3. The pitcher may not bring his pitching hand into contact with his mouth or lips while on the mound, although exceptions can be made in cold weather if both managers agree. Penalty: automatic ball called.

   Other reasons for an automatic ball being called include
   - applying a foreign substance to the ball;
   - spitting on the ball, on either hand, or on the glove;
   - rubbing the ball on the glove, body, or clothing;
   - defacing the ball; and
   - pitching a "shine" ball, spitball, mudball, or "emery" ball.

4. The pitcher may rub the ball in his bare hands.

5. The pitcher may not intentionally throw at a batter. If he does, the umpire may expel the pitcher and his manager or may warn the pitchers and the managers of both teams.

6. A manager or coach may make two trips to the mound during an inning to talk to the pitcher. On the second trip, the pitcher must be removed.

Batting

Batting rules that have not been previously stated include the following.

1. Players must hit in the batting order decided by the manager.

2. A batter cannot leave the batter's box once the pitcher comes set or begins his windup.

3. Both of the batter's feet must be in the batter's box (the lines are part of the box). If the batter hits the ball—either fair or foul—with one or both feet on the ground entirely outside of the box, he is automatically out.

4. A batter may request time, but the umpire does not have to grant this request. If a batter refuses to take his position in the batter's box, the umpire will order the pitcher to pitch and call each pitch a strike, no matter the location.

5. A batter makes an out when

   - his fair or foul fly ball is caught by a fielder;
   - a third strike is caught by the catcher;
   - a third strike is not caught by the catcher when first base is occupied before two are out;
   - he bunts foul on the third strike;
   - an infield fly rule is called (see page 26);
   - his fair ball touches him before touching a fielder (such as on a bunt);
   - after hitting a ball in fair territory, he hits the ball with his bat a second time (unless the umpire judges that the batter did not intend to interfere with the ball);
   - after a third strike or a hit into fair territory, he or first base is tagged before he touches first base;
   - he runs outside the three-foot line toward first base, interfering with the first baseman taking the throw or with a fielder fielding the ball;
   - he interferes with the catcher's fielding or throwing;
   - he uses a bat that has been tampered with (i.e., a bat that has been filled, hollowed, grooved, covered with paraffin or wax, or otherwise altered) to increase hitting distance; or
   - a runner on first intentionally interferes with the second baseman or shortstop on a double play opportunity (if the runner leaves the baseline to try to "take out" the pivot man, both the runner and the batter are automatically out).

Base Running

The following are base-running rules that have not been previously covered.

1. A runner is entitled to an unoccupied base when he touches it before he is put out.

2. The baseline belongs to the runner. A fielder not in the act of fielding the ball cannot block the path of a runner between any two bases. In such a case the ball is dead and the runner is awarded the base he would have reached, in the umpire's judgment, had he not been obstructed.

3. A runner is out when

   - he is tagged by a fielder with the ball while not on a base (however, a runner can run or slide past first base without risking being tagged out if he returns immediately to first base without stepping or turning to second);
   - he fails to reach the next base before a fielder tags him or, when he is forced to advance because the batter has become a runner;
   - he runs out of the baseline (more than three feet away from a direct line between the bases), unless he is doing so to avoid interfering with a fielder fielding a batted ball;
   - he intentionally interferes with a thrown ball, or hinders a fielder making a play on a batted ball;
   - two runners occupy the same base and one runner is tagged with the ball;
   - a runner is hit by a batted ball in fair territory before it touches a fielder or an umpire (unless he is on a base and an infield fly rule has been called);
   - he passes a runner on the base paths;
   - he misses a base in advancing to the next base and a fielder appeals before the next pitch by touching the base with the ball in his possession;
   - he fails to touch each base in order; or
   - he intentionally interferes with a fielder or the ball in trying to break up a double play—in this case both the runner and the batter are out.

SCORING

A win can be recorded in any of the following situations:

- When the home team is ahead after the visiting team bats in the top of the ninth inning
- When the home team, tied or behind going into the bottom of the ninth inning, scores the winning run in the bottom of the ninth
- When the home team, losing in the bottom of the ninth inning, fails to score (the visitors win)
- When the teams are tied after nine innings, and the game goes into extra innings, where it is played until one team has scored more than the other at the end of a complete inning
- When the game is shortened for bad weather, if it has gone at least five innings and one team is ahead (or 4 1/2 innings if the home team is ahead)
- When the umpire declares a forfeit

EQUIPMENT

Balls, bats, bases, and batter's helmets were described under "Terms." The catcher's glove may not be more than 38 inches in circumference and not more than 15.5 inches from top to bottom. The first baseman's glove may be a maximum of 12 inches from top to bottom and 7.75 inches across the palm. In addition to gloves, catchers wear other protective gear: a helmet, face mask, chest and throat protectors, and shin guards. Players may not wear pointed spikes on their shoes.

OFFICIALS

The umpire-in-chief (home plate umpire) is in full charge of the game. Any umpire may disqualify any player, coach, or manager for objecting to decisions or for unsporting conduct or language. The umpire's decision on any judgment call is final and may not be appealed. A manager may, however, appeal any call that he believes goes against the rules.

For common umpire signals, see figure 5.2.

MODIFICATIONS

Baseball leagues begin with players as young as 5 years old and go on through the teen years and, of course, beyond. To make the game safe, fun, and appropriate for younger players who are just beginning to develop their talents, various organizations and leagues modify their playing rules. The rules most often modified pertain to the following areas:

- **Length of game:** Youth leagues typically play between 5 and 7 innings; as the players age, they play more innings. Some leagues have time limits; for example, no inning may start after the game has gone 1.5 hours.
- **Distance between bases and to fences:** Distance between bases varies from 50 feet at the youngest levels to 60 to 80 feet in the preteen years to the major league distance of 90 feet by teen years. Fences down the lines are usually less than 200 feet until the players are 11 or 12 years old; the distance increases as the players get to mid and late teens, with many leagues having 300-foot fences at that point. In center field, the fences typically begin at 200 feet and increase to 275 feet by age 12 and 350 feet by mid teens.
- **Pitching:** Many leagues make concessions for the abilities of youngsters to pitch. See "Coach-Pitch" and "T-Ball."
- **Base running:** Younger divisions of youth leagues typically have "no lead-off" and "no stealing" rules. Older divisions may lead off and steal.
- **Other modifications:** Youth leagues also limit the number of innings young pitchers may pitch in one game and in one week, and many 8-and-under leagues use a safety (softer) ball. Younger divisions often allow up to 12 players on defense and have no infield fly rule.

Coach-pitch and T-ball are two of the major ways in which the game is modified. For specific rules modifications for youth baseball, contact the organizations listed at the end of the chapter.

Time out

Strike

Player is out

Runner is safe

▶ Figure 5.2   Common umpires' signals in baseball.

Coach-Pitch

Coach-pitch is a step between T-ball and regular baseball (player-pitch). A coach or another adult pitches to the batters because the pitchers are not able to throw the ball over the plate consistently. With coach-pitch, batters have more of an opportunity to practice their hitting and are less likely to be hit by pitches.

Coach-pitch is usually recommended for ages 8 and under. Some leagues use a pitching machine instead of an adult.

T-Ball

Many 8-and-under leagues play T-ball instead of baseball. In T-ball the batter hits the ball off a tee. This results in the ball being put in play more regularly and is appropriate for leagues with young and unskilled players who cannot bat or pitch very consistently. General rules for T-ball include the following, though they are often varied:

- All players on the roster bat.

- An inning is over when nine players have hit or three outs are made, whichever occurs first. The ninth batter must attempt to score; his scoring or his being put out will end the inning, if three outs have not already been made.

- No bunting is allowed. The ball must travel at least 25 feet in fair territory; a 25-foot arc is drawn from foul line to foul line.

- Balls not hit beyond the 25-foot arc are foul balls.

- A "pitcher" on the mound must be in contact with the pitching rubber and make a pitching motion before the batter swings.

- Three misses constitute a strikeout.

- No stealing or leading off is allowed.

- Nine players are on defense (many leagues allow all the players on defense).

- Each player must play at least two innings in the field.

- The coach of the defensive team may stand beyond the infielders and instruct his players.

- A regulation game is by innings or hours— often 6 innings or 1.5 hours.

ORGANIZATIONS

All-American Amateur Baseball Association
www.aaba.net

Amateur Athlete Union's Baseball
P.O. Box 1000
Lake Buena Vista, FL 32830-1000
407-934-7200
www.aaubaseball.org

American Legion Baseball
700 N. Pennsylvania Street
Indianapolis, IN 46206
317-630-1369
www.baseballlegion.org

Babe Ruth League
1770 Brunswick Pike
Trenton, NJ 08638
609-695-1434
www.baberuthleague.org

Little League Baseball
www.littleleague.org

National Amateur Baseball Federation
P.O. Box 705
Bowie, MD 20718
301-262-5005
www.nabf.com

National Federation of State High School Associations
P.O. Box 690
Indianapolis, IN 46206
317-972-6900
www.nfhs.org

National Semi-Professional Baseball Association
8437 Bell Oaks Drive, 184
Newburgh, IN 47630
812-402-8457
www.ezteams.com/NSPBA

Pony Baseball
www.ponybaseball.org

USA Baseball
P.O. Box 1131
Durham, NC 27702
919-474-8721
www.usabaseball.com

U.S. Amateur Baseball Association
P.O. Box 55622
Seattle, WA 98155
425-776-7130
www.usaba.com

U.S. Baseball Congress
8437 Bell Oaks Drive, 184
Newburgh, IN 47630
812-402-8457
www.ezteamz.com/usbc

Basketball

Basketball began with 13 fundamental rules that have been added to and amended greatly over the years since the game's beginnings in 1891. Invented by James Naismith, basketball first featured nine players per team because Naismith had 18 students in his YMCA Training School. In a few years that number was changed to five per side, a metal ring with a net replaced the original peach baskets that players shot at, and running with the ball was eliminated.

Basketball first became an Olympic sport in the 1936 Berlin Olympics. It is a widely enjoyed participant sport, with leagues for all ages and abilities and more than 30 million people who play the sport, from recreation levels on up, in the United States.

The rules in this chapter are general basketball rules, with specific references at times to high school, college, and professional play. How the game is modified at the international level and the youth level is noted toward the end of the chapter.

Objective: To win by scoring more points than the other team.

Scoring: One point per successful free throw; two points per two-point field goal; three points per three-point field goal.

Number of Players: Five per team.

Length of Game: 32 minutes (high school), 40 minutes (college), or 48 minutes (professional).

Overview: A team advances the ball by dribbling and passing, and attempts to score. A shot that does not go into the basket is usually rebounded by a player. If that player is on offense, she can either shoot or set up another scoring opportunity. If the player who rebounds is on defense, she and her team advance the ball down court and try to set up their own scoring opportunity. After a made basket, the player who throws the ball in may run the length of the baseline with the ball. On any inbounds play other than a made basket, the player who throws the ball in must establish, and may not move, a pivot foot before releasing the ball. The player must throw the ball in within five seconds, or it is turned over to the other team.

COURT

Court sizes vary according to the level of play. In high school, the court is 50 feet by 84 feet; in college and the National Basketball Association (NBA), it is 50 feet by 94 feet. The *free-throw line* at all three levels is 15 feet from the basket. The *free-throw lane*, which borders the free-throw line, is 12 feet wide in high school and college and 16 feet wide in the NBA. This lane has a semicircle with a six-foot radius from the center of the free-throw line.

At least three feet of unobstructed space should lie beyond the *sidelines* and *end lines* (or *baselines)* that mark the boundaries of the court. The court is split in half by a *center line,* around which are two *center circles.*

Two *coaching boxes* are behind the sidelines, 28 feet long and extending toward center court from each end line. See figure 6.1 for standard court attributes.

Court

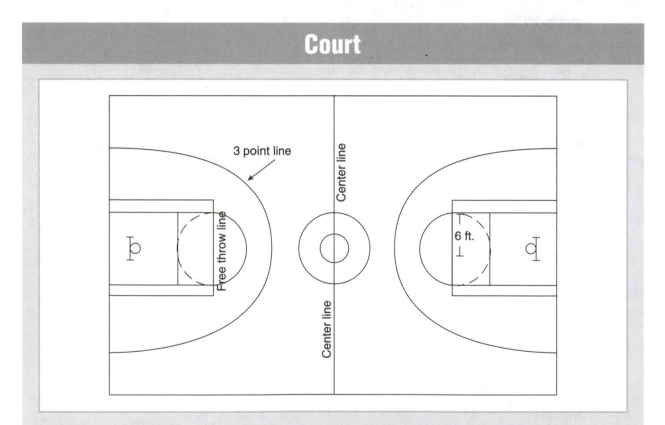

▶ Figure 6.1   Dimensions for courts vary according to the level of play, but many of the same features are included on all courts.

Adapted from White 1990.

TERMS

These terms are not described elsewhere in this chapter.

To **dribble** is to bounce the ball on the floor, using one hand at a time. (Dribbling with both hands at once is "double dribbling," a violation that results in a turnover.) Players may move on the court or be stationary when they dribble. The dribble ends when the ball is caught by the dribbler, who cannot dribble again until another player touches the ball.

A team's **frontcourt** is that half of the court that includes its basket. The **backcourt** is the half of the court that includes the other team's basket. No part of the end line or the center line is considered part of the frontcourt.

A **held ball** occurs when each of two players from opposite teams has a firm grasp on the ball or when an opposing player places a hand on the ball to prevent an airborne player from attempting a pass or shot. The team with the possession indicator in its favor is awarded the ball out of bounds.

Incidental contact occurs when opponents are in equally favorable positions to perform normal defensive or offensive movements, and contact (even severe contact) is made, such as in going for a loose ball. No foul is called. Similarly, a blind screen may be ruled incidental contact, regardless of the violence of the collision.

A **pass** is the movement of the ball by a player who throws, bats, or rolls the ball to another player.

A **pivot** occurs when a player holding the ball keeps one foot at a point of contact with the floor while stepping in any direction. Picking up the pivot foot before dribbling or getting rid of the ball is a traveling violation.

A **rebound** occurs when a player controls possession of a shot missed by either a teammate (offensive rebound) or an opponent (defensive rebound).

A **screen** occurs when an offensive player reaches a desired position first, causing a de-fensive player to go around him and delaying the progress of the defender. The offensive player must have feet planted and remain stationary.

Substitutes are alternative players who may enter a game by reporting to the scorer and being beckoned by an official. Substitutes may enter during a dead ball and when time is out (except in college, where a substitute may enter after a successful field goal in the last minute of a game and in overtime). A substitute may not enter a game for a player shooting a free throw unless that player is injured.

Verticality applies to ascertaining who has legal position. A defender who has already es-tablished position and who raises her hands and arms within her vertical plane is in legal position and shouldn't be charged with a foul if an offensive player causes contact. The de-fender can leave her feet within this plane, but cannot "belly up," or use the lower part of the body to contact the offensive player outside the vertical plane.

PLAYERS

A team consists of five players. Typically, but not always, a team will play two guards (a point guard, considered the team's playmaker, and an off guard or shooting guard), a small forward, a power forward, and a center or post player. These are loosely defined roles; players may be defined differently in different systems. Players are sometimes referred to by position numbers (which have nothing to do with their uniform numbers):

1. Point guard
2. Off guard or shooting guard
3. Small forward
4. Power forward
5. Center or post

PLAY

Game length and other time factors differ according to the level of play; see table 6.1. The shot clock governs the time a team is

Table 6.1   Game Length and Time Factors

Level	Length	Overtime	Shot clock	Timeouts
High school	Four 8-min quarters	3 min	None	Four per game
College	Two 20-min halves	5 min	30 sec women; 35 sec men	Four per regulation (three per televised game); one per overtime
Professional	Four 12-min quarters	5 min	24 sec	Seven per regulation plus one 20-sec timeout per half; three per overtime
International	Two 20-min halves	5 min	30 sec	Two per half

allowed to be on offense before attempting a shot. If the ball does not leave the shooter's hand before the clock expires, or if the shot does not touch the rim or go into the basket, a shot clock violation is called and the ball is given to the other team. The clock is stopped at the end of each period and when an official blows a whistle for

- a violation,
- a foul,
- a held or jump ball,
- a ball that goes out of bounds,
- suspension of play because of an injury to a player,
- suspension of play for any other reason,
- when the shot clock sounds (if the shot is in the air when the clock sounds and the shot hits the rim, the clock is ignored and play continues without time stopping), and
- timeouts.

Defense

When a defender is guarding a player who has the ball, the maximum distance between the two players is 6 feet. (No minimum distance is required.) To establish legal position, the defender must have both feet on the floor, with the torso facing the opponent. If the opponent is airborne, the defender must have established a legal position before the other player left the floor and must maintain that position.

When a defender is guarding a player who does not have the ball, the defender must give the opponent time and up to two steps to avoid contact. If the opponent is airborne, the defender must have established a legal position before the other player left the floor and must maintain that position.

Examples of legal use of hands and arms include when a defender vertically extends hands and arms, reaches to block or slap the ball away, or hits the hand of the opponent when the ball is in contact with the opponent's hands. If the extension is not vertical and any contact hinders the offensive player, the movement is not legal. Defenders may use their hands to protect their faces or bodies in absorbing a charge from an opponent, but they can't use their hands to push the offensive player away. Defenders cannot use any part of their bodies to force their way through screens or to hold a screener and then push that player away.

In professional basketball a team cannot play a *zone defense,* in which each defender is assigned a certain portion of the court, rather than an individual player. In college and high school, zone defenses are allowed, as are *man-*

to-man defenses, in which each player defends a specific opponent.

Fouls

A foul occurs when a player or coach breaks a rule in any of a variety of ways. A player is disqualified and removed from a game after being assessed five fouls (high school and college) or six fouls (professional). Specific fouls include these:

- **Away from the ball** is a foul committed by a player in a play not involving the player with the ball.

- **Blocking** is illegal contact by a defender, impeding the progress of an offensive player.

- **Charging** is illegal contact by an offensive player by pushing or moving into the defender's torso.

- **Delay of game** is called when a player prevents the ball from being promptly put into play, such as after a made basket or in batting the ball away from an opponent before the player can throw the ball inbounds.

- A **double personal** occurs when two opposing players commit personal fouls at about the same time. No free throws are awarded; in professional ball, the team in possession of the ball at the time of the fouls retains possession; if neither team was in possession, a jump ball is used to put the ball into play. In college, the alternating-possession arrow determines the team that gets possession.

- A **double technical** is called when two opposing players commit technical fouls at about the same time. In college, each team receives two free throws, and the alternating-possession arrow determines which team gets possession. In professional ball, this penalty is handled the same way as a double personal foul.

- In professional ball, two free-throw attempts are awarded for an **elbow foul**. If the contact is made above shoulder level, the player throwing the elbow may be ejected. In college and in high school play, excessive swinging of elbows—even without making contact—may result in a foul.

- A team calling a timeout when it has no timeouts left is assessed a technical foul for **excessive timeout.** The timeout is granted, but two free throws and the ball out of bounds are awarded to the opposing team.

- A defender cannot **face guard**—that is, place a hand in the face or eyes of the opponent she is guarding from the rear if the opponent does not have the ball. Such a play results in a technical foul.

- In the NBA, **fighting** results in technical fouls assessed against those involved and automatic ejection. No free throws are awarded.

- In both college and the pros, a **flagrant foul** results in two free throws awarded to the offended team and possession of the ball. Any player committing a flagrant foul is automatically ejected in college; a professional player may be ejected at the discretion of the official.

- Defenders cannot **hand check**—that is, use their hands to check the progress of offensive players when those players are in front of them.

- If either an offensive or a defensive player **hangs on the rim**, a technical foul is assessed. The only exception is if a player hangs on the rim to protect himself or other players from injury.

- In college, an **intentional foul** occurs when a player commits a personal foul without attempting to directly play the opposing player or the ball. It does not depend on the severity of the foul; it depends on whether the official judges the foul to be intentional. Holding or pushing a player in full view of an official, in order to stop play or shoving a player in the back as she is attempting a lay-up that cannot be defended are examples of intentional fouls. The penalty for such fouls is two free throws and the ball out of bounds.

- Any player on offense can commit an **offensive foul.** If a defender has established legal position in a dribbler's path, the dribbler cannot make contact with the opponent. A screener cannot move into an opponent after setting a legal screen. A shooter cannot charge into a defender who has established legal position and who maintains that position.

- The term **personal foul** covers a wide variety of contact fouls that players can commit, including holding, pushing, charging, tripping, and illegally interfering with a player's progress.

- A **player-control** foul is another term for charging—when the dribbler commits an offensive foul by charging into a defender who has established legal position.

- In professional ball, a **punching foul** results in one free throw being awarded, and the ball out of bounds. The player throwing the punch—whether it connects or not—is automatically ejected. (In college this foul would be handled the same as a flagrant foul.)

- A **technical foul** is a foul committed by anyone—players on the court or bench, coaches, other team officials—that does not involve contact with the opponent while the ball is alive. Examples of technical fouls include use of profanity, delay of game, excessive timeouts, unsporting conduct, and hanging on the rim (except to prevent injury). Two free throws and the ball are awarded the offended team when a player commits a technical foul. If a coach, substitute, or other team personnel commits a technical foul, two free throws are awarded (and in college, the offended team would retain possession of the ball). A player who commits two technical fouls is removed from the game. A coach who commits two technical fouls is removed from the competition area.

- **Throwing the ball**, or any object, at an official is a technical foul and cause for possible ejection.

- **Unsportsmanlike conduct** is a technical foul resulting from any of numerous unsporting actions, including disrespectfully addressing an official, trying to influence an official's decision, arguing with an official, taunting an opponent, inciting undesirable crowd reactions, throwing items on the court, and so on. The penalty is two free throws and the ball out to the opposing team.

SCORING

When the ball enters the basket from above and remains in or passes through the net, a goal is scored. If that goal is scored with at least one of the shooter's feet on or inside the three-point line, a *two-point field goal* is scored. If neither of the shooter's feet is on or inside the three-point line, a *three-point field goal* is scored. After releasing the ball, the shooter may touch the three-point line or land inside the line and still be awarded three points on a successful shot. If a goal is mistakenly scored in the opponent's basket by a defender, two points are awarded to the nearest offensive player.

A successful *free-throw* attempt counts as one point. If the free throw is not made but the rebound is tapped in, the player who tapped it in is awarded two points. Free throws must be attempted within 10 seconds.

Defensive players and offensive players alternate positions along the free-throw lane, with the defensive team getting the positions closest to the basket. The shooter must remain behind the free-throw line until the ball touches the basket. The players in the lane must remain in their positions on the free-throw lane until the ball leaves the shooter's hands.

A player who is fouled while attempting a two-point field goal gets two free throws; a player gets three free throws if fouled during a three-point field goal attempt. One free throw is awarded a player who is fouled while making a field goal. After a certain number of fouls are committed in a quarter or a half, a team may be in the *bonus* situation, where the next player fouled (not in the act of shooting or as the result of taking a charge from an offensive player) receives a chance to make a free throw. If the first free throw is successful, that player receives a bonus of one more free-throw attempt. Bonus free throws are awarded as follows:

- **High school:** The one-and-one bonus is awarded on the 7th, 8th, and 9th team fouls of each half. Beginning with the 10th team foul of each half, the team fouled gets two free throws, regardless of the outcome of the first free throw.

- **College:** The one-and-one bonus is awarded beginning with the 10th foul in a half.

- **Professional:** Two free throws are granted for each foul after four fouls in a quarter (or three in overtime).

The penalty for most technical fouls is two free throws and the ball out of bounds to the team attempting the free throws. Any player on the floor may be named by the coach to attempt free throws awarded from a technical foul.

VIOLATIONS

Violations occur when players break the rules in a way that does not involve contact. Violations include the following:

- When a team is in possession of the ball in its frontcourt and the ball goes into the backcourt (last touched by an offensive player), an offensive player cannot touch the ball until a defensive player does. If an offensive player does touch the ball first, a **backcourt violation** is called, and the ball automatically goes to the defensive team. If, however, the ball was deflected into the backcourt by a defender, then an offensive player may retrieve the ball in the backcourt.

- **Basket interference and goaltending** are called when a player touches the ball or the basket when the ball is on or within the basket. A player cannot touch the ball when it is in the cylinder (the basket extended upward) or touch the ball if it is in flight downward toward the basket and has a possibility of entering the basket. Defensive basket interference and goaltending result in two points for the offense; offensive basket interference results in no points and the ball out of bounds to the defense.

- **Double dribble** is called when a player stops her dribble and then resumes it. A player can resume a dribble, however, if the ball has been batted out of her hands or if a pass or fumble has been touched by another player.

- A player cannot intentionally miss a **free throw**. The penalty is the awarding of the ball out of bounds to the opposing team.

- A player cannot intentionally **kick** the ball or **strike** it with his fist. Doing so results in the ball being given out of bounds to the other team.

- Any ball that goes **out of bounds** is awarded to the team opposing the player who last touched the ball.

- Any shot that does not beat the **shot clock** results in the ball being turned over to the other team. If the ball is released before the clock expires and hits the rim after the buzzer goes off, no violation has occurred.

- **Traveling** is called when a player advances with the ball without dribbling it.

- A player making a **throw-in** (throwing the ball inbounds) may not carry the ball onto the court; hold the ball longer than five seconds; touch the ball on the court before another player has touched it; leave the designated throw-in spot (except after a made basket); or step over the boundary line while still touching the ball.

EQUIPMENT

The ball is round, with a circumference of 29.25 to 30 inches for men and 28.5 to 29 inches for women. A men's ball weighs 20 to 22 ounces; a women's ball weighs 18 to 20 ounces. The ball has a leather cover with eight panels joined by rubber ribs. (Balls with synthetic covering may be used if both teams agree.)

The backboard, which supports the basket, can be either 6 feet by 4 feet or 6 feet by 3.5 feet for college and high school play; professional basketball uses only the smaller size. In high school play, a fan-shaped backboard may be used. A 24- by 18-inch rectangle is centered on the backboard, behind and above the basket. The bottom and sides of the backboard are padded, as is the backboard support.

The basket is an orange metal ring, 18 inches in inside diameter. A white cord net, 15 to 18 inches in length, hangs from the basket. The upper edge of the basket is 10 feet above and parallel to the floor. The nearest point of the basket is 6 inches from the backboard.

Other equipment includes

- a scoreboard,
- a game clock, and
- a possession indicator (which indicates which team will get possession of the ball in the next held ball or double-foul situation).

OFFICIALS

A referee and one or two umpires, depending on the level of play, call fouls and violations and make all on-court calls. A scorekeeper operates the scoreboard and records the play; a timekeeper operates the game clock; and a shot clock operator is in charge of the shot clock.

For common officials' signals, see figure 6.2.

MODIFICATIONS

Because basketball is so widely popular and is played by young and old, skilled and unskilled, many organizations adapt the rules to fit their members better. Two major groups who have rule variations are youth and international basketball.

Youth Basketball

Variations differ from organization to organization; following is an overview of the types of rules that are adapted for youths.

- The size of the ball and the court is generally smaller.
- The basket height is lowered to give youths a reasonable chance to score and to help them learn proper shooting technique.

- The free-throw line is closer to the basket. The younger the players, the closer the line (compared to the standard 15-foot free-throw line).
- The length of the game is shorter and a shot clock is often not used for the younger levels.
- Officials are not as strict in calling all violations and fouls, and they often help instruct the players in terms of what constitutes violations and fouls. Violations that are typically not called strictly by the book, especially for younger levels, include traveling, double dribble, and backcourt violations.

International Rules

The Fédération Internationale de Basketball Amateur (FIBA) regulates international play for Olympic and other international competitions. Some of the major differences between FIBA rules and the rules presented earlier in this chapter include the following:

- The size of the court is 28 meters long by 15 meters wide. The free-throw lane is 3.6 meters wide at the free-throw line, widening to 6 meters at the baseline. The 3-point arc is a semicircle that is 6.25 meters from the basket at all points.
- Game length is four 10-minute periods with, if necessary, one or more 5-minute overtimes.
- The shot clock is 24 seconds.
- All held balls result in jump balls.
- A player fouls out after committing five fouls.
- A team is in the bonus foul situation when it has committed four team fouls in a period.
- A maximum of five players—three defensive and two offensive—may occupy the free-throw lane places during a free throw.

Jump ball

Foul

Pushing or charging

Holding

Technical

Blocking

Points scored (1 or 2)

Lane violation

Three-point goal

(continued)

▶ Figure 6.2 Common officials' signals for basketball.

Three-point field goal attempt

Intentional foul

Traveling

Illegal dribble

Three-second violation

Player control foul

▶ Figure 6.2 *(continued)*

42

ORGANIZATIONS

Continental Basketball Association
P.O. Box 6650
1412 W. Idaho Street, Suite 235
Boise, ID 83707
208-429-0101
www.hoopsonline.com

International Amateur Athletic Federation
201 01
17 Rue Princesse Florestine BP 359
MC-98007, Monaco Cedex
(377) 93 10 88 88
www.iaaf.org

National Association of Basketball Coaches
of the United States
9300 W. 110th Street, Suite 640
Overland Park, KS 66210
913-469-1001
www.nabc.ocsn.com

National Basketball Association
645 Fifth Avenue, 110th Fl.
New York, NY 10022
212-826-7000
www.nba.com

National Collegiate Athletic Association
700 W. Washington Street
P.O. Box 6222
Indianapolis, IN 46206-6222
317-917-6222
www.ncaa.org

National Federation of State High School
Associations
P.O. Box 690
Indianapolis, IN 46206
317-972-6900
www.nfhs.org

USA Basketball
5469 Mark Dabling Boulevard
Colorado Springs, CO 80918
719-590-4800
www.usabasketball.com

Youth Basketball of America
10325 Orangewood Boulevard
Orlando, FL 32821
407-363-9262
www.yboa.org

Bowling

Bowling was introduced in North America in the 1600s. Tenpin bowling, which is currently played, is believed to have sprung up when ninepin bowling was declared illegal in Connecticut in the 1840s.

The American Bowling Congress and the Women's International Bowling Congress standardized rules and equipment in the early 1900s. One of bowling's attractions is that it can be played by young and old, large and small, male and female. Bowling is the 7th most popular recreational activity in the United States, with 40 million participants. Its greatest growth is at the youth levels. The rules described in this chapter are for tenpin bowling.

Objective: To score the most points by knocking down pins with a ball rolled down a lane.

Scoring: Depends on the number of pins knocked down; scoring is increased by *spares* and *strikes* (see "Terms").

Number of Players: Played either between individuals or between teams, with up to five players on a team.

Length of Game: Ten frames.

Overview: Players take turns, rolling one frame at a time. In team play, players must bowl in the order they have designated and switch lanes after every frame, bowling five frames on their own lane and five on their opponent's. A player delivers two balls in each of the first nine frames, unless she scores a strike on the first ball by knocking down all the pins (in that case, only one ball is delivered). In the 10th frame, the player delivers either two or three balls. If she scores a strike, she rolls two more balls. If she scores a spare (by knocking down all the pins in two attempts), she rolls one more ball.

LANE

The *lane,* or alley, measures 60 feet from the *foul line* to the center of the head (first) pin (see figure 7.1). The total length of the lane, to the back of the *pin deck,* where the pins stand, is 62.85 feet. A lane's width is 41 to 42 inches.

The *pins* are wood, plastic-coated wood, or synthetic material. Each pin is 15 inches tall and weighs between 3 pounds, 6 ounces and 3 pounds, 10 ounces. Pins are set 12 inches apart from each other in a triangular pattern on the pin deck.

The approach, or *runway,* which ends at the foul line, is a minimum of 15 feet. Grooved *gutters* (channels) are on either side of the lane to catch errant balls.

TERMS

A **double** occurs when a player rolls two consecutive strikes.

An **error** is made by a player who leaves any pins standing in a frame, unless the pins left standing after the first delivery constitute a split.

A **frame** consists of two deliveries by a player (unless the first delivery is a strike, in which case the frame is over).

A **spare** is scored by a player who knocks down any remaining pins on the second delivery of the frame. The player scores 10 points plus the number of pins he knocks down on his next delivery.

A **split** refers to a setup of pins left standing after the first delivery, when the head pin is down and the remaining pins are far apart.

A **strike** is recorded by a player who knocks down all the pins on her first delivery. A strike cannot occur on the second delivery, even if no pins were knocked down on the first delivery. A strike counts 10 points plus the number of pins the player knocks down on her next two deliveries.

A **triple,** or **turkey,** refers to three successive strikes by one player.

SCORING

Except when a strike is scored, the number of pins knocked down by the player's first deliv-

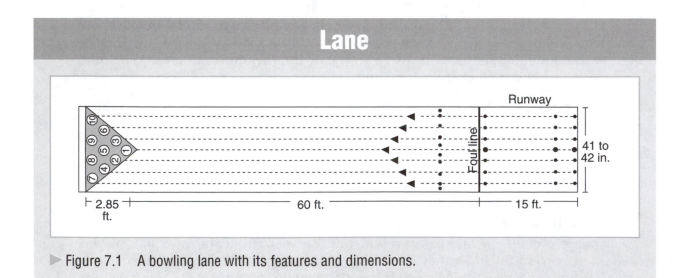

Lane

▶ Figure 7.1   A bowling lane with its features and dimensions.

1	2	3	4	5	6	7	8	9	10
☒	☒	☒	7 | 2	⑧ /	F | 9	☒	7 /	9 | —	☒ ☒ | 8
30	57	76	85	95	104	124	143	152	180

▶ Figure 7.2   This scorecard shows strikes were bowled in frames 1-3. The bowler knocked down seven pins on the first ball in frame 4 and two pins on the second ball. Frame 10 shows two strikes and two pins left standing.

Courtesy of American Bowling Congress/Women's International Bowling Congress/*Young American Bowling Congress 1995-1996 Playing Rules Book.*

ery is marked next to the small square in the upper right corner of that frame (see figure 7.2). The number of pins the player knocks down on the second delivery is marked down inside the small square. If none of the pins is knocked down by the second delivery, the player marks the score sheet with a minus sign.

When a player scores a strike, he marks an "X" in the small square in the upper right-hand corner of that frame. His final score for that frame will be 10 (for the strike) plus however many pins he knocks down in his next two deliveries. For example, if he rolls three consecutive strikes, his score for that first frame is 30 points. The score for a perfect game—12 strikes—is 300.

Fouls

A foul occurs when any part of the player touches any part of the lane or the foul line during or after a delivery. On a foul, the delivery counts, but any pins knocked down are not recorded. Except in the case of a deliberate foul, the player who fouls on her first delivery still would be allowed her second delivery, but any pins knocked down on the first delivery would first be respotted.

Pinfalls

Pinfalls are legal when pins are knocked down by the ball or by another pin, including a pin that rebounds from a side panel, rear cushion, or sweep bar when the bar is at rest on the pin deck. A pin that leans and touches the

kickback or side partition is also considered to have legally fallen. These pins are called "dead wood" and must be removed before the next delivery.

Pinfalls are not legal when

- a ball leaves the lane before reaching the pins,
- a ball rebounds from the rear cushion and knocks down any pins,
- a pin is touched by the mechanical pin-setting equipment,
- a pin is knocked down while dead wood is being removed,
- a pin is knocked down by a human pin-setter, or
- the bowler fouls.

Any pins that have illegally fallen on a player's first delivery must be respotted before the second delivery. A pin that rebounds onto the lane and remains standing is not considered to have been knocked down.

If the pins are improperly set and the player delivers a ball, the delivery and pinfall count. Once a delivery has been made, the pin position cannot be changed, unless the pinsetter moved or misplaced a pin.

Dead Ball

When a dead ball is called, the delivery does not count. Any pins knocked down with a dead ball must be respotted, and the player receives a new delivery. A dead ball occurs in the following cases:

- After a delivery, a player immediately reports that one or more pins were missing from the setup.
- A human pinsetter interferes with any standing pin before the ball reaches the pins.
- A human pinsetter interferes with a downed pin before it stops rolling.
- A player bowls out of turn or on the wrong lane.
- A player is interfered with during delivery. (The player may choose to accept the resulting pinfall.)
- Any pin is knocked down as a player delivers the ball but before the ball reaches the pins.
- The ball contacts a foreign obstacle on the playing surface.

Provisional Ball

When a protest involving a foul, legal pinfall, or dead ball is made and is not immediately resolved, a provisional ball can be rolled. A record of both scores (with and without the provisional ball) for the frame is kept, and the protest is referred to the league board or tournament director for a decision.

The procedures for rolling a provisional ball vary according to the situation. For the first ball of a frame, or the second ball in the 10th frame if the first ball was a strike, these rules apply:

- For a protested foul, the player completes the frame and then bowls one provisional ball at a full setup of pins.
- For a protested pinfall, the player completes the frame and then bowls one provisional ball at the same setup that would have occurred had the disputed pin or pins not fallen.
- For a protested dead ball, the player completes the frame and then bowls a complete provisional frame.

For a spare attempt or third ball of the 10th frame, these rules apply:

- For a protested foul or illegal pinfall, no provisional ball is necessary.

- For a protested dead ball, the player bowls a provisional ball at the same setup that was standing when the disputed ball was bowled.

EQUIPMENT

A ball is made of a nonmetallic composition (usually a plastic or urethane compound) with a circumference no greater than 27 inches and a weight of no more than 16 pounds. It can have up to five holes for finger grips.

OFFICIALS

Officials can be used for both scoring and judging fouls, but automatic scoring and foul-detection devices are typically used.

ORGANIZATIONS

American Bowling Congress
5301 S. 76th Street
Greendale, WI 53129
800-514-2695
www.bowl.com

Professional Womens Bowling Association
7171 Cherryvale Boulevard
Rockford, IL 61112
815-332-5756
www.pwba.com

Professional Bowlers Association
719 Second Avenue, Suite 701
Seattle, WA 98104
206-332-9688
www.pba.org

The National Bowling Association
377 Park Avenue South, 7th Fl.
New York, NY 10016
212-689-8308
www.tbainc.org

USA Bowling
5301 S. 76th Street
Greendale, WI 53129
800-514-2695
www.bowl.com

Women's International Bowling Congress
5301 S. 76th Street
Greendale, WI 53129
800-514-2695
www.bowl.com/bowl/wibc

Young American Bowling Alliance
5301 S. 76th Street
Greendale, WI 53129
800-514-2695
www.bowl.com/bowl/yaba

8

Boxing

© Empics

Boxing dates back more than 5,000 years. It became a more formally organized sport in 18th-century England; bare-knuckle contests were the norm until the 1870s, when padded gloves were introduced.

The sport is contested at both amateur and professional levels; boxers who become professionals cannot return to amateur status. Amateur boxing begins at age eight and continues through several age divisions and weight categories. The length and number of rounds depend on the division. Boxing grew in popularity in the 1900s in the United States, but because of its violent nature it has had a controversial history and has declined in popularity in recent years.

Objective: To score points by landing *scoring blows* on the opponent.

Scoring: Determined by the number of scoring blows a boxer lands each round (see "Scoring," page 54).

Number of Boxers: Two.

Length of Match: Three to five rounds (typically three), each round lasting one to three minutes.

Overview: The boxers attempt to land legal blows and score points. If a boxer is knocked down, the referee begins to count to 10 (see "Count," page 53). For the ways in which a boxer can earn a decision (win), see "Decisions," page 54.

RING

The *ring* is a square, 16 to 20 feet long on each side, measured from inside the *ropes* (see figure 8.1). The ring is bordered by at least four ropes, made of manila, a synthetic, or plastic and not less than one inch in diameter. The apron of the ring extends at least 2 feet beyond the ropes. The floor of the ring is not more than 4 feet above ground.

TERMS

A referee may **caution** a boxer for a foul. The action does not stop for a caution.

A referee begins a **count** one second after a boxer is down. If a boxer is not ready to resume the bout by the count of 10, the bout is over.

A **decision** is a win.

A boxer may be **disqualified** for fouls that have resulted in three warnings.

A boxer is **down** when a part of his body other than his feet touch the floor, when he is hanging on the ropes, or when he is standing but semiconscious and not fit to continue.

A **low blow** is a hit delivered below the beltline. This is a foul.

A boxer receives a **mandatory eight count** after he has been down. If he is ready to go after a count of eight, the bout resumes. Even if he is ready to go before eight, the referee will count to eight before allowing the bout to resume.

A **round** is a determined length of time, depending on the division, in which the

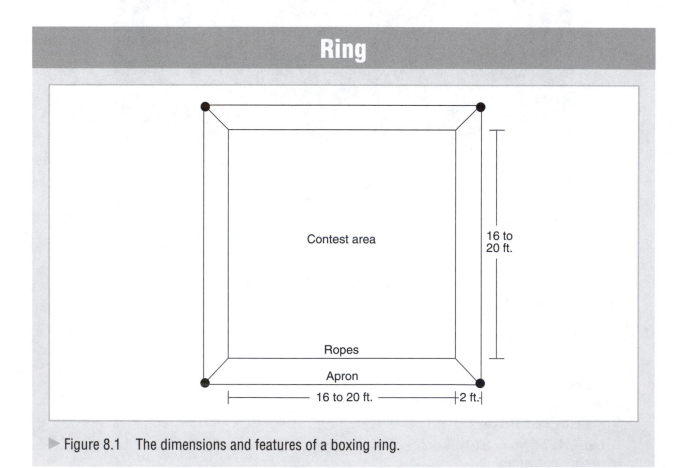

Ring

Contest area

Ropes

Apron

16 to 20 ft.

16 to 20 ft.

2 ft.

▶ Figure 8.1   The dimensions and features of a boxing ring.

boxers compete before breaking. The number of rounds varies depending on the competition.

RSC refers to body injuries to one boxer that are severe or excessive enough to cause the referee to stop the bout and declare the opponent the winner.

RSCH refers to head blows sustained by a boxer sufficient to cause the referee to stop the bout and declare the opponent the winner.

A referee may issue a **warning** to a boxer for a foul.

BOXERS

Boxers weigh in on the day of competition. A boxer must weigh more than the minimum for the weight class shown in table 8.1, and no more than the maximum for the weight class he desires to box in. Women may compete against other women, although various medical restrictions apply (e.g., pregnant women may not compete).

COMPETITION

During each bout, referees must be prepared to count and to watch for fouls.

Count

If a boxer is knocked down during a round, the referee begins to count to 10, with one second between numbers, indicating each second with his hand. The count begins one second after the boxer is down. The opponent must go to a neutral corner; the referee will not start or continue the count until the opponent does so.

The bout never continues before the count of eight, even if the downed boxer rises and is ready to continue before then. If the boxer is unable to continue at the end of the count, the bout is over and the opponent wins.

If a boxer is down at the end of a round, the referee will count as usual. If a boxer is ready to continue before the count of eight but then falls before being hit again, the referee resumes counting from the count of eight.

Table 8.1 Weight Classes		
Class	**Pounds**	**Kilograms**
Light flyweight	106	48
Flyweight	112	51
Bantamweight	119	54
Featherweight	125	57
Lightweight	132	60
Light welterweight	139	63.5
Welterweight	147	67
Light middleweight	156	71
Middleweight	165	75
Light heavyweight	178	81
Heavyweight	201	91
Super heavyweight	over 201	over 91

Adapted from United Sates Amateur Boxing, Inc. 1995.

If both boxers are down at the same time, counting continues as long as one remains down. If both remain down past the count of 10, the bout is stopped and the boxer who has the most points wins. If a boxer has three counts in one round, or four counts in a bout, the bout is stopped and the opponent wins.

Fouls

A referee may caution, warn, or disqualify a boxer who commits a foul. A referee may caution a boxer without stopping the bout; he must stop the bout to issue a warning. If a referee warns a boxer about a particular foul, he may not later issue a caution for the same foul. Three cautions for the same foul require a warning. A boxer will be disqualified if he receives three warnings in one bout.

Examples of fouls include

- hitting below the belt, holding, tripping, kicking, or butting;
- using head butts or blows;
- hitting with the shoulder, forearm, or elbow;
- pushing or shoving;
- pressing an arm or elbow in the opponent's face;
- pressing the opponent's head back over the ropes;
- hitting the opponent's back, neck, kidneys, or back of head;
- hitting with an open glove;
- hitting while holding the ropes;
- hitting an opponent who is down or who is rising;
- holding and hitting;
- locking the opponent's arm or head;
- not stepping back when ordered to break;
- using aggressive or offensive language; and
- spitting out the mouthpiece.

SCORING

A scoring blow is one that lands directly with the knuckle part of the closed glove on any part of the front or sides of the head or body above the belt. In case of a flurry of blows from both boxers, the boxer who has had the better exchange in the rally is credited according to the degree of his superiority.

At the end of each round, the more skillful boxer for that round is awarded 20 points and the other boxer proportionately fewer. If boxers are judged equal for that round, they both receive 20 points. No extra points are awarded for a knockdown.

If the winner of a round committed a foul, his opponent receives one point. (If the score was 20-19, it becomes 20-20.) If the loser of a round committed a foul, he loses one point. (If he lost the round, 20-19, the score becomes 20-18.) If the round is tied, the boxer who committed a foul has one point subtracted.

Electronic scoring was introduced in the 1992 Olympics. Five judges record scoring blows on keypads linked to a mainframe computer; for a blow to be recorded by the computer, three of the five judges must record the blow within a one-second interval. Scores are reported in terms of the number of blows recognized by a majority of the judges over the course of the bout. For example, a 29-25 win for the Red corner indicates that Red was credited with 29 blows, while Blue was credited with 25.

Decisions

Types of decisions are as follows:

- **Win by points:** The boxer with the most points wins.
- **Win by retirement:** If a boxer quits a bout because of injury or fails to resume after a round break, the opponent wins.
- **Win by referee stopping contest:** A referee may stop a bout if a boxer is being outclassed or injured, or if he has reached the compulsory count limit. A referee may stop a bout for excessive body injury (RSC) or as a result of head blows (RSCH).
- **Win by disqualification:** If a boxer is disqualified, the opponent wins.
- **Win by walkover:** If a boxer fails to appear within three minutes of the bell, the opponent wins.

Injury

If the referee believes a boxer is unable to continue because of injury, he may stop the bout and declare the opponent the winner. This decision is the referee's, although he may consult with a doctor. The ringside physician also has the right to terminate a bout for medical reasons. If the referee consults a doctor, he must abide by the doctor's recommendation.

EQUIPMENT

Approved headgear and custom-made or individually fitted mouthpieces must be worn. Gloves are 10 ounces for weight classes up to 156 pounds, and 12 ounces for heavier weight classes, except for masters competitors, who wear 12-ounce gloves, regardless of weight.

OFFICIALS

The referee controls the bout. He uses three basic commands: "Stop," "Box," and "Break" (the latter in breaking a clinch). The referee may terminate a match at any time if it is too one-sided or if a boxer is endangered.). The referee also issues cautions and warnings and may disqualify a boxer for fouls.

The judges independently judge the merits of the boxers and determine the winner. Either five or three judges are present. A timekeeper keeps time for each round and between rounds. During championship events, a three- or five-panel jury checks the scorecards of the judges to ensure points and penalties are correctly recorded.

ORGANIZATIONS

USA Boxing
1 Olympic Plaza
Colorado Springs, CO 80909-5778
719-866-4506
www.usaboxing.org

International Boxing Federation
134 Evergreen Place, 9th Fl.
East Orange, NJ 07018
973-414-0300
www.ibf-usba-boxing.com

© Empics

9
Canoeing and Kayaking

Canoeing and kayaking offer several forms of competition, including flatwater, slalom, and wildwater racing. This chapter will focus on those three types of competitions.

Flatwater's beginnings are traced to the early 1900s; the first sporting association for kayakers was founded in Copenhagen in 1924, and the first European Championships were contested in 1933. Slalom got its beginnings in Switzerland in 1932, coming from the idea of ski slalom. It began on flatwater and soon moved to whitewater. It is popular in North America and Europe and is gaining interest on other continents as well. Wildwater canoeing began in 1959, with most courses between four and six kilometers; sprint courses between 500 and 1000 meters were added in 1988.

Overview: *Flatwater* competitions take place on unobstructed courses of varying lengths; the fastest time wins. In *slalom* racing, competitors negotiate a rapid river course defined by gates. The object is to record the fastest time and not accrue any penalties in negotiating the course. The time of the run, in seconds, plus the penalty points, determines a competitor's final score; low score wins. In *wildwater* competitions, the start is directly upstream or downstream; no angled starts are allowed. Boats are held in the starting position until the start; competitors may use only standing starts. Individual starts are separated by at least 30 seconds; team starts have intervals of at least one minute.

TERMS

A **brace** is a defensive maneuver in which a kayaker uses a paddle blade and hip action to keep upright.

A boat is **broached** when it is pinned to a rock.

Class I to VI is the whitewater river rating system, from easiest to most difficult.

The **deck** is the top of the boat, which keeps the water out.

An **eddy** is a calm spot in whitewater, just downstream of a rock.

Flotation bags, filled with air, are fitted on either side of a kayak's walls to provide buoyancy in case of a capsize.

A **J lean** is named for the shape of a competitor's spine when she leans into a boat tilt with her body weight centered over the boat.

Kayak paddle blades are **offset**, which means that the blades face in different directions. The difference in blade direction is usually about 70 degrees.

A **spray skirt** fits around the rim of the boat and around the competitor's waist to keep water out.

A **sweep** is the primary stroke used to turn a boat.

FLATWATER

Course requirements, procedures, and equipment for flatwater competition follow. Variations for slalom and wildwater racing are noted on pages 59 and 60, respectively.

Men's flatwater events include the 200-meter, 500-meter, 1,000-meter, and 5,000-meter; women's races include the 200-meter, 500-meter, and 5,000-meter. A race involves at least three kayaks or canoes; if heats are necessary, lots are drawn to place competitors into the heats. Heats are not used, however, for 5,000-meter races. Lots are also used to determine the starting position.

At the start of a race, the bows of the boats must be on the starting line and stationary. An official uses a starter's pistol to begin the race. The starter may recall the race to realign the boats. Any racer who makes two false starts is disqualified. If a racer breaks a paddle within the first 25 meters, the starter will recall the race.

Course

The start and finish are at right angles to the course and are marked by red flags. The 25-meter distance, from which competitors can be recalled for a fresh start, is marked by yellow flags. Each boat has an individual course at least 5 meters wide at the beginning. For races up to 1,000 meters, the course is straight and in one direction. For races beyond 1,000 meters, turning points are permitted. Turning points are marked by at least six diagonally divided flags, with one half in red and one half in yellow.

Competition

A competitor may not take pace or receive assistance from boats not in the race. Such boats may not proceed on the course, even outside the boundary buoys. In races up to 1,000 meters, competitors must stay in their marked lanes. In 5,000-meter races, they may go outside their lanes as long as they do not obstruct other competitors.

In races with turns, competitors must make the turns counterclockwise. If two competitors are approaching a turn together, the competitor on the outside must leave room for the competitor on the inside if the inside competitor's bow is even with the front edge of the cockpit of the outside boat. A competitor may touch a turning buoy as long as she doesn't gain an advantage from the touch.

A craft that is being passed cannot obstruct the craft overtaking it. The boat that is passing must, however, keep clear of the boat it is overtaking. A competitor who causes a collision may be disqualified.

A competitor finishes a race when the craft's bow crosses the finish line with all the crew members in the boat. In case of a tie for a position that determines which boat will advance to the next level of competition, if not enough lanes are available to accommodate both boats at the next level, the two boats race again. This race takes place one hour after the last race of the day. If the two tie again, lots are drawn to determine who advances.

Equipment

Canoes and kayaks may be constructed of any material; electric or electronic devices, such as pumps, are not allowed. Kayaks may have one steering rudder and may be propelled only with double-blade paddles. Canoes may not have a steering rudder or any guiding apparatus; Canadian canoes may be propelled only with single-blade paddles. The paddles may not be fixed to the boat.

SLALOM

In individual slalom competitions, each craft is allowed two runs, the best of which counts. In team competitions, either one or two runs may be allowed. Team members may be substituted between runs.

Competitors may make standing starts only. Starts may be directly upstream or downstream; starts angled into or against the current are not allowed. Boats are held in position by the starter's assistant until the start. In team events, the second and third boats must be stationary until the first boat begins. Start intervals are 45 seconds or greater. Slalom competitions are guided by rules covering gate and course negotiation, penalties, finish line and point calculation, and equipment.

Course

The course must be entirely negotiable and provide the same conditions for right-handed and left-handed paddlers. Ideally, the course should require reverse maneuvers and consist of natural and artificial obstacles. The course must be at least 300 meters wide and 600 meters long, with 20 to 25 gates. The last gate must be at least 25 meters before the finish.

The current velocity must not be less than 2 meters per second. Competitors are allowed a training run on the course before the race.

Negotiating Gates

Competitors negotiate gates according to the established direction. A gate consists of two suspended poles painted with five green and five white rings for downstream gates and five red and five white rings for upstream gates. The poles are between 1.2 and 3.5 meters apart and are 3.5 to 5 centimeters in diameter. The lower end of each pole should be about 15 centimeters above the water.

The gates are numbered, and competitors must negotiate them in numerical order. Negotiation begins when a competitor crosses the line between the two poles or when a competitor's boat, body, or paddle touches a pole. Negotiation of a gate ends when a competitor begins to negotiate the next gate, or when she finishes the race.

To correctly negotiate a gate, a competitor must

- maneuver his boat and body between the poles on the correct side of the gate;
- cross his boat between the poles at the same time as his body crosses between;
- pass at least his entire head between the poles, and in the proper direction; and
- not touch a pole with his body, paddle, or boat for a faultless negotiation.

Penalties

Competitors are penalized for incorrect gate negotiations and other acts as follows.

- *5 points*—touching one or both poles while correctly negotiating the gate. Repeated touching of the same pole or poles is penalized only once.

- *50 points*—touching one or both poles while incorrectly negotiating the gate. Intentionally pushing a gate to facilitate negotiation, crossing a gate line while the body is upside down, and negotiating the gate in the wrong direction are each a 50-point penalty. Missing a gate and failing to cross the finish line within 15 seconds of teammates are also 50-point penalties.

A competitor is not penalized for undercutting a gate or for making repeated attempts at a gate, as long as she does not touch the poles or pass her body across the line between the poles. A competitor cannot be penalized more than 50 points at any one gate.

On the Course

A competitor who is being overtaken must give way if the section judge whistles for him to do so. The competitor who is passing, however, must be attempting to negotiate the course properly. If he is passing because the competitor ahead has missed a gate, he cannot hinder the competitor as he approaches. Any competitor who is hindered may repeat the run if authorized to do so by the chief judge.

A craft is considered capsized when it has turned upside down and the competitor has left the boat. After a capsize, a competitor may not negotiate any further gates. An Eskimo roll is not a capsize.

Finish and Point Calculations

A competitor finishes when her body crosses the finish line (in team competition, when the first body in the boat crosses the line). In team events, all three craft must finish within 15 seconds of each other. The time for team events begins when the first boat starts and ends when the last boat finishes.

A competitor's or team's point total is figured by adding the time of the run, in seconds, plus penalty points. For example, a running time of 135.8 seconds plus 55 penalty points equals a final score of 190.8. If two competitors are tied, the one with the better noncounting run is placed ahead of the other competitor. A competitor who accepts outside assistance or leaves his boat is disqualified.

Equipment

Each boat must have handles attached no more than 30 centimeters from the bow and the stern. Handles may be an integral part of the boat construction or may be loops of rope. A competitor cannot tape the handles. If a competitor breaks or loses a paddle, she may use an extra paddle that she carries on the boat.

WILDWATER

In wildwater competitions, a craft being overtaken by another craft must allow passage if the competitor on the overtaking craft shouts, "Free!" If a competitor sees another in real danger, he must help him or risk disqualification for life. A competitor may resume competition after capsizing. If two or more competitors record the same score, the tie stands.

Course

The course must be at least three kilometers long, and part of it must be Class III difficulty. As an alternative to a single run, competitors may be required to make two runs of 500 to 1,000 meters each, with the results being an aggregate of both runs. This latter event is called a Wildwater Sprint event. A boat must be able to navigate the complete course without touching bottom. Dangerous passes may be marked with gates to indicate the correct channel. Competitors may take a training run a day before the competition.

Equipment

Wildwater boats must be rudderless. As with flatwater boats, kayaks are propelled only with a double-blade paddle and Canadian canoes only with a single-blade paddle.

OFFICIALS

Officials who supervise competitions include chief officials, starters, aligners, 25-meter judges for flatwater racing, course and turning point judges, finishing line judges, timekeepers, and boat controllers.

ORGANIZATIONS

International Canoe Federation
Calle de la Antracita 7, 40
E-28045 Madrid, Spain
011-34-91-5061150
www.canoeicf.com

© Empics

10 Cricket

At a glance, cricket may seem a bit like baseball. It is played on a grassy field and has, after all, bowlers (who act much as pitchers do in baseball) and batters. Cricket, like baseball, is played in innings, and the team in the field tries to get the batters out and to stop them from scoring runs; the team with the most runs wins.

But with rules governing play with leads of 200 runs or more and notes for test matches extending up to five days, it's easy to see that cricket is indeed quite distinct from baseball.

Cricket, in fact, is the older of the two sports, with records of games being played in London in the early 1700s. The Marylebone Cricket Club (MCC), formed in 1787 in London, drew up the code by which the game is played and has continued as the governing body for the sport ever since. The first official cricket club in America was formed at Haverford College, near Philadelphia, in 1833, but the sport has never caught on in the states as it has in other countries.

Objective: To score the most runs.

Number of Players: Eleven per side.

Length of Game: One or two innings. An innings, which is a singular term, is finished when all 11 batters on the batting team have come to bat and 10 have been put out, one after the other (the last batter does not have to be put out; more on that later). The team in the field then bats in the same way.

Overview: Bowlers deliver balls to batters, who hit the balls and attempt to score as many runs as possible. For a more complete overview, see "Play" on page 65.

FIELD

The field is an open, oval expanse of closely cropped turf divided into two equal halves by an imaginary line running down the middle of the *pitch* (see figure 10.1). From the point of view of a right-handed striking batter as he faces the bowler, the right side of the ground is the *off side*; the left side is the *on* (or *leg*) *side*. The field is encircled by a roped or chalked *boundary line*. There is no official size for the field, but most high-level contests are played on fields with diameters of 150 to 200 yards.

Wickets are placed opposite each other, 22 yards apart. Each wicket is made of three poles, or *stumps*. The stump closest to the batter is the *leg stump*; the stump in the middle is the *center stump*; and the stump farthest from the batter is the *off stump*. The wickets are 28 inches high and 9 inches wide. Set in grooves on the tops of the stumps are two *bails*—cylindrical pieces of wood that measure 4.38 inches in length.

Running 4 feet in front of and parallel to each wicket is a 12-foot *popping crease*. Any time a batter is away from his wicket and beyond his popping crease, he may be put out. If any part of his body or his bat is behind the line, he may not be put out. Intersecting the popping crease are two lines, 8 feet, 8 inches apart,

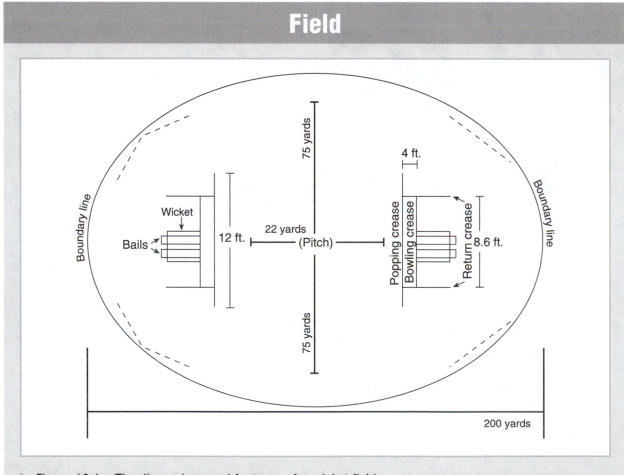

▶ Figure 10.1   The dimensions and features of a cricket field.

running back toward the wicket. These are the *return creases*. These creases mark the area in which the bowler may operate.

The *bowling crease* runs parallel to and 4 feet behind the popping crease. The wickets are set on this crease. The *pitch* is the stretch of turf between the two wickets; it's usually the width of the area between the two return creases. The grass on the pitch is very short and smooth; in many instances the pitch is artificial turf.

TERMS

A **back-up** is the nonstriker's, or nonbatter's, "lead-off" of his popping crease when he expects to run. As the bowler releases his delivery, the nonstriker goes over his popping crease, taking a few steps toward the opposite wicket.

A **beamer** is a fast, head-high delivery.

A **bouncer** is a brushback—a pitch delivered short and fast so that it will bounce up at the batter's head.

A **boundary** is a "four" (a ground ball hit over the boundary line) or a "six" (a fly ball onto or over the boundary line).

A batter is **bowled** when the delivery gets by him and knocks a bail off his wicket. This is similar to a baseball strikeout.

Any number of runs may score when a fair delivery does not touch the batter or his bat and gets by the wicketkeeper; this is called a **bye.** (This is similar to a passed ball in baseball.)

The **center** (or middle) **stump** is the center pole of the wicket.

A batter makes a **century** when he scores 100 runs in a single at-bat (roughly equivalent to rushing for 100 yards in American football).

A **cutter** is a medium-paced delivery that spins or bounces into or away from the batter.

A **dead pitch** is one that bounces low and straight—an easy pitch to hit.

A **declaration** is a strategy in which the team batting may stop before all of its batters are

out; this is usually done to allow enough time to get the opponents out.

A **duck** signifies an at-bat in which the batter doesn't score any runs.

Fall of wicket refers to an out; "the sixth wicket fell" means the batting team has made its sixth out.

Follow on is a strategy in a two-innings match that allows the team that bats first, if ahead by a certain number of runs, to reverse the second-innings batting sequence.

A **four** is a ground ball that goes into or beyond the boundary line; this automatically scores four runs.

A **grubber** is a delivery that's rolled on the ground.

A **hat trick** occurs when a bowler takes three wickets on three successive deliveries.

A **leg-bye** is a run scored from a delivery that hits the batter's body.

The **leg stump** is the pole of the wicket closest to the batter.

A **maiden** is an over in which no runs are scored off the bat.

No ball signifies an illegal delivery; the batting team gets an automatic run.

Off side is the half of the playing area that the batter is facing.

The **off stump** is the pole of the wicket farthest from the batter.

On side is the half of the playing area behind the batter.

An **over** is a set of six fairly delivered balls to one wicket. The direction of the deliveries switches to the opposite wicket at the end of each over.

The **pitch** is the area between the two wickets.

A **quick single** is a run scored on a shallow hit, similar to a baseball bunt.

A **shooter** is a fast delivery that stays low.

A **short run,** which does not count as a run, occurs when a batter fails to touch part of his body or his bat behind the popping crease when running.

A **six** is six runs automatically scored when a fly ball goes on the full onto or beyond a boundary line.

A **sticky wicket** is a damp pitch that's drying out, causing the ball to bounce and become difficult to hit.

Stonewalling is batting with the intention of not getting out, rather than trying to score runs.

A **strike rate** is the average number of runs a batter makes per 100 deliveries.

A **stump** is the name for a wicket's three individual poles. A wicket is often referred to as "the stumps."

A **wide** is called by the umpire when the bowler doesn't deliver the ball within reach of the batter. This results in a penalty run for the opponents.

PLAYERS

Officially there are 11 players per side. The lineup is set before each innings and may not be changed without the consent of the opposing captain. If both sides agree, more or less than 11 may play, but no more than 11 may field. The traditional cricket uniform is white or cream pants, shirts, sweaters, and shoes. Club insignias are on players' caps.

A substitute may field for a teammate only if the teammate is injured or ill. If a fielder has to leave for another legitimate reason, and the opposing captain consents, a team may substitute for the fielder. However, no substitute may play for the wicketkeeper or be allowed to bat or bowl.

A player who was substituted for may return to bat, bowl, or field. If he was gone for more than 15 minutes, however, he must be on the field for the length of time he was gone before he may bowl. A runner may run for a batter who is ill or injured. He must wear the same protective equipment that the batter wears. An injured batter is out when his runner is put out.

Bowlers

The bowler may take a "runup" before delivering, but he must have at least part of his front foot behind the popping crease, and part of his back foot inside the return creases, when he releases the ball. Failure to do so results in the umpire calling *no ball,* which gives the opponents a penalty run. A no-ball will also be called if the bowler throws the ball. A no-ball does not count as part of the over.

The bowler must deliver the ball within reach of the batter. Failure to do so will result in the umpire calling a *wide,* which also results in a penalty run for the opponents. A wide does not count as part of the over.

The bowler most often will try to "attack the off stump" (keep the ball outside) and bounce the ball at the wicket, not too close to the batter. Most bowlers don't want to bowl short; when the ball bounces far from the batter, a high, easily hit long hop results. Bowlers also usually stay away from *full tosses,* which are deliveries that reach the batter in the air; these are easiest of all to hit. Bowlers often try to vary the angle of their deliveries, sometimes bowling *over the wicket* (e.g., on the left side of the wicket of the bowler who is right-handed) and sometimes *around the wicket* (on the right side of the wicket if the bowler is right-handed).

Batters

A skilled batter doesn't just swing indiscriminately for the boundary. Rather, he may start out swinging with a high-percentage, vertical stroke, deflecting or spoiling a bowler's good deliveries, and using various strokes for various deliveries, including baseball-like "cross-bat" strokes and "sweep or reverse-sweep" strokes to sweep the ball to his left or right; he may even go over the popping crease to meet the ball and drive it straight over the bowler's head.

Regardless of the stroke or situation, the batter doesn't want to give the fielders a chance to catch a ball in the air. The skilled batter may score a century (100 runs) during an at-bat; he may also be able to "carry his bat" (outlast all his teammates until he's the last batter not out).

Fielders

The *wicketkeeper* is the only player who wears gloves; he wears one on each hand and acts much like a baseball catcher. He positions himself opposite the bowler and behind the batter who is batting. The other nine fielders vary their positions, according to the skills of the bowler and the batter, but in loose terms they fit into these positions:

• One or more **slips** play behind the wicket-keeper, to the off side of the field. The faster the bowler is, the more slips might be employed, expecting the batters to hit, in baseball terminology, "foul balls."

• A **gully** stands behind the slip for deeper-hit balls.

• A **point,** a **cover,** and a **mid-off fielder** stand on the off side, beginning with the point about 15 yards from the batter; these fielders are 5 to 10 yards apart from each other. They attempt to stop balls from getting past their side of the field.

• **Mid-ons, mid-wickets, square legs,** and **fine legs** are on the on side, or leg side, of the field. Mid-ons play farthest from the striking batter; square legs and fine legs play closest. A fine leg plays behind the batter, while a square leg plays in front of him.

A team may shift to play a batter *finer* (closer to parallel to the line of the pitch), or *squarer* (at more of a right angle to the line of the pitch).

Other rules regarding fielders include the following:

• No more than two on-side fielders may be behind the popping crease when the bowler delivers the ball. The umpire will call "no ball" if more than two are on side behind the popping crease.

• Until the batter makes contact with the ball or the ball strikes the batter or goes past him, no fielder may be on the pitch except the bowler, or "no ball" will be called.

• When fielders' protective helmets are not in use, they are placed behind the wicket-keeper. If a ball in play strikes a helmet, the batting team is awarded five penalty runs.

PLAY

A batter stands at each wicket. The bowler for the team in the field, much like a baseball pitcher, delivers a ball to the batter standing near the opposite wicket. In simple terms, the ball must not be thrown—and a throw involves straightening the arm. A locked arm is permissible, but so too is an arm that remains bent throughout.

The batter may swing and miss any number of times; he cannot "strike out," as in baseball. He also cannot hit a "foul ball," because all territory is "fair"—even if he hits the ball to the side or behind him. Batters do not have to run after hitting the ball, but if they choose to, they score a run each time they cross the opposite popping creases (see figure 10.1, page 62). Each time they both make it safely from one wicket to the other while the ball is in play, their team scores a run.

The batters carry their bats with them when they run. This can be an advantage, because the bat is considered an extension of the batter's arm, and he can reach over with his bat to touch the popping crease to score a run. Each time a batter hits a fly ball over the boundary line (similar to a "home run" in baseball), his team gets six runs; each time a ground ball goes over the boundary line, his team scores four runs. This is true whether or not a fielder has touched the ball or is in possession of it when it crosses the boundary line.

A batter continues to hit until the fielding team can get him out. One way to get a batter out is for the bowler to sneak a delivery by him, knocking at least one bail off his wicket. Other ways to get a batter out are detailed in "Scoring and Violations" on page 66.

Because a batter is at each wicket, the direction of bowling is reversed every six deliveries. A bowler bowls a sequence of six fair deliveries toward one wicket, and then another fielder becomes the bowler and bowls a sequence of six fair deliveries toward the opposite wicket. The six fair deliveries is called an over, and this pattern continues throughout the match. The fielding team may change bowlers for every over, and a bowler may bowl multiple overs, but the bowler may not bowl two overs in a row.

The wicketkeeper acts similar to a baseball catcher; he is the only player with gloves (he has, in fact, one on each hand). He shuttles from wicket to wicket after every over; he is always behind the wicket opposite the bowler.

Batters always bat in pairs, one at each wicket; therefore the last (11th) batter does not have to be put out, because he cannot bat alone. Once the 10th is retired, the innings is over. Even so, a normal two-innings match can go on for days. At the end of the match, the team with the most runs wins. (Quite often a team will score more than 200 runs.) If the team batting second needs 200 runs to win, and scores 200 when, say, its seventh batter is hitting, then the contest is over and the win is scored "200 for 7," signifying that the team scored the winning run on its seventh wicket, or batter. The teams draw, regardless of the score, if it is not possible to finish the match. If the match is finished with the score even, it is a tie.

"*Limited overs*" cricket, typically played in one day, is becoming more popular. The length of the game is controlled by the number of overs each team is allowed. A "40-over" match is one in which each team bats for 40 overs (that is, each team gets 240 legal deliveries). Typically, not all batters get to bat in limited overs.

SCORING AND VIOLATIONS

A team scores one or more runs in these situations:

- When a batter hits a fly ball over the boundary line, that's worth six runs.
- When a batter hits a ground ball that goes over the boundary line, that's worth four runs.
- When both batters cross the opposite popping crease, one run is scored.

- When the fielding team claims "lost ball," the batting team gets six runs—or the number that it had already scored on the play, if that's more than six.
- When the opposing bowler delivers a *wide ball* (one that's out of reach of the batter) or a *no ball* (an illegal delivery), the batting team adds five runs to what it has already scored on the play when a fielder illegally stops the ball.
- When a *bye* is called, any number of runs may be scored.
- When a *leg-bye* is called, one run is scored.

A batter is out when he

- allows a delivery to knock a bail off his wicket (in which case he is "out, bowled");
- hits a ball caught in the air by a fielder ("out, caught");
- uses his body to block a delivery from hitting his wicket, even if unintentional ("out, leg before wicket");
- is not over the popping crease when a fielder throws a ball and knocks the bail off the wicket that the batter is approaching, or when a fielder holds the ball and knocks the bail off by hitting it ("run out");
- crosses the popping crease while trying to hit the ball and the wicketkeeper grabs the ball and knocks the bail off his wicket before the batter can return ("out, stumped");
- touches a ball in play ("out, handled the ball");
- hits a ball twice ("out, hit the ball twice");
- intentionally interferes with a fielder ("out, obstructing the field"); or
- breaks his wicket while receiving, or preparing to receive, a delivery ("out, hit wicket").

The following rules fall under the category of maintaining fair play:

- No player may rub the ball on the ground, rub an artificial substance on the ball, or take any other action to alter the condition of the ball, except to dry a wet ball or to remove mud from a ball.
- If a fielder intentionally obstructs a batter in running, the umpire will signal "dead ball" and allow any completed runs, plus the run in progress, to score.
- Bowling fast, short-pitched balls is not fair if it is intended to, or likely to, injure the batter. The umpire may call a "no ball" and caution the bowler.
- Bowling fast, high, full pitches—deliveries that pass, on the fly, above the batter's waist height—will result in the umpire calling "no ball" and cautioning the bowler.
- Wasting time is unfair and results in a caution.
- Any player damaging the pitch to assist a bowler will be cautioned by the umpire.
- Unless the bowler makes a play on him, the nonstriker may not attempt to steal a run during the bowler's runup. The umpire will signal "dead ball" and order the batters to return to their original wickets.

A ball is ruled dead when

- it settles in the hands of the wicketkeeper or the bowler;
- it goes over the boundary;
- a batter is out;
- it lodges in the equipment or clothing of a batter or umpire;
- it lodges in a protective helmet of a fielder;
- it is lost; or
- the umpire calls "over" or "time."

EQUIPMENT

The ball is hard, weighing, when new, not less than 155.9 grams and not greater than 163 grams. The ball when new must measure not less than 8 3/16 inches and not more than 9 inches. It is red, with a single-stitched seam down the middle, made of cork and wool and bound in leather. The bat is paddle-shaped. It is made of willow and may be of any weight. Its maximum length is 38 inches and maximum width is 4 1/4 inches. The batter wears protective gear: padded leg guards, padded gloves, and a helmet with a face guard. The wicketkeeper wears two flat, long-cuffed leather gloves. He also wears leg pads.

OFFICIALS

Two umpires officiate a match; one umpire stands near each wicket.

ORGANIZATIONS

Association of Cricket Umpires and Scorers
5 The Glade
Enfield
Middlesex, Greater London EN2 7QH, England
44 181 363 9397

Marylebone Cricket Club
Lord's Cricket Ground
London NW8 8QN, England
44 071 289 5686

International Cricket Council
ICC Development Office
The Clock Tower
Lord's Cricket Ground
London NW8 8QN, England
+44 (0) 7266 1818

© Empics

11 Cross-Country Skiing

A petroglyph on a rock wall in Norway depicts a skier on long skis. Dating from 2000 B.C., this petroglyph attests to the longevity of Nordic, or cross-country, skiing. Scandinavian immigrants sparked interest in cross-country skiing in the United States in the 19th century. Advances in equipment helped to create two distinct forms of skiing: downhill (Alpine) and cross-country. The latter experienced a boom in the United States in the 1970s, and in the 1980s two forms of cross-country skiing evolved: classical (traditional) skiing in tracks and freestyle (skating) out of tracks, on groomed trails. Nordic downhill, which combines both Alpine and Nordic elements, has also emerged as a type of skiing. Cross-country skiing is popular both as recreation and as competitive sport.

Objective: To record the fastest time.

Number of Competitors: There are individual and team events; see "Competitors" on page 71.

Length of Course: From 5 to 50 kilometers.

Overview: Competitions include individual, relay, and pursuit events, as well as combination events, which take place over two days and include both classical and freestyle forms of skiing.

COURSE

Cross-country courses range from 5 to 50 kilometers; they are marked with various colored boards, arrows, and ribbons, depending on the competition. A course must be at least three to four meters wide and prepared so that skiers can safely compete. An individual's two ski tracks are set 17 to 30 centimeters apart, measured from the middle of each track. The tracks are 2 to 5 centimeters deep.

A typical course consists of

- one-third uphills, with climbs between 9 and 18 percent, plus some steeper, short climbs;
- one-third rolling terrain, with short climbs and downhills and height differences of one to nine meters; and
- one-third varied downhills.

Table 11.1 shows rules for height differences, maximum climbs, and total climbs.

TERMS

A **christie** is a skidded turn in which both skis skid on the same edges.

Cross-country downhill skiing is a combination of Alpine and Nordic skiing also known as "telemarking."

A **diagonal stride** is the most common cross-country maneuver for gliding across flat terrain and up hills. It employs arm and leg actions similar to walking.

A **diagonal V** is a skating maneuver in which the skier glides aggressively uphill with the skis in a V-shaped position.

Double poling is a maneuver in which a competitor uses both arms to push simultaneously on the poles to provide momentum.

A **gliding herringbone** is a maneuver used to slide uphill with skis in a V shape.

A **herringbone** is a maneuver used to step uphill with skis in a V shape.

A **kick double pole** refers to pushing off with both poles while also pushing off from the leg to provide more power. This is also known as *single-step double pole.*

A **marathon skate** is a technique that combines double poling with an extra push from an angled or skating ski. Skiers use this to gain extra power in tracks.

Poling refers to a skier planting the poles to increase momentum or to guide through a turn.

The **power side** is the side on which poling occurs during skating moves.

Sideslipping refers to skidding on the skis to the side and forward down a hill.

Sidestepping refers to lifting one ski at a time across the snow to move sideways.

A **skate turn** is a technique used to accelerate around turns, using the skis in a V shape. The competitor steps off one ski and onto the other, bringing the first ski parallel.

Skating with no poles occurs when the skier steps off one ski, glides onto the other, and then glides back to the first ski.

A **snowplow** is a downhill maneuver a skier uses to control speed by angling the skis in an A shape and pressing them into the snow.

Table 11.1   Height and Climb Regulations

Distance (km)	Maximum height differential (m)	Maximum single climb (m)	Maximum total climb (m)
5	100	50	150 to 225
10	150	80	250 to 450
15	200	100	400 to 650
30	200	100	800 to 1,200
50 and longer	200	100	1,400 to 1,800

Adapted from United States Ski and Snowboard Association 1993.

A **telemark turn** occurs when the skier sinks into a curtsy and the skis form one long curve.

V1 is a skating maneuver that combines skating with double poling. The skier poles once for every two steps. This maneuver is done on groomed snow with no tracks.

V2 is a fast skating technique that combines double poling with skating. The skier poles twice for every two steps. As with V1, this maneuver is done on groomed, trackless snow.

A **wedge turn** is a turn made with the skis in an A-shape.

COMPETITORS

Cross-country skiing offers competition for all levels of interest. Men, women, persons with special needs, seniors, and youth can all enjoy the sport at various distances and tracks of difficulty. Those categories are broken down as follows:

- **Men:** 10-kilometer, 15-kilometer, 30-kilometer, 50-kilometer, and 70-kilometer; 4 × 10-kilometer relay; pursuit races; and overall
- **Women:** 5-kilometer, 10-kilometer, 15-kilometer, 20-kilometer, and 50-kilometer; 4 × 5-kilometer relay; pursuit races; and overall
- **Disabled men:** 5-kilometer, 10-kilometer, 10-kilometer pursuit, 20-kilometer, and 30-kilometer; 3 × 5-kilometer relay; and overall
- **Disabled women:** 5-kilometer, 7.5-kilometer pursuit, 10-kilometer, and 20-kilometer; 3 × 5-kilometer relay; and overall

Competition is categorized in junior, senior, and masters divisions.

- **Seniors:** At least 21 years old during the competition year
- **Masters:** At least 30 years old; masters divisions are split into five-year categories (30-to-34, 35-to-39, and so on)

- **Juniors:**
Junior 5	9 to 10 years old
Junior 4	11 to 12 years old
Junior 3	13 to 14 years old
Junior 2	15 to 16 years old
Junior 1	17 to 18 years old
Older junior	19 to 20 years old

RACING

Competitors use one of two skiing techniques: classical or freestyle. *Classical skiing* is what most people associate with traditional cross-country skiing: using a diagonal stride, double-poling, and using a herringbone technique without a gliding phase. Skiers cannot skate in a classical race. For individual competitions, skiers follow a single track. *Freestyle skiing* employs skating methods, including marathon and no-pole skating. This is normally a faster method than classical skiing.

Competitors must follow the marked course from start to finish, using their marked skis and their own means of propulsion. They cannot be paced or pushed. In individual competitions, a competitor may exchange poles, but not skis. During relays and combined competitions, a competitor may exchange one ski if it is broken or damaged.

A competitor may not wax, scrape, or clean her skis during competition, with one exception: In classical skiing, a competitor may scrape her skis to remove snow and ice and add wax if necessary. She must do this on her own, outside the track. A competitor who is being overtaken must give way on the first demand, unless he is in the final 200 meters of the course. This is true in classical competitions even if two tracks are in use.

Start

The starter calls, "Attention," 10 seconds before the start, then counts down beginning at five. The competitor's feet must be stationary and behind the start line; the poles should be over the start line and stationary. If electric timing is used, the competitor may take off anywhere from three seconds before to three seconds after the command to go. If he starts more than three seconds before, he must go behind an extension of the start line outside the start gate.

The following starts are used in competitions.

• **Single** or **double start:** One or two skiers begin, and after a specified interval—either 30 or 60 seconds—another skier or pair of skiers starts.

• **Group** or **mass start:** Competitors are divided into groups. Individual starting places are at least 1.5 meters apart. The start line is an arc of a circle, with a radius of 100 meters. For the classical technique, the first 100 to 200 meters is marked with parallel tracks that the competitors must follow. The number of tracks are cut in half over the next 100 meters and converge into two or three tracks shortly after that. For the freestyle technique, competitors ski in 100 to 200 meters of parallel tracks; they cannot use skating techniques in the tracks. The course then opens up into at least 100 meters without tracks.

• **Pursuit start:** The winner of the first combined competition starts first; the second-place finisher starts second; and so on. The start intervals are the same as the differences between the competitors' times from the first day's results. The first 200 meters must be prepared at least 6 meters wide. A *modified pursuit start* may be used when time differences are substantial. The bottom half of the field may use a mass start one minute after the last person from the top half of the field has started.

• **Reverse finish order start:** The slowest competitor from the first day begins first; then the next slowest; and so on. They start in intervals of 10, 15, or 30 seconds. A modified version of this is to have the bottom half of the field begin in a mass start, and then after two minutes pass, the first skier from the top half begins, followed in intervals by the rest.

Finish

The final 200 meters should be as straight as possible. For classical competitions, the final 200 meters is set with three tracks; for freestyle competitions, the final 200 meters is prepared at least 9 meters wide. A competitor finishes when he contacts the electric beam in electric timing, or, in hand timing, when his first foot crosses the finish line. Times are recorded to one-tenth of a second.

EQUIPMENT

Skis may be made of any material. They must be at least as long as the height of the skier, minus 10 centimeters; they cannot be longer than 230 centimeters. The middle of the ski must be between 43 and 47 millimeters wide. The tips must be curved at least 5 centimeters for classical skis or 3 centimeters for freestyle skis. The tail must not rise more than 3 centimeters. Skis must weigh at least 750 grams per pair. Both skis must be constructed in the same way and be of the same length. Edges may not face upward. The running surface can be smooth or slightly grooved. Scale patterns, to aid climbing, are allowed. There are no limitations for boots and bindings.

A skier's poles must be of equal length; they may not be longer than the competitor's height, nor shorter than the distance from hip to ski. The poles' length must be constant; they may not have telescopic qualities. They also may not have any springs or mechanical devices to assist in pushing off. Poles have no weight restrictions. Poles may be constructed with differences between them. A grip must attach to the shaft, but there are no limits on the grip's material or design nor on the shaft's material.

OFFICIALS

A competition committee is responsible for conducting the technical aspects of the competition. The committee includes a chief of competition, a competition secretary, and chiefs of course, timekeeping, stadium, and, at large competitions, security.

ORGANIZATIONS

US Ski and Snowboard Association
www.ussa.org

12
Curling

© Empics

Curling dates back to 16th-century Scotland; originally it was played on frozen ponds, and players used stones of varying shapes, which often curved, or "curled," as they slid down the ice (some believe this is how the name "curling" was arrived at). Players used brooms to clear the snow in the stone's path.

The game was introduced to North America in the 18th century by immigrants. By the 1850s, curling clubs had sprung up in various Canadian and northern U.S. cities. In the 20th century the game moved indoors and equipment was standardized. Today there are more than one million curlers in Canada and about 16,000 in the United States, curling has spread to 37 countries, and it is an Olympic medal sport.

Objective: To score the most points by getting stones within the 12-foot circle called the "house" and closer to the tee than those of the opponents.

Scoring: Determined after each end of 16 stones is completed; a stone that is within a six-foot radius of the tee and is closer to the tee than any opponent's stone scores a point.

Number of Players: Two teams of four players.

Game Length: 8 or 10 ends (innings); 10 for championship play.

Overview: Player 1 from team A delivers a stone, followed by player 1 from team B. Each player shoots two stones per end. While one player shoots, two teammates sweep the ice, if necessary, to help the stone travel farther. Some rocks may not be scoring rocks but may be placed to block or guard other rocks that are in scoring position. The team that scores in an end goes first in the next end.

TERMS

A **bonspiel** is a recreational tournament.

A **cashspiel** is a tournament with cash prizes.

A **championship** is a tournament leading to national or international play.

An **end,** with some similarities to an inning in baseball, is a portion of the game in which all eight players (four per team) deliver two stones each. Scoring is determined at the completion of each end; a game lasts 8 or 10 ends.

The **house** is the scoring area of the rink, with a 12-foot diameter and a tee at the center.

A **match** is a contest between two or more teams on each side; the winner is determined by the total number of points or by games won.

A **skip** is the team captain. Only the skip or the acting skip can be in the house when the opposition is throwing.

PLAYERS

Each of the four players on a team delivers two stones during each end, delivering alternately with her opponent. The established rotation must be maintained throughout the game. A team may not substitute for more than one of the original players in a competition (or one male and one female in mixed competition), but any number of substitutions are allowed for that one player (or couple, in mixed competition). In championship play, substitutes may only be eligible team members.

PLAY

Players from each team alternate delivering stones; each player shoots two stones per end. Teammates sweep the ice for their team's shots, helping to guide the stone. The stone that is closest to the tee and that is within a six-foot radius of the tee scores a point; other stones, while not scoring points, can aid a team's efforts by blocking the path of other stones delivered after it. Once an end of 16 stones is completed, the team that scores goes first in the next end.

Stones

A stone (or "rock") is removed from play when it

- rolls over or comes to rest on its side or top,
- does not clear the far hog line (see figure 12.1) and has not struck another stone in play,
- comes to rest beyond the back line, or
- hits a side board or touches a side line.

A stone's position is not measured until the last stone of the end is delivered, unless a skip requests that a stone be measured to determine whether it is in play. All 16 stones are delivered in an end unless the players in charge of the house agree on a score for that end or one of the teams concedes the game.

If a running stone is touched by either a player or equipment of the playing team, the stone is removed from play. The opposing skip may choose, however, to place the stone where she thinks it would have ended up if not touched, if she believes it is to her oppo-

Rink

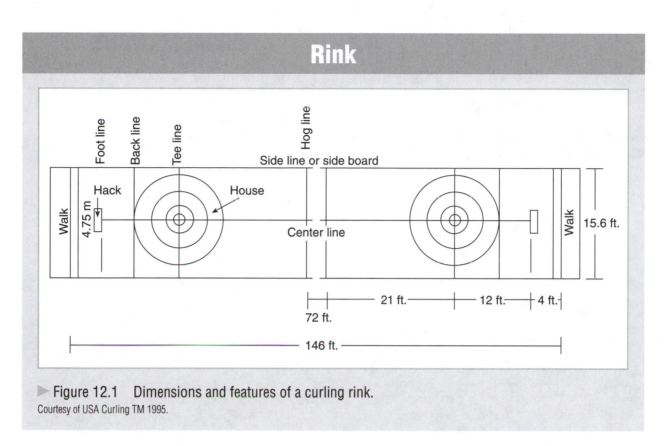

► Figure 12.1   Dimensions and features of a curling rink.
Courtesy of USA Curling TM 1995.

nents' advantage to have the stone removed. She may also reposition any stone inside the hog line at the playing end that would have been displaced had the running stone not been touched.

If a running stone is touched by an opponent or opponent's equipment, the skip of the playing team may place the stone where he believes it would have come to rest had it not been touched.

Delivery

Right-handed players deliver stones from the hack (a rubber foothold) on the left side of the center line; left-handers play from the hack on the right side of the center line. A stone is removed from play if this rule is violated.

The player must release the stone before the stone reaches the nearer hog line. Otherwise, the stone is removed from play. Any displaced stone hit by a stone released in violation of this rule will be replaced in its original position to the satisfaction of the opposing skip.

Sweeping

Players may sweep between the tee lines for their teammates' delivered or struck stones. They may not sweep for their opponents' stones between the tee lines. Neither the sweeper nor her equipment may touch the stone at any time.

Behind the tee line, only one player from each team—the skip or acting skip—may sweep at any one time. A player may not begin sweeping an opponents' stone until it reaches the tee line. If the delivering team's choice is not to sweep behind the tee line, that team may not prevent the opposing team from sweeping the stone.

EQUIPMENT

Stones are circular and weigh no more than 44 pounds, with a circumference no greater than 36 inches. Stones must be at least 4.5 inches in height. Brooms or brushes are used for sweeping. Players may not wear shoes that damage or mark the ice; shoes should be flat-soled and grip the ice well for walking.

OFFICIALS

An umpire supervises the game and settles any disputes between opposing skips.

ORGANIZATIONS

United States Curling Association
1100 Center Point Drive
Box 866
Stevens Point, WI 54481
715-344-1199
www.usacurl.org

Cycling

Today's bicycles, whether for the road, for off-road, for the track, or simply for recreation, bear little resemblance to the early models, which were made entirely of wood and were essentially two wheels attached to a hobby horse. These wooden models, first created in 1817, gave way in the 1870s to metal bikes with solid rubber tires. Pneumatic tires came on the scene in 1888, and 3-speeds and 10-speeds first appeared in the 1960s.

The invention of the bicycle was followed almost immediately by the start of bicycle racing, which developed gradually over the years. By the 1890s racing as we know it today had begun, and the first Tour de France was held in 1903. Bicycle racing was initially seen as an endurance sport, with distances that often exceeded 500 kilometers per day, but developments in bicycle manufacturing and the expansion of paved roads slowly changed the emphasis to speed.

Overview: Bicycle races today take many shapes and forms within the three main types of racing: *track racing*, *road racing*, and *off-road racing*. Road racing is the most popular brand of cycling, with the annual Tour de France, covering 3,900 kilometers in approximately 24 days, well known to even the most casual of fans. Off-road racing has evolved from recreational off-road bicycling and is a fast-growing sport in itself. There are numerous types of races contested on the track (see "Track Racing" on page 78).

Races are held for individuals and for teams, over one or more events. Depending on the event, the object of cycling is to finish first, to finish with the overall best time, or to score the most performance points.

TERMS

A **criterium** is a circuit road race held on a course closed off to traffic. Primes (sprints) are held within the race.

A **cyclocross** is a race held on rough terrain, about 75 percent of which is traversable on bike.

A **handicap start** is one in which the faster riders either ride longer or start later.

A **keirin** is a paced sprint, held on a velodrome, in which a motorized bike leads a pack of riders, accelerating until the next-to-last lap, upon which the pacer drops out and the riders sprint for the finish.

A **mass start** is a race where all riders begin on the same line.

In a **miss-and-out** race, the last rider on designated laps is forced to withdraw from the race.

In a **pursuit race,** riders begin at equal intervals around the track. The race is run until one rider catches the others or until a certain distance is covered, as specified in advance.

A **stage race** is a series of road races for individuals and teams.

In a **time trial,** riders compete one at a time over a fixed distance.

RIDERS

Riders compete in both individual and team competitions, which may be further classified according to gender and age. Age groups normally are in five-year groupings (30-34, 35-39, and so on). Junior age groups are 10-12, 13-14, 15-16, and 17-18.

RACING

Cyclists begin a race in one of three ways: all with holders; all with one foot on the ground; or all with a rolling start. Holders cannot step over the starting line. When a rolling start is used on a track, at least one neutral lap is taken to ensure a fair start. A race is begun with a signal—usually a gun or a whistle.

Any rider who appears to present a danger to the other competitors may be disqualified. Pushing or pulling among riders is prohibited in all races except the *madison* (see page 79); no rider may hold back or pull an opponent. A cyclist may not progress unaccompanied by a bicycle. A cyclist who crashes may run with his bike.

The last lap is indicated by the ringing of a bell. A cyclist finishes a race when her front tire first penetrates the finish line. Should two or more track riders tie for a place in which there is a prize, they may ride either the full distance or a shorter distance, as determined by the chief referee, to determine their places.

Track Racing

Track races are held on an oval track, usually .16 to .54 kilometer in length (see figure 13.1). The track is usually slightly banked on the straightaways and more so on the turns. Marked lines include the *starting line* (if it doesn't coincide with another line), the *200-meter line* (placed 200 meters before the finish line), two *pursuit finish lines* (in the middle of the two straightaways), and a *finish line*.

Track races include the following:

• **Handicap:** Faster riders must travel farther or must start later than the other cyclists.

• **Individual pursuit:** Racers start at equal intervals around a track. The race is run until one rider catches all the other riders; any rider passed by another must withdraw from the race.

• **Keirin:** Up to nine riders compete in a paced event for five laps on tracks of 333 meters or less, or for four laps on longer tracks. A pacer

Track

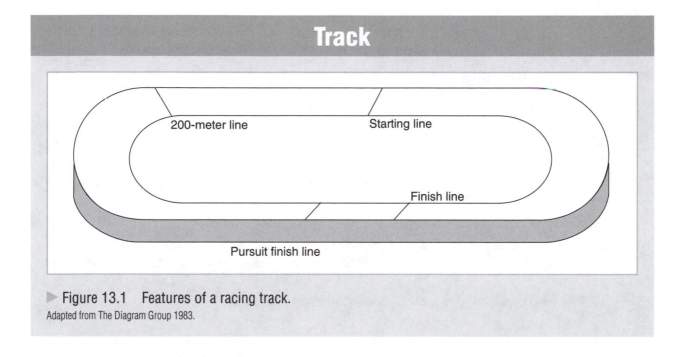

200-meter line

Starting line

Finish line

Pursuit finish line

▶ Figure 13.1   Features of a racing track.
Adapted from The Diagram Group 1983.

rides a motorized bike. Sprint rules apply; during the first lap, the speed is about 45 to 50 kilometers per hour. On the next-to-last lap, the pacer gradually accelerates and then moves off the track.

• **Madison:** Teams of two or three riders each compete in a relay points race. No more than two members of a team may ride at the same time. Sprints for points are conducted the same as in a points race. In case of a mishap, a teammate may take over until the injured rider returns. If a bicycle is judged to be damaged, then the team involved is not penalized any laps while its rider is off the track.

• **Mass start:** All riders start from the same point at the same time. The race is run over a specified number of laps; lapped riders are normally removed from the race.

• **Miss-and-out:** In this mass-start race, the last rider over the line on designated laps is eliminated. This may occur on every lap, every other lap, or on some other announced schedule. Either the winner is the last rider left, or the race is run until a specified number of riders remains, at which point a free lap may be followed by a sprint lap to determine the finish.

• **Omnium:** Riders compete for points in a set of races; final places are determined by total points for all the events, with points being awarded in each event on a 7-5-3-2-1 basis for first place through fifth. A tie is broken by the rider who has the most first-place finishes; if still tied, the rider who has the most second-place finishes wins, and so on. If still tied, the rider who placed highest in the final event wins.

• **Points:** Riders begin in a mass rolling start; sprints for points are held on designated laps. On these laps, the first four riders are awarded points (5, 3, 2, and 1). The number of points is doubled on the sprint nearest the midpoint of the race and on the final sprint.

• **Sprint:** A sprint is a series of short races with a small number of competitors. The rounds may be preceded by a flying start 200-meter time trial to seed or select riders. Round-robin sprints, held with a small number of riders, pit each competitor in an individual race against every other competitor. In championship formats, riders are advanced through qualifying sprints to the finals.

• **Tandem sprint:** Tandem sprints are run over the integral number of laps nearest

Special Race Rules

These rules apply to mass-start, handicap, miss-and-out, madison, and point races:

- Leaders must occupy the sprinters' lane unless they are able to do otherwise without interfering with other riders.
- A rider must pass on the outside unless the rider ahead is riding above the sprinters' line.
- In the homestretch on the last lap, riders must ride a straight line parallel to the edge of the track.
- Riders may not ride on the blue band below the track surface.
- If a crash causes a hazard to other riders, the race may be "neutralized"—the riders ride slowly around the top of the track, maintaining their positions, until the race may be safely resumed.
- Riders who crash may receive assistance in restarting.

to 1,500 meters for the particular track. No more than four tandems are raced together (no more than three on tracks shorter than 333 meters).

• **Team pursuit:** Various team pursuit races involve two or more riders per team. Typically four riders are on the track in a pursuit race.

• **Time trial:** Riders compete one at a time over a fixed distance. In a kilometer time trial, two riders start at the same time, on opposite sides of the track.

Road Racing

A road course may be out-and-back, around a circuit, from place to place, or any combination of these, but the course may not cross itself, forcing riders to cut through other riders. A marker denotes the final 1,000 meters. A white flag indicates the final 200 meters, which should be a straightaway.

If the road is open to traffic, riders must keep to the right of the center line. A rider may pass on either side of another rider. If the lead riders are stopped by a temporary road closure (such as at a train crossing), the race is neutralized and all riders begin at the same time intervals as their arrival at the closure. If the lead rider or riders make it through and others are stopped,

this is an unforeseeable incident, and no compensation is allowed.

Riders may exchange food and drink among themselves. A rider who suffers a mishap may be helped back on her bike and may be pushed for 10 meters.

Road races fall into the following categories:

• A **criterium** is a circuit race held on an 800-meter to 5-kilometer course that is closed to traffic. Riders on different laps may work with each other, but no rider may drop back to assist a rider who has broken away from the pack. Primes, or sprints within the race, are either held at preassigned times or designated by a bell preceding the lap that will begin the prime. Lapped riders are not eligible for primes.

• A **cross-country time trial** may be an individual or team event. A rider who takes pace from another rider closer than 25 meters ahead or 2 meters to the side will receive a time penalty.

• **Cyclocross** takes place on rough terrain, no more than half of which is paved. About 75 percent of a cyclocross course can be covered on a bicycle. The lap is at least one kilometer long; no jumps (such as ditches or streams) should be longer than 1 meter, and no artificial barriers should be higher than

40 centimeters. Bicycles may be exchanged in case of mechanical failure.

- **Individual road races** include mass-start races and handicap races. Lapped riders may be called off the course. Riders on different laps may not pace one another.

- An **individual time trial** may be out-and-back, circuitous, or point-to-point. Riders start at intervals (typically one minute apart). No rider may match pace (draft) with another rider closer than 25 meters ahead or 2 meters to the side. Time penalties are given for such violations.

- A **stage race** is a series of road races for individual riders and teams. The maximum duration is 10 days of racing, except that national tours may have up to 20 days of racing. Rest days are not included in this count; at least one rest day must be given for an event 10 days or longer. Up to two stages may be held in one day. Riders are not compensated for time loss if they take a wrong turn. A rider in an accident within a kilometer of the finish receives the same time as the last riders of any group she was riding with. Riders receive points for individual finish placings and hill climbing. Riders also receive time bonuses for finish order (e.g., 30 seconds off for first place, 20 seconds off for second, and so on).

- In a **team time trial,** two or more riders make up one team. The starting interval between teams is typically two minutes. Teammates on different laps may not work together; the team is disqualified for this violation. Teammates may exchange food, drink, and repair tools.

Off-Road Racing

Following is a very truncated version of the regulations for off-road racing in general and for its specific races. Racers must begin and complete the event on the same bicycle. Any repairs must be made by the racer; no outside support is permitted. Spare parts and tools must be carried by the racer. Riders who shortcut or cut trail switchbacks will be disqualified.

- **Cross-country:** Water and food are available only in designated zones. Riders have the right-of-way over racers pushing bicycles. Lapped riders must yield to other riders. A rider cannot bodily interfere with another rider's progress.

- **Dual slalom:** Each rider gets at least one qualifying run. The fastest qualifier is seeded against the slowest, and so on. The winner of each head-to-head competition moves on to the next heat. A rider who gets a jump start is penalized 1.5 seconds. Riders must ride around gates; a missed gate costs 1.5 seconds. Other 1.5-second penalties include changing from one course to another, not passing both wheels around a gate, interfering with the other rider, and not finishing in possession of the bike. Ties are broken by comparing the overall times on the course that both riders completed.

- **Observed trials:** Low score wins. The first dab (hand or foot touching ground) costs 1 point; the second dab, 2 points; the third and fourth, 3 points each; and the fifth and subsequent dabs, 5 points each. Two or more dabs at the same time cost 5 points. Other penalties include riding outside the limits with either tire, 5 points; breaking the ribbon or knocking down a marker, 5 points; sliding one foot on the ground, 3 points; gate foul, 5 points; exceeding the event time limit, 5 points; and preriding the course, 100 points.

- **Ultra endurance:** No mechanical support other than wheel changes in designated areas is permitted.

EQUIPMENT

Bicycles may be no more than two meters long and 75 centimeters wide; tandem bicycles may be up to three meters long. Bicycles may be propelled only by the riders' legs. They may have no protective shield to reduce wind resistance. Wheels may be either spoked or of solid construction. Handlebars should be solidly plugged; ends that point up or forward or provide support for the rider's forearms are allowed only in time trials and pursuits.

For track races, only a bicycle with a single-cog fixed wheel (one gear on the rear wheel) and without derailleurs may be used. For road races, only a bicycle with a freewheel (multiple gears on the rear wheel) and one working brake on each wheel shall be used. Riders must wear a protective helmet and a jersey that covers the shoulders. Footgear must be fully enclosed. Eye protection is recommended, as is additional helmet padding for downhill and dual slalom events.

OFFICIALS

Races are officiated by a head referee, assistants, starters, timers, and judges.

MODIFICATIONS

Off-road racing has grown in recent years, drawing on the enthusiasm of off-road recreational cyclists. The brief overview of this sport's rules comes from the National Off-Road Bicycle Association.

Off-road competitions include the following:

- **Cross-country competition** is held on a circuit course of forest and field roads and trails as well as paved and unpaved gravel roads.

- A **downhill race** is a time trial in which the finish is lower than the start.

Competitors typically start in 30-second intervals.

- In **dual slalom,** two riders race head-to-head down two parallel slalom courses.

- A **hill climb** is a mass start or a time trial of sustained climbing in which the finish is higher than the start.

- **Observed trials** are races over an obstacle course, in which riders attempt to maneuver the course without putting down a foot (dab). Each dab adds a point to the rider's score. Low score wins.

- **Point-to-point** is the same as cross-country but on a point-to-point course.

- **Stage races** involve a series of different events leading to an overall score or time. These races may be held over one or several days.

- **Ultra endurance** is an event in excess of 75 miles.

ORGANIZATIONS

USA Cycling
One Olympic Plaza
Colorado Springs, CO 80909
719-866-4581
www.usacycling.org

14
Equestrian

© Empics

The Olympic history of events involving horses dates back to 682 B.C., when chariot races were contested at Greece's 25th Olympiad. In the modern Olympic era, the full program of *dressage, show jumping,* and *three-day eventing* was introduced in 1912. Equestrian is the only Olympic sport in which humans and animals are teamed up and in which men and women are pitted against each other on absolutely equal terms.

USA Equestrian, the national governing body for the sport, annually sanctions more than 2,500 competitions across the United States. In addition, there are numerous nonsanctioned equestrian events as well, with competitors at all levels.

Objective: To score the most points.

Disciplines: Dressage, show jumping, three-day eventing.

Scoring: In *dressage,* competitors are judged and score points based on their performance in numerous criteria. In *show jumping,* the team of horse and rider that covers the course in the shortest time with the fewest jumping faults wins. In *three-day eventing,* the team of horse and rider with the fewest penalties wins.

Main Elements: In *dressage,* a horse and rider perform prescribed tests that include walking, trotting, and cantering. In *show jumping,* horse and rider go through at least one change of direction and over at least eight obstacles. In *three-day eventing,* horse and rider compete in dressage, cross country, and stadium jumping.

TERMS

A **canter** is a three-beat gait, similar to a gallop (see "Dressage").

A **clean round** signifies that a jumper has completed a course within the allotted time and without incurring any jumping faults.

A **combination** is two or three jumps taken in quick succession, separated by only a stride or two. If a horse stops or runs out at any part of the combination, it must rejump the entire series.

A **curb** is a bit with leverage action that works on the top of the horse's head, the chin, and the bars of the mouth.

A **gait** is a pace: a walk, trot, canter, or gallop, or varying speeds of each, as well as the rack and slow gait of the American saddlebred horse.

A **hand** is a unit of measurement equaling four inches. A horse is measured from the ground to the top of its shoulder, which is called the *withers*.

A **knockdown** occurs when a horse or rider lowers an element of a jump that establishes the height of an obstacle.

A **snaffle** is a bit that works directly on the corners of the horse's mouth.

A **trot** is a two-beat gait, faster than a walk and slower than a canter (see "Dressage").

DRESSAGE

The discipline of dressage displays and tests the complete training of the horse as demonstrated through the walk, trot, and canter. A horse and rider perform a prescribed test in an enclosed, flat arena. The requisite movements, such as transitions between gaits, circles, or lead changes, must come at markers designated by letters placed along the outside of the arena. Each test reviews the basics of training, as demonstrated through the collection or extension of stride and lateral movements. The horse and rider are judged according to numerous criteria; the highest score wins.

Following are brief descriptions of the main elements of dressage (the word is French for "training").

- **Walk:** The horse's walk is a marching gait in which the footfalls of the horse's feet follow one another in "four time." There are four types of walks—*collected, medium, extended,* and *free*—that should demonstrate the proper training of the horse.

- **Trot:** The horse's trot is a gait of "two time" on alternate diagonal legs (left front, right hind and vice versa) separated by a moment of suspension. The trot is judged by its general impression, the elasticity and regularity of the steps, and the rhythm and balance. The *collected, working, medium,* and *extended* trots should demonstrate the training of the horse.

- **Canter:** The horse's canter should be light and cadenced with a regular stride. The gait is "three time"; there is a moment of suspension when all four feet are in the air before each stride begins. The canter is judged on general impression, the regularity and lightness of the gait, and the rhythm. The proper training of the horse is demonstrated through four canters: the *collected, working, medium,* and *extended* canters.

- **Reinback:** The Reinback is an equilateral, retrograde movement in which the feet are raised and set down by diagonal pairs moving backward.

Performance and Judging

During a test, the horse and rider may perform the following figures and movements:

- *Volte*—a circle with a diameter of 6, 8, or 10 meters.

- *Serpentine*—S-pattern movements demonstrating changes of direction
- *Figure eight*—two voltes of equal size, joined at the center

The following factors are judged: collection and balance, correct outline of the horse, and impulsion. A judge may warn a competitor of an error in the test, such as a wrong turn or incorrect movement, by ringing a bell. Subsequent errors are penalized by two points, then by four, and then by elimination. Riders perform some of the tests from memory, although at the lower levels, the tests may be read to them.

Judges rate performances on a scale of 0 to 10, with 0 being "not executed" and 10 being "excellent." Judges award collective marks for gaits, impulsion, submission, and rider's position and seat.

SHOW JUMPING

In show jumping, the horse and rider jump a course of a minimum of eight obstacles, attempting to make jumps that are "clean" (i.e., that do not knock down the obstacle) within the time allowed. The team of horse and rider that covers the course in the shortest time with the fewest jumping faults wins.

Jumpers are scored on faults incurred while on the course, including disobediences, falls, knockdowns, touches, and time penalties. In combinations, each obstacle is scored separately. If a horse refuses to jump or runs out at one element, it must repeat the entire combination. Ties involving championships must remain tied; classes with a tie for first place, only, will be decided by a jump-off.

Course

The course must include at least one *change of direction* and at least eight *obstacles*. At least three of the first eight obstacles must be spread obstacles. Obstacles can consist of combinations, spreads, single rails, gates, and brush. (Note: Certain categories of competitions have variances to the type of obstacles used.) The height of *obstacle rails* ranges from 2 feet, 9 inches to 6 feet.

Water obstacles must be at least 16 feet wide at the face and have at least an 8-foot spread of water; they may be up to 15 feet long. For every foot in length, they may have two inches in depth of water. They may have an obstacle no higher than 2.6 feet on the take-off side. Knocking down or displacing such an obstacle is not a penalty.

Penalties

Horse and rider may be penalized for disobediences, knockdowns and touches, falls, and time penalties. Following are examples of disobediences:

- Refusal to jump (stopping in front of the obstacle and then backing up or circling to make the jump)
- Run-out (evading or passing the obstacle)
- Loss of forward movement (when the horse comes to a standstill before attempting the obstacle)
- Circling

THREE-DAY EVENTING

The three-day event, previously known as "combined training," is the all-around test of the horse. The event consists of dressage, cross country, and stadium jumping. Each test takes place on a separate day.

It begins with the *dressage test*, which is similar to a dressage competition. The *cross country test* is a test of endurance and consists of four phases; these follow one another without interruption. Phase A begins at a trot or a slow canter; this is called "roads and tracks." Phase B is the steeplechase; this phase is normally carried out at the gallop over obstacles. Phase C is again roads and tracks, reverting back to a trot or a slow canter. The final phase, D, is "cross country," normally carried out at the gallop over obstacles where horse and rider negotiate solid jumps, ditches, banks, and streams. Cross country is considered the heart of the sport. The final test, *stadium jumping*, requires the horse and rider to compete on a show jumping course within an arena. The team of horse and rider completing the three days of competition with the fewest penalties is the winner.

OFFICIALS

A ground jury is responsible for adjudicating and judging the event, although additional judges may be appointed for dressage and jumping events. An appeals committee addresses any protests or charges.

ORGANIZATIONS

USA Equestrian
4047 Iron Works Parkway
Lexington, KY 40511
Phone: 859-258-2472
www.equestrian.org

15
Fencing

© Empics

Fencing originated from a form of combat and began as a sport in either Italy or Germany—both claim to have originated the sport—in the 14th or 15th century. Three innovations in the 17th century led to fencing's popularity: the development of the foil (with a padded tip to reduce the risk of injury); the development of a set of rules that limited the target to certain areas of the body; and the creation of the wire-mesh mask.

Fencing is one of the few sports that have been contested at every Olympic Games. There are about 450 dedicated fencing clubs in the United States with about 500 additional organizations that offer fencing classes. Nearly 17,000 people in the United States belong to the U.S. Fencing Association, the national governing body for the sport.

Objective: To touch and not be touched; the winner is the fencer who accumulates the appointed number of touches first.

Number of Fencers: Two.

Scoring: A fencer scores by touching the opponent's target area with the point of the weapon (for *foil* and *épée*) or with its edges (*sabre*).

Length of Bout: Three minutes or until one fencer scores five touches.

Winning: If no fencer has reached the appointed number of touches within three minutes, various rules apply to determine the winner (see "Scoring" on page 89).

Overview: When the command "Fence" is given, the bout begins. The weapon must be held and used with one hand only; a fencer may not change hands during a bout unless permitted to do so because of injury. After each valid touch, the fencers return to the on-guard lines.

When two fencers are in contact, the bout is stopped. In foil and sabre all contact is pro-hibited. In épée, no intentional contact is allowed. When a bout is temporarily halted, it is resumed at the spot where it was halted until a touch is made. When a fencer leaves the strip, the bout is halted. A fencer is not penalized for accidentally leaving the strip (e.g., in being jostled).

FIELD

The field of play is a strip of even surface of wood, linoleum, cork, rubber, or other material (see figure 15.1). The strip is 1.5 to 2 meters wide and 17 to 18 meters long, 14 meters of which is in bounds. If the strip is mounted on a platform, the height of the platform can be no higher than .5 meter. If the competition is judged with electrical apparatus, the strip must be covered by metal or a metallic mesh to neutralize touches made on the ground.

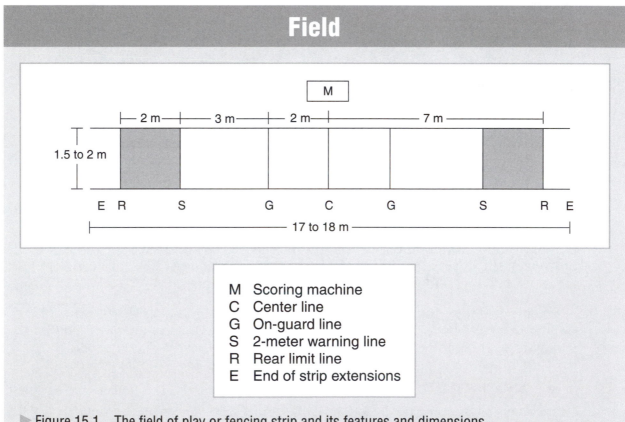

▶ Figure 15.1   The field of play or fencing strip and its features and dimensions.
Adapted from the United States Fencing Association 1994.

TERMS

The **attack** is the initial offensive action made by extending the arm and continuously threatening the opponent's target.

A **bout** is a timed, scored match in a competition.

A **competition** is the aggregate of bouts or matches that determine a winner. Competitions are distinguished by weapon. They can also be categorized by gender, age, or other classification, and by individual or team events.

A **compound attack** is one made in more than one movement.

A **counterattack** is an offensive or an offensive-defensive action made during the opponent's offensive action.

A **counter-riposte** is an offensive action of a fencer who has parried the riposte.

A **direct attack** is one made in the same line.

An **indirect attack** is one that changes lines on the way in.

A **parry** is a defensive action made to prevent the attack from arriving.

Redoublement describes a new action against an opponent who has parried without riposting or who has retreated from or evaded the action.

A **remise** is a simple and immediate offensive action that follows an attack, without withdrawing the arm, after the opponent has parried or retreated.

A **reprise** is a new attack performed immediately after a return to the on-guard position.

A **riposte** is an offensive action that may be immediate or delayed, depending on the speed and execution of the action.

FENCERS

Fencers compete in individual or team competitions, and in various age divisions and classifications, including the following:

- Senior
- Under 19
- Under 16
- Under 14
- Under 12
- Under 10
- Wheelchair

SCORING

Fencers score by making legal touches on valid targets. Following is an overview for scoring in foil, épée, and sabre competitions.

Foil

To score a touch, the point must touch the target, which is the trunk of the opponent and which is covered with a metallic cloth vest called a lamé. When an opponent's tip hits the vest, it sets off a light and a buzzer on the scoring machine on the side of the fencer who hit. A valid hit is signified by a colored light; an invalid (off target) hit is signified by a white light. The limits of the target are the collar (six centimeters above the collarbone), the seams of the sleeves, and the tops of the hipbones (see figure 15.2).

If the score is tied when time runs out, one minute is added, a coin is tossed, and the bout continues until a single touch is scored or time runs out. The coin toss determines who has priority if the score remains tied. If the score of the bout is 0-0 after three minutes of fencing and no touch was scored after the extra minute, then the score is recorded as V0-D0 in favor of the fencer with the priority. If a touch is scored in the additional minute, the score would be V1-D0 in favor the person scoring the touch.

Épée

The touch must be made on the target, with the point. The target is the whole of the fencer's body, including clothing and equipment. Bouts are for five touches. The fencer who hits first gets a point; if both fencers hit within 1/25th of a second, each scores a point.

For épée fencers, double touches still count. If double touches arrive when the score is 4-4,

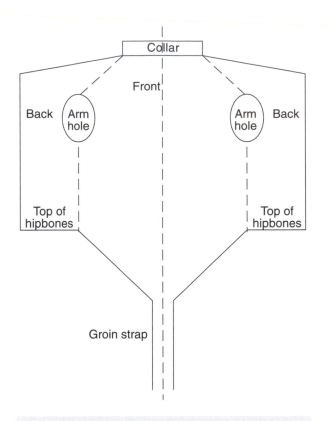

> ▶ Figure 15.2   A point is scored when the foil point touches the target. The boundaries of the target are the collar, seams of sleeves, and the tops of the hipbones.
> Adapted from United States Fencing Association 1994.

nothing is written on the score sheet. The score remains 4-4 and the fencers do not return to the center.

Sabre

Touches made with the cutting edge, the side edge, or the back edge of the blade are valid. Hitting with the guard of the weapon is not valid and is penalized. Touches with the point that graze the target or cuts that slip along the opponent's body are not valid. The target comprises the entire body above a horizontal line between the top of the folds formed by the thighs and the trunk when in the on-guard position.

When time expires before a fencer reaches five touches, the final score is arrived at by adding the number of touches to the leader's score to reach five and adding the same number of touches to the other fencer's total. If the two fencers are tied, the time limit is off, the score is set at 4-4, and the next touch wins.

EQUIPMENT

All weapons are composed of a flexible steel blade that comes to a tip; a grip, which may include a handle and a pommel (which locks the handle onto the tang of the blade); and a metal guard between the blade and the hilt, to protect the hand. The guard can be padded; for electrical weapons, it contains the connector to which the body cord is attached.

A fencer's outfit must be white or a light color on the torso. The rest of the clothing may be of a different, singular color. The glove's cuff must cover about half of the forearm of the sword arm. The mask is made of mesh.

OFFICIALS

Fencing bouts are directed by a referee, who may be assisted by judges. Judges are required when there is no metallic strip and in the final bout of a competition. Scorers and timekeepers are also used. When a judge sees a touch arrive, she raises her hand to advise the referee. The judges and the referee vote on the "materiality of the touch" to decide whether to award a touch to the fencer. Each judge's opinion counts as one vote; the referee's opinion counts as a vote and a half.

In bouts judged with a scoring machine, the referee places himself in view of the machine, and the materiality of the touch is indicated by the machine. Only touches that are registered by the machine are counted as such.

ORGANIZATIONS

United States Fencing Association
1 Olympic Plaza
Colorado Springs, CO 80909-5778
719-866-4511
www.usfencing.org

16
Field Hockey

© ImageState

Modern field hockey dates back to Princeton in the late 1700s. The sport was introduced to Harvard in 1901 and soon caught on at many women's colleges in the eastern United States. The game is played by both women and men at high school, college, and club levels. In the United States it is popular among women, especially in the East, but not among men. In Olympic competition, India, Great Britain, and Pakistan tend to dominate.

Objective: To score more goals than the opponents.

Scoring: A goal is scored when an attacking team member plays the ball within the shooting circle and it completely passes the goal line between the goal posts. The ball may be deflected by a defender and still count as a goal, but it may not go outside the shooting circle.

Players: 11 players per side, including a goalkeeper for each side.

Length of Game: Two 35-minute halves.

Overview: A game begins with a center pass, in which a member of the attacking team hits the ball from the center line to a teammate. Players on a team pass the ball to each other and attack the opponents' goal. A game is also restarted with a center pass after a goal is scored; the opponents scored upon put the ball into play.

FIELD

The field is 100 yards long and 60 yards wide (see figure 16.1). It has a *center line* marking and two *25-yard line* markings. The *shooting circles* are 16-yard semicircles in front of the goal. *Penalty spots* for penalty strokes are marked 7 yards in front of each goal. The *goals* are 4 yards wide, 7 feet high, and at least 4 feet deep. Each goal has a *backboard* 18 inches high spanning the width and sides of the goal. Goals are netted loosely to prevent the ball from rebounding onto the field.

TERMS

A **bully** is a play that restarts action by employing a face-off between two opponents who tap each other's sticks three times and then attempt to play the ball.

A **center pass** is used to begin play and to resume play after a goal has been scored. It takes place at the center line and involves a member of the attacking team passing the ball back to a teammate.

Dangerous play is any action that endangers any player, including raising the ball, tackling from the wrong position, and playing the ball while lying on the ground.

A **flick** occurs when a player pushes the ball and raises it off the ground.

A **free hit** is given for a foul committed outside the shooting circle.

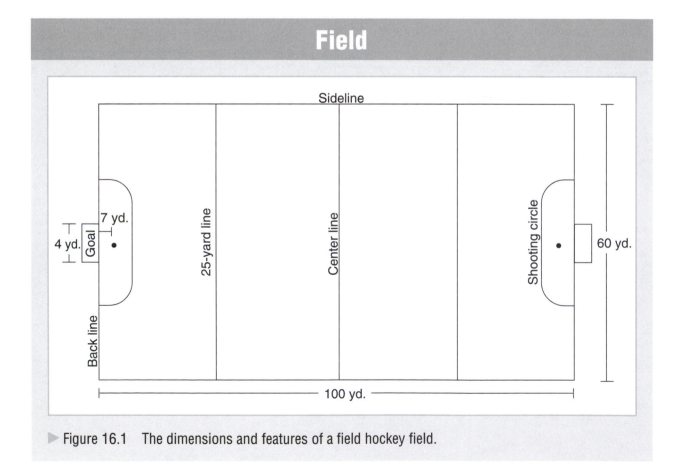

▶ Figure 16.1   The dimensions and features of a field hockey field.

A **penalty corner** results from a foul committed inside the circle; an attacker hits the ball from a point on the goal line at least 10 yards away from a goal post.

A **penalty stroke** occurs from a foul committed inside the circle if the defenders have intentionally fouled. An attacker shoots at goal from 7 yards away, in a one-on-one confrontation with the goalkeeper.

PLAYERS

A team has 16 players in international matches, 11 of which may be on the field at one time. Players wear uniforms and may wear guards for shins, ankles, and mouths. Goalkeepers may wear upper body protectors and must wear different colored shirts from those of either team. Goalkeepers also wear protective helmets and may wear protective padding on their legs and elbows.

A team captain wears a distinctive armband. Time is not stopped for a substitution, except when a goalkeeper is replaced; the substitute may enter the field only after the player coming out is off the field. Players coming in and out may do so only at the center line or some other designated area.

PLAY

Scoring the most goals during the allotted game time is the purpose of field hockey. In doing so, players must follow specific guidelines.

- During a pass back, opponents must be at least 5 yards from the ball. The player passing back must move the ball at least 1 yard and may not play the ball again until another player has played it.
- A field player may only play the ball with the flat side of the stick. A goalkeeper may use any part of her body to stop the ball within the shooting circle so long as she has a stick in her hands.
- A bully is a play used to restart a game when each team commits a simultaneous foul, when the ball lodges in the goalkeeper's pads, or when time is stopped

for an injury or for any other reason. Two opposing players face each other where the stoppage happened, with the ball between them and all other players at least 5 yards away. (If the occurrence happened inside the shooting circle, the ball is placed 16 yards from the goal line, even with the edge of the circle.) Each of the two players taps her stick on the ground, on her side of the ball, and then taps the flat face of the opponent's stick three times, over the ball. At this point the players may attempt to put the ball into play.

- When a ball goes out of bounds it is put back into play according to where and how it went out.
- When the ball goes out over a sideline, play is restarted by a member of the opposing team. The restart occurs where the ball went out, but the player does not have to be wholly in or out of bounds.
- When the ball goes out over a back line, play restarts in one of three ways:
  1. When the attack knocks the ball out of play, a defender puts the ball back into play up to 16 yards from, and opposite, where it crossed the back line, parallel with the sideline.
  2. When the defense unintentionally knocks the ball out of play over a back line, an attacker restarts play on the side line 5 yards from the corner flag nearest where the ball went out.
  3. When the defense intentionally knocks the ball out of play over a back line, the attacking team is awarded a *penalty corner* on the back line, 10 yards from the closer goal post (see "Penalties"). A player may be in this position as long as she is not passed the ball.

PENALTIES

Penalties are awarded for fouls that clearly disadvantage the player or team fouled. (For fouls, see sidebar "Rules of Conduct.") An umpire may award a free hit, a penalty corner, or a penalty stroke.

Rules of Conduct

Players may not

- intentionally play the ball with the rounded side of the stick;
- participate in a play without a stick in hand;
- play the ball above shoulder height with the stick;
- lift their sticks over the heads of players;
- use their sticks dangerously or play the ball in a way that is likely to lead to dangerous play;
- hit, hook, hold, or strike another player's stick or uniform;
- catch or stop the ball with the hands (except in protection);
- use their bodies to propel the ball;
- use their feet or legs to support the stick in a tackle;
- intentionally raise the ball from a hit, except for a shot at goal;
- intentionally raise the ball over a long distance so that it lands in the shooting circle;
- approach within 5 yards of a player receiving a pass in the air (the ball must be played and on the ground); or
- use their bodies or sticks to shield the ball from an opponent (obstruction).

Free Hit

A free hit is awarded for a foul by an attacker or for an unintentional foul by a defender outside the shooting circle. The hit takes place at or near where the foul occurred.

Penalty Corner

A penalty corner is awarded when the defense commits an intentional foul, when the defense intentionally plays the ball out of bounds over their back line, or when the defense unintentionally fouls an attacker within the circle who does not have the ball. An attacker takes a penalty corner from a spot on the back line 10 yards from a goal post. At least one of the attacker's feet must be out of bounds; no other player may be within 5 yards. The other attackers must be outside the circle. Not more than five defenders, including the goalkeeper, may be behind the back line; the remaining defenders must be beyond the center line.

An attacker may not attempt a shot at goal until the ball has come to a complete rest out-side the circle. If the first shot at goal is a drive, the ball must cross the goal line no higher than the backboard for a goal to be scored, unless it touches a defender or a defender's stick while in flight. The attacker putting the ball into play may not score directly.

Penalty Stroke

A penalty stroke is awarded when the defense commits an intentional foul in the circle to prevent a goal from being scored, or when the defense unintentionally fouls in the circle, thereby preventing a probable score. A penalty stroke is also awarded when the defense persists in breaking the back line at penalty corners.

Time stops when a penalty stroke is taken. The player taking the stroke stands behind the ball, which is placed 7 yards from the goal. All other players, other than the goalkeeper, must stand beyond the 25-yard line. The goalkeeper may not move until the attacker plays the ball. The attacker may push, scoop, or flick the ball from the penalty spot, raising the ball to any height. She may touch the ball only once, and she may not feint before she touches it. If the player scores a goal, the game restarts with a pass back. If the player doesn't score, the game restarts with a defender playing the ball 16 yards in front of the center of the goal line.

EQUIPMENT

The ball is spherical, weighing 5.5 to 5.75 ounces, with a circumference of 8.8 to 9.25 inches. Its surface is smooth. The stick has a flat side and a rounded side. The maximum length of the curved head, measured from the lowest part of the flat face, is 4 inches. The stick must weigh between 12 ounces and 28 ounces. The diameter of the shaft must not exceed 2 inches.

OFFICIALS

Two umpires control the game. Each umpire is primarily responsible for play on his half of the field, diagonally from the near left corner to the far right corner as he faces the field.

ORGANIZATIONS

U.S. Field Hockey Association
1 Olympic Plaza
Colorado Springs, CO 80909-5778
719-866-4567
www.usfieldhockey.com

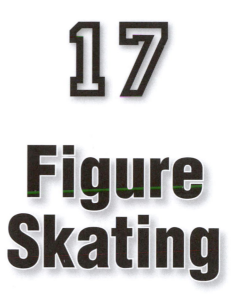

Figure Skating

In the early 20th century, figure skating competitions and tests became established in the United States and in Canada; figure skating was an Olympic sport in 1908 and was reintroduced to the Winter Games in the first Winter Olympics in 1924. In 1976 ice dancing was added as an Olympic sport. Competitions are held in various events, including *singles skating, pairs skating, ice dancing,* and *synchronized team skating,* which is the fastest growing part of the sport. The grace, strength, and athleticism of figure skating have made the sport popular among athletes and spectators. While skaters at all levels and ages compete in figure skating, the rules in this chapter pertain to senior-level events.

Objective: For individuals, pairs, and teams to score points for technical merit and for presentation.

Start: The order of skating is based on an officials' draw; competitors must begin their programs within two minutes of being called to perform.

Length of Program: Ranges from 2 minutes, 40 seconds for the short program to 4 minutes, 30 seconds for free skating.

Music: Except for compulsory dances, competitors choose their own music; for free skating and short programs, vocals are not allowed.

Scoring: Each competitor or pair receives two marks on a scale of zero to six; the two marks cover the most important aspects of the competition (such as technical merit and artistic impression). Competitors may finish within 10 seconds of their allotted time. For every 10 seconds they go beyond that, .1 is deducted from their marks. They receive no marks if they skate 30 seconds or more beyond their allotted time plus the 10-second allowance.

RINK

The rink consists of a smooth ice surface, typically 100 feet by 200 feet (minimum size is 85 feet by 185 feet). It has rounded corners and a low wall.

TERMS

Following is a short list of the terms of figure skating.

A **crossover** is the most efficient way to gain speed on a curve and can be done skating forward or backward.

Death spirals are pair moves where the man performs a back pivot and the lady circles around the man on one foot with her body bent backward and her head toward the ice.

A **double jump** is a jump with two complete revolutions and allowable further rotation of less than 360 degrees.

Edges are sustained one-foot glides on a curve with the body of the skater leaning into the center of the curve.

A **flying spin** is a spin that begins with a jump in which the position of the spin is evident during the jump. Sit spins and camel spins are the two most common flying spins. There are also death drops, butterflies, and flying change sit spins.

Footwork includes steps, turns, and edge and directional changes that are performed by the skater in a deliberate way and in time to the music to connect other moves.

A **half-revolution jump** is a jump of one-half revolution (180 degrees) in the air.

A **lift** is when one partner (usually the man) assists the jumping partner in a continuously ascending and descending movement, limited to three revolutions of the lifting partner. In ice dancing, the man may not lift his arms over his shoulder to assist the woman.

A **Mohawk turn** is a turn from forward to backward, or vice versa, from one foot to the other; the curve of the exit edge continues the curve of the entry edge. There are many variations of Mohawk turns.

A **pattern** of a dance is the dance's design. A pattern can be *set*, in which the steps are prescribed; *optional*, which allows for more than a set pattern; and *border*, in which the pattern is laid out progressively around the rink, never repeating at the same place in the rink.

A **single jump** is a jump of one complete revolution and allowable further rotation of less than 360 degrees.

A **spin** is a move in which the skater continuously rotates in small circles. Spins can be rotated forward and backward in a variety of positions.

A **spiral** is a move in which the upper body bends forward at the hip, with the body almost parallel to the ice, and the head and the free leg are up, with the free leg past the horizontal level.

A **throw** is a combination of a lift and jump in which the man assists the lady on the takeoff by lifting and "throwing" her. The lady continues the rotation and lands the jump without assistance on a back outside edge.

A **twist** is a pairs move in which the man lifts and throws the lady in the air before catching her at her waist and lowering her to the ice. Unlike a traditional throw, where the throwing action looks as if it carries the lady horizontally across the ice, in a twist, the lady is thrown vertically into the air. The man has to exit on one foot from this lift.

SKATERS

Skaters must wear clothing that is modest and dignified, not garish or theatrical. They may choose clothing that reflects the character of the music, but they will be marked off for clothing considered inappropriate. Men must wear full-length trousers, not tights. Men's clothing must have sleeves. Ladies must wear skirts or pants that cover the posterior and the hips. Unitards and bare midriffs are not allowed, and clothing must not have excessive decoration.

COMPETITION

Each program, be it singles or doubles competition, has specific rules and objectives.

Short Program for Singles

The short program consists of eight required elements with connecting steps, to be completed in 2 minutes, 40 seconds (the program can be shorter if all the required elements are completed). Jumps, spins, and step sequences are common to short programs. Judges award two marks on a scale of zero to six; the first mark is for required elements, the second is for presentation. Judges consider the following in marking for the required elements:

- **Jumps**—height, length, technique, and clean starting and landing of required jumps
- **Spins**—strong, controlled rotation of spins; number of revolutions and speed of rotation; height (for flying spins)
- **Step sequences**—difficulty of steps; swing, carriage, and flow

Judges consider the following in marking the presentation: Harmonious composition, difficulty of steps, speed, use of the ice surface, easy movement and sureness in time to the music, carriage and style, originality, and expression of the character of the music.

Free Skating Singles (Long Program)

Free skating consists of a program including jumps, spins, steps, and other linking movements executed with a minimum of two-footed skating in harmony with nonvocal music. A program lasts 4 minutes for ladies and 4 minutes, 30 seconds for men. The skater may choose the elements of the program. Special attention is given to choreography, expression, interpretation of the music, and intricacy of footwork. The skater must use the full ice surface. A well-balanced senior singles program must contain jumps, jump combinations, spins (a minimum of four spins of different natures), and step sequences.

Judges award two marks on a scale of zero to six; the first mark is for technical merit, the second for presentation. For technical merit, the factors considered are performance difficulty, variety, and cleanness and sureness. For presentation, factors considered include harmonious composition, speed, use of the ice surface, easy movement and sureness in time to the music, carriage and style, originality, and expression of the character of the music.

Pairs Skating

Pairs skating is performed by two skaters (a woman and a man) skating in unison and harmony to nonvocal music. Skaters perform moves of single skating either symmetrically (mirror skating) or in parallel fashion (shadow skating), executing spins, lifts, partner-assisted jumps, and similar moves, linking their moves with harmonious steps. Judges give special attention to the selection of an appropriate partner; a serious imbalance in physical characteristics that impairs the skaters' unison will be reflected in their marks for technical merit and presentation.

In a short program for pairs, skaters must perform eight required elements with connection steps within 2 minutes, 40 seconds; the program may be shorter if all the required elements are completed.

These elements include

- one overhead lift (minimum of two revolutions of the lady),
- one twist lift (double),
- one solo jump (double or triple),
- one solo spin (with one change of foot and minimum of two positions),
- one combination pairs spin (one change of foot and minimum two positions),
- one death spiral,

- one spiral-step sequence, and
- one step sequence (circular, straight line, or serpentine).

Judges award two marks from zero to six, one for the required elements and one for presentation. Judges give special attention to choreography, unison, expression, interpretation of the music, and intricacy of the footwork. Partners may separate, but they must always give the impression of unison and harmony. They must keep movements on two feet to a minimum.

A senior pairs program (long program) must contain three to five different lifts (one but not more than two of which must be a twist lift); one throw jump; two different solo jumps; one jump sequence; one pairs spin combination; one solo spin; one death spiral; a pairs spin or a second death spiral, different from the first one; a step sequence using the full ice surface; and a sequence of spirals or arabesques, turns, pivots, or spread eagles, using the full ice surface.

Ice Dancing

A dance couple is composed of a woman and a man. Ice dancing includes compulsory dances, an original dance, and free dancing. Theatrical poses are forbidden. Skaters skate closer together and ice dancing programs include difficult footwork sequences performed in dance hold. Ice dancing often looks like ballroom dancing on ice, but couples may perform any variety of dance styles.

Compulsory dances consist of set pattern dances and optional pattern dances set to music. Judges watch for accuracy of positions, steps, and movements; placement of steps and use of the ice surface; upright body carriage and flowing motion; close and effortless unison; timing to the music; and expression of the character of the music. The length of the dance varies. Judges give couples two marks on a scale of zero to six, one for technique and one for timing and expression.

In *original dance,* couples dance to music with a prescribed tempo; only music with constant and regular tempo may be used. The dance may be 2 minutes, 30 seconds and may not be a free dance. Two lifts are allowed, but no more.

They may last 5 seconds. The skaters may not separate except to change dance holds. Judges award two marks on a scale of zero to six, one for composition and one for presentation.

In *free dance,* couples may express the character of their chosen music without performing any prescribed steps. The dance lasts 4 minutes and must contain combinations of new or known dance movements with technical aspects that show the athleticism of dancing. Dancers may perform all steps and turns; they may perform free skating movements that are appropriate to the music's character. They may separate to execute intricate footwork and to change holds and positions, provided the separation does not exceed five meters or 10 seconds. At least one skate of each partner must be on the ice at all times, except during jumps and lifts. Judges award two marks on a scale of zero to six, one for technical merit and one for artistic impression.

Synchronized Team Skating

Synchronized team skating includes a junior short program, a senior short program, and free skating. Depending on the level and type of program, the competition lasts from 2.5 minutes to 4.5 minutes. The short program for senior and junior competition consists of these required maneuvers: circle, line, block, wheel, and intersection. Required step sequences include turns, counters, rockers, mohawks, and choctaws.

In synchronized free skating, teams skate to the music of their choice and include elements such as circles, wheels, lines, blocks, and intersections, all linked harmoniously through transitions. Men and women may skate on the same team. Teams can vary their number of elements, but must include them all and not excessively repeat an element. Judges pay special attention to choreography, expression, and interpretation of the music chosen.

Senior teams must do four different holds; junior and collegiate teams must do three; and junior classic teams must do two different holds. No lifts are allowed, and no jumps of more than one revolution. Also, teams cannot step or jump over hand-clasped or outstretched arms or lie or kneel for prolonged times at any time.

EQUIPMENT

Blades must be standard stock blades that are generally available to figure skaters. The cross section of the blades may be slightly tapered.

OFFICIALS

Officials for skating competitions include a referee, assistant referees, and an odd number of judges (three to nine). The referee is in overall charge of the event and decides on any disputes not specifically covered in the rules.

ORGANIZATIONS

United States Figure Skating Association
20 First Street
Colorado Springs, CO 80906
719-635-5200
www.usfsa.org

18
Football

American football evolved from rugby, which was a spin-off from soccer. Early roots of the modern game can be traced to a college game played in 1869 between Princeton and Rutgers universities. Each team had 25 men on the field; the game more resembled soccer than football, as running with the ball, passing, and tackling were not allowed. Harvard and McGill universities played a game in 1874 that combined elements of rugby and soccer; this game caught on in eastern U.S. schools and developed into the beginnings of modern football.

Early rules included playing with a round ball and needing to make 5 yards in three downs. Rules have continually evolved to make the game fair, exciting, and less violent. From its beginnings in America on college campuses, football has grown into a widely popular sport in the United States, where it is played in youth leagues, in high schools, and professionally. Football rules are played all over the world, although it is not a great spectator sport outside the United States. There is a National Football League (NFL) Europe league, made up mostly of American players, with rules basically the same as in the NFL in the United States.

The rules in this chapter are general football rules, with specific references to both National Collegiate Athletic Association (NCAA) rules and NFL rules. Important modifications for other levels and variations of the sport are addressed near the end of the chapter. It is important to note that different rules apply for high school, college, and pro levels.

Objective: To score the most points via touchdowns, extra points, field goals, and safeties.

Number of Players: 11 per team on the field.

Scoring: A touchdown is worth six points; teams can try for one-point (kicking) or two-point (running a play from scrimmage) conversions after a touchdown; a field goal is worth three points; a safety is worth two.

Length of Game: Four 15-minute quarters in the NFL and college; four 12-minute quarters in high school.

Overview: The team on offense tries to advance the ball down the field and score a touchdown by crossing the goal line with the ball or, alternatively, to kick a field goal through the goal posts. The team on defense tries to regain possession of the ball by intercepting a pass in the air, recovering a fumble, stopping the offense from making 10 yards in four downs (plays), or forcing the offense to punt (kick) the ball to them.

FIELD

The *playing field* is 53.33 yards wide by 120 yards long (see figure 18.1). The length of the field is marked by boundary lines called *sidelines*. The end zones, located at both ends of the field, are 10 yards deep, bordered by a goal line in front and an end line in back. The two goal lines are 100 yards apart. Any part of the goal line is considered part of the end zone; any part of the end line and the sideline that borders the end zone is considered out of bounds.

The front and back corners of the end zones are marked with pylons. These pylons are out-of-bounds. The field is lined, width-wise, at intervals of 5 yards; along the sidelines each

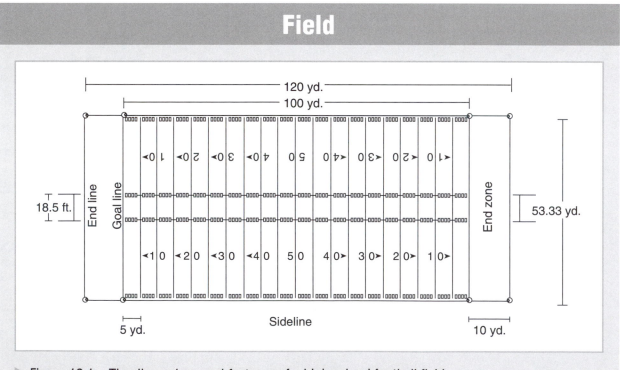

▶ Figure 18.1   The dimensions and features of a high school football field.
Adapted from the National Football League 1994.

yard is marked. Yard lines are numbered every 10 yards in multiples of 10; these numbers are 2 yards long. Inbounds lines, or *hash marks,* run parallel to the yard lines. Hash marks are set 70.75 feet from each sideline in professional football and 53.25 feet from each sideline in college football.

Goal posts are at the back of each end zone, with a horizontal crossbar 18.5 feet in length and 10 feet above the ground. The crossbar is directly above the end line. Two vertical posts extend 30 feet above the crossbar and are topped by ribbons measuring 4 inches by 42 inches.

TERMS

Following are brief explanations for terms that are not described elsewhere in this chapter.

A **dead ball** occurs when a ball carrier is downed or out of bounds, when a quarterback drops to his knee, when a ball carrier slides feet first, when a ball carrier is held or otherwise restrained so that his forward progress is stopped, when a pass drops incomplete, when a kick receiver does not attempt to run out a kick from the end zone, when a fair catch is made, when a field goal attempt passes the crossbar, or when an official sounds his whistle. When the ball is dead, the play is over.

A **free kick** happens when a kick is "free" (undefended) during a kickoff and after a safety. A team may also choose to free kick immediately following a fair catch of a punt. A free kick may be a drop kick, place kick, or punt. This is true for high school and pro football, but not college.

A **fumble** occurs when a player loses possession of the ball while the play is still in progress.

During a kickoff, the kicking team may put on a play—an **onside kick**—to retain possession of the ball. The kick must travel 10 yards or first touch a player on the receiving team before the kicking team can recover the ball.

A player or a ball is **out of bounds** when either has touched a boundary line (or touched ground beyond the boundary line).

Special teams is a term used for the units on the field during kickoffs, placekicks, and punts.

A **touchback** occurs when a ball is dead on or behind a team's own goal line, provided the ball's impetus came from an opponent and it is not a touchdown.

PLAYERS

Offensive and defensive units have 11 players each. Player positions are designated depending on the system and terminology employed by the coach. Generally speaking, on offense, players are the quarterback, running backs, wide receivers, tight end, and offensive linemen (center, tackles, and guards).

On defense, players are generally identified as defensive linemen (ends and tackles), linebackers, and defensive backs (cornerbacks and safeties).

Special teams are the units on the field when kicking takes place—during a kickoff, a field goal attempt, a point-after conversion attempt, or a punt. Primary among these players are the holder (who receives the snap and holds the ball for the placekicker), the placekicker (who kicks field goals and extra points), the punter, and the kick returners (who return kickoffs and punts).

Substitutes may enter a game during a dead ball (when play is out). A player is not limited to a certain number of times he may enter a game, but neither team may have more than 11 players on the field at the snap of the ball.

PLAY

Before the game, the winner of a coin toss either opts to receive the kickoff or chooses which goal his team will defend. At the end of the first and third periods, the teams change goals. To start the second half, the team that lost the pregame coin toss chooses between the same two privileges.

The game begins with a kickoff at the kicking team's 30-yard line in the NFL, 35-yard line in college, or 40-yard line in high school play. All players on the kicking team must be behind the yard line from which the ball is kicked, and all players on the receiving team must be no closer than 10 yards away from the kickoff line.

If the kickoff goes out of bounds without being touched by a receiver, the receiving team may elect to take the ball either where it went out of bounds or 30 yards beyond the kickoff line. If the kick touches a receiver and then goes out of bounds, the receiving team puts the ball into play at the yard line where the ball went out of bounds.

Each team normally huddles before a play, to call the play and coverage. (Sometimes an offensive team will go without a huddle and go directly to the line of scrimmage, where the quarterback will call the play through coded signals.) The players line up on the line of scrimmage before the snap of the ball. The offensive team must have at least seven players on its line at the snap. Offensive players not on the line must be at least 1 yard behind it.

After the ball is snapped, the offensive team may advance the ball by running with or passing it. While a team may only attempt one forward pass during a down, it may attempt multiple backward passes or laterals. Backward passes may be advanced by both teams even if the ball touches the ground before a receiver secures possession.

An airborne NFL receiver must come down with *both feet in bounds* (on the ground in the playing field) while in possession of the ball in order to record a legal reception. At other levels, *only one foot needs to be in bounds*. In the NFL and in high school, if a receiver is pushed out of bounds but would have landed inbounds otherwise, the catch is allowed.

In the NFL, a ball carrier may fall and get back up and continue running if he is not tackled or touched by a defender while on the ground. In amateur play, once a runner touches any part of his body to the ground, except for his hands and feet, he is considered down.

During each play, offensive players attempt to block defenders to protect the passer and ball carrier. The defense attempts to tackle the ball carrier or knock him out of bounds, or to intercept or knock down a pass. A defender records a sack when he tackles the quarterback for a loss of yardage during a pass attempt.

The offensive team has four downs, or plays, to advance 10 yards from the line of scrimmage at the first down. A team may, in certain instances, be awarded a first down (a new set of four downs) on a defensive penalty, even if the necessary 10 yards are not made.

In many cases if a team has not made a first down in three plays, it will punt (kick) the ball to the opponents on the fourth down. The player receiving the punt may attempt to catch and advance the ball, let it roll dead (it may not be recovered by the kicking team if it does not touch a player on the receiving team), or call for a fair catch by waving a hand above his helmet. The kicking team may not touch a player who has signaled for a fair catch, unless the player fumbles.

SCORING

A player scores a touchdown (six points) when he possesses the ball and the ball touches the plane of, or crosses over, the opponent's goal line. A touchdown can be made by running with the ball, by catching a pass, or by recovering a fumble on or over the opponent's goal line. The defense may intercept a pass, return a kick, or recover a fumble or blocked punt and return it for a touchdown.

After a touchdown is scored, a team has the choice of attempting a one-point or two-point try, or conversion. In the NFL, the ball is placed at the 2-yard line for a conversion attempt; in amateur football, the ball is placed at the 3-yard line. A one-point conversion is scored by kicking the ball through the uprights. A two-point conversion is scored by an offensive player possessing the ball on or over the goal line (in what normally would be considered a touchdown).

A field goal (three points) is scored by place-kicking or dropkicking the ball through the opponent's goal post uprights (though drop-kicking is rare in modern football). If the kick is no good and the ball is beyond the opponent's 20-yard line, the ball is given to the opponents at the line of scrimmage. If the unsuccessful kick was attempted from on or inside the 20-yard line, the ball is given to the opponents at the 20-yard line. If, however, the kick is blocked and recovered by the opponents, the ball goes to the opponents at the spot where the ball is downed, regardless of the yard line.

A safety (two points) is scored when the defense tackles behind the opponent's own goal line. A safety is also scored if the offense maintains possession of the ball out of bounds on or behind its own goal line. Examples of safeties are a runner or quarterback being tackled in his own end zone or a punt being blocked and going out of bounds beyond the goal line. Following a safety, the team that was just scored upon kicks off from its own 20-yard line.

FOULS AND PENALTIES

Many rules in football are geared for safety. On the following pages are brief explanations of common violations, listed in alphabetical order, that result in penalties. The length of the penalty appears at the end of each listing.

- **Batting or kicking the ball:** A player may not bat a ball toward the opponent's end zone or bat a ball in any direction in the end zone. Although stripping the ball (raking the ball from the player's grasp) is legal, attempting to bat the ball in a player's possession is not legal. Neither is kicking any loose ball or ball in a player's possession. *10 yards*

- **Defensive holding:** No defensive player can tackle or hold an opponent other than the ball carrier. *10 yards*

- **Delay of game:** A team must put the ball into play in the allotted time (40 seconds from the end of the previous play, or 25 seconds after a timeout, measurement, injury, or other delay). *5 yards*

- **Double (offsetting) foul:** When live-ball fouls are committed by both teams, the penalties offset each other, and the down is replayed at the previous spot.

- **Encroachment:** No part of a player's body may be in the neutral zone and no contact may occur before the ball is snapped. The neutral zone is a space the length of the ball between the offense's and defense's scrimmage lines. *5 yards*

- **Fair catch interference:** A player signaling for a fair catch of a punt must be given the opportunity to make the catch before the ball hits the ground. No contact may be made by a defender unless the ball has touched the receiver or touched the ground. *15 yards*

- **False start:** A false start occurs when an offensive player, once in the set position, moves in such a way as to signify the snap of the ball. *5 yards*

- **Helping a runner:** No offensive player can assist a runner (other than blocking for the runner) or use *interlocking interference* to aid a runner. Helping a runner includes pushing him or lifting him. *10 yards in NFL play; 5 yards in NCAA play*

- **Illegal contact:** A defender may make contact with an offensive receiver who is in front of him and within 5 yards of the line of scrimmage. Beyond 5 yards, or if the receiver has moved beyond the defender, the defender may not make contact that impedes or restricts the receiver. Incidental contact is legal, as long as it does not significantly impede the progress of the receiver or create a distinct advantage for the defender. *15 yards and automatic first down*

- **Illegal forward pass:** A team may make one forward pass from behind the line of scrimmage (a player with the ball may not cross the line of scrimmage and then retreat behind it and throw a pass). Any other forward pass is illegal with penalties as follows: for passing from a point beyond the line of scrimmage—*5 yards from the spot of the pass and loss of down;* for a second forward pass thrown, or for a pass thrown after the ball was returned behind the line of scrimmage—*loss of down from the previous spot;* for a forward pass not from scrimmage—*loss of 5 yards from the spot of the pass.*

- **Illegal motion:** Only one offensive player—a backfield player—may be in motion before the snap. The motion can be parallel to, or backward from, the line of scrimmage. Any other motion by other players—including movement of head, arms, or feet and swaying of the body—is illegal. *5 yards*

- **Ineligible player downfield:** Before a pass is thrown, an offensive lineman (unless he is designated as an eligible receiver) may not lose contact with an opponent and advance beyond the line of scrimmage. *5 yards*

- **Intentional grounding:** A passer may not throw an incomplete pass without a realistic chance of completing it in order to avoid being tackled. (A quarterback may stop the clock, however, by receiving a snap and immediately throwing the ball to the ground in front of him.) *loss of down 15 yards from previous spot*

- **Offensive holding:** No offensive player, in attempting to block, may use his hands to grab or obstruct a defender, except to initially contact the defender. The hands cannot be used to hang onto or encircle the opponent or to restrict his movement. *10 yards*

- **Offside and encroachment:** A player is offside when any part of him is beyond the line of scrimmage when the ball is put into play. *5 yards*

- **Pass interference:** Once a ball is thrown, no player may hinder the progress of an opponent who has a chance to catch the pass. Incidental contact that does not impede a player or affect his chance to catch the ball is legal. Restrictions on pass interference end once the pass is touched. *15 yards for offensive pass interference*

The following personal fouls result in penalties.

- **Blocking below the waist:** Players on the receiving team on a kickoff or punt cannot block below the waist. After a change of possession, neither team may block below the waist. *15 yards*

- **Chop block:** No offensive player may block a defensive player at the thigh level or below while the defender is being blocked by another offensive player. *15 yards*

- **Clip:** Except for close-in line blocking, no player may clip an opponent below the waist from behind. *15 yards*

- **Crackback block:** An offensive lineman aligned 7 yards or more from a middle lineman may not clip or contact a defender below the waist while he is within 10 yards either way of the line of scrimmage. *15 yards*

- **Grabbing the face mask:** No player may grasp the face mask of an opponent. *5 yards for incidental grasping and 15 yards for twisting, turning, or pulling the mask*

- **Head slap:** A defensive player may not contact an opponent's head with his palms except to ward him off the line. This exception may not be a repeated act during a single play. *15 yards*

- **Piling on:** Players may not pile on a runner after the ball is dead or intentionally fall upon any prostrate player. *15 yards*

- **Roughing the passer:** After the passer has released the ball, the rusher may make direct contact only up through the rusher's first step. After the first step, the rusher must attempt to avoid contact and not "drive through" the rush. Even if the timing of the contact is legal, a rusher may not be unnecessarily rough, club the passer's arm, or hit the knee or below if the rusher has a direct route to the passer. This is a good safety rule but it is not followed in high school play. *15 yards*

- **Roughing or running into the kicker:** No defensive player may run into or rough a kicker unless the defender has touched the ball or the kicker initiates the contact. There is no penalty if a defender is blocked into the kicker. *5 yards for running into the kicker and 15 yards for roughing the kicker*

- **Striking, kicking, or clubbing:** No player may strike with his fists, club, kick, or knee another player in the head, neck, or face. *15 yards*

- **Tripping:** No player may intentionally trip an opponent. *10 yards*

- **Too many players on the field:** A team may not have more than 11 players on the field at the snap of the ball. (There is no penalty for having fewer than 11.) *15 yards*

- **Unnecessary roughness:** This call covers a variety of illegal actions, including spearing with the helmet, tackling out of bounds, throwing the runner to the ground after the ball is dead, running or diving into a player who is obviously out of the play, and kicking an opponent above the knee. *15 yards*

- **Unsportsmanlike conduct:** This call is used for any unsporting act, including baiting, taunting, or using abusive or threatening language; unnecessary physical contact with an official; and jumping or standing on another player in an attempt to block a kick. *15 yards*

EQUIPMENT

The ball is oval shaped, leather bound, and inflated to a pressure 12.5 to 13.5 pounds per square inch; it weighs 14 to 15 ounces. It is 11 to 11.5 inches long and 28 to 28.5 inches at its largest circumference. (Youth league footballs are smaller.)

Players wear helmets, face masks, pads, and other protective equipment. This gear includes shoulder, chest, rib, hip, thigh, knee, shin, elbow, wrist, and forearm pads. Jerseys must cover all pads on the torso and upper body. Pants must cover the knee, and stockings must cover the lower legs from the feet to the bottom of the pants. Metal and aluminum cleats are prohibited. Conical cleats with tips measuring less than .375-inch in diameter are also prohibited. Nylon cleats with flat steel tips are permitted.

A crew of three operates yardage chains on the sidelines. The chains are 10 yards long and are attached to two sticks 5 feet in height. The down marker has four flip-over numbers (1, 2, 3, and 4) on a stick 4 feet in height. These numbers denote the down that is coming up (see page 104), and the marker is placed at the nose of the ball.

A play clock is used between plays. Various levels have rules denoting how much time can run off a play clock (which begins at the end of one play and ends with the snap of the ball beginning the next play) before a team is penalized for delay of game. In the NFL, it's 40 seconds between plays; in the NCAA, 25 seconds are allowed from the time the ball is ready to be put into play to the snap.

Game Clock

From high school on up, teams get three timeouts per half. For games tied at the end of regulation time, overtime is played. In the NFL, overtime is begun with a coin toss and a kickoff, and the first team to score wins. In college and high school, each team has a chance to score in the overtime. The clock starts when

- the ball is snapped after a timeout;
- the ball is placed ready to play after a penalty; or
- an official spots the ball at the inbounds mark following an out-of-bounds play, and the referee gives the ready signal (except in the last two minutes of the first half and last five minutes of the game, when the clock doesn't start again until the next snap). *Note*: In NCAA play, the clock doesn't start on any kickoff until a player on the receiving team touches the ball.

The clock stops when the ball is out of bounds; when a pass drops incomplete; when a play is completed during which a foul occurs; when two minutes remain in a half (NFL only); when a first down occurs (college only); when a period expires; when a field goal, safety, or touchdown is scored; when an official signals timeout; or when a down involving a change of possession is completed.

If time expires as a play is in progress, time is not called until the play is completed. If either team commits a foul on the last play of a period, the offense may run another play. If the offense commits a foul on the last play of a half, the half is over.

OFFICIALS

Any official may rule on any foul; there is no territorial division in this regard. While each official has many duties, the main duties for each include the following.

- The **referee** has general control; he has the final say in any disagreement, including score and number of downs. He starts and stops play, spots the ball after each play, signals coaches for the two-minute warning (in NFL play) and when they have used their timeouts, and announces penalties.

- The **umpire** watches for scrimmage line violations. He records timeouts, watches for line violations on short passes, and assists the referee in ball possession decisions close to the line. He is also in charge of legality of equipment.

- The **linesman** watches primarily for offside, encroachment, illegal motion, and other violations occurring on the line before or at the snap. He is in charge of the chain crew.

- The **line judge** operates on the opposite side of the field from the linesman. He is responsible for timing the game and for spotting violations, including illegal motion and illegal shift, on his side of the field. He assists on calls of holding, encroaching, offside, forward laterals, and false starts, and he marks the out-of-bounds spot of all plays on his side.

- The **back judge** operates on the middle of the field as the line judge, 20 yards deep. He counts the number of defensive players and watches the eligible receivers on his side of the field, concentrating on action in the area between the field judge and the umpire. He signals when time is out and when the ball is dead, and he assists in calls regarding legal catches. He also judges whether field goals are good.

- The **side judge** operates on the same side as the head linesman, 20 yards deep. He counts the number of defenders and watches the eligible receivers on his side. He watches the action between the umpire and the field judge and assists on calls regarding legal catches, fumble recoveries, and out-of-bounds plays.

- The **field judge** is primarily responsible for covering kicks and forward passes that cross the goal line. He times the halftime and timeouts and the time between plays. He also assists on calls regarding legal catches, fumble recoveries, and out-of-bounds plays. He is positioned on the line judge's side of the field.

For common officials' signals, see figure 18.2.

MODIFICATIONS

Football can be played in various forms, including flag, touch, Canadian, and arena football, which is played indoors on smaller fields. Youth leagues also have rule variations to enhance players' safety and make the sport more appropriate for kids. Following are some of the basic differences in the rules for flag and touch football, Canadian football, youth football, six-man football, and eight-man football.

Flag and Touch Football

Flag and touch football have several variations. For general guidelines see table 18.1.

Contact blocking allows contact between the opponent's waist and shoulders. Blockers must be on their feet before, during, and after the block; no cross-body blocks or rolling blocks are allowed. An open-hand, straight-arm block is permitted; the blocker may not lock his hands together.

Screen blocking allows no contact with the opponent's body. Blockers must be on their feet before, during, and after the block.

A game lasts 48 minutes (two 24-minute halves). The clock runs continuously for the first 22 minutes of a half; it stops as with regular football rules during the last two minutes of a half. Teams get three timeouts per half, lasting one minute each. A team may take no more than two timeouts in the last two minutes of a half. In regular season overtime games, team A starts with a first-and-goal on the opponents' 20-yard line. Team B then gets a chance to score in the same situation. The game is continued in this fashion until the tie is broken. Team B always gets a chance to tie or win. In

Delay of game

Holding

Illegal motion

First down

Pass interference

Roughing kicker

Missed kick, penalty refused, or incomplete pass

(continued)

▶ Figure 18.2 Common football officials' signals.

Timeout

Touchdown

Personal foul

Illegal use
of hands

Illegal contact

Offside

▶ Figure 18.2 (continued)

Table 18.1	Flag and Touch Football		
Game	Players per team	Blocking	Field
Flag	8	Contact	53 1/3 yd × 100 yd
Touch	7	Contact	53 1/3 yd × 100 yd
Screen flag	7	Screen	53 1/3 yd × 100 yd
Ineligible linemen flag	9	Contact	53 1/3 yd × 100 yd
4 on 4	4	Screen	25 yd × 40 yd

championship games, overtime is decided by sudden death—the first team to score wins.

In flag football, when a flag is removed from the ball carrier, the play is over. In touch football, the play is dead when the ball carrier is legally touched. A new set of downs is awarded each time a team advances to the next zone (a regulation field is divided into five zones of 20 yards each).

In 4 on 4, there are no-run zones from each 5-yard line to the goal line, and from 15-yard line to 15-yard line (i.e., 10 yards across midfield).

Points are awarded as follows:

- Touchdown = six points
- Touchdown made by a woman (in coed play) = nine points
- Extra point (from the 3-yard line) = one point
- Extra point (from the 10-yard line) = two points
- Return of extra point by defense = two points

A team may choose to attempt the extra point from either the 3-yard line or the 10-yard line.

Canadian Football

Canadian football is similar to American football. The following list includes some of the significant differences:

- The playing field is 65 yards by 165 yards; goal lines are 110 yards apart.
- The goal posts are on the goal line.
- The end zone is 25 yards deep.
- Teams play with 12 players each.
- Teams have three downs to gain 10 yards.
- Fair catches on punts are not permitted.
- A punt that is not returned from the end zone results in one point awarded to the kicking team.
- Each team gets one timeout per half, to be used only during the last three minutes of a half.

- There is no sudden death; overtime games have two five-minute periods.
- The ball is placed on the 5-yard line for extra point conversions; one point is awarded for kicking an extra point; two are awarded for running or passing the ball over the goal line.

Youth Football

Many leagues have both age and weight classifications. Some have a mandatory play rule, with players required to play a minimum of plays per game, depending on the number of players on the team. Leagues for younger players (11 and under) often choose to use an 80-yard field. The smaller field is also used for six-man and eight-man leagues. Periods last 10 to 12 minutes, with two-minute breaks between the first and second periods and between the third and fourth periods, as well as a 15-minute halftime.

Six-Man Football

A few of the differences in the six-man game follow:

- The offense must advance the ball 15 yards in four downs.
- At least three offensive players must be on the line of scrimmage at the snap.
- The ball may not be run directly across the line of scrimmage; it may, however, be advanced by passing, kicking, or lateraling behind the line of scrimmage (the player receiving a lateral may then run across the line).
- Kickoffs are made from the 30-yard line.
- On a touchback, the ball is brought out to the 15-yard line (on an 80-yard field).

Eight-Man Football

A few of the differences in the eight-man game follow:

- At least five offensive players must be on the line of scrimmage at the snap.
- Backs and the right and left ends are eligible to receive passes.

- Direct running across the line of scrim-mage is allowed.

ORGANIZATIONS

National Football League
280 Park Avenue
New York, NY 10017
www.nfl.com

Pop Warner Football
586 Middletown Boulevard, Suite c-100
Langhorne, PA 19047
www.popwarner.com

U.S. Flag and Touch Football League
7709 Ohio Street
Mentor, OH 44060
440-974-8735
www.asftl.com

19

Golf

G olf is believed to have had its beginnings in 15th-century Scotland, where players first used wooden balls and then leather balls stuffed with feathers. Golf was introduced in the United States in the late 1700s and has grown in popularity with the advent of improved equipment, professional tours, and television coverage.

Today golf is popular worldwide; in the United States nearly 26 million golfers go to the greens at least once a year. Nearly half of those are between the ages of 18 and 39, and another 28 percent are 50 or older.

Objective: To use as few strokes as possible to hit the ball into a series of holes arranged on a course.

Scoring: In *stroke play*, the side (individual player or partners) that has the lowest total score wins; in *match play*, the winner is the side that leads by a number of holes that is greater than the number of holes left.

Overview: The order of play is determined by a draw. Partners can decide their own playing order. The side that wins the hole in match play or scores the lowest in stroke play "takes the honor" by going first at the next tee. If each side scores the same on a hole, the side that teed first at that hole retains the honor.

In match play, if the sides are tied at the end of regulation, play continues until one side wins a hole, which ends the match. In stroke play, if sides are tied at the end of the round, they may play until one side has a lower score on a hole. This is a sudden-death playoff. In tournaments, ties are sometimes broken by an 18-hole playoff, after which sudden death applies.

COURSE

While courses vary in hole lengths, design, and playing characteristics, they share common components (see figure 19.1). A standard course contains 18 *holes* usually between 100 and 600 yards long; each hole is on a putting green and is 4.25 inches in diameter and at least 4 inches deep. Each hole has a *teeing ground* from which play for that hole begins. The most forward point from which the ball may be played is designated by *tee markers*; the farthest point back from which a ball may be teed is two club lengths behind these markers.

The *fairway* lies between the teeing ground and the *putting green,* which is the short-cropped surface around the hole. The *apron* (short collar) around the green is not considered part of the green. *Hazards*—both bunkers and water hazards—lie between and around the teeing ground and the green. The *rough* is the longer grass and rough terrain bordering the fairway and green.

The *flagstick* is a movable pole about 8 feet long that is placed in the hole to show the position of the hole on the putting green.

TERMS

A player is said to **address the ball** when he takes his stance and grounds the club in preparing to strike the ball.

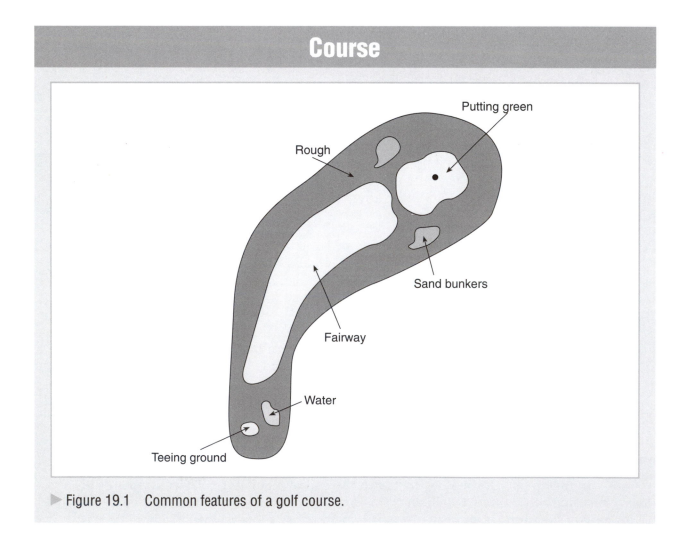

Course

▶ Figure 19.1   Common features of a golf course.

An **approach shot** is a shot that is made to hit the ball onto the green.

A **birdie** is one stroke under *par.*

A **bogey** is one stroke over par; a **double-bogey** is two strokes over.

A **bunker** is an area of the course usually filled with sand. It is also considered a hazard.

A **caddie** carries a player's clubs and offers advice on how to play holes.

Casual water is a temporary accumulation of water.

A **chip shot** is a low approach shot from a position close to the green.

A **divot** is a piece of turf dug from the ground by the clubhead.

A **draw** is a controlled right-to-left shot for a right-handed player (as opposed to a *hook,* which curves sharply to the left).

A player **drives** the ball when she strikes it from the tee on a par 4 or 5.

An **eagle** is two strokes under par.

A **fade** is a controlled left-to-right shot for a right-handed player (as opposed to a *slice,* which curves sharply to the right).

A **halved hole** occurs when each side scores the same on a hole.

A **hazard** is any bunker or water hazard.

A **hook** is a shot that curves sharply to the left (or to the right, for a left-handed player).

Loose impediments are natural objects on the course, such as pebbles or leaves, which are not embedded in the ground.

Obstructions are any artificial objects except for out-of-bounds markers or objects that are an integral part of the course.

Out describes the first nine holes; **in** signifies the second, or back, nine holes.

Boundary markers denote all areas that are **out of bounds;** play is not allowed out of bounds.

Par is the number of strokes that an expert player is expected to take to hole out. The

Table 19.1 Yardage Guidance for Par

Par	Men (yd)	Women (yd)
3	Up to 250	Up to 210
4	251 to 470	211 to 400
5	471 to 690	401 to 590
6	691 and over	591 and over

USGA Handicap System Manual © 2002 United States Golf Association.

yardage guidance for par is shown in table 19.1.

A **pitch** is a high shot near the green that is intended to roll minimally after landing.

A group may **play through** when the group ahead of them is slowing them down.

"Rub of the green" is the term used when a ball is deflected or stopped by something or someone other than anyone part of a match or competitor's side in stroke play.

A **shank** is a shot that goes off to the right (or to the left, for a left-handed player).

A player's **"short game"** refers to her pitching, chipping, and putting.

A **slice** is a shot that curves sharply to the right (or to the left, for a left-handed player).

Winter rules allow for improving the lie of the ball on the fairway (but not closer to the hole); check local rules.

PLAY

Golf is a unique sport in that there are rules governing play and etiquette both on and off the actual area of play, along with general standards of etiquette no matter where you are on the course.

Through the Green

The following rules apply to play "through the green," which is the entire course except for the teeing ground, the putting green of the hole being played, and all hazards.

• No player may give advice to anyone other than her partner. A player may receive advice from her partner, from her caddie, or from her partner's caddie.

• A player will be penalized for discontinuing play unless the committee has discontinued play or is ruling on a disputed play, or the player believes there is danger from lightning.

• In stroke play, when there is doubt as to procedure, the player may play another ball after announcing this to his fellow competitor. The player reports the facts to the committee before signing his card; if the rules allow for play of the second ball, the player's score for the hole is what it was with the second ball.

• A player dropping a ball must hold the ball at shoulder height and arm's length and drop it. Examples of when a ball may be dropped without penalty are when it rolls into or out of a hazard, onto a putting green, out of bounds, or more than two club lengths away from or closer to the green.

• A ball embedded in a closely mown area may be lifted, cleaned, and dropped as close as possible to the spot but not closer to the hole.

• When a ball is in a hazard—either a bunker or a water hazard—a player may not test the condition of the hazard, touch the ground or water of the hazard, or touch or move loose impediments in the hazard. If the ball is in a water hazard, a player may take a one-stroke penalty and either (a) play a ball from the spot it was last played, or (b) drop a ball behind the hazard. The player may also play the ball from the water, if possible.

• To identify a ball (except in a hazard), a player may lift a ball she believes to be her own and clean it as necessary for identification. She must then return it to the same spot.

• A ball in motion touched by an outside agency is played where it lies. In stroke play, if it is touched by the player, his partner, caddie, or any of his own equipment, he incurs a two-

stroke penalty and plays the ball where it lies; in match play, he loses the hole.

• A player may lift her ball if it is interfering with or assisting play. This may not be done while another ball is in motion. In stroke play, a player requested to lift her ball may choose to play first rather than lift.

• A player must play the ball as it lies. He may not improve the position of his ball, the area of his swing, or his line of play. This includes moving or bending anything growing, tamping down grass, replacing old divots before the shot, and so on. Loose impediments may be removed, however.

• When lifting a ball, a player must first mark the position of the ball. If the position is not marked, the player incurs a one-stroke penalty.

• The line of play may be indicated by anyone, but no one may stand on or close to the line while the stroke is played. (See also "line of play" in "On the Green.")

• If there is reason to believe a ball is lost out of bounds or outside a water hazard, a player may take a one-stroke penalty and play a provisional ball as close as possible to the spot where the original ball was played. A ball is defined as "lost" if the player has searched for five minutes, if the player has put another ball into play, or if the player has continued to play with the provisional ball. If the original ball is found within five minutes, it must be played, even if it is in an unplayable lie or water hazard.

• If a ball is moved by the player, partner, caddie, or equipment, the ball is replaced and a one-stroke penalty is incurred. If the ball is moved by the opponent in match play (except during a search), the opponent is assessed a one-stroke penalty. In stroke play, no penalty is assessed a fellow competitor for moving a ball. A ball moved by another ball is set back in place.

• If a ball is played from outside the teeing ground in match play, the opponent may ask for the shot to be replayed (no penalty) or let the stroke played stand. In stroke play, there is a two-stroke penalty, and the ball must be replayed.

• A player may not play a practice stroke except when between two holes. Then she may practice putting or chipping on or near the teeing ground of the next hole, provided the practice does not unduly delay play. Note that a practice swing is not a practice stroke.

• A player is not necessarily entitled to see the ball when playing a stroke.

• In striking the ball, the player must fairly strike at the ball and not push or scoop it. Any player who strikes the ball twice on the same stroke receives a one-penalty stroke (two strokes total).

• If a ball falls off a tee while a player is addressing it, he may replace it with no penalty. But if the player swings at the ball, whether the ball is moving or not, the stroke counts.

• A player may declare her ball unplayable anywhere, unless it lies in or is touching a water hazard. She may take a one-stroke penalty and play a ball as near as possible to the spot where the last shot was played. Or she may drop a ball within two club lengths of where the unplayable ball lies (but not nearer to the hole) and add a penalty stroke. A third option is to take a penalty stroke and drop a ball behind the unplayable lie, keeping that spot between the hole and the drop area. There is no limit to how far back a player may drop the ball.

• When a player plays a wrong ball (any ball other than the ball in play or a provisional ball) while in match play, he loses the hole. The only exception is if the ball is played from a hazard; in this case, no penalty is incurred, the stroke does not count, and the player places another ball in the spot from which the wrong ball was played. In stroke play, playing a wrong ball brings a two-stroke penalty.

On the Green

The following rules apply to play "on the green."

• A player may clean a ball when she lifts it. She must mark and replace the ball where she lifted it.

• The flagstick may remain in place, be attended, be removed, or be held up to indicate position. The flagstick may not be moved once a ball is in motion, unless it is attended. If a ball rests against a flagstick and falls in the hole when the flagstick is picked up, the ball is considered holed on the previous stroke.

• A line of play for putting may be pointed out before the stroke, but the putting green may not be touched and no mark may be laid on it to indicate the putting line. In match play, breaking this rule results in loss of the hole; in stroke play, the player incurs a two-stroke penalty.

• If a ball from off the green strikes and moves a ball on the green, there is no penalty and the ball moved is returned to its original position. If a player on the green strokes a ball that hits another player's ball, there is a two-stroke penalty in stroke play. There is no penalty in match play for this.

• A player cannot take a practice stroke on the green prior to completing play of the hole.

General Etiquette

The following rules are matters of courtesy and safety:

• Before swinging, the player should make sure that no one is in a position to be hit with the club or ball.

• The player who has the honor should be allowed to play before the next player tees off.

• While a player is addressing or stroking the ball, no one should talk, move, or stand directly behind the ball or the hole.

• Players should play without delay.

• Players searching for a ball should signal the players behind them to pass when it becomes apparent that the ball will not be found quickly. In most cases they should not complete the five-minute search time before letting players behind them play through.

• When players complete a hole, they should immediately leave the green and record their scores elsewhere.

- Among players with similar abilities, two-ball matches have precedence over three-ball and four-ball matches. Players in the latter two matches should invite two-ball matches to pass through.
- A single player should give way to a match of any kind.
- Any match playing a whole round is entitled to pass a match playing a shorter round.
- A player should smooth over any holes and footprints she makes before leaving a bunker.
- A player should replace any turf he cuts through the green and repair any damage on the green made by the ball. Damage to the green made by golf spikes should be repaired after the hole is completed. All divots should be replaced and tamped down.
- Players should not damage the green by leaning on their putters.
- A player should call "fore" if she thinks her ball may hit another person.
- A player should not take his golf bag, cart, extra clubs, or any other equipment onto the green or tee.
- A player attending the flagstick should take care that her shadow does not fall across the line of the putt.
- Players should place an identification mark on their golf balls.

SCORING

Players are responsible for keeping their own scores. In stroke play, players add each stroke and penalty stroke to arrive at their total scores. At the end of a round, each player should review and sign his scorecard before turning it in. If a player signs for a lower score for a hole than he shot, he is disqualified. If he records a higher score for a hole, that score stands. No changes on the scorecard may be made once it is turned in to the committee.

Handicaps allow players of varying abilities to compete fairly against each other. Handi-caps are determined by a player's recent play. A player with a 10 handicap who shoots an actual 100 would finish with a net score of 90.

EQUIPMENT

A maximum of 14 clubs is allowed. The clubs are carried in a golf bag; players may carry the bag or transport it in a hand- or motorized cart. The three types of clubs include the following:

- **Woods:** The clubhead is wood (modern woods also have metal, carbon, and titanium heads); these clubs are used for longer shots. Woods are numbered 1 through 10; the most commonly used are 1, 3, and 5.
- **Irons:** The clubhead is usually steel, and the club has a shorter shaft than a wood. Irons are used for shorter shots and are numbered 1 through 10, plus the wedges.
- **Putters:** There are many styles of clubheads; putters are usually all metal and are used on the putting green.

The ball is dimpled and has a synthetic shell. It weighs not more than 1.62 ounces and is not less than 1.68 inches in diameter. On a teeing ground the ball is placed on a tee, which is a peg about 2 inches long. The tee allows the player to drive the ball.

MODIFICATIONS

Variations of games are as follows:

- **Match:** One player or side plays against another. In a *threesome*, one player plays against two, and each side plays one ball. In a *foursome*, two players play against two others, with each side playing one ball and partners alternating shots.
- **Three-ball:** Three players each play against one another. In *best-ball*, one player plays against the better ball of two others or best ball of three others.

- **Four-ball:** In *four-ball,* two players play against two others in match-play format, with only the best ball (best score) of each team counting.

- **Four-ball stroke:** Two competitors team up, each playing her own ball; the lower score of the two balls for each hole is counted. In *bogey* and *par* competitions, players play against a fixed score at each hole. For example, par on a hole is the "opponent"; the winner is the golfer who is furthest ahead of par.

- **Stableford:** Points are awarded in relation to a fixed score at each hole. For example, a birdie is worth three points, a double bogey or worse scores zero points. Table 19.2 shows how points are awarded in Stableford play; the person scoring the most points wins.

The United States Golf Association suggests that junior handicaps be used to give young golfers a sense of accomplishment. For example, an adult par 5 hole might become a junior par 8.

The paraphrased text is reprinted with permission from *The Rules of Golf* © 2002-2003 United States Golf Association.

Table 19.2 How Points Are Awarded in Stableford Play

Hole played in . . .	Points
More than one over fixed score	0
One over fixed score	1
Fixed score	2
One under fixed score	3
Two under fixed score	4
Three under fixed score	5
Four under fixed score	6

USGA Handicap System Manual © 2002 United States Golf Association.

ORGANIZATIONS

United States Golf Association
P.O. Box 708
Far Hills, NJ 07931
908-234-2300, ext. 1346
www.usga.org

20 Gymnastics

The roots of gymnastics can be found in ancient Greece, but the modern development of the sport began in 19th-century Germany, where much of the sport's apparatus—the rings, the horse, and the bars—were developed. Immigrants brought the sport to the United States. Men competed in gymnastics in the first modern Olympics in 1896; women began Olympic competition in 1936.

Historically, Germany, Russia, Bulgaria, Romania, and Japan have dominated the world championships and Olympic Games. Recently, the United States, China, Ukraine, and Romania have enjoyed greater successes. Gymnastics is a highly popular Olympic sport; for the past three to four Olympic Games, artistic gymnastics has had the highest viewer ratings of all the Olympic coverage.

Gymnastics is most popular among the youngest age groups, with children being introduced to the sport as early as two years of age. USA Gymnastics has more than 80,000 registered members (athletes, coaches, judges, and administrators). Male and female gymnasts compete in various events, attempting to score the highest number of points possible through their performances. High score wins.

Events: Women compete in four artistic events (*vault, uneven bars, balance beam,* and *floor exercise*). Men compete in six artistic events (*floor exercise, pommel horse, rings, vault, parallel bars,* and *horizontal bar*). Gymnasts also compete in *trampoline and tumbling, sports acrobatics, group gymnastics,* and *rhythmic gymnastics.*

Starting an Event: Gymnasts begin their exercise when a green light is lit or when the judge signals for them to begin.

Continuing an Event: If gymnasts fall during an exercise, they have 30 seconds to remount and continue.

Scoring: Scoring is based on judges' evaluations; see "Scoring and Evaluation" and the sections on individual events for more information.

TERMS

An **acrobatic element** is a salto (somersault) or handspring executed from a stand or a run.

The **difficulty** of an element is categorized into one of six value groups (A, B, C, D, E, or Super E), based on the strength and physical requirements of the movement.

An **element** is the smallest independently executed movement in gymnastics, with definite starting and ending points.

An **element of flexibility** shows an extreme range of motion in one or more joints (e.g., shoulders, hips, or spine).

An **element of flight** is a movement in which the gymnast releases a grip, executes a distinct flight phase, and regrips the apparatus.

An **element of strength** is a movement where gravity is conquered slowly or where a gymnast achieves balance through static force.

An **element of swing** is a dynamic movement executed with great amplitude and without stopping or visibly showing strength.

An **exercise** is the complete presentation of all the elements. *Compulsory exercises* contain specific criteria that the gymnast must meet; *optional exercises* have specific requirements but also allow for the gymnast's preferences.

A **gymnastics element** is a nonacrobatic move, such as performing a body wave, separating the legs, rolling, or jumping.

A **hold part** refers to the gymnast's holding his body for two seconds in a prescribed position.

GYMNASTS

The primary age of competitive participants is between 6 and 18. Collegiate athletes finish active participation around age 22 and some men are competitive into their 30s. Gymnasts must wear proper attire (leotards). They may wear bandages and slippers or socks. Gymnasts must begin their exercise within 30 seconds once they are given the signal. On the horizontal bar and rings, a coach or another gymnast may assist a gymnast into a hanging position.

WOMEN'S ARTISTIC EVENTS

Women compete in the following events: vault, uneven bars, balance beam, and floor exercise (see figure 20.1).

Vault

The vault table is 5.2 feet long, 3.9 feet high, and 14 inches wide. It is made of wood on a metal frame and has a thin layer of padding covered with leather or vinyl. In compulsories, women get one attempt; in optionals, they get two. In individual finals, both optional vaults are scored and averaged. In apparatus finals the two vaults must be different. The vaulter runs down a runway, springs off a springboard, and vaults over the table. She is judged on four portions of the vault, including

- the first flight phase (from the springboard to the table),
- the support phase (pushing off the table),
- the second flight phase (from the table to the dismount), and
- the landing.

Uneven Bars

The upper bar is 7.75 feet high; the lower bar is 5.2 feet high. The bars are 11.4 feet long.

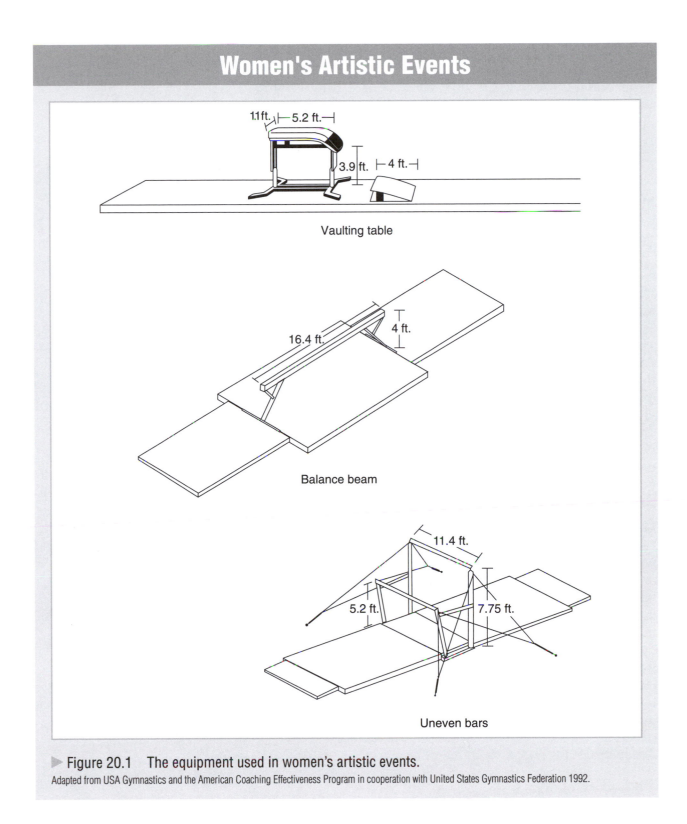

1.1 ft. — 5.2 ft. —

3.9 ft. — 4 ft. —

Vaulting table

16.4 ft.   4 ft.

Balance beam

11.4 ft.

5.2 ft.   7.75 ft.

Uneven bars

▶ Figure 20.1   The equipment used in women's artistic events.

Adapted from USA Gymnastics and the American Coaching Effectiveness Program in cooperation with United States Gymnastics Federation 1992.

Trampoline and Tumbling

- Power tumblers perform on elevated spring runways, demonstrating speed, strength, and skill while performing explosive somersaults with multiple twists and flips.
- On the trampoline, gymnasts perform individually or in pairs, the latter in synchronized trampoline, where gymnasts on two separate trampolines must perform identical 10-skill routines at the same time.
- Double mini-trampoline is a relatively new sport that combines the horizontal run of tumbling with the vertical rebound of trampoline.

They are made of wood or fiberglass, with a metal support. The evaluation begins with the gymnast's takeoff from the board or floor. The exercise must include at least 10 elements. The exercise must contain at least one directional change (a 180-degree pirouette, for example) and at least two flight elements of at least a B value. The exercise must include at least three bar changes. Elements must be performed without pause and without an intermediate swing.

Balance Beam

The balance beam is 16.4 feet long, 4 feet high, and 4 inches wide. The beam is wood padded with foam rubber and covered with synthetic or real suede. The evaluation begins with the takeoff from the board or floor. The exercise must last from 70 to 90 seconds. A gymnast may use two static holds on the beam; additional pauses result in deductions. The routine must include both acrobatic and gymnastics elements. Acrobatic elements include forward, backward, or sideways flight; gymnastics elements include leaps, turns, hops, step combinations, balance elements, and body waves. The gymnast must execute at least

- one 360-degree turn,
- one acrobatic series of two or more flight elements,
- one gymnastics series of two or more elements,
- one mixed series of two or more elements (gymnastics/acrobatic), and

- one element or connection close to the beam (i.e., not standing).

Floor Exercise

The floor exercise lasts between 70 and 90 seconds. The exercise is done to music and begins with the first gymnastics or acrobatic movement. Stepping outside of the floor area (a square measuring 12 meters on each side) results in a deduction of one-tenth point. The exercise should consist of both acrobatic elements and gymnastics elements (turns, leaps, jumps, balance elements in various positions, and body waves). It should include dynamic change between slow and fast movements and must be done in harmony with the music. The gymnast must perform

- one gymnastics series with three elements;
- one mixed series with three elements; and
- two acrobatic series, one with two saltos and one with one salto; all three saltos must be different.

Rhythmic Events

Rhythmic gymnastics involves body movements and dance set to music and performed while handling small equipment: rope, hoop, ball, clubs, and ribbon. An individual exercise lasts 60 to 90 seconds; a group exercise lasts for two to two and a half minutes. Gymnasts may perform three pre-acrobatic elements, such as rolls, but no handsprings or aerials are allowed.

Each routine must contain at least four elements of B difficulty and four of A difficulty; in finals competitions, a C and D element are also required. The routine must cover the entire floor and include leaps, pivots, balances, and flexibility movements.

The base score for an individual is 9.60; a senior gymnast may earn up to .40 bonus points for a maximum of 10.00. A junior gymnast may earn up to .20 bonus points for a maximum of 9.80. A group begins with a base score of 19.20 and may earn a maximum of .80 bonus points for a possible 20.00 score.

During an exercise, the ball may be thrown, caught, rolled, and bounced. The rope may be thrown, caught, swung, and twirled. The hoop may be thrown, caught, swung, and passed through. The clubs may be thrown, caught, and swung. The ribbon may be thrown in loops, circles, and spirals.

MEN'S ARTISTIC EVENTS

Men compete in the following events: the floor exercise, pommel horse, rings, vault, parallel bars, and horizontal bar (see figure 20.2).

Floor Exercise

The floor exercise lasts up to 70 seconds. The gymnast must use the entire floor area—a square measuring 12 meters on each side. He may step on, but not over, any boundary line. He also may not pause for more than one second in his routine, unless he is holding a static element.

The exercise should consist of acrobatic jumps and include acrobatic and gymnastics elements of flexibility and balance. Examples of errors, for which points are deducted, include attaining a low height during a jump, not having the knees and shoulders in a straight line during a standing scale, and stepping outside the floor area.

Pommel Horse

The pommel horse is 3.4 feet high and 5.3 feet long. The gymnast performs circular and pendulum swings on the horse, using various positions of support, and utilizing all three parts of the horse. The gymnast must execute leg circles with the legs together; he must perform two scissors (open-leg swings) in an optional connection. He must perform at least one B value element on one pommel with three hand placements. He may not pause during the routine, and the dismount must be at least a C value. Errors, for which points are deducted, include not using all three parts of the horse equally, not executing a scissor, and performing more than 40 percent of the exercise with the legs straddled.

Rings

The rings are 8.4 feet above the mat. The gymnast must perform swing, strength, and hold parts, in about equal proportions. The gymnast executes these parts in a hang position, to or through a support position, and into a handstand position, with straight arms. The gymnast should not let the ropes swing; points are deducted for this. He must perform at least two handstands, one from swing and one from strength, and one static strength part.

Types of errors for which a gymnast is penalized include touching the ropes with his feet or any part of his body, using too many strength elements, and not holding strength elements level or for two seconds.

Vault

Male gymnasts vault over the vault table lengthwise (i.e., from end to end). A gymnast runs up, jumps onto a springboard, and executes single or multiple rotations around the body's transverse and longitudinal axes before and after touching the vault table. The vault is judged on its start value, on the flight from the springboard to the table, on the body position during execution, and on the push off from the table to a landing position.

Male gymnasts perform only one vault except during apparatus finals, when they complete two different vaults and have their scores averaged.

Errors resulting in penalties include opening or straddling of the legs while going from the board to the horse or while on the table, insufficient height off of the table, deviation

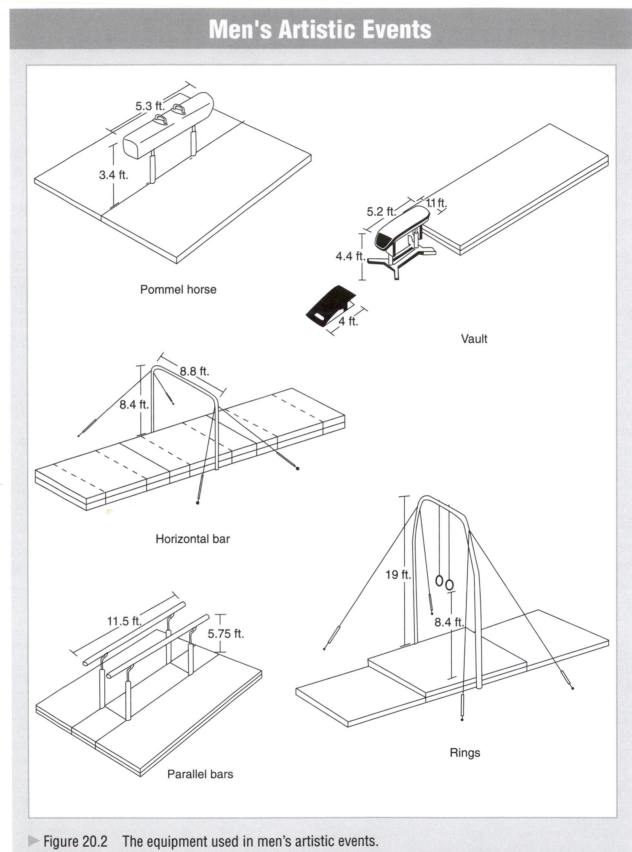

Pommel horse

Vault

Horizontal bar

Parallel bars

Rings

▶ Figure 20.2   The equipment used in men's artistic events.

Adapted USA Gymnastics and the American Coaching Effectiveness Program in cooperation with United States Gymnastics Federation 1992.

from the axis of the table during the vault or during the landing, and insufficient distance during landing.

Parallel Bars

The parallel bars are 5.75 feet high and 11.5 feet long. The gymnast performs elements of swing and flight both above and below the bars. He can execute elements in a side position and elements of strength. He must perform at least one swinging part and one element from a hang or through a hang while releasing both hands. He may not perform more than three hold parts or unnecessarily straddle his legs. Other errors that may result in penalties include walking during a handstand, touching the bars or floor with any part of his body other than his hands on the bars, and not holding strength parts for the required two seconds.

Horizontal Bar

The horizontal bar is 8.4 feet high and 8.8 feet long. The gymnast performs elements of uninterrupted swing, including giant swings (360-degree rotations), turns, and flight elements. He may perform a one-arm swing. The routine must include at least one release-and-regrasp of the bar, slowing flight. The gymnast will be penalized for errors, including stopping in a handstand or any other position, executing swing elements with strength, deviating from the direction of the movement, bending his arms during a circular swing, and failing to regrasp the bar after a flight element.

SCORING AND EVALUATION

Compulsory exercises are set routines that every gymnast must complete. (Beginning in 1997, compulsories were eliminated from international competition.) Each competitor begins compulsories with 10 points.

Women competing in *optional exercises* begin with 9.40 points; they may earn .60 bonus points for performing extremely difficult skills or combinations, to reach a maximum of 10 points. Men competing in optional exercises begin with 8.8 points, and they may earn a maximum of 1.2 bonus points, for a maximum total score of 10. Each exercise has specific requirements and deductions, the latter based on types of errors made.

In competitions with six judges, the high and low scores are thrown out; the remaining four scores are added and then divided by four to arrive at an average score. The allowable difference between the two middle scores decreases as the scores increase.

Scoring is further affected by six *difficulty values,* ranging from easy (A) to highest (Super E) difficulty and value. Also, different events have different requirements; if these requirements are not successfully completed, points are deducted. Gymnasts can earn *bonus points* for extremely difficult skills and combinations.

Gymnasts have points deducted for *faults.* For women, point deductions range from .05 to .20 point for a small fault, to .25 to .40 point for a medium fault, to .45 point or more for a major fault. For men, small faults result in a deduction of .10 point; medium faults, .20 point; large faults, .30 point; and falls, .50 point. Examples of faults include

- breaking form;
- touching the apparatus or floor for balance;
- incorrectly positioning hands or legs;
- interrupting an upward movement;
- losing balance during, or not completing, a dismount;
- bending arms in a handstand, or falling out of the handstand;
- stepping outside the floor area during a floor exercise;
- falling off an apparatus; and
- failing to start on time.

OFFICIALS

Up to seven judges evaluate each routine.

MODIFICATIONS

To make the sport safer and more appropriate for younger athletes, various organizations have modified events (for instructional classes, not for competition) in the following ways:

- For the *balance beam*, gymnasts may use a lower or wider beam.

- For the *floor exercise*, gymnasts may be allowed to use "cheese-wedge" mats to assist them with their rolls, and larger mats may be used to assist their rotational movements.

ORGANIZATIONS

USA Gymnastics
Pan American Plaza, Suite 300
201 S. Capitol Avenue
Indianapolis, IN 46225
317-237-5050
www.usa-gymnastics.org

21

Handball

Handball's origins date back to ancient Rome. The game was played on dirt floors in Ireland in the Middle Ages and was brought to the United States by 19th-century Irish immigrants. Little about the sport has changed since its introduction into America, except that it now uses a smaller, harder ball and a smaller court. Handball is most popular in the United States, Canada, Mexico, Ireland, and Australia.

Handball can be played on a four-walled, three-walled, or one-walled court. The rules for the main body of this chapter are for four-wall handball. The "Modifications" section addresses three-wall and one-wall rule differences.

Objective: To win rallies and score points by serving or returning the ball so that the opponent cannot keep the ball in play.

Scoring: A rally is won when one player cannot return the ball before it hits the floor twice, or when a player returns a ball that hits the floor before it hits the front wall; only the serving player or team can score.

Number of Players: Two players (singles) or four players (doubles).

Game Length: First team to 21 points.

Match Length: Best two of three games; the third game (the tiebreaker) is played to 11 points.

Overview: The winner of a coin toss chooses to serve or receive to begin the game. The other player or side chooses for the second game. To begin a tiebreaker, the player or team with the most points in the first two games chooses. If both sides have scored the same number of points, another coin toss is used to begin the tiebreaker.

COURT

A standard four-walled court is 20 feet wide, 20 feet high, and 40 feet long (see figure 21.1). The recommended minimum height for the back wall is 14 feet. The short line is parallel to the front and back walls; its outside edge is 20 feet from the front wall. The service line is parallel to the short line and its outside edge is 5 feet in front of the short line.

The service zone is the area between the outer edges of the short line and the service line. The service boxes are located at each side of the service zone. Each service box is marked by a line parallel to the side wall, 18 inches from the wall. The receiver's restraining lines are 5 feet behind the short line. They are parallel to the short line and extend 6 inches from each side wall.

TERMS

An **ace** is a legal serve that eludes the receiver.

An **avoidable hinder** is interference that the offending player could have avoided; penalty is loss of serve or a point for the opponent.

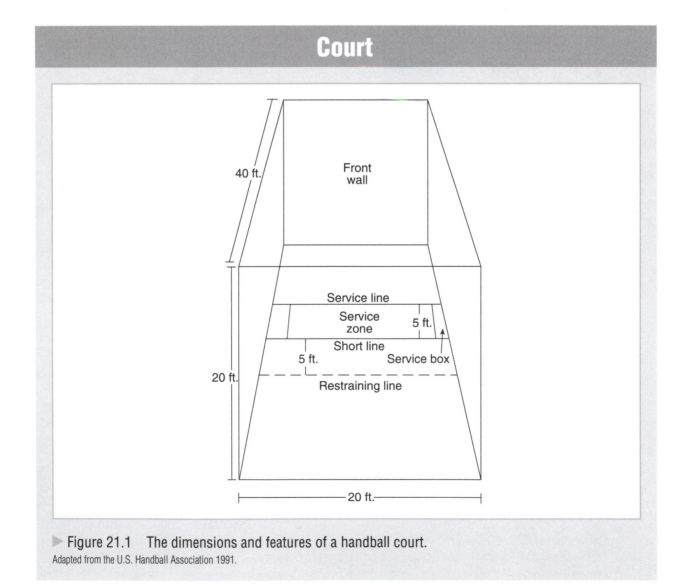

Court

▶ Figure 21.1   The dimensions and features of a handball court.
Adapted from the U.S. Handball Association 1991.

A **back wall shot** is one that is made from a rebound off the back wall.

A **ceiling shot** is one that is hit directly to the ceiling.

A **court hinder** occurs when an erratic bounce is caused by an obstacle, construction abnormality, or wetness on the court.

A **crotch ball** is one that hits the juncture of any two walls, any wall with the floor, or any wall with the ceiling.

A **defensive shot** is one that is made to get the opponent out of an offensive position but is not made with the intent of winning the rally.

A **dig** is made by a player who retrieves a low shot.

A **fault** is an illegally served ball.

A **fly shot** is one that is played before it bounces.

A **foot fault** occurs when a portion of the server's foot is outside the service zone before the served ball passes the short line.

A **hinder** occurs when a player accidentally hinders an opponent from making a shot, or hinders the flight of the ball. A hinder is not penalized but is replayed.

A **hop serve** is a serve that has spin on it, causing it to hop to the right or the left.

A **kill shot** is one that hits the front wall so low that the opponent has no chance to return it.

A **lob** is a soft shot high on the front wall.

An **offensive shot** is one intended to win a rally.

A **passing shot** is one that is driven past an opponent's reach on either side.

A **point** can be scored only by the server or serving team.

The **service line** is the line parallel to and 5 feet in front of the short line.

The **service zone** is the area of the court between, and including, the short line and the service line.

The **short line** is the line halfway between, and parallel to, the front and back walls.

A **sideout** occurs when the receiving player or team wins a rally and gains the serve.

PLAYERS

Two, three, or four players can play handball. Games played by three players are called cut-throat. The player serving plays against the other two; the serve rotates. The rules for singles apply to the server; the rules for doubles apply to the two other players.

PLAY

The fundamental rules of play are found in the rules for serving, returning serve, and rallies.

Serving

The server serves from anywhere in the *service zone* (see figure 21.1 on page 132). A *foot fault* is called if any part of either foot is beyond the outer edge of either service zone line. The server must remain in the service zone until the ball passes the *short line.*

The server must come to a complete stop before beginning a serve by bouncing the ball. She may bounce and catch the ball several times before beginning her serve, but when she begins her serve she must bounce the ball once and hit it. More than one bounce is a fault; bouncing the ball outside the service zone is also a fault.

The serve must strike the front wall first, and it must hit beyond the short line. It may touch one of the side walls. As soon as a rally ends, the referee calls either "point" or "sideout," and the receiver has 10 seconds to get into position. When the receiver is in position, or when 10 seconds elapse, whichever comes first, the referee announces the score and the server has 10 seconds to serve.

A server may commit one service fault. If he commits two faults on the same serve, he loses his serve. In doubles, the first serving team gets only one serving turn—when the receiving team wins the rally, it wins the serve.

After that, both players on a team get a serving turn each time they gain the serve. The serving order of the partners is kept throughout the game. Each player continues his serve until the opponents score a *sideout*.

It is not necessary for partners on the receiving team to alternate receiving the serve. The server's partner must stand within the service box until the ball passes the short line. A violation is a foot fault. Other faults include

- short serve—one whose first bounce hits before or on the short line;
- three-wall serve—a serve that hits the front wall and two other walls before hitting the floor;
- ceiling serve—a serve that hits the ceiling before hitting the floor;
- long serve—a serve that hits the back wall before hitting the floor;
- out-of-court serve—one that hits the front wall and then goes out of the court without touching the floor; and
- two consecutive screen serves—serves that pass too close to the server or the server's partner, obstructing the receiver's view.

The first screen serve is called a "defective serve" and is not penalized; the server serves again. Other defective serves that are replayed with no penalty include serves that hit the server's partner in the air (on the bounce results in a fault), straddle balls (serves that travel between the server's legs), court hinder (a serve that bounces erratically because of a court obstruction or wetness), and a ball that breaks on the serve.

The server loses her turn when she

- misses the ball while attempting to serve,
- serves so that the ball strikes anything other than the front wall first,
- serves so that the ball strikes her,
- strikes her partner with the serve when her partner's foot is outside the service box,
- commits two consecutive service faults,

- hits a crotch serve—a serve that hits the crotch in the front wall (if the serve hits a crotch in the back wall or side wall, after legally hitting the front wall first and going beyond the short line, it is legal),
- serves out of order, or
- goes beyond her allotted 10 seconds in serving.

Return of Serve

The receiver must stand at least 5 feet behind the short line until the serve is struck. Not doing so will result in a point for the server. No part of the receiver may extend on or over the plane of the short line when contacting the ball. A violation results in a point for the server. The receiver may go beyond the short line, however, after hitting the ball.

The receiver must return the ball before it strikes the floor twice. A serve can be returned before it strikes the floor. A return of serve can hit the back wall, one or both side walls, and the ceiling before it touches the front wall, but it must touch the front wall before it strikes the floor.

Rallies

A rally is played out until one side cannot legally return the ball. Teams alternate hits—team A is obligated to return team B's hit, and vice versa—but partners on a team do not have to alternate hits. In doubles play, both partners may swing at a ball, but only one player can touch it.

The front or back of the hand may be used to hit a ball; the wrist or any other part of the body may not be used. If a rally needs to be replayed for any reason, any previous fault against the server is voided. A player loses a rally if she intentionally hinders her opponent from returning the ball. A rally is replayed for *dead-ball hinders,* such as unavoidable interference or contact.

SCORING AND PENALTIES

Scoring and penalties are affected by avoidable hinders and technicals.

Avoidable Hinders

An avoidable hinder results in a sideout if the offending player was serving, or a point if the player was receiving. A player commits an avoidable hinder when he

- doesn't move out of the way to allow his opponent a shot;
- moves into a position that blocks his opponent as he is about to return the ball;
- moves into the path of the ball just struck by his opponent;
- pushes his opponent;
- obstructs his opponent's view just before his opponent is about to strike the ball; or
- interferes in any way with the opponent's stroke, including restricting the opponent's follow-through.

Technicals

An offender loses one point for a technical, which may be assessed for frequent complaints, profanity, arguing, threats made to the opponent or the referee, excessive kicking or throwing the ball between rallies, failure to wear proper eye protection, or for any unsporting behavior. A technical does not result in a sideout or affect the serve order.

If a technical occurs between games, the offending player begins the next game with a negative score. Three technicals in a match result in a forfeit. A warning, with no point deduction, may be given instead of a technical. This is at the discretion of the referee. A player may be assessed a technical without first receiving a warning.

EQUIPMENT

The ball is rubber or synthetic, with a 1.9-inch diameter, with a variation of .03 inch. It weighs 2.3 ounces, with a variation of .2 ounce. Players must wear gloves that are light in color and made of soft material or leather. The fingers may not be webbed, connected, or removed, and the gloves may not have holes that expose skin.

Players may not use any foreign substance, tape, or rubber bands on the fingers or palms outside the gloves. They may wear metal or hard substances underneath if, in the referee's opinion, this does not create an advantage for the player wearing them. Players must change gloves when they become wet enough to dampen the ball.

Customary handball attire includes full-length shirts; players may not wear shirts cut off at the torso. Their shoes must have soles that do not mark or damage the floor. Players must wear protective eyewear at all times during play.

OFFICIALS

The referee is in charge of the match and makes all decisions regarding points, equipment, protests, and hinders. A linesman and a scorer are used for larger events.

MODIFICATIONS

Three-wall handball is played on a court that is 20 feet wide and 40 feet long. The three-wall game abides by four-wall rules, except for the following:

- Recommended length for side walls is 44 feet, extending 4 feet beyond the long line, which runs parallel to the front wall and whose outer edge is 40 feet from the front wall.
- Shirts are not required for outdoor play unless requested by an opponent.
- A *long serve* is one that hits the front wall and rebounds past the long line before touching the floor.
- During tournament play, a referee awards the server a point when the receiver catches a serve the receiver assumes to be long.
- A *long ball* is one that hits the front wall and doesn't bounce until it is past the long line.

One-wall handball is played on a court measuring 20 feet wide and 34 feet long.

One-wall play abides by four-wall rules, except for the following:

- The wall is 16 feet high.
- A long line, parallel to the wall, is marked 34 feet from the wall.
- A minimum of 6 feet of floor, and ideally 20 feet, should extend beyond each side line; 16 feet should extend beyond the long line.
- The short line runs parallel to the wall, 16 feet from the wall.
- Two service markers, at least 6 inches long, extend from the sidelines, parallel with the short and long lines and halfway between them. The imaginary extension of these lines indicates the service line.
- The serving zone is the floor between the short line, the sidelines, and the service line.
- The receiving zone is the floor beyond the short line, inside and including the sidelines and long line.

- Shirts are not required in outdoor play unless requested by an opponent.
- The server's partner must stand outside the sidelines, straddling the extended service line until the served ball passes him.
- If a player attempting to play a ball is blocked by an opponent who has stood still after hitting her shot, no hinder is called.
- If a ball hits an opponent on the way to the wall, this is always a hinder, regardless of whether the referee believes the ball had a chance to hit the wall on the fly.
- During a rally, if a player on the serving side hinders an opponent, the serving side begins the next serve with a fault.

ORGANIZATIONS

United States Handball Association
2333 N. Tucson Boulevard
Tucson, AZ 85716
www.ushandball.org

22

Ice Hockey

The history of ice hockey is a bit murky: some claim that it originated from play by British soldiers on frozen Lake Ontario in 1855, while residents of Halifax, Nova Scotia, say the sport had already begun there. Hockey is likely a descendant of a sport called bandy, developed in England in the late 18th century. The first set of rules were developed at McGill University in Montreal in 1879. Hockey was first played in the United States in the 1890s, and today is most popular in North America and northern Europe. The National Hockey League was formed in 1917.

Women's ice hockey began in the 1890s. More than 100 years later, in 1998, women's hockey became an Olympic medal sport. The only rule difference between men's hockey and women's is that there is no body checking in the women's game.

Objective: To score a goal by shooting a puck into the opponents' goal; the team that scores the most goals wins.

Number of Players: Six per team.

Length of Game: Three 20-minute periods; each team gets one 30-second timeout.

Overtime: If the score is tied at the end of regulation, a five-minute overtime is played. The first team to score wins. If the score is still tied at the end of overtime, the game is a tie. In team competition, a victory is worth two points, while a tie is worth one.

Overview: A game begins with a face-off (see page 140). Face-offs are also used to begin each period and to resume play after a penalty or other stop in action. Players advance the puck toward the opponents' goal by skating with the puck or passing it. The puck must be in motion at all times. A player may take the puck behind his own goal one time; otherwise, the team possessing the puck must advance it toward the opponents' goal.

RINK

The rink has an ice surface; its components are shown in figure 22.1. The rink is divided into thirds by two *blue lines,* each of which is 60 feet from the nearest goal. The blue lines separate the rink into three zones: the *defending zone,* where the goal is defended; the *neutral zone,* or central portion; and the *attacking zone,* where the goal is attacked.

The *center spot,* 12 inches in diameter, is inside the *center circle,* which has a 15-foot radius. Two *face-off spots* are 5 feet from each blue line, and 44 feet apart, in the neutral zone. The *end zone face-off spots* are 20 feet from each goal line and 44 feet apart. These spots are in *end zone face-off circles* with a 15-foot radius.

The *goal cages* are 6 feet long by 4 feet high, centered on the *goal lines,* which run the width of the rink, 11 feet from the end of each rink.

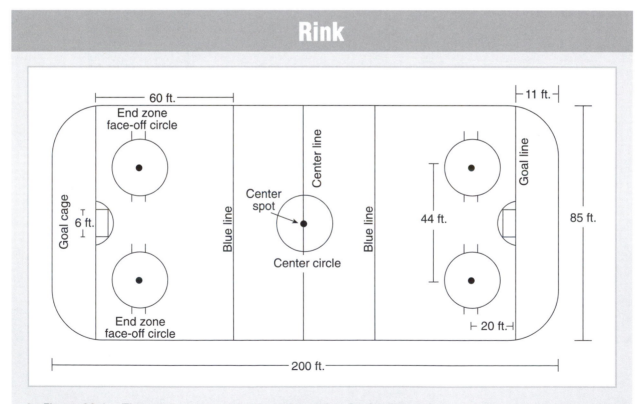

► Figure 22.1   The components and dimensions of an ice hockey rink.
Adapted from White 1990.

The *goal crease* is 4 feet by 8 feet, centered on each goal line. It is delimited by a semicircle with a radius of 6 feet.

The *referee's crease* is a semicircle with a 10-foot radius at the center of one side. The boards around the rink are white wood or fiberglass, 40 to 48 inches high. Safety glass, 40 to 48 inches high, rises above the boards. Players' benches are on one side of the rink, opposite the penalty box.

TERMS

Following are terms that are not described elsewhere in this chapter.

A player receives an **assist** when her pass leads to a teammate's scoring a goal. No more than two assists are allowed on any one goal. An assist counts for one point in the player's record.

A **body check** is the use of the body to block a player's progress.

A **breakaway** occurs when a player in control of the puck has no defenders between him and the opponents' goal.

Butt-ending is using the end of the stick in a jabbing motion.

Charging is called when a player jumps into or uses more than two steps to skate into another player.

A team **clears a puck** when it gets the puck away from the front of its goal.

Control of the puck is determined by the last player to propel the puck in a desired direction.

Cross checking occurs when a player holds her stick above the ice in both hands and impedes an opponent's progress with it.

Delayed offside is called when an attacking player precedes the puck across the attacking blue line but the defending team possesses the puck and is in position to bring it out of its defending zone without any delay or contact with an attacking player. If the defending team advances the puck out of its defending zone, no offside is called.

A **drop pass** is one that is left behind for a teammate.

A **flat pass** is one that doesn't leave the surface of the ice.

A **flip pass** is one that travels through the air.

A player **freezes** the puck in an attempt to stop play.

A **goal** (one point) is scored when the puck crosses the goal line between the goal posts and under the crossbar. If a defender accidentally knocks the puck into his own goal, the opponents are awarded a goal. If a puck deflects off an official and across the goal line, the goal does not count.

A goal does not count if an attacking player is in the **goal crease** (a marked area in front of the goal) when the puck crosses the goal line, or if an attacking player bats or kicks the puck across the goal line.

A **hat trick** is accomplished by a player who scores three goals in one game.

High sticks means carrying or using the stick above shoulder height.

A **hip check** occurs when a player uses her hip to knock an opponent in possession of the puck off balance.

Hooking is called when a player uses his blade to interfere with an opponent's progress.

When a player goes **intentionally offside** to try to gain a stoppage in play, the puck is faced off at the end zone face-off spot in the defending zone of the offending team.

Possession of the puck is determined by the last player touching it (including deflections).

A team is in a **power play** when it has more players on the ice than its opponent.

A **rebound** is a puck that bounces off the goalkeeper or the goal post.

A **save** is recorded by a goalkeeper who prevents a goal from being scored.

A team is **short-handed** when it has fewer players on the ice than its opponent. This occurs because of penalties. When a goal is scored against a short-handed team, the minor or bench minor penalty that caused the team to be short-handed is ended and the penalized player returns to action.

A **slap shot** is a shot taken by a player lifting her stick in a backswing before hitting the puck.

Slashing is called when a player hits, or tries to hit, an opponent with his stick.

A **slow whistle** refers to a play in which an official raises his arm in preparation for blowing his whistle for an infraction, depending on how the play turns out. For example, a delayed offside situation results in a slow whistle. The whistle will be blown in this case if the defending team does not advance the puck out of its defending zone and an attacker is offside.

Spearing occurs when a player uses her stick blade to stab an opponent.

A **wrist shot** is taken by a player who does not lift his stick off the ice before hitting the puck.

PLAYERS

Each team has 6 players on the ice: a goalkeeper, 2 defensemen, and 3 forwards. (Actually, all 6 players are defensemen when the other team has possession of the puck.) In most leagues, a team can dress 20 players, including two goalies. The team captain is the only player who can discuss calls with the referee.

Players may be changed at any time, but the player or players leaving the ice must be within five feet of the bench, and out of play, before the change is made. For minor injuries, play is not stopped. For injuries in which the player can not leave the ice, play is continued until the injured player's team has possession of the puck and is not in scoring position. At the officials' discretion, play may be stopped immediately for any severe injury, no matter who has possession of the puck.

PLAY

Following are rules pertaining to face-offs, passes, offside, and the puck.

Face-Offs

A referee or linesman drops the puck between two opposing players whose stick blades are on the ice. Each player faces the opponent's end of the rink and tries to hit the puck to a teammate. No other players may be in the face-off circle or within 15 feet of the players facing off. Players must stand on the side during the face-off, and no substitutes may enter the game until the face-off is complete.

Face-offs may not take place within 15 feet of the goal or side boards. If an attacker in his team's attacking zone causes play to stop, the face-off occurs at the nearest face-off spot in the neutral zone.

If a defender in his team's defensive zone causes play to stop, the face-off occurs at the point of stoppage. Any stoppage of play in the neutral zone results in a face-off at the point of stoppage. If play is stopped between the end of the rink and the end face-off spots, the face-off occurs at the nearest end face-off spot.

Passes

A player in one zone may not pass forward to a teammate in another zone. A player in the defending zone may pass to a teammate at the center line, but the puck must pass the center line before the receiver does. The position of the puck, and not the players, determines from which zone the pass was made and received.

Once a player leaves the defending zone, she may not pass back to that zone unless her team is playing short-handed. If a player from the neutral zone enters the attacking zone after the puck has been passed into that zone, she is eligible to play the puck. The same is true for any player entering a new zone after the puck has entered that zone. If an attacking player passes the puck back toward her own goal while in the attacking zone, an opponent may play the puck anywhere regardless of whether she was in the same zone when the puck was passed.

Offside

An attacking player is offside if he is in the attacking zone before he receives the puck. Similarly, an attacking player already beyond the center line is offside if he receives the puck from a teammate in the defense zone. Both skates must be past the line when the puck enters the zone for a player to be offside. An offside call results in a face-off.

If a defender reaches the puck and passes or skates with it into the neutral zone, an attacking player is not offside. Similarly, if a player moves across the line before the puck but is in control and moving the puck forward, he is not offside.

Puck

Specific rules for handling the puck include the following:

- **Out of bounds:** If the puck goes out of bounds, it is faced off from where it was shot or deflected.
- **Lodged or frozen:** If the puck becomes lodged in the netting outside the goal, or becomes "frozen" between opposing players, the puck is faced off at the nearest face-off spot—unless the referee believes an attacking player caused the stoppage, in which case the face-off takes place in the neutral zone.
- **Player on puck:** If a scramble takes place and a player accidentally falls on the puck, play is stopped and a face-off occurs.
- **Striking an official:** Play is not stopped when a puck strikes an official. If a puck strikes an official and deflects into the goal, however, the goal does not count.

Also, players may kick the puck in any zone, but a goal may not be scored by kicking the puck, whether or not the kick was intentional. If a player on a team that is not short-handed shoots a puck across the center line and past the opponents' goal line (icing the puck), play is stopped, and a face-off occurs at the end face-off spot of the offending team. If, however, a goal is scored on the shot, the goal counts. Finally, players on the attacking team may not enter the attacking zone before the puck does. Such a violation results in a face-off in the neutral zone.

PENALTIES

When a player whose team is in possession of the puck violates a rule, the referee immediately blows his whistle and imposes the appropriate penalty. The game is resumed with a face-off. If the player who commits the penalty is on the team that is not in possession of the puck, the referee blows his whistle and imposes the penalty after the play is completed. The kinds of penalties are discussed next.

Minor Penalty

Any player, other than the goalkeeper, sits in the penalty box for two minutes; no substitutes are allowed. The goalkeeper's penalty may be taken by a teammate. A sampling of minor penalties includes delay of game, dislodging the net from its moorings, falling on the puck, handling the puck, holding an opponent, hooking, interfering with an opponent who is not in possession of the puck, interfering with the goalkeeper, playing with a broken stick, and tripping.

Depending on the severity of the offense, minor penalties may be assessed for

- board checking or checking from behind (minor or major),
- charging (minor or major),
- cross checking (minor or major),
- elbowing, kneeing, or head-butting (minor or major),
- high sticks (double minor or major),
- slashing (minor or major), or
- roughing (minor or double minor).

Bench Minor Penalty

A coach may remove any one of his players from the ice, except the goalkeeper, to serve this two-minute penalty. If a team is short-handed by one or more minor or bench minor penalties, and the opposing team scores, the first penalty assessed is terminated.

Major Penalty

Any player, except for the goalkeeper, who commits a major offense serves a five-minute penalty. No substitution is allowed. If a player commits three major penalties in a game, he is ejected from the game. Major penalties may be assessed for

- elbowing or kneeing an opponent and causing injury,
- fighting,
- grabbing or holding an opponent's face mask,
- hooking or cross checking and causing injury,
- slashing and injuring an opponent, or
- spearing or butt-ending with the stick.

Misconduct Penalties

Players may incur misconduct penalties, game misconduct penalties, and gross misconduct penalties. Team personnel may also incur gross misconduct penalties.

Any player, except the goalkeeper, who commits a *misconduct penalty* must sit for 10 minutes. This player may be replaced immediately. A player whose misconduct penalty has expired must remain in the penalty box until a stoppage in play. When a player commits a misconduct penalty and either a major or a minor penalty at the same time, his team must put a substitute player in the penalty box to serve the major or minor penalty.

For a *game misconduct penalty,* a player is suspended for the duration of the game, but a substitute is allowed. If a player accumulates three game misconducts during the season, she is suspended for one game. For each subsequent game misconduct, that player's suspension increases by one game.

A *gross misconduct penalty* may be levied against any player or team personnel. It results in suspension for the rest of the game. Acts

resulting in misconduct or game misconduct penalties, depending on the severity of the violation, include

- abusing officials;
- continuing to dispute after receiving a penalty;
- continuing to fight after being ordered to stop;
- entering the referee's crease while officials are in it consulting;
- being the first player to intervene in an altercation;
- leaving the players' bench or penalty bench to enter an altercation;
- using obscene, profane, or abusive language or gestures;
- physically abusing officials;
- shooting a puck out of reach of an official who is retrieving it;
- spearing an opponent;
- throwing the puck or any equipment out of the playing area;
- touching or holding an official in any way; and
- using threatening or abusive language to incite an opponent.

Match Penalty

The player is replaced for the rest of the game and ordered to the locker room. A substitute may replace this player after five minutes of playing time have elapsed.

Match penalties are assessed for

- deliberately injuring an opponent,
- attempting to injure an opponent, or
- kicking or attempting to kick another player.

Goalkeeper's Penalty

A teammate may serve a goalkeeper's minor or major penalty. If a goalkeeper incurs three major penalties in one game, he is ruled off the ice and a substitute goalkeeper may take his place. A goalkeeper must serve his own misconduct or match penalty, but his place on the ice may be taken by a substitute.

Delayed Penalty

If a third player of a team is penalized while two teammates are serving penalties, the penalty time of the third player doesn't begin until the first teammate's penalty time elapses. Nonetheless, the third player must go to the bench immediately and be replaced by a substitute, who may play until the third player's penalty time officially begins.

Penalty Shot

A penalty shot may be awarded for numerous reasons. The following list includes some of the common violations that result in a penalty shot:

- Falling on the puck, holding the puck, or gathering the puck into the body when the puck is within the goal crease (goalkeeper exempted)
- Interfering with an opponent in possession of the puck and with no defender between her and the goalkeeper
- Throwing a stick or any object at the puck in the offending player's defending zone (if a goal is scored on the play, no penalty shot is given)

The referee places the puck on the center face-off spot, and the player taking the penalty shot attempts to score on the goalkeeper. The player may take the puck anywhere in the neutral zone or in his own defending zone, but once the puck crosses the blue line into the attacking zone, it must be kept in forward motion, and once it is shot, the play is complete. No goal may be scored on a rebound. While the penalty shot is being taken, all other players except the two involved withdraw to the sides of the rink on the attacker's side of the center line.

If a goal is scored on a penalty shot, play resumes with a face-off at center ice. If the goal is not scored, play resumes with a face-off at

one of the end face-off spots in the zone in which the penalty shot was attempted.

EQUIPMENT

The puck is hard rubber, 1 inch thick and 3 inches in diameter. It weighs between 5.5 and 6 ounces. The stick is wood or another approved material; its maximum length is 60 inches from the heel to the top of the shaft. Its blade can be no longer than 12.5 inches and must be between 2 and 3 inches wide. Tape can be used to reinforce the stick.

The blade of the goalkeeper's stick may be up to 15.5 inches long. Its maximum width is 3.5 inches, except at the heel, where it may be 4.5 inches. The shaft extending up from the heel, for up to 26 inches, is 3.5 inches wide. Goalkeepers wear leg guards, chest protectors, gloves (one to block shots, the other to catch shots), helmets, and full face masks.

All protective equipment—padded pants and pads for shins, hips, shoulders, and elbows—must be worn under the uniform. All players must wear a helmet with a chin strap. Behind each goal, a red light is turned on when a goal is scored.

OFFICIALS

The referee is in charge of the game and of the other officials: two linesmen, who watch for rules violations; two goal judges, who are stationed behind the goals and determine whether a goal has been scored; a penalty timekeeper, who records all the penalties and keeps the time for the players in the penalty box; an official scorer, who records all game data; and a game timekeeper, who runs the game clock.

See figure 22.2 for officials' signals.

MODIFICATIONS

All players at junior level or younger (19 years old or under) must wear face masks. Players at the pee wee level or younger (12 or under

Holding

Cross checking

Tripping

Charging

Hooking

Boarding

Icing

Misconduct

Interference   *(continued)*

▶ Figure 22.2   Common officials' signals for ice hockey.

Slashing

High-sticking

Spearing

Kneeing

Elbowing

Unsportsmanlike conduct

▶ Figure 22.2 *(continued)*

for boys; 13 to 15 for girls) must wear mouth-pieces. To make the game more appropriate for younger hockey players, sometimes a shorter rink is used (about 185 feet long instead of 200 feet long), and the goal posts are 12 to 15 feet from the end of the rink, instead of the standard 11 feet.

ORGANIZATIONS

USA Hockey
1775 Bob Johnson Drive
Colorado Springs, CO 80906-4090
719-576-8724
www.usahockey.com

23

Judo

© Bongarts/SportsChrome

Judo is a martial art that was developed from jujutsu (also called *jujitsu*) by Professor Jigoro Kano in Japan in 1882. *Ju* means gentleness; *do* means way. While judo is concerned with attacks and defenses against an opponent, it also develops physical conditioning and total health. More than 4 million worldwide participate in judo; about 40,000 in the United States take part.

As in other martial arts, competitors are grouped into various skill levels. Judo skills involve a combination of knowledge, speed, timing, balance, and coordination of mind and body. Judo is a form of wrestling that emphasizes throws, pins, holddowns, chokes, and arm locks. Competitions are often highlighted by spectacular throws. Timing and technique are the keys to a competitor's success.

Objective: To defeat the opponent by using the opponent's own force.

Scoring: Points are scored with various throws and techniques; the competitor with the most points wins.

Contest Length: Five minutes for men and women; three minutes for juniors (real contest times).

Contest Ends: A competitor scores *ippon* (one point) or two *waza-ari* (which equal one point; see "Scoring"); a competitor is awarded *sogo-gachi* (compound win); a competitor wins because of default, disqualification, or injury; or contest time expires.

Overview: To begin a contest, the competitors stand facing each other, bow, and take one step forward. The referee then calls out, "hajime," to begin the competition. Competitors attempt to score points by using various techniques to throw, pin, or hold down their opponents (see "Scoring"). The referee may temporarily halt a match, during which the competition clock stops, when

- one or both competitors go outside the competition area,
- a competitor performs a prohibited act (see "Prohibited Acts"),
- a competitor is injured or ill, or

- the competitors are entangled on the ground and not making progress.

COMPETITION AREA

The competition area is a mat that is at least 14 meters by 14 meters and no more than 16 meters by 16 meters (see figure 23.1). The mat is made of pressed straw or foam. It is divided into two zones in which competition may take place: a *danger zone,* in red, and the *contest area,* generally in green. The danger zone is usually 1 meter wide, on the outside of the contest area, which is at least 8 meters by 8 meters, and no more than 10 meters by 10 meters. The area outside the danger zone is called the *safety area;* it is 3 meters wide.

TERMS

Hantei is a call by the referee for a judge's decision.

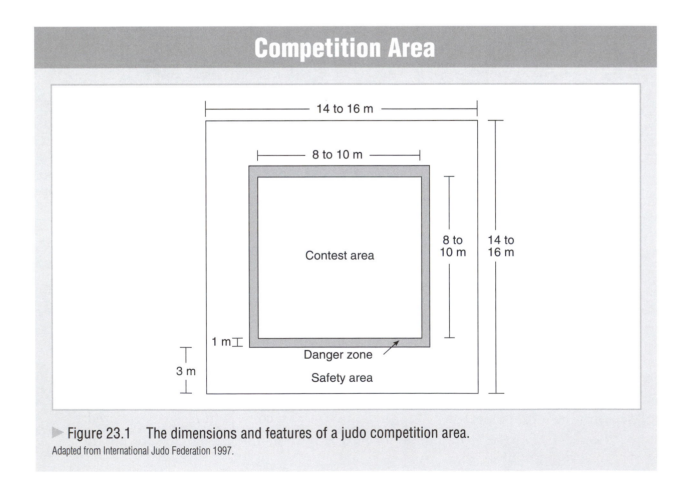

▶ Figure 23.1   The dimensions and features of a judo competition area.
Adapted from International Judo Federation 1997.

A **hike-wake** is called when the match is a draw.

Ippon is one point; **waza-ari** is a half-point; **yuko** is a score less than a waza-ari; and a **koka** is a score less than a yuko.

A **shiai** is a judo contest, which is fought on a mat called a **tatami.**

In a judo competition, the attacker is called a **tori.**

In judo, technique is called **waza.**

A **yusei gachi** is a win by the judges' decision.

COMPETITORS

Each contestant wears a white, off-white, or blue *judogi* (uniform). The judogi jacket must be long enough to cover the thighs, and the arms of the jacket must reach the wrist joints when the arms are extended down. The trousers must reach to the ankle joints. Each contestant wears a belt, with the color corresponding to grade level, over the jackets. Fingernails and toenails must be cut short.

The United States Judo Association has 12 degrees for junior competitors (16 years old and younger). They range from Junior First Degree through Junior Twelfth Degree. Senior ranks, for those 17 years old and older, are split into two categories:

- Beginner (six ranks, with sixth-class rank being lowest and first-class rank being highest)
- Black belt ranks (ranging from lowest rank at first degree to highest rank at tenth degree)

SCORING AND PENALTIES

Competitors score points based on the moves they successfully execute and the penalties they incur.

Scoring

A competitor scores an *ippon,* worth one point and a victory, when she

- throws her opponent largely on her back with considerable force, control, and speed;
- pins her opponent's back and at least one shoulder to the mat (*osaekomi*) and the opponent is unable to get away from this hold within 25 seconds;
- causes her opponent to give up because of the hold she is using; or
- employs a strangle technique or arm lock from which her opponent submits.

If a competitor is penalized *hansoku make* (see "Prohibited Acts"), her opponent is awarded ippon and the match.

Waza-ari is worth one-half point. A competitor scores waza-ari when he throws his opponent, but the technique is not deserving of ippon (e.g., one of the elements of force, control, speed, or being largely on the back is missing). A contestant also scores waza-ari when he holds his opponent's back and at least one shoulder to the mat and the hold lasts 20 seconds or more, but less than 25 seconds. If a competitor is penalized *keikoku* (see "Prohibited Acts"), his opponent is awarded waza-ari. If a competitor scores two waza-ari, which equal an ippon, he wins the match. A referee will call *sogo-gachi* (compound win) when a contestant already has waza-ari and his opponent is penalized keikoku.

A *yuko* is awarded when a competitor throws her opponent but her technique is lacking in two of the elements necessary for ippon. For example, the opponent thrown may not be largely on her back, or the throw itself may have been lacking in speed or force. If a contestant is penalized *chui* (see "Prohibited Acts"), her opponent receives a yuko.

A *koka* is awarded when a competitor throws his opponent onto the buttocks or side of the hip. An osaekomi that goes beyond nine seconds is worth a koka.

Prohibited Acts

There are four types of prohibited acts for which a contestant may be penalized:

- A *shido* is a minor infringement.
- A *chui* is a serious infringement.

- A *keikoku* is a grave infringement; a chui and one more infringement of any kind equal keikoku.
- A *hansoku make* is a very grave infringement; a keikoku and one more infringement of any kind equal hansoku make.

A few examples of each type of infringement follow.

A shido may be called for stalling or preventing action, adopting an excessively defensive posture, or failing to attack. A chui may be called for applying leg scissors to the opponent's trunk, neck, or head; kicking the opponent's hand or arm to be freed from his grip; or bending back the opponent's fingers to break his grip.

Keikoku may be called for attempting to throw an opponent by winding a leg around her leg while facing in the same direction and falling backward onto her, locking joints (except for the elbow joints), acting in a way that could injure the opponent's neck or spinal cord, lifting an opponent who is lying on the mat and slamming her back onto the mat, or applying techniques outside of the contest area.

The gravest infringement, hansoku make, may be called against a competitor who dives head first onto the mat while performing, or attempting to perform, various techniques or who intentionally falls backward when an opponent is clinging to his back.

EQUIPMENT

Judges use chairs, placed on either end of the safety area and diagonally opposite each other. A scoreboard is used to show points and penalty points for each contestant. Clocks are used to time the match and to time the length of each osaekomi.

OFFICIALS

One referee and two judges conduct the match. They are assisted by contest recorders and timekeepers.

ORGANIZATIONS

United States Judo Association
21 North Union Boulevard
Colorado Springs, CO
719-633-7750
www.usja-judo.org

© Empics

Karate

The origins of karate are somewhat obscure, but the martial art dates back to at least the 17th century in the Okinawa Prefecture of Japan. In its early stages, karate was an indigenous form of closed-fist fighting; *kara* means *empty* and *te* means *hand*. Karate conditions both body and mind, and its numerous styles are enjoyed by people of all ages and skill levels. Competition as we know it today began in the 1950s. People as young as 6 years old can compete in karate in various age, weight, and experience level groups; karate is popular among youths and young adults in America. It is estimated that more than 1 million people participate in karate competitions in the United States.

Overview: The sport includes competition in *kumite* (free-fighting), *kata* (forms), and *weapons kata* (forms with weapons). Both team and individual competitions are held.

A tournament may consist of kumite, kata, weapons kata, or all three. Individual matches are divided by weight classifications; in team kumite matches, each team must have an odd number of participants. The coach determines his team's fighting order (from one to five) before the match begins. A kata team consists of three people performing in synchronization.

Objective: In kumite competition the objective is to score *ippon* (one point), *nihon* (two points), or *sanbon* (three points) by performing techniques according to specific criteria. The contestant with the highest score wins. In kata or weapons kata the objective is to receive the highest score of the judges.

Scoring: In kumite, the first contestant to score 8 points above his opponent wins. In kata and weapons kata, contestants are judged and awarded points based on their performance and mastery of the requisite skills.

COMPETITION AREA

The kumite competition area is a matted square, 8 meters on each side (see figure 24.1). The area may be elevated up to 1 meter above the floor. If it is elevated, it should measure 10 meters on each side, with the outer 2 meters being a safety area. Two parallel lines, each 1 meter long, are 1.5 meters from the center of the competition area. The contestants are positioned on these lines. A line .5 meter long and perpendicular to the contestants' lines is 2 meters from the center of the competition area. This is the referee's line. A warning line is drawn 1 meter inside the edges of the mat on all four sides.

TERMS

An **ippon** is a score awarded to a contestant who has performed a punch or strike according to these criteria: good form, correct attitude, vigorous application, proper timing, correct distance, and perfect finish.

A **nihon** is worth two points. It is awarded for kicks, combination techniques, or punches to the back, or for unbalancing the opponent and scoring.

A **sanbon** has a value of three points. It may be earned by performing high level (face) kicks or by sweeping the opponent and scoring with a punch, kick, or strike.

A **hansoku** is a foul that results in a victory for the contestant fouled.

A win by **kiken** is awarded a contestant if her opponent is absent, withdraws, or is withdrawn.

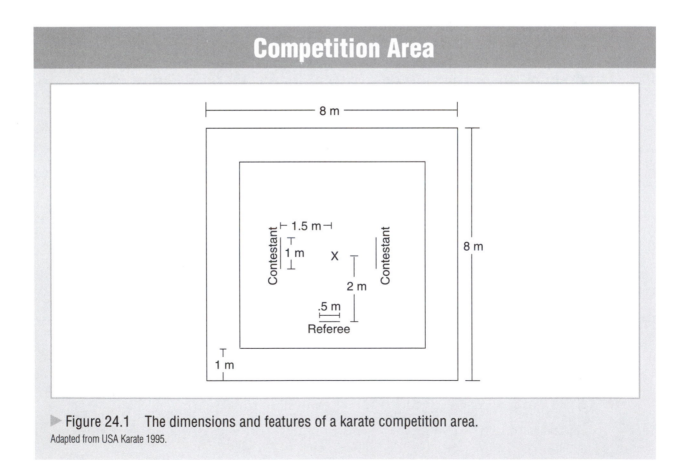

▶ Figure 24.1   The dimensions and features of a karate competition area.
Adapted from USA Karate 1995.

Shikkaku means "disqualification." A contestant is awarded the victory if his opponent commits an act leading to shikkaku.

Hajime is the command to start a match and to continue the match after a command to stop.

Yame is the command to stop. Yame may be called in the middle of a bout as well as at the end.

CONTESTANTS

Competitions may be held according to age group, experience level, and weight.

Age Group

- **Junior:** 6 to 17 years old
- **Adult:** 18 and over
- **Senior:** 35 and over
- **Senior advanced, male and female:** ages 35 to 44, ages 45 and over

(In weapons kata, age groups may be combined. Male and female contestants may not compete against each other.)

Experience Level

- **Beginner:** Not more than one year of experience; 7th to 10th *kyu* or equivalent
- **Novice:** One to two years of experience, green belt, or 4th to 6th kyu or equivalent
- **Intermediate:** Two to three years of experience, brown belt, or 1st to 3rd kyu or equivalent
- **Advanced:** Three or more years of experience or black belt

Weight

- **Junior age group:** May be divided into divisions at the discretion of the tournament director.
- **Adult, advanced; male:** Under 132 pounds (60 kilograms); 132 pounds (60 kilograms) to 143 pounds (65 kilograms); 143 pounds (65 kilograms) to 154 pounds (70 kilograms); 154 pounds (70 kilograms) to 165 pounds (75 kilograms); 165 pounds (75 kilograms) to 176 pounds (80 kilograms); and 176 pounds (80 kilograms) and over.
- **Adult, beginner, novice, and intermediate; male:** Under 154 pounds (70 kilograms); over 154 pounds (70 kilograms).
- **Adult, advanced; female:** Under 117 pounds (53 kilograms); 117 pounds (53 kilograms) to 132 pounds (60 kilograms); 132 pounds (60 kilograms) and over; open weight (no limitation).
- **Adult, beginner, novice, and intermediate; female:** Under 132 pounds (60 kilograms); 132 pounds (60 kilograms) and over.

COMPETITION

Karate has three disciplines—kumite, kata, and weapons kata. Rules and guidelines to each follow here.

Kumite

The referee, judges, and contestants take their positions and exchange bows in the prescribed manner, and the match begins. When a referee sees a scoring technique or a penalty, he stops the match, awards an ippon, waza-ari, or penalty, and orders the contestants to take their original positions to restart the bout.

When a contestant scores 8 points above her opponent, the referee stops the bout and declares her the winner. Whether or not a contestant has scored 8 points, each bout between adult males is finished after three minutes; women's and junior bouts are limited to two minutes. If the score is tied at the end, a majority vote among the referee and judges determines the winner. If the referee and judges believe neither contestant exhibited superiority, an overtime period begins. The first contestant to score wins.

A contestant wins a match by scoring ippons, nihons, or sanbons, or a combination thereof, to attain 8 points more than his opponent.

No technique will score if a contestant delivers it outside the competition area. Similarly, effective scoring techniques delivered simultaneously by both contestants cancel each other out. A referee will temporarily stop a bout when there is a penalty or a score; when either or both of the contestants are out of the competition area; when a contestant needs to adjust his uniform; when a contestant breaks, or is about to break, a rule; when a contestant grabs his opponent but does not immediately execute an effective technique; when a contestant falls or is thrown and no effective techniques occur; or when a contestant is injured and cannot continue.

Kata

When the competitor's name is called, she stands on the designated line, bows to the panel of judges, and announces the name of the kata that she will perform. (The four major styles of karate recognized by the World Karate Federation are goju-ryu, shito-ryu, shoto-kan, and wado-ryu. Within these four styles, there are eight approved compulsory katas for the first two rounds.) She then performs the kata. At the end of the kata she returns to the line and awaits her score.

In the first round, the competitor performs a kata from the approved compulsory list. In the second round, she performs a different kata from the compulsory list, and in the remaining rounds, she may perform any kata from the approved list not previously performed. *Repechage* is commonly used to chart rounds.

Each round of kata pairs contestants up against each other, with the winner succeeding to the next round.

In kata, contestants receive scores according to how well they demonstrate

- competence and a clear understanding of the principles involved in the chosen kata;
- correct focus, use of power, balance, and proper breathing; and
- other points within the kata.

In team kata, movements are synchronized, but the kata should not be altered in rhythm or timing for the sake of synchronization. In either individual or team kata, if a contestant interrupts or varies a kata, the contestant (or team) is disqualified.

In team competitions, the three team members performing face the chief judge. Movements must begin and end in unison; otherwise points are deducted. Points are also deducted for momentary imbalances and brief pauses. If a contestant completely loses balance, falls, or comes to a distinct halt, she is disqualified.

Weapons Kata

Weapons kata is judged using the same criteria as open-hand kata, with the additional criterion of demonstrating the characteristics of the weapon used. A contestant must perform a kata that does not endanger people or property; loss of control of the weapon results in disqualification. Weapons are inspected before the competition to ensure that they are in good shape and are of authentic design and proper weight. Weapons include the following:

- **Bo:** A hardwood staff, either the height of the contestant or 6 feet.
- **Sai:** A metal club with blunt edges and a sharp point; two hooks face outward from the grip. While held hooked between the thumb and forefinger, this piece should extend beyond the tip of the elbow one to two inches.
- **Tonfa:** Two hardwood sticks, round or square, with a handle off one side about 6 inches from the end.
- **Nunchaku:** Two hardwood sticks held together by a cord the length of the competitor's wrist.
- **Kama:** A bladed weapon, like a scythe; the blade is at least 6 inches long. The handle may not have a rope or cord attached to it.
- **Ieku:** An oar, about 5.5 feet long with a handle about 3.25 inches long and a blade about 2.25 feet long.
- **Nunti:** A 6-foot bo with a manji sai attached to one end.

- **Kuwa:** A garden hoe with a round or oval-shaped 4-foot-long handle with a 4-inch by 10-inch rectangular curved blade at one end.

LEGAL AND ILLEGAL ACTS

A contestant may attack an opponent in the head, face, neck, abdomen, chest, back (excluding shoulders), and side. The following acts are illegal:

- Contact to the throat
- Excessive contact to the head, face, or neck; attacks to these (and all) areas must be controlled
- Attacks to the groin, joints, or instep
- Open-hand attacks to the face
- Dangerous throws that cause injury
- Direct attacks to the arms and legs
- Repeated exits from the competition area
- Wrestling, pushing, or grabbing without immediately executing a technique
- Reckless actions
- Faking injury to gain an advantage

Such acts are penalized on the following scale:

- *Chukoku* is a warning called for minor infractions.
- A *keikoku* may be imposed for minor infractions for which a contestant has been previously warned. An ippon is added to the opponent's score.
- A *hansoku-chui* is usually imposed for a major infraction or for an infraction in which a keikoku has been previously issued. A nihon is added to the opponent's score.

- A *hansoku* is a very serious infraction that raises the opponent's score to 8 points (victory). Hansoku may be imposed for an infraction for which a hansoku-chui has previously been imposed.
- A *shikkaku* is a disqualification from the match, with the victory going to the opponent. Shikkaku may be called when a contestant takes an action that harms the honor and prestige of karate.

Note: The referee can award any of these penalties for the first penalty. Each succeeding penalty must be awarded at a higher level, even if it is a less serious infraction.

EQUIPMENT

Each contestant wears a white, unmarked karate gi. The back of the gi may be numbered. The jacket must cover the hips but hang no lower than mid-thigh. The jacket sleeves may not reach less than halfway down the forearm but must not extend beyond the wrists. The pants must cover at least two-thirds of the shins. Men wear groin cups. Mitts and mouth guards are mandatory in kumite; soft shin pads are allowed.

OFFICIALS

Matches are officiated by a match area referee, judges, arbitrators, and a scorekeeper.

ORGANIZATIONS

USA Karate Federation
1300 Kenmore Boulevard
Akron, OH 44314
330-753-3114
www.usakarate.org

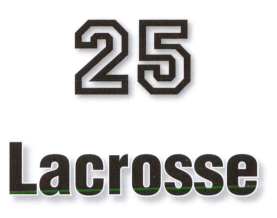

Lacrosse

© Empics

Lacrosse originated in North America, where it was played by Native Americans in what is now Canada and New York. French missionaries playing the game thought the sticks they used resembled the bishop's staff, or *crozier;* thus they called it "la crosse." Certainly the biggest rule change from its early days centers on the length of the game and field: When Native Americans played the sport, a game stretched on for days and the goals could be 15 miles apart!

Rules in place by 1860 remain pretty much the standard for the women's game as it is played today. The men's game evolved in the 1930s and has a different set of rules. The men's game is more popular than the women's, though women's programs are growing. More than 250,000 people play lacrosse in the United States, and countries that compete internationally include Sweden, Germany, and the Czech Republic.

Major League Lacrosse is an outdoor professional league that debuted in 2001; the National Lacrosse League, an indoor professional league, began in the mid-1980s. Nearly 25,000 men play lacrosse in college; about 5,500 women do so as well. More than 72,000 boys and 15,000 girls play lacrosse in high school. About 125,000 youths participate in recreational lacrosse programs across the country.

Objective: To score more goals than the opponents.

Number of Players: 12 per side for women; 10 per side for men.

Length of Game: Two 25-minute halves for women (30-minute halves for collegiate women); four 15-minute quarters for collegiate men.

Scoring: One point for each goal (see "Scoring").

Overview: Players use long-handled sticks to throw, catch, and scoop the ball and to try to throw the ball into the opponents' goal. Women's rules limit stick contact and prohibit body contact; men's rules allow some stick and body contact. Lacrosse is a combination of basketball, soccer, and hockey and requires quickness, speed, and endurance.

TERMS

Blocking occurs when a player moves into the path of an opponent who has the ball without giving the opponent a chance to stop or change direction without contact.

Body checking occurs when a defender moves with an opponent without making body contact, but causing her to slow, change direction, or pass off.

The **critical scoring area** is at each end of the field, where the attacking team shoots for a goal. It runs from approximately 15 meters in front of the goal circle to 9 meters behind the goal circle and 15 meters to either side of the goal circle. It is not marked on the field.

Cross checking occurs when a defender tries to dislodge the ball from his opponent's crosse by tapping it with his own crosse.

A **deputy** is a player on the defensive goalkeeper's team who may enter the goal circle when her team is in possession of the ball and the goalkeeper is out of the goal circle.

The **8-meter arc** is the area in front of each goal circle, intersecting the circle and the goal line extended, and connected by an arc marked 8 meters from the goal circle.

Free space to goal describes the path to goal within the critical scoring area, defined by two imaginary lines extending from the ball to the outside of the goal circle.

Marking is the term used to describe guarding an opponent within a stick's length.

A **penalty lane** is the path to goal that is cleared when a free position is awarded to the attacking team within the critical scoring area in front of the goal line. All players must clear this lane.

A **pick** is a technique used by a player without the ball to force an opponent to take a different direction. The player must give the opponent time to see the pick and react to it.

Slashing is viciously or recklessly swinging a crosse at an opponent's crosse or body. Contact doesn't have to be made for the umpire to call a foul.

A **slow whistle** occurs when an attacking team is fouled on a scoring play within the critical scoring area; the play is finished and the umpire assesses a foul only if the attacking team does not score a goal.

The **12-meter fan** is a semicircle in front of each goal circle, bounded by an arc 12 meters from the goal circle.

WOMEN'S LACROSSE

Women's lacrosse is distinctly different from the men's version of the game. One main difference is in the women's game, body contact is prohibited, and stick contact is limited.

Women, therefore, don't require protective gear beyond mouthguards; the much more physical game played by the men require male players to wear helmets and protective padding.

The stick, or crosse, has a much shallower pocket for women, requiring them to cradle the ball to keep it from falling out as they run up the field. (The men's crosse has a deep pocket that allows them to run easily downfield with the ball.) The field itself is different; in women's lacrosse, there are no set boundaries, while in men's lacrosse boundaries are set. Women play with 12 players per team on the field; men, with 10.

Field

The field has no set boundaries, but an area measuring 110 meters by 64 meters is desirable (see figure 25.1). The goals are 92 meters apart, with 9 meters of playing space behind each goal line, running the width of the field. Minimum width is 55 meters. The goal circles, 8-meter arcs, 12-meter fans, and center circle are as shown in figure 25.1.

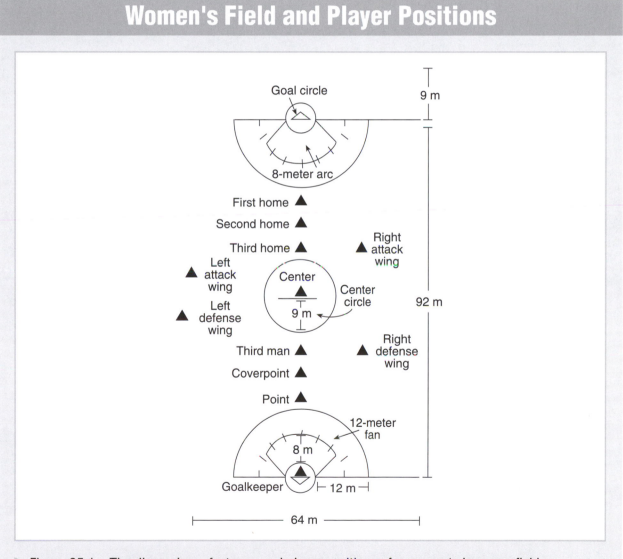

Women's Field and Player Positions

▶ Figure 25.1   The dimensions, features, and player positions of a women's lacrosse field.

Adapted from U.S. Women's Lacrosse Association 1996.

The goals are of wood or metal, 6 feet high and 6 feet wide. A goal line is marked between the two goal posts. Netting is attached to the posts and is firmly pegged to the ground 6 feet behind the center of the goal line.

Players

Twelve players for each team may be on the field at one time. Players wear composition or rubber-soled shoes; spikes are not allowed. Goalkeepers may wear padding on their hands, arms, legs, shoulders, and chests; they must wear helmets with face masks, throat protectors, and chest protectors. All players must wear mouth guards. Substitutions are unlimited and may be made at any time the ball is not in play. Players may reenter the game.

Play

The maximum regulation playing time is 50 minutes (60 minutes in college play), split into halves with up to a 10-minute halftime. The clock stops after a goal is scored and on every whistle in the last two minutes of each half. If a team is leading by 10 or more goals, the clock does not stop after a goal. In high school and college, each team may take one timeout per half.

A game starts with a *draw*—two opposing players toeing the center line, their crosses held in the air, parallel to the center line. The umpire places the ball between the players, calls, "Ready," and blows the whistle. The players pull their sticks up and away, lifting the ball into the air. All other players must be outside of the center circle during the draw. The team that has the ball attempts to score a goal by advancing the ball down the field by carrying, throwing, rolling, or batting it.

If the ball goes out of bounds, it is given to the nearest player. If two players of opposing teams are an equal distance from the ball, the game is restarted with a *throw*. The players stand one meter apart; the umpire, standing four to eight meters away, throws the ball in the air so that the players take it as they move toward the field. No other players may be within four meters of the players taking the throw. A throw also is taken when the ball lodges in the clothing of a player or umpire or when two players commit offsetting fouls.

Only one player (the goalkeeper or her deputy) may be in the *goal circle* (see figure 25.1 on page 159). Within the goal circle, the goalkeeper must clear the ball within 10 seconds. She may use her hands and body to stop the ball, as well as using her crosse. She may also use her crosse to reach out and bring the ball into the goal circle, provided no part of her body is grounded outside the circle. When the goalkeeper leaves the goal circle she loses all goalkeeping privileges.

Scoring

A team scores a goal when the ball passes completely over the goal line, between the posts, and under the cross bar of the opponents' goal. A goal counts if it bounces off a defender and goes into the goal.

If, however, the ball is last touched by an attacking player, it must be propelled by the player's crosse; a goal does not count if the ball bounces off an attacking player and goes into the goal. A goal may also be disallowed if the ball enters the goal after the whistle has blown, if the attacking player or her crosse breaks the plane of the goal circle, or if any other attacking player is in the goal circle. In addition, a goal may be disallowed if an attacking player interferes with the goalkeeper or if the umpire rules the shot or follow-through dangerous.

Fouls

Players may be called for major, minor, or goal circle fouls. *Major fouls* include

- rough or reckless checking or tackling;
- slashing;
- holding a crosse around the face or throat of an opponent;
- hooking an opponent's crosse;
- blocking;
- remaining in the 8-meter arc for more than three seconds, unless marking an opponent within a stick's length;

- setting picks, detaining or tripping an opponent, or charging or backing into an opponent; and
- shooting dangerously.

Minor fouls include

- guarding a ground ball with the player's foot or crosse,
- checking or tackling an opponent's crosse when the opponent is trying to gain possession of the ball,
- touching the ball by hand (by anyone other than the goalkeeper),
- throwing a crosse,
- drawing illegally,
- taking part in the game without holding a crosse,
- intentionally delaying the game, and
- deliberately causing the ball to go out of bounds.

Goal circle fouls may be called when

- a field player enters the goal circle or holds her crosse over the goal circle line,
- the goalkeeper allows the ball to remain within the circle for more than 10 seconds,
- the goalkeeper reaches beyond the circle to play the ball,
- the goalkeeper draws the ball into the circle while she is partially grounded outside the circle, or
- the goalkeeper steps back into the circle while she has the ball.

A player may be given a *misconduct* or *suspension* for playing in a rough, dangerous, or unsporting manner. The penalty for a misconduct or suspension violation is the same as for major fouls (see "Penalties").

Penalties

The penalty for major and minor fouls is a *free position* awarded to the player who was fouled. The player with the free position may run with the ball or throw it with her crosse. All other players must be at least 4 meters away.

When a defender commits a major foul within the 8-meter arc, the free position is awarded at the spot of the foul. When a defender commits a minor foul within the 12-meter fan, the player fouled takes the free position at the nearest spot, with her defender at least 4 meters away. This is an *indirect free position,* and the player taking this position may not take a shot until another player has played the ball.

The penalty for a goal circle foul by the defense is an indirect free position taken 12 meters out to either side, level with the goal line. The exception here is for an illegal deputy; this is treated as a major foul.

A slow whistle occurs on a major foul; the referee throws a signal flag and allows the attacking players to continue a scoring play in the critical scoring area. If the attackers score a goal, the referee does not assess the foul; if the attackers don't score, the referee assesses the foul.

Equipment

The ball is rubber; it is solid yellow and not less than 20 centimeters or more than 20.3 centimeters in circumference. It weighs between 142 grams and 149 grams.

The field crosse is made of aluminum, fiberglass, gut, leather, nylon, plastic, rubber, or wood; the head of the crosse is triangular. The pocket is strung with four or five thongs, with 8 to 12 stitches of cross-lacing. The crosse is 36 to 44 inches long. The head is 7 to 9 inches wide and 10 to 12 inches long. Its pocket may have a maximum depth of 2.5 inches. Maximum overall weight is 20 ounces. The goalkeeper's crosse is 36 to 48 inches long and may weigh a maximum of 26 ounces.

Officials

An umpire, a scorer, and a timer officiate the game.

MEN'S LACROSSE

Men's lacrosse, as noted in the section, "Women's Lacrosse," is very different—and much more physical—than the women's game.

For a few of the basic differences, refer back to "Women's Lacrosse" on page 158.

Field

The field is 110 yards long by 60 yards wide (see figure 25.2). A center line runs across midfield. While the field itself is 60 yards wide, its three major portions—the defensive area, the wing area, and the attack area—are 40 yards wide, with 10 yards on either side of these portions of the field extending to the sidelines. The defensive area begins at a team's own end line and measures 35 yards long; the wing area is 40 yards long, with its center being midfield; and the attack area is 35 yards long and ends at the opponents' end line.

The two goals have openings 6 feet wide and 6 feet high. Goal posts are made of metal pipe and joined by a crossbar. Each goal is centered between the sidelines and is 15 yards from the nearest end line; the goals are 80 yards apart. Each goal has a mesh net fastened to the posts, crossbar, and ground

7 feet behind the center of the goal. Each goal has a goal crease—a circle with a 9-foot radius—drawn around it. The center of the crease is the midpoint of the goal line. The goal areas are marked at each end of the field by lines 40 yards long, centered on the goal and parallel to and 20 yards from the goal line at that end of the field.

Players

A team is made up of 10 players in the following designations: goalkeeper, defense, midfield, and attack. Four players at most, not counting the goalkeeper, may use long crosses 4.5 feet to 6 feet long.

A team may play with less than 10 players if some players have been injured or expelled, as long as onside provisions are maintained. Substitutes may enter the game when officials have suspended play, or "on the fly," with one player entering the field from the table area after the player he is replacing has left the field by the table area.

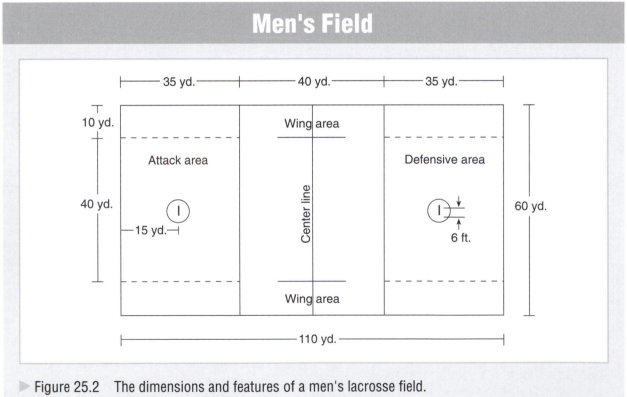

▶ Figure 25.2   The dimensions and features of a men's lacrosse field.
Adapted from National Collegiate Athletic Association 1996.

Play

A game lasts 60 minutes (four 15-minute quarters). Intervals of 2 minutes separate the first and second quarters and the third and fourth quarters; halftime lasts 10 minutes. After each period in regulation time, the teams change goals. Each team gets three timeouts per game, with no more than two taken in one half. If the game is tied at the end of regulation, sudden-death overtime is played in 4-minute periods until a goal is scored. Teams get one timeout each per sudden-death period.

The ball is put into play to begin the game, and after each goal, with a face-off between two opposing players at the center of the field. The referee places the ball between the two players' crosses and blows a whistle to begin the action, and the two players attempt to take control of the ball.

After gaining possession of the ball in its defensive area (see figure 25.2 on page 162), a team must advance the ball past the defensive area line within 10 seconds or turn the ball over to its opponents. The team clearing the ball may throw the ball back across the defensive area line one time on each restart.

After crossing the center line in possession of the ball, the attacking team must advance the ball into the attack area within 10 seconds. Once the ball is in the attack area, players may take it back outside that area, unless warned to "keep it in" (this warning occurs automatically in the final two minutes of regulation if the team in possession is winning). If a team takes the ball outside the attack area, a new 10-second count begins, and the attacking team must advance the ball inside the attack area before it expires, or lose possession of the ball.

A player may body check an opponent who has the ball or who is within 5 yards of a loose ball. The check must be from the front or side, above the waist and below the neck.

When a player who has the ball steps on or over a boundary line, or when his crosse touches on or beyond the boundary line, the ball is out of bounds and is awarded to the opponents. On a restart, no player may be within 5 yards of the player with the ball.

If the ball becomes caught in a player's crosse, the referee will count four seconds. If the player has not freed the ball by then, the ball is awarded to a team according to the alternate-possession rule. The team that wins the coin toss to begin the game gets first possession; possessions alternate after that for plays in which the official cannot determine which team should be awarded the ball.

If the ball becomes caught in a player's uniform or equipment other than his crosse, the ball is immediately awarded in accordance with the alternate-possession rule.

A team is offside when it has fewer than three men in its attack half of the field, or fewer than four men in its defensive half of the field. In such cases, a technical foul (see "Fouls") is called against the offending team.

Within the goal crease area, the goalkeeper may stop the ball with any part of his crosse or body, including batting it with his hands; however, he may not catch the ball. If the ball is outside the crease area, he may not touch the ball with his hands, even if he is within the crease area. No opponent may make contact with the goalkeeper while he is in the crease area, whether or not the goalkeeper has the ball. An attacking player may not be in the crease area at any time. A defending player with possession of the ball, including the goalkeeper, may not enter the crease area. If a defending player gains possession of the ball within the crease area, he must get rid of the ball or leave the crease area within four seconds.

Scoring

A team scores a goal when the ball passes from the front and completely through the imaginary plane formed by the rear edges of the opponents' goal line, the goal posts, and the crossbar.

A goal does not count when

- it passes the goal's plane after the period-ending horn or whistle,
- it passes the goal's plane while an attacking player is in the goal crease area,
- the attacking team has more than 10 men on the field (including the penalty area),

- the attacking team is offside as the goal is scored, or
- an official has whistled the play dead for any reason.

Fouls

Players may be called for personal, technical, and expulsion fouls. *Personal fouls* include illegal body checking, slashing, cross checking, tripping, unnecessary roughness, unsporting conduct, and using an illegal crosse. A player committing a personal foul is suspended for one to three minutes, depending on the severity of the foul. The ball is given to the team fouled. A player who commits five personal fouls in a game is disqualified and may be replaced by a substitute when any penalty time for the fifth foul is over. *Technical fouls* are less serious in nature than personal fouls. They include violations of rules that aren't covered under personal fouls and expulsion fouls. Examples of technical fouls include holding, pushing, offside, crease violations, illegal offensive screening, interference, and stalling. A player must serve a 30-second penalty if his opponents had possession of the ball at the time of his foul; if his team had possession of the ball, the ball is awarded to the opponents for a technical foul. A player is assessed an *expulsion foul* for fighting. That player is suspended from the game and from the next game. He may be replaced after three minutes.

Equipment

The ball is rubber, weighing between 5 and 5.25 ounces and having a circumference between 7.75 and 8 inches. The crosse is made of wood or synthetic material. It is 40 to 42 inches long for a short crosse, or 52 to 72 inches long for a long crosse. The goalkeeper's crosse may be 72 inches or less. The circumference of the crosse handle may be no greater than 3.5 inches; the head at its widest point is between 6.5 and 10 inches. The head for the goalkeeper's crosse may range from 10 to 12 inches in width.

All players must wear protective helmets and mouthpieces. They must also wear protective gloves, shoulder pads, shoes, and jerseys. The goalkeeper must wear protective goalkeeper equipment.

OFFICIALS

A referee, umpire, and a field judge control the game. At least two officials must be used; a fourth may be used as a chief bench official.

ORGANIZATIONS

U.S. Lacrosse
113 W. University Parkway
Baltimore, MD 21210
www.lacrosse.org

International Lacrosse Federation
www.intlaxfed.org

United States Club Lacrosse Association
www.uscla.com

Netball

Netball seems to have evolved from an early version of basketball (i.e., scoring when the ball was successfully thrown into a basket placed in a higher position than the players at each end of a court area). This game developed in the United States. Originally the game was known as nine-a-side basketball, and it became most popular in Australia and New Zealand. The game was then played outdoors, with rings on the goal posts instead of baskets.

Today netball is played by more than 1.5 million people in more than 40 countries, including Commonwealth countries. In 1960 an international code of play was introduced, and in 1963 the first world championships were held in England, where Australia and New Zealand established themselves as the dominant teams. Australians have been the world champions for almost all of the years since 1963.

Netball is predominantly a game for women, but men also play in mixed and also men's-only teams. Players' ages range from 7 years to masters, with the most of those participating between the ages of 20 and 40.

Objective: To score more goals than the opponents.

Number of Players: Seven players on the court per team.

Scoring: A goal may be scored by one of two scoring players on each side.

Length of Game: Four 15-minute quarters.

Overview: The game starts (and restarts after every goal) by a center pass taken alternately by the opposing center players, from the center circle in the middle of the center third of the court. The center pass and all subsequent passes must be caught or touched by a player who is standing or who lands in whichever third the ball is in (the ball must not pass over a complete third without being touched).

COURT

The court is 100 feet long by 50 feet wide. It is divided into three equal areas, called *thirds* (see figure 26.1).

PLAYERS

Each team consists of up to 12 players, 7 of whom are on the court at the same time. All on-court players wear identification letters front and back that delineate their playing position and the areas of the court into which they may move. These are the court areas in which each player is allowed:

- Goal shooter (GS): 1, 2
- Goal attack (GA): 1, 2, 3
- Wing attack (WA): 2, 3
- Center (C): 2, 3, 4
- Wing defense (WD): 3, 4
- Goal defense (GD): 3, 4, 5
- Goalkeeper (GK): 4, 5

PLAY

At the start of play, all players must be in their respective goal thirds and are free to move; the defending center is in the center third and free to move, and the attacking center is in the center circle ready to pass the ball.

The attacking center may throw to one of four teammates who are allowed, by virtue of

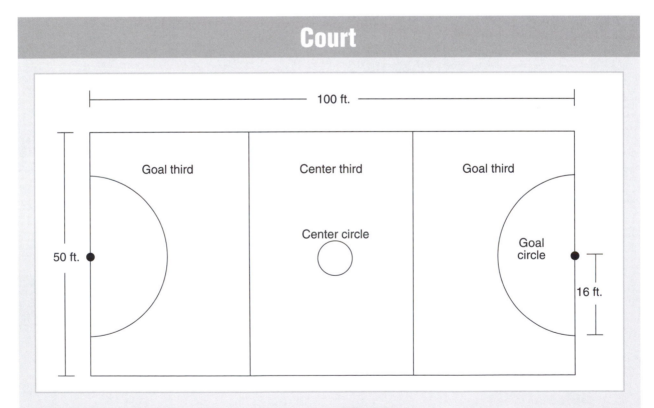

▶ Figure 26.1   The dimensions and features of a netball court.
Adapted from Shakespear 1997.

their playing positions, to enter the center third. Those players are the wing attack, goal attack, wing defense, and goal defense. The attacking team then tries to move the ball down court into the goal circle where one of two players, the goal attack or the goal shooter, attempts to score a goal. Only these two players may attempt to shoot goals and then only from the goal circle, which is a semicircle centered on the goal line with a radius of 16 feet.

Footwork

When a player catches the ball, she must pass it within three seconds and obey the footwork rule. Footwork is one of the most important of the netball skills and does not allow the player with the ball to reground the grounded foot once it has been lifted, unless the ball has been released (thrown). Skilled players who jump to catch the ball while in the air are able to land on one foot, step onto the other foot, lift the first foot, and then throw the ball before that foot is placed on the ground. That sequence could read something like this: Land on the left foot, step onto the right foot, lift the left foot, throw the ball, and put the left foot back onto the ground.

Passing

There are many passing options, including the bounce, the lob, the drop back, the two-handed pass, and the most common single-handed shoulder pass. If a ball goes out of court it is returned to play by any member of the non-offending team who is allowed in the area from where the ball is to be thrown in.

Injury or Illness

Play may be stopped for injury or illness for up to two minutes. During the injury time, both teams may make positional or team changes, but the injured or ill player must be involved in her team changes or substitutions. There is no limit to the number of substitutions that may be made, provided the players used are in the starting 12 listed at the beginning of the game.

SCORING

A goal is scored when the ball is thrown over and completely through the goal ring by either the goal shooter or the goal attack. The 10-foot goal post has a goal ring with a 15-inch diameter, which is projected horizontally 6 inches from the post. The post is centered on the goal line. Should any other player other than the goal shooter or goal attack throw the ball through the goal ring, no goal is scored and play continues.

INFRINGEMENTS AND PENALTIES

Netball infringements are classified into two main groups: minor infringements and major infringements. The minor infringements include not releasing the ball within three seconds of receipt, throwing the ball over a third of the court, using incorrect footwork, moving offside into an area not part of a player's designated playing area, moving out of court, and breaking at center pass. The penalty for minor infringements is a free pass, taken by any member of the nonoffending team who is allowed in the area where the infringement occurred. In the case of an out of court, this free pass is actually a throw in.

The major infringements include obstruction, contact, and intimidation, and are penalized with a penalty pass, or penalty pass or shot. In this penalty, the offending player must stand out of play until the ball has been released. This penalty is taken from where the infringer was standing; the ball must be released within three seconds and the footwork rule must be obeyed. The umpire may conduct a toss-up if there is a simultaneous infringement or action by any two opposing players.

One of the major rules, obstruction, has three elements: distance, arms, and interference. Players must be 3 feet from the player with the ball if they wish to use their arms to defend. If they do not use their arms, they may be within that 3-foot distance. It is possible for both attacking and defending players to infringe this rule, and they would then be penalized. If there is the legal distance between an attacking and defending player and the attacking player lessens the distance, there is no obstruction infringement. Players may use outstretched arms to catch a thrown ball, to attempt to catch a feint pass, or to rebound a shot at goal.

There are also rules regarding contact. Although netball is a contact sport, no player may cause contact to occur by moving into the path of a moving player or by standing so close that contact becomes inevitable. During attacking or defending, or in contesting for the ball, contact may occur, but whether it is accidental or deliberate, it may not interfere with the play of an opponent. Illegal contact may occur through leaning on an opponent, pushing, tripping, or any other form of physical contact.

Players and officials are expected to uphold the rules and the spirit of the game at all times. Should players infringe this area, they may be penalized with an appropriate penalty, which may include an on-court penalty, a warning, a suspension, or an ordering off, depending on the severity of the infringement.

EQUIPMENT

The ball may be made of leather, rubber, or similar material. It measures 27 to 28 inches and weighs 14 to 16 ounces.

OFFICIALS

Match officials are the umpires, scorers, and timekeepers. Team officials are the coach, assistant coach, manager, captain, and two primary care personnel.

ORGANIZATION

International Federation of Netball Associations
+44 (0) 121 4464451
www.netball.org

27 Racquetball

Racquetball is a fast-paced game played with a hollow rubber ball and strung rackets. It was created in 1949 by combining the rules of squash and handball, and by 1970 about 50,000 people were playing regularly in the United States. That figure has grown today to about 7.5 million Americans and about 15 million people worldwide.

Objective: To win rallies and score points by serving or returning the ball so that the opponent cannot keep the ball in play.

Number of Players: Two, three, or four.

Scoring: Points are scored only by the serving side; a rally is won when one player or side cannot return the ball before it hits the floor twice, when a player or side returns a ball that hits the floor before it hits the front wall, or when an avoidable hinder is called.

Length of Match: The best two of three games. (In professional play, matches are the best three of five games to 11 points.)

Length of Game: The first two games are played to 15 points; if a third game is necessary, it is played to 11 points.

Overview: The winner of a coin toss chooses to serve or receive to begin the game. The player or side beginning the first game as server will begin the second game as receiver. To begin a third game, the player or side that scored the most points during the first two games gets the choice to serve or receive. If the point totals are equal, another coin toss is required.

In singles, the server continues to serve as long as she wins each rally. She earns one point for each rally won. When she loses a rally, her opponent gains the serve.

In doubles, to begin a game, player 1 of team A serves until his team loses a rally. Team B then gains the serve. From then on, when the first server of a team loses the serve, it is called an *out serve* and the serve goes to the second player on the team. When the second server loses the serve, it is a *sideout,* and the opponents gain the serve.

COURT

The court is 20 feet wide by 40 feet long (see figure 27.1). The court is 20 feet high, with a back wall at least 12 feet high. The short line is midway between the front and back walls.

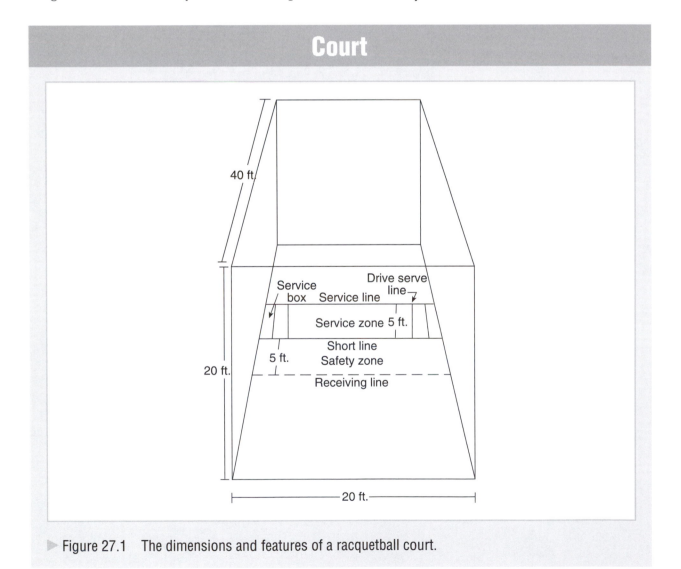

▶ Figure 27.1   The dimensions and features of a racquetball court.

The service line is 5 feet in front of the short line. The service zone is the space between these two lines.

Service boxes are on either end of the service zone; they are 18 inches wide. Drive serve lines are marked by lines parallel to the side walls; these lines denote the drive serve zone, which is 36 inches wide. The receiving line is 5 feet behind the short line. The safety zone is that space between the receiving line and the short line.

TERMS

An **avoidable hinder**—such as blocking an opponent or impeding an opponent's return and taking away an offensive opportunity—results in the loss of the rally.

A **crotch serve** is one that hits the juncture of the front wall and the floor at the same time. This serve results in an out.

A **dead-ball hinder**—such as when a ball that would have otherwise reached the front wall on the fly hits an opponent or when body contact hinders a return—results in a replay, with no penalty. The server receives two serves after such a hinder. This can also be a court hinder—such as when the ball hits the lights and bounces poorly, or hits the door latch, and so on.

A **dead-ball serve**—such as from a court hinder or a broken ball—is replayed, but no previous fault serve is canceled.

The **drive serve lines** are 3 feet from and parallel to each side wall, within the service zone. Along with the side walls, they define a 17-foot drive serve zone.

Fault serves result from a variety of violations: foot faults, short serves, three-wall serves, ceiling serves, long serves, and so on. Two consecutive fault serves result in an out.

A **game** is normally played to 15 points.

A **match** is the best two of three games.

Out serves result from various serves, including consecutive fault serves, missed serve attempts, fakes, and touched serves. The player loses her serve on an out serve.

A **rally** is all the play, beginning with the return of serve.

The **receiving line** is a broken line parallel to, and 5 feet behind, the short line. The receiver may not break the plane of the receiving line until the serve has done so.

The **safety zone** is the 5-foot area between the receiving line and the short line. The receiver may not be in this zone until the served ball has either bounced on the floor inside the zone or else crossed over the receiving line.

Service boxes are at the end of each service zone; they are marked by lines parallel with the side walls. The boxes are 18 inches wide.

The **service line** is parallel to, and 5 feet in front of, the short line. The space between the service line and the short line is known as the service zone.

The **service zone** is the 5-foot area between the short line and the service line.

The **short line** is midway between, and parallel to, the front and back walls.

A **sideout** occurs when a player or side loses the serve to the opponent.

A **technical foul** may be called for a variety of reasons, including profanity, excessive arguing, and slamming the racket on a wall or floor. A technical warning results in no points deducted; a technical foul results in one point taken away from the offender.

A **tiebreaker** game, to 11 points, is played if the opponents split the first two games of a match.

A **volley** is a ball hit in the air before it hits the floor.

PLAYERS

Players may play in singles matches (two players) or doubles (four players). A nontournament game consisting of three players—called "cutthroat"—may also be played. In this version the server plays against the other two players; the serve rotates among the three players.

PLAY

The rules of play are outlined in these categories: serving, return of serve, rallies, hinders, and timeouts.

Serving

The server has 10 seconds to serve once the score has been called. It is the server's responsibility to make sure the receiver is ready before she serves. A receiver may signal she is not ready by raising her racket above her head or by turning her back to the server. These are the only two acceptable signals.

The server serves from any place within the service zone. Neither the ball nor any part of either foot may be beyond the service zone lines when the server begins her motion. The server may step over the front service line if portions of both feet remain on or inside the line until the served ball passes the short line.

Once the server begins her motion, she must bounce the ball once and hit it with her racket. The ball must strike the front wall first and then strike the floor on its first bounce beyond the back edge of the short line. A serve can hit one of the side walls before hitting the floor.

A player may hit a drive serve between himself and the side wall nearest to him if he remains outside of the three-foot drive service zone. In doubles, players must maintain their order of serve. That order can be changed between games.

The server's partner must stand with his back to the side wall and with both feet within the service box until the ball passes the short line. A violation results in a foot fault, unless the partner enters the safety zone (the area between the short line and the receiving line); in this case the server loses his serve.

A dead-ball serve results in no penalty; the server is given another serve. Dead-ball serves include court hinders (e.g., the ball bounces irregularly because it hit a wet spot or irregular surface) and balls that break on the serve.

A server may have one fault serve; a second fault results in a handout or a sideout. Among fault serves are foot faults (for either the server or the partner), short serves (those that hit the floor on or in front of the short line), three-wall serves (those that hit the front wall and both side walls before striking the floor), ceiling serves (those that hit the front wall and then the ceiling, with or without touching a side wall), and long serves (those that hit the back wall before hitting the floor or go out of the court).

Out serves, which result in either a handout or a sideout, may be called for a number of occasions, including when the server executes two consecutive fault serves; when the server totally misses an attempted serve; when a served ball rebounds and touches the server or the server's racket; and when a served ball is stopped or caught by the server or the server's partner. Other instances in which an out serve is called include when the ball strikes any surface other than the front wall first; when a player hits a "crotch serve"—one that hits the juncture of the front wall and floor, front wall and side wall, or front wall and ceiling; and when a player serves out of order (any points scored by the player serving out of order are subtracted).

Return of Serve

The receiver may not enter the safety zone until the ball bounces or crosses the receiving line. The receiver may try to return the ball before it strikes the floor, but the ball must pass the plane of the receiving line first. The receiver's racket or body may break the plane of the receiving line on the follow-through.

A receiver may not intentionally catch or touch an apparently long serve until the referee has made the call or the ball bounces twice. Violation results in a point for the server. A receiver must return a serve before it strikes the floor twice. The return must hit the front wall before it touches the floor. It may hit any combination of walls and ceiling beforehand.

Rallies

During a rally—all the play that follows the serve—a player may hit the ball only with the head of the racket, which may be held in one or both hands. Switching the racket from one hand to the other, or removing the wrist thong, results in a loss of the rally. Other losses of rally result when a player

- touches the ball more than once on a return;
- carries the ball (slings or throws it, rather than hitting it);
- fails to return the ball before it bounces twice;
- fails to hit the front wall on the return, before the return strikes the floor;
- hits himself or his partner with the ball;
- commits an avoidable hinder (see "Hinders"); or
- hits the ball out of the court before the ball has first hit the front wall.

The ball remains in play until it touches the floor a second time, no matter how many walls the ball hits, including the front wall. A player may swing at a ball and miss in a return attempt as long as he hits it before it bounces twice.

In doubles, both partners may attempt to return the ball; no alternating is necessary. Only one player may strike the ball on a return, however. If a return strikes the front wall, bounces once and goes into the gallery or through any opening, the ball is dead, and the server receives two serves. Whenever a rally is replayed, the server begins with two serves.

If a ball breaks during a rally, the rally is replayed. If a foreign object enters the court during a rally, play is stopped and the rally is replayed.

Hinders

A *dead-ball hinder* results in a replay with no penalty; the server receives two serves. The receiver must make a reasonable effort and have a reasonable chance to make a return before a referee will call a hinder. Some examples of dead-ball hinders include when the ball hits a door knob or bounces irregularly due to rough surface, when the ball hits an opponent (unless it's obvious the ball would not have reached the front wall), when body contact occurs (if the contact prevents a player from being able to make a reasonable return), and when an offensive player is screened from the ball passing close to a defensive player.

An *avoidable hinder* results in loss of the rally. An avoidable hinder does not necessarily mean the act was intentional. Examples of avoidable hinders include when a player does not move enough to allow her opponent a shot straight at the front wall as well as a cross-court shot; when a player's movement, or lack of movement, impedes his opponent's swing; when a player's position blocks her opponent from reaching or returning a ball; and when a player moves into the path of, and is struck by, a ball just hit by an opponent.

Timeouts

Each player or team may take up to three 30-second timeouts in games to 15, and two 30-second timeouts in games to 11. If a timeout is called after the serve has begun, or when the player or team has none left, a technical foul (loss of point) is called for delay of game. A player is awarded up to 15 cumulative minutes of injury timeout.

The referee may award a player or team a timeout of up to two minutes, if all regular timeouts have been used, to change or adjust equipment. A two-minute break is given between the first two games; a five-minute break is given between games two and three. In international rules, equipment timeouts may be given without being charged to a player or team.

EQUIPMENT

The ball is 2.25 inches in diameter and weighs about 1.4 ounces. The racket may not exceed 22 inches in length; it must have an attached wrist cord. The racket may be made of any material deemed to be safe. It is strung with gut, nylon, or a combination of materials.

Players are required to wear protective eyewear designed for racquetball; it must meet or exceed approved standards. Shoes must have soles that do not mark or damage the floor.

OFFICIALS

A referee is in charge of the match; two line judges and a scorekeeper may assist the referee. The referee makes all decisions regarding rules.

MODIFICATIONS

This section highlights major rules modifications affecting play for various groups and divisions.

Eight-and-Under Multi-Bounce

This multi-bounce game is for those eight years old and under. The ball is in play until it stops bouncing and begins to roll, with the following stipulations: A player may swing at it only once and must hit it before it crosses the short line on the way back to the front wall. If the ball bounces from the front wall to the back wall on the fly, it may be hit from anywhere on the court, including beyond the short line.

Tape is used to mark two parallel lines on the front wall: one 3 feet above the floor, and the other 1 foot above the floor (measuring from the bottom of the lines). A ball that hits between the 1- and 3-foot lines must be returned before it bounces three times. A ball that hits below the 1-foot line must be returned before it bounces twice. A ball that hits on or above the 3-foot line can be returned on any bounce. All games are played to 11 points.

One-Wall

The wall is 20 feet wide and 16 feet high. The floor is 20 feet wide and 34 feet to the back edge of the long line. The court should extend 3 to 6 feet beyond the long line and the side lines for the safety of the players.

The back edge of the short line is 16 feet from the wall. Service markers—lines at least

6 inches long—are parallel to, and midway between, the short and long lines. The service zone is the entire area between and including the short line, side lines, and the service line. The receiving zone is the entire area behind the short line, including the side lines and the long line.

Three-Wall

Three-wall can be played with either a short side wall or a long side wall. With a short side wall, the front wall is 20 feet wide and 20 feet high; side walls are 20 feet long and 20 feet high, tapering to 12 feet high at the back end of the court. The rest of the court dimensions are the same as for a four-wall court.

With a long side wall, the court is 40 feet long. The walls may taper from 20 feet high to 12 feet high by the back end of the court. All other markings and dimensions are the same as for a four-wall court. A serve that goes beyond the side walls on the fly is an out. A serve that goes long, but is within the side walls, is a fault.

Wheelchair

The standard rules apply, with the following exceptions:

- Body contact includes wheelchair contact. Such contact may be either a dead-ball or an avoidable hinder.
- The ball is not dead until the third bounce.
- If a player intentionally leaves his chair, he automatically loses the rally.
- The serve may take place from anywhere within the service zone.
- Maintenance delays for chair repair may not take more than five minutes. A player may have two maintenance delays per match.
- In multi-bounce play, the ball may bounce any number of times, but the player may swing at it only once. The ball must be struck before it crosses the short line on its way back to the front wall. The receiver cannot cross the short line once the ball hits the back wall.

There are also modifications of rules for visually- and hearing-impaired players.

Men's and Women's Professional Tour

The following modifications apply to competitions in both the Men's International Racquetball Tour and the Women's International Racquetball Tour. Modifications generally are the same, except for screen serves. Matches are the best three of five games, which are played to 11 points each. Each game must be won by at least two points. Each player receives a single one-minute timeout per game. The rest period between games is two minutes, except between the fourth and fifth games, when five minutes are allowed.

Players are allowed only one serve to put the ball into play. No court hinders are called. Screen serves are replayed without penalty, except that on the women's tour, two consecutive screen serves (serves that are screened) result in an out. Line judges are not used.

ORGANIZATIONS

United States Racquetball Association
1685 W. Unitah
Colorado Springs, CO 80904-2921
719-635-5396
www.racquetball.org

International Racquetball Tour
www.irt-tour.com

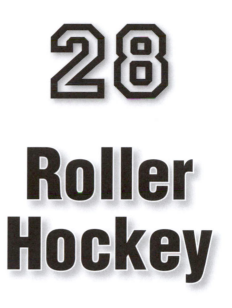

Roller Hockey

Roller hockey is traced to 1878 London, where it is reputed to have its beginnings; in the 1880s several Midwestern cities in the United States formed leagues and adopted rules of play. Professional play began in 1991 with the formation of Roller Hockey International, but the game is much more popular at the amateur level. USA Roller Sports has 32,000 members, and the sport enjoys wide popularity in many countries, most notably in Spain, Portugal, and Italy and throughout South America.

Roller hockey is a fast-paced game, employing many of the moves and tactics of ice hockey. Its equipment is also similar to that used in ice hockey. There are, however, two major differences: Roller hockey is a noncontact sport, and it offers hardball, puck, and softball hockey variations. In hardball hockey, players use a hard, black cork or rubber ball, and wooden, cane-style sticks. Softball hockey uses a low-impact, lightweight plastic ball and cane-style plastic sticks, adaptable for players of all sizes. The softball variation is commonly employed in Junior Olympic leagues and leagues for players new to the game.

Objective: To score more goals than the other team.

Scoring: A goal is scored when the ball completely crosses the goal line between the two vertical posts of the goal mouth.

Number of Players: Two teams of five players each.

Length of Match: Two periods of 20 or 25 minutes each, depending on scheduling (senior category); two periods of 20 minutes each (junior category); two periods of 15 minutes each (schoolboy category).

Overview: A match begins with a face-off. The team with the ball or puck attempts to weave its way through the opponent's defense to get a shot on goal. The defenders try to steal the ball or puck, intercept a pass, or block a shot and gain control of the ball or puck. Play is continuous except for timeouts, injuries, face-offs, penalties, and penalty shots. After each goal, play is resumed with a face-off at the center circle.

PLAYING AREA

The playing surface is 90 feet wide by 180 feet long, or dimensions that are similar (see figure 28.1). The surface should not be longer than 200 feet and should have a 1:2 ratio of width to length. A retaining barrier surrounds the surface to help keep the ball in play.

Goal cages are 15 feet from the end barriers. Goal lines are drawn across the mouths of the goals and extend across the width of the floor. The cages are not secured to the floor. They may be any size, but a recommended size is 67 inches wide by 41 inches tall by 36 inches deep. The cage's frame is covered with netting strong enough to withstand any shot. In front of the cages are goal creases, semicircles with a radius of 3.5 feet.

Five face-off circles are on the floor, one in the center and four toward the corners, about 20 feet out from each goal line and about one-quarter the distance from the side barriers. The face-off circles have a 10-foot radius, and the circle in the middle, where the referee drops the ball for a face-off, is 1 foot in diameter. A center line, running the width of the floor, separates the floor in equal halves. A penalty box is on one side of the court, and two players' benches are on either side of the box.

TERMS

Boarding is a violation that occurs when a player cross checks, elbows, body checks, or trips an opponent, causing her to crash into the boards.

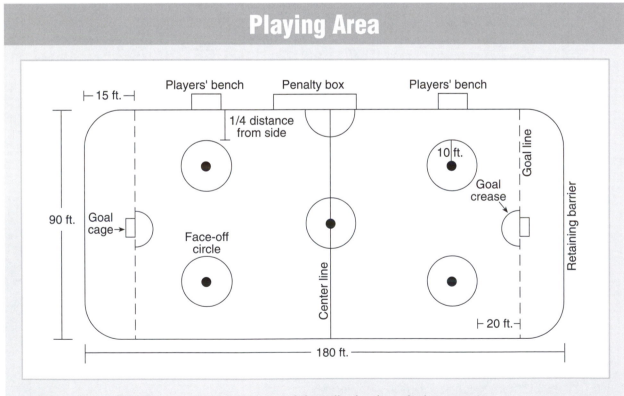

▶ Figure 28.1   The dimensions and features of the roller hockey playing area.

Adapted from USA Roller Skating.

Butt-ending is a violation called when a player uses the shaft of the stick above the upper hand to jab, or attempt to jab, an opposing player. It can be a violation even if the player makes no physical contact.

Charging is a violation called when a player runs or jumps into an opponent.

Chopping is a violation that occurs when a player taking a shot chops the ball by hitting it with the sharp edge of the stick. Players may hit the ball only with the flat part of the blade.

Cross checking is a violation by a player who checks another by extending his arms with both hands on the stick and making contact with the opponent above the waist.

Elbowing is a violation called when a player uses an elbow to foul an opponent.

High-sticking is a violation that occurs when a player carries her stick above her shoulder. A player doesn't have to make contact for a referee to call a violation.

Holding is a violation called when a player holds an opponent with his legs, hands, feet, or stick, or in any other way.

Hooking is a violation that occurs when a player uses his stick to hook and impede, or attempt to impede, an opponent's progress.

Intentional delay is a penalty called when a player deliberately delays the game (e.g., deliberately holding the ball against the boards while not being checked). Play is resumed with a face-off at the nearest face-off circle adjacent to the offender's goal (in hardball the other team gets the ball).

Interference is a violation resulting in a penalty. Examples of interference include a player who impedes the progress of an opponent who doesn't possess the puck, or a player who deliberately knocks a stick out of an opponent's hand, or one who prevents a player from regaining her dropped stick.

Kicking the ball is legal in all zones, but a goal cannot be scored by an attacking player kicking the ball in (unless it deflects in off a defender other than the goalkeeper). In hardball, players may not play the ball with their feet.

Lofting the ball is a penalty called when a player intentionally lofts the ball above the height of the goal cage.

Overtime does not occur except during tournament play; otherwise, games may end in a tie. In tournament play, teams play a five-minute overtime; the first to score wins. If the score is still tied after five minutes, five players from each team each get a shot on goal. If the score remains tied, the teams alternate taking shots until one team scores and the other team fails to score.

Slashing is a violation that occurs when a player slashes with her stick to impede the progress of an opponent. The player doesn't need to make physical contact for this to be a violation.

Spearing, or attempting to spear an opponent, is a violation called when a player stabs at an opponent with the point of the stick blade. The player doesn't need to make contact for the referee to call a foul.

Throwing the stick to stop a goal from being scored is not legal. This results in a penalty shot for the offended team.

Tripping is a violation that occurs when a player uses a stick, knee, foot, arm, hand, or elbow to trip an opponent.

PLAYERS

Players may not play the ball if they are skating with a damaged skate or broken stick, holding onto the barrier, not using mandatory safety equipment, or holding onto the goal cage (except for the goalkeeper).

Local leagues develop divisions based on age, skill level, and size. USA Roller Sports recommends coed play for ages up to 13. It also recommends that team members wear similar shirts, with numbers on the backs of the shirts or on the sides of helmets. A coach may make substitutions at any time during play. A team may have no more than five players on the floor at one time.

FACE-OFFS

A referee uses a face-off to begin a game or a new period; to restart play after a timeout, after a player has scored a goal, or after action has displaced a goal cage; and to reset action if he cannot see the play for an extended period. The referee will also call for a face-off if the ball is frozen between two opposing players, if it becomes stuck in the netting outside the goal, or if it goes out of play and the referee is not certain who touched it last. If the referee can identify which team touched it last, the opposing team gets to play the ball from the point at which it went out of bounds.

Face-offs that are used to begin a game or period or to resume play after a goal occur at the center circle. All other face-offs take place at either the center circle or one of the other four face-off spots, depending on where the ball is when the referee calls for the face-off.

Two opposing players, with their backs to their own goals, face each other at the face-off spot, about one stick length apart. The full blade of each one's stick must be on the floor, and all other players must be at least 10 feet away and on their own sides of the floor. The referee drops the ball at the face-off circle to resume play.

PENALTIES

A referee can call three types of penalties, depending on the severity of the act: minor, major, and misconduct penalties. A referee will warn a player for the first minor infraction; for each subsequent minor violation, the player will spend two minutes in the penalty box. Players are penalized five minutes for major infractions, and either 10 minutes or expulsion from the game for misconduct penalties.

Goalkeepers do not have to serve minor penalties; the coach appoints a teammate who was on the floor at the time to serve the penalty for the goalkeeper. Goalkeepers are required to serve their own major and misconduct penalties.

A coach may substitute for a player serving a minor or a misconduct penalty, but not for a player assessed a major penalty. (In hardball the players must serve their own penalties.) A referee waits until the play has finished before calling a minor penalty on a player whose team possesses the ball. The referee stops play immediately, however, for a major or misconduct penalty.

If the offended team scores on a play where the referee could call a minor penalty, the referee does not call the penalty. He calls major and misconduct penalties, regardless of the play.

The referee uses one of three cards to note the severity of the penalty: a *yellow card* for minor penalties, a *blue card* for major penalties, and a *red card* for misconduct penalties.

Minor Penalties

Minor penalties may be called for

- chopping,
- displacing the goal cage,
- falling on the ball,
- handling the ball,
- high-sticking,
- intentionally delaying the game,
- interference, or
- lofting.

A minor or major penalty, depending on the severity of the act, is called for unnecessary physical contact, including

- boarding,
- butt-ending,
- charging,
- cross checking,
- elbowing,
- holding,
- hooking,
- kicking,
- kneeing,
- slashing,
- spearing, or
- tripping.

Major and Misconduct Penalties

A major penalty is called for fighting or for throwing a stick (unless the referee awards a penalty shot). A minor, major, or misconduct penalty may be assessed for abuse of officials and other misconduct, including

- using obscene, profane, or abusive language or gestures;
- showing disrespect for any official;
- banging the boards with a stick or other equipment;
- intentionally shooting the ball out of reach of an official who is reaching for it;
- delaying in going to the penalty box;
- touching or holding an official;
- continuing, or attempting to continue, a fight; or
- throwing anything onto the floor.

Penalty Shot

A referee awards a penalty shot to restore a scoring opportunity that was illegally taken away. The referee designates the player to take the shot; only this player and the goalkeeper are involved in the play. The player begins with the ball in the center circle and attempts to score. (In hardball the shot is taken from the top of the penalty area.) The designated player must keep the ball in motion toward the opponent's goal. Once she shoots and either scores or misses, the play is over; she may not play a rebound. If the player scores a goal, play resumes with a face-off in center circle; if the player doesn't score, she may still play the ball.

EQUIPMENT

The ball or puck must be suitable for roller hockey and commercially available. Sticks are made of wood, plastic, or other similar material. They cannot have any projections, but players may wrap tape around the blade to reinforce it. A stick may be no longer than 62 inches from heel to end of shaft, and not more than 12.5 inches from the heel to the end of the blade. In hardball, sticks are 39 inches long with 2-inch blades.

The goalkeeper's blade may be no wider than 5 inches at any point, except at the heel,

Rule Recommendations

Although each league may develop its own regulations regarding certain procedures, USA Roller Sports recommends these rules:

- A game consists of two 15-minute halves with a 3-minute halftime.
- The teams switch sides at halftime.
- Players use a commercially available ball suitable for roller hockey.
- No more than 10 players and 2 goalkeepers are allowed per team.
- A team with less than 4 players at the start must forfeit.
- If a team drops below 3 players during a game, it must forfeit.
- Each team should have two one-minute timeouts per game. A coach or player on the team possessing the ball may call timeout, or one may be called during a stop in the action.
- No timeouts are allowed in overtime.
- In tournament play, a team receives two points for a win, one point for a tie, and no points for a loss.

where it may not exceed 5.5 inches. It must not exceed 15.5 inches in length from the heel to the end of the blade. The widened portion extending up the shaft of the blade may not exceed 24 inches from the heel and may not be wider than 5 inches. (In hardball most goalkeepers play with a player stick.)

When a player's stick breaks, he must retrieve a new one from his bench. When a goalkeeper's stick breaks, he may receive a new one from a teammate, but it may not be thrown on the floor to the goalkeeper; it must be handed to him.

Players wear in-line or quad (conventional) skates with no protruding parts. Protective equipment that players may use includes helmets with full-protection face masks and chin straps, gloves, shin guards, knee pads, and mouthpieces. Goalkeepers must wear approved leg guards, face masks, gloves, chest protectors, pads, and, at the league's discretion, blocker and catching gloves. In hardball, goalie's masks are not required.

OFFICIALS

A referee is in complete charge of the game. Optional officials include an assistant referee, a goal judge, a scorer, and a timekeeper. Referee signals for roller hockey and ice hockey are very similar. For drawings of ice hockey/roller hockey referee signals, please see pages 144-145.

ORGANIZATIONS

USA Hockey
1775 Bob Johnson Drive
Colorado Springs, CO 80906-4090
719-576-8724
www.usahockey.com

Rowing

© Empics

The oldest known reference to a "regatta" was found in a document dating from 1274 in Venice, Italy. Racing was common in Venice in the 1300s and began in London in the mid-1400s. The first race in the United States took place in New York in 1756; in 1852, Harvard defeated Yale in an eights race in the first intercollegiate contest of any sport.

Rowing became an Olympic sport in 1896, and recreational rowing came into its own in the United States with the more durable and seaworthy shells of the 1970s. Rowing is most popular in the collegiate Northeast and Pacific Northwest, but it is gaining in popularity throughout the United States, especially in the East and Midwest, and is gaining force as a high school sport as well.

Objective: To finish with the fastest time.

Number of Lanes: From three to eight.

Number of Rowers: Depends on the race; see table 29.1 on page 186.

Length of Course: 2000 meters for sprint races; 1000 meters for masters courses; head races vary in distance.

Overview: Rowing races (other than head races) are held on courses that have no bends or turns. Head races are longer races (generally 2 to 4 miles) held primarily on rivers; the courses include the bends in the river. Some boats have a coxswain, who steers the boat but does not row, and a crew who rows; other boats have only rowers (a boat may have one, two, four, or eight rowers, not including a coxswain). Rowers sit with their backs to the forward movement of the boat.

Competitions, known as *regattas,* include sculling events, in which each rower uses two oars, and sweep boats, in which each rower uses one oar. A head race consists of crews who start a few seconds apart and race the clock. Events may be categorized by boat, gender, age, weight, or skill level.

COURSE

A race course is 2,000 meters long (except for masters courses, which are 1,000 meters long) and is wide enough to hold three to eight lanes. If a buoy system is used, each lane is 12.5 to 15 meters wide; without a buoy system, each lane is 15 to 20 meters wide; a lane width of 15 meters is recommended.

A *Class A* course has no bends or turns on the course or runoff area; a current of less than 1 meter per minute; at least six lanes, though eight are preferred; and a water depth of at least 3 meters throughout the course. It also has

- at least 5 meters between the course perimeter and the shore or any obstacle;
- no fixed obstructions on the course;
- use of a buoy system for lanes, with buoys marking the lanes every 10 to 12.5 meters (the first 100 meters and the last 250 meters use different-colored buoys);

- a starting station with a platform or stake-boat solidly anchored;
- two steering markers behind the center of each lane; and
- distance markers every 250 meters.

A *Class B* course is the same as a Class A course, with the following exceptions: Water current may not exceed 6 meters per minute; there must be a minimum of four lanes; water depth must be sufficient to ensure safe racing; and obstacles nearer than 5 meters from the perimeter must be marked. Other distinctions of a Class B course include the following:

- Fixed obstructions must not interfere with, or create a hazard for, a crew.
- A buoy system is not required, but overhead lane markers every 250 meters define the lane boundaries.
- A single marker may be used for steering markers.
- Distance markers are placed every 500 meters; these may consist of painted stripes on the shore.

A *Class C* course does not meet the standards for a Class A or B course, but does meet the requirements for length, width, and uniform conditions for all crews.

TERMS

A **coxswain** is a competitor who does not row or physically participate in propelling the boat forward, except to steer.

A **crew** consists of all competitors in the boat, including the coxswain.

A **head race** pits crews who race on a course at different times against one another. Their finish times determine their placement.

A **regatta** is a combination of different events that are considered a single unit.

A **scull** refers to the shell in which rowers use two oars. It also refers to the events in which each rower uses two oars.

The **starting area** is the first 100 meters of the course.

Sweep refers to an event in which each rower uses a single oar.

A crew **washes** another crew when the water turbulence from the oars and the wake of the leading shell affect the progress of the trailing crew.

CREWS

Each member of a crew wears identical clothing, although headgear is optional for each competitor. Junior competition is for those 18 and younger; a "Junior B" competition may be held for those 16 and younger. Masters competition is for those 27 and older, broken into age groups. Age for masters competition is determined by averaging the ages of the crew, minus the coxswain. Each rower must be a master but need not fall into the specific age category.

In the United States, male coxswains may compete in female events and vice versa (except for elite-level events such as the National Team Trials). A coxswain for a men's crew must weigh at least 120 pounds; for a women's crew, a coxswain must weigh at least 110 pounds. Coxswains who do not meet the weight requirement may carry dead weight, placed as close to their torso as possible, to meet the requirement.

Competitions may also be categorized by skill (intermediate, senior, and elite). In addition, a lightweight crew may compete against similar crews, with each men's crew averaging no more than 155 pounds per rower with no rower weighing more than 160 pounds. For women, a lightweight crew must average no more than 125 pounds with no rower weighing more than 130 pounds.

RACING

Racing rules can be categorized by those concerning the start, the race in progress, and the finish.

Start

Crews are required to be at their starting stations two minutes before the start. The aligning judge makes sure that each boat is aligned with the starting line's plane. When alignment is secured, the judge holds aloft a white flag until the start of the race. If alignment is lost before the start, the judge raises a red flag.

Once aligned, crews are polled individually by the starter to make sure they are ready. After the crews are polled, ready, and aligned, the starter raises a red flag overhead and gives the command to begin—a verbal "Attention!" and then "Go!" accompanied by a downsweep of the flag.

A starter also may use a quick start, dispensing with the polling procedures. A countdown start, in which the starter counts down from five and then gives the normal starting commands, also may be used. During the countdown start, crews must ensure they are ready; the starter will not recognize a crew signaling that it is not ready.

Once a crew rows out of the starting area, which is 100 meters long, the crew may not protest the start as unfair. If a crew's bow crosses the starting line before the signal to begin is given, it is assessed a false start. More than one crew may be assessed false starts on one start. The race is recalled, the offending crews are warned, and the race is restarted. If a crew commits two false starts in one race, it is excluded from the race.

Race in Progress

Crews that row out of their assigned lanes do so at their own risk. If they are out of their own lane and interfere with a crew in its proper lane, the referee will tell the offending crew to alter its course. A crew that does not alter its course may be asked to stop. If a crew interferes with another crew while out of its lane (clashing oars, washing the opposing crew, or forcing the other crew to alter its course to avoid collision), the interfering crew may be excluded. If the interference was slight and did not alter the race results, the referee may issue a lesser penalty.

A crew must maintain its racing cadence as indicated by strokes per minute. It may be penalized for not maintaining the cadence if so instructed by the referee. A crew may not receive outside assistance or coaching during a race. Such assistance may result in exclusion.

If the referee believes a crew has not had a fair chance to win, place, or advance, due to either interference or unfair course conditions, the referee may elect to advance the crew or to rerow the race with some or all of the participants. The referee may elect to stop a race in progress in such a case.

Officials may impose the following penalties on a crew:

- **Reprimand:** This is an informal caution and has no immediate effect upon the crew.
- **Warning:** A crew that has been given two warnings in the same race is excluded. A false start counts as a warning.
- **Exclusion:** Officials may rule that a crew is excluded from the event but may compete in other events.

- **Disqualification:** A crew that is disqualified is removed from the event and from all remaining events in the same regatta. This occurs when a crew flagrantly or intentionally breaks the rules.

Finish

A crew finishes a race when its bow or any part of its hull touches the plane of the finish line. If two crews tie in a finals race, they rest and then rerow to determine places. In some cases a tie is awarded without a rerow. If a tie occurs in a race that advances crews, the referee will allow all the crews that tied to advance, if possible; if not, they will rerow after a rest.

EQUIPMENT

All load-bearing parts of a boat must be firmly fixed to the boat, although the rowers' seats may move along the boat's axis. "Sliding riggers," where the oar's support is not fixed in one place, are forbidden in normal competition. For boat categories, see table 29.1.

Table 29.1	Boat Categories				
Number	Boat name/oar	Coxswain	Abbreviation	Minimum weight (lb)	Minimum weight (kg)
1	Single/scull	No	1x	30.86	14
2	Double/scull	No	2x	59.53	27
2	Pair-without/ sweep	No	2–	59.53	27
2	Pair-with/sweep	Yes	2+	70.55	32
4	Four-without/ sweep	No	4–	110.23	50
4	Four-with/sweep	Yes	4+	112.44	51
4	Quad/scull	No	4x	114.64	52
4	Quad-with/scull	Yes	4x+	116.85	53
8	Eight/sweep	Yes	8+	205.03	93
8	Octuple/scull	Yes	8x	213.85	97

Adapted from U.S. Rowing Association 1996.

Each boat must have a supple or plastic ball, four centimeters in diameter, on its bow, to protect against injury and to provide visibility. A sweep oar must be at least five millimeters thick, measured three millimeters from the blade's tip; a scull oar must be at least three millimeters thick, measured two millimeters from the tip. Each boat must have footgear that allows for quick release, without needing to use the hands, in case the boat capsizes.

In a race, each boat has a numbered card attached to its bow. The number indicates its race lane. If equipment breaks before a crew passes the 100-meter starting area, the crew may signal the referee, who will stop the race. The referee will restart the race after the crew has had time to repair equipment.

OFFICIALS

Officials who oversee rowing competitions include a chief referee, a referee, a starter, a judge at start, a chief judge, and other judges. A jury comprised of the chief referee and four other officials will hear and decide any protests.

Each race is followed by at least one referee (the primary judge), who may be aided by additional referees. These additional referees may withdraw if the primary judge is satisfied with how the race is proceeding. The primary judge must remain with the race, however, to keep the total elapsed time.

ORGANIZATIONS

U.S. Rowing
201 S. Capital Avenue, Suite 400
Indianapolis, IN 46225
317-237-5645
www.usrowing.org

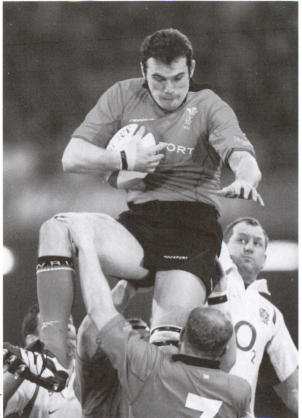

© Empics

30 Rugby Union

Rugby Union got its beginnings in 1823 when a young man named William Webb Ellis of Rugby School in England broke the rules of Foot-the-Ball (soccer) by picking up the ball and running with it. About half the players on both sides stopped playing because this clearly was in violation of the rules. But the other half took no heed, and as Ellis recklessly made his way down the field toward his opponents' goal, many defenders became among the first to try to tackle a ball carrier, and many teammates became among the first to move alongside the ball carrier, hoping to catch a pass.

Cambridge University immediately adopted the new sport, making local rules, but Rugby School itself did not officially consent to play the game until 1841—18 years after Ellis picked up the ball and ran with it. By 1871, however, laws for Rugby Union were in place, and the game was quickly spreading. Today it is a worldwide sport, popular in England, Wales, Scotland, France, and other European countries, as well as Australia, New Zealand, and South Africa. The United States won Olympic gold medals in 1920 and 1924—the last two Olympics in which rugby was played. Rugby's popularity waned in the United States after the sport was dropped from the Olympics, but interest revived in the 1960s and 1970s. Today there are about 1,200 rugby clubs in the United States, and the sport is gaining in popularity on college campuses for women as well as for men.

Objective: To score the most points.
Number of Players: 15 players per side.

Scoring: Five points for a try; two points for a kick scored after a try; three points for a goal scored from a penalty kick; three points for a dropped goal (dropkick).

Length of Game: 80 minutes—two 40-minute halves with a 5-minute halftime.

Overview: The team that kicks off makes a drop kick from the center of the halfway line, while the receiving team stands on or behind its 10-meter line. If the ball doesn't reach the 10-meter line, the receiving team may choose either to field another kickoff or to form a scrummage at the center.

The teams attempt to score by carrying, passing, kicking, and grounding the ball in *in-goal*. After the kickoff, any player who is *onside* (whose progress is not ahead of the ball) may catch or pick up the ball and run with it; pass, throw, or knock it to another player; kick or otherwise propel it; tackle, push, or shoulder an opponent holding it; fall on it; take part in a scrummage, ruck, maul, or line-out; or ground the ball in in-goal.

FIELD

The field of play is rectangular; it is not wider than 70 meters and not longer than 100 meters from goal line to goal line (see figure 30.1). The in-goal areas are each between 10 meters and 25 meters deep. A halfway line runs the width of the field at the center of the field. On both sides of the halfway line, 10-meter lines are marked in broken lines, 10 meters from the halfway line. Broken 5-meter lines run parallel to, and 5 meters inside, the touch lines (sidelines). Two 22-meter lines are on either end of the field, each 22 meters from a goal line.

Solid lines 15 meters inside the touch lines, intersect the goal lines, the 22-meter lines, and the halfway line. The top edge of the

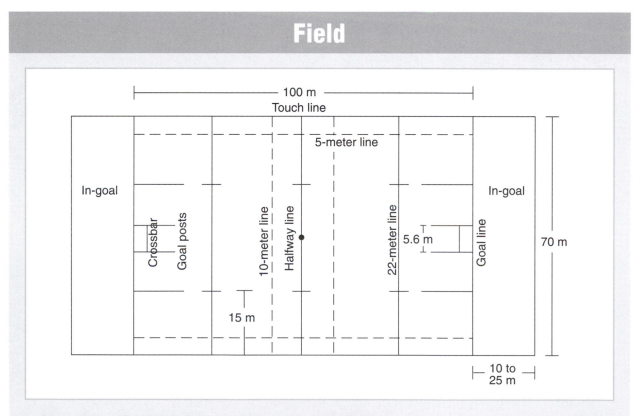

▶ Figure 30.1   The dimensions and features of a rugby field.
Adapted from Powell 1976.

goal's crossbar is 3 meters high; the goal posts are 5.6 meters apart. Corner posts are at least 1.2 meters high.

TERMS

The **dead-ball line** is the line at the end of the in-goal area.

A **drop out** is a dropkick taken on or behind the 22-meter line; the opponents may not cross the line until the kick is made.

A **fair catch** may be made by a player within her 22-meter area or her in-goal. She must catch the kick and shout, "Mark!" She is awarded a free kick for a fair catch.

A **free kick** is awarded to a team after a fair catch or minor infringement. The team may not score a dropped goal from a free kick.

In-goal is the area bounded by a goal line, the touch-in-goal lines, and a dead-ball line. It includes the goal line and goal posts but excludes the touch-in-goal lines and dead-ball line.

A **knock-on** (or "throw-forward") occurs when the ball travels toward the opponents' dead-ball line after a player loses possession of it or propels or strikes it with his hand or arm, or when the ball strikes a player's hand or arm and touches the ground or another player before it is recovered.

A **line-out** is a set play with a member of one team throwing the ball inbounds between two lines of players, with each line defending its own goal.

A **maul** is formed by players from both teams, on their feet and converging on the ball carrier. It ends when the ball is on the ground, when a ball carrier emerges from the maul, or when the referee calls for a scrummage.

A player is **offside** in general play when her team is in possession of the ball and she is in front of it. She may not take part in the play, but she is not penalized unless she plays the ball, obstructs an opponent, or comes within 10 meters of an opponent waiting to play the ball.

A player is **onside** in general play when he is behind the ball. He may take part in the play when he is onside.

A **penalty kick** may be taken by any player of the offended team. The kick must be taken at or behind the prescribed mark. When awarded a penalty kick, a team may opt to kick, to dropkick for goal, or to put in the ball in a scrum. The opponents may not interfere with a penalty kick.

A **ruck** occurs when the ball is on the ground and players from each team are on their feet, in physical contact, **driving over the ball from a position originating behind the ball.** If the ball becomes unplayable, a scrummage is ordered.

A **scrummage**, or *scrum,* is a set play where one team puts the ball into play between players from both teams.

The ball is in **touch** when it touches on or beyond a touch line (out-of-bounds line) or is carried by a player on or beyond a touch line.

A **touch-down** is scored when a player grounds the ball (touches the ball to the ground) in his in-goal. A **try,** worth five points, is scored when a player grounds the ball in his opponents' in-goal.

PLAYERS

Players wear appropriate uniforms. Players may not wear anything with dangerous projections, such as buckles or rings. They may only wear International Rugby Board-approved shoulder pads. They may wear circular studs on their shoes, not exceeding 18 millimeters in length or 13 millimeters in diameter at the base. Players may wear shin guards and elastic knee and elbow pads. They may also wear soft leather scrum caps to protect their ears.

Players normally may only be replaced when injured. No more than six players per team may be replaced.

PLAY

Most of the fundamental rules of play are covered in tackling, scrummages, line-outs, rucks, and mauls.

Tackling

A player is tackled when he is brought to the ground or when the ball comes in contact with the ground while the player is holding it. If one or both of the player's knees are on the ground or if he is on top of another player who is on the ground, the ball carrier is considered tackled. Once tackled, a player must immediately release or pass the ball and move away.

Once a player is tackled, the next player to play the ball must be on his feet. A player who goes to the ground to get the ball must immediately get up or pass or release the ball. Failure to do so may result in a penalty. It is illegal to prevent a tackled player from passing or releasing the ball or to impede him from moving away from the ball after he has passed or released it. It is also illegal to pull the ball from a tackled player's possession while on the ground, to fall intentionally on a tackled player who possesses the ball, or to fall intentionally on other players lying on the ground near the ball.

Scrummage

A *scrummage*, or scrum, is a set play where one team puts the ball into play between two groups of players. A scrum is formed at the place of infringement. At least eight players from each team are involved in a scrum—at least three in the front row and two in the second row. The players must be stationary, and the middle line must be parallel to the goal lines until the ball is put into play.

The middle player in each front row is the *hooker*; the players on either side of her are the *props*. Each front row crouches with heads and shoulders no lower than hips and not farther than an arm's length from their opponents' shoulders. The players bind to each other, hooking arms around the bodies of the teammates next to them.

The team not responsible for the infraction puts the ball into play; or, if no infraction occurred, the ball is put into play by the team that was advancing the ball. The player putting the ball into play stands one meter from the scrum, between the two front rows. She holds the ball with both hands between her knees and ankles, and with a single forward movement puts the ball into play between the two front rows. Once the ball enters the "tunnel" between the rows, the front row players attempt to gain possession of it with their feet. If the ball comes out of either end of the tunnel, it is put in again.

Line-Out

A line-out is a set play that occurs when a ball has gone in touch (out of bounds). The ball is thrown in by a member of the team whose opponents last touched the ball before it went in touch. A member of one team throws the ball inbounds between two lines of players— one line consisting of his teammates and the other of his opponents. The team throwing the ball in determines the maximum number of players on the line. The two lines stand a meter apart. On the throw-in, the ball must first touch the ground or a player at least five meters from the touch line. Players may not charge an opponent, except to tackle him or play the ball, and they may not hold, push, or obstruct an opponent not carrying the ball.

The line-out ends when a ruck or maul forms and all the players' feet move beyond the original line on which the ball was thrown in; when a ball carrier leaves the line-out; when the ball is passed, knocked back, or kicked from the line-out; or when the ball becomes unplayable.

Ruck

Each player joining a ruck must bind with at least one arm around the body of a teammate; failure to do so results in a free kick for the opponents.

A player in a ruck may not

- return the ball into the ruck,
- pick up the ball with hands or legs,

- handle the ball except to score a try or touchdown,
- intentionally collapse the ruck or jump on other players,
- intentionally fall or kneel in the ruck, or
- interfere with the ball while lying on the ground.

If the ball becomes unplayable in a ruck, a scrum is ordered.

Maul

The players in a maul must be on their feet; they must be in physical contact with each other; and their heads and shoulders must be no lower than their hips. A player in a maul may not jump on top of other players in the maul, collapse the maul, or try to drag a player out of the maul. To be in the maul, a player must be bound to it and not merely alongside it.

SCORING

A try (five points) is scored when a player grounds the ball in her opponents' in-goal. A try may be scored in a scrum or ruck if a team pushes its opponents over its goal line and the ball is grounded in-goal by an attacking player. A try is awarded when the ball is grounded while held on the goal line or when a held ball is in contact with the ground and a goal post. A try may also be awarded if a team probably would have scored a try except for a foul by its opponents. After a try, a team can take a place-kick or dropkick at goal, worth two points. The kick is made anywhere on a line opposite where the try was scored. (Thus, it's an advantage to score near the center of the goal line, so that the kick's angle is not too sharp.) The kicker's team must be behind the ball when it is kicked. The opponents must be behind the goal line until the kicker approaches the ball; at that point they may attempt to block the kick.

A penalty kick, taken by any player of the offended team, is taken with the kicker's teammates behind the ball, except for the placer. The kicking team may kick for goal, kick for touch, or kick ahead for possession or territo-

rial advantage. If the kick at goal goes over the crossbar and between the goal posts, it is worth three points. The opponents may not interfere with the kick and must retreat 10 meters from the mark where the kick is being taken. A drop out is a dropkick taken on or behind the 22-meter line. If the ball is kicked into touch, the opponents may accept the kick, have the ball dropped out again, or have a scrummage formed at the 22-meter line.

FOULS

Fouls may be called for obstruction, unfair play, misconduct, dangerous play, unsporting behavior, retaliation, or repeated infringements. If the team fouled has an advantage, the referee does not have to whistle for the foul.

Obstruction occurs when a player running for the ball pushes or shoves an opponent also going for the ball; shoulder-to-shoulder contact is not considered obstruction. Obstruction is also the call when an offside player willfully blocks or prevents an opponent from reaching a teammate carrying the ball. A penalty kick is awarded for obstruction.

Unfair play and *repeated infringements* occur when a player deliberately wastes time or knocks or throws the ball into touch, touch-in-goal, or over the dead-ball line. These infractions result in free kicks. The opponents of a player who deliberately plays unfairly or repeatedly breaks the law of the game will be awarded a penalty kick.

Misconduct and *dangerous play* include

- striking, kicking, tripping, or trampling an opponent;
- tackling early, late, or dangerously;
- charging or obstructing an opponent who has just kicked the ball;
- holding, pushing, or obstructing an opponent who is not holding a ball, except in a scrum, ruck, or maul; and
- intentionally collapsing a scrum, ruck, or maul.

A player guilty of misconduct or dangerous play is cautioned or ordered off the field for

10 minutes. A cautioned player who repeats the offense must be ordered off and may not play anymore in the match.

OFFSIDE

When a player of the team in possession of the ball is closer to the opponent's goal than the ball is, that player is offside. This means she may not take part in the play and faces possible penalty. A player can also be offside in scrums, rucks, mauls, and line-outs.

A player may be penalized while in an offside position if she plays the ball or obstructs an opponent. She may also be penalized if she comes within 10 meters of an opponent waiting to play the ball and does not retire promptly. She may not move toward an opponent waiting to play the ball or to the place where the ball is pitched until she is put onside.

A player is offside in the following situations:

• A player is offside during a scrum if he joins the scrum from the opponents' side, if he doesn't retire behind the offside line or to his goal line, whichever is nearer, or if he places a foot in front of the offside line.

• In situations not involving a line-out, a player is offside if she joins the ruck or maul from her opponents' side; joins it in front of her hindmost teammate; doesn't join the ruck or maul, or unbinds from it, but fails to retire behind the offside line without delay; or advances beyond the offside line but doesn't join the ruck or maul.

• When a ruck or maul takes place at a line-out, a player is offside if he joins the ruck or maul from his opponents' side, joins it in front of his hindmost teammate, or is in the line-out but is not in the ruck or maul and does not retire behind the offside line.

• A player participating in a line-out is offside if she advances beyond the line-of-touch before the ball has touched a player or the ground, unless she is advancing while jumping for the ball. After the ball has touched a player or the ground, a player is offside if she is not carrying the ball and advances beyond

the ball, unless she is attempting to tackle the ball carrier. A player who is not participating in the line-out is offside if she goes beyond the offside line before the line-out ends.

ONSIDE

Except for a player who is within 10 meters of an opponent waiting to catch a kick, a player who is offside is made onside when he retires behind the teammate who last kicked, touched, or carried the ball; when the teammate carrying the ball runs in front of him; or when a teammate runs in front of him after coming from the place, or behind the place, where the ball was kicked. A player who is offside may also be made onside when an opponent carrying the ball has run 5 meters, when an opponent kicks or passes the ball, or when an opponent intentionally touches the ball and does not catch or gather it.

KNOCK-ON AND THROW-FORWARD

A knock-on occurs when the ball is propelled toward the opponent's dead-ball line after a player loses possession of it or strikes it with her hand or arm. A throw-forward occurs when the ball carrier passes the ball forward toward the opponents' dead-ball line. Neither a knock-on nor a throw-forward may occur intentionally; the penalty is a penalty kick at the place of infringement. If the play is unintentional, a scrummage is formed.

IN-GOAL

Touch-in-goal occurs when the ball touches a corner post, a touch-in-goal line, or the ground or a person on or beyond the line. The flag is not part of the corner post. When the ball becomes dead in in-goal, a scrum is formed 5 meters from the goal line, with the attacking team putting the ball into play. If a player carries the ball into in-goal but is held and cannot ground it, the ball is dead. The ball is also dead if a defender kicks, knocks, or carries the ball into his own in-goal area and the ball becomes dead.

IN TOUCH

The ball is in touch (out of bounds) when it touches on or beyond a touch line or when it is carried by a player who touches on or beyond a touch line. A player may be in touch and kick or propel the ball with his hand if the ball does not cross the plane of touch. A player may also catch and deflect a ball into the playing area if it has crossed in touch, but the player's feet have not.

BALL OR PLAYER TOUCHING REFEREE

If the ball or a ball carrier touches a referee, play continues unless the referee believes a team has gained an advantage. In this case he orders a scrummage and the team that last played the ball puts it in. If a player carrying the ball touches the referee while in her opponents' in-goal, before she can ground the ball, she is awarded a try.

EQUIPMENT

The ball is oval and is 280 to 300 millimeters long. It is 760 to 790 millimeters in circumference, from end to end, and 580 to 620 millimeters in circumference around the middle.

OFFICIALS

A referee is in charge of the match. Two touch judges, one on each side of the field, assist the referee.

MODIFICATIONS

Rugby League Football is similar to Rugby Union Football. The main differences include the following:

- Each side has 13 players per side instead of 15.
- A try is worth four points; a conversion is worth two. A penalty goal nets two points, and a drop goal counts for one point.
- A tackled player is allowed to retain possession of the ball temporarily.
- Ground gained by a kick into touch does not count, unless the ball lands in the field of play before it bounces into touch.

ORGANIZATIONS

United States Rugby Football Union
3595 E. Fountain Boulevard
Colorado Springs, CO 80910
719-637-1022
www.usarugby.org

© Empics

31 Soccer

Soccer is based on 17 main laws, which have been refined since the game's modern beginnings in Great Britain in 1863. The sport was first known in Britain as association football; this was shortened to A-soc, and, finally, soccer. The sport's popularity in the United States lagged until the 1970s, when youth leagues began to flourish. Soccer is a popular sport worldwide, especially in Argentina, Brazil, England, Germany, and Italy. In the United States, it is second only to basketball in youth participation (about 7.7 million U.S. youths play soccer). About 18 million people play soccer at least once a year in the United States, nearly half of those regularly in soccer leagues. The game is popular in the United States both recreationally and at youth and high school levels.

Objective: To score as many points as possible by putting the ball into the opponents' goal.

Number of Players: Eleven per side (for short-sided games, see "Modifications" on page 201).

Scoring: A goal (one point) is scored when the ball completely crosses the goal line under the crossbar and between the goal posts.

Length of Game: Two 45-minute halves with a 5-minute halftime.

Overview: The player who begins the game by kicking off may not touch the ball again until another player has. Players must use their feet, heads, or chests to play the ball; with the exception of the goalkeeper—and of making a *throw-in*—players may not use their hands or arms. The game proceeds with each team attempting to control the ball, move it down the field, and score a goal.

FIELD

See figure 31.1 for the components and dimensions of a soccer field.

TERMS

An **advantage** refers to a situation in which the referee calls "Play on!" despite a foul—because the team that would be given a free kick already has the advantage of a scoring or passing opportunity.

A **corner kick** is awarded the opposing team when a player kicks the ball over his own goal line. For a corner kick, all opposing players must be at least 10 yards from the ball.

A **direct free kick** occurs after any of nine fouls (see page 200).

A **foul** (see page 200) results in a direct or an indirect free kick for the opposing team at the spot of the foul.

A **goal** (see "Scoring" on page 197) may not be scored directly from a *kickoff, goal kick,* or *throw-in*. A goal may be scored directly from a *corner kick,* from an opposing goalkeeper's punt, or by an attacker carrying the ball in on her chest or between her knees or feet. An attacking player may not use her hands or arms to throw, carry, or propel the ball across the goal line.

A **goal kick** occurs after a player kicks the ball over the opposing team's goal line. The opposing team is awarded the goal kick. Opposing players must be outside the penalty box; the ball may be kicked by either the goalkeeper or another player. It must be kicked beyond the penalty box area to be put into play. The player who kicks the ball may not touch the ball again until another player has done so.

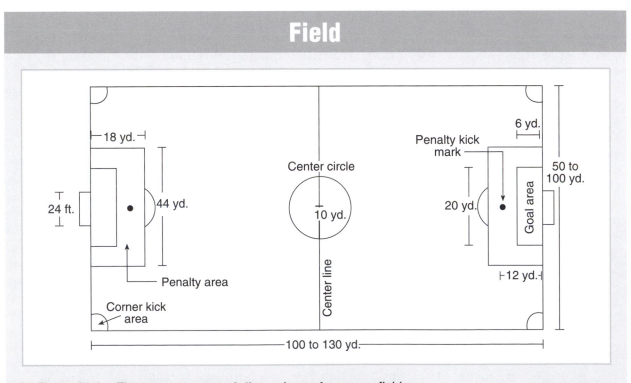

Field

▶ Figure 31.1   The components and dimensions of a soccer field.
Adapted from American Coaching Effectiveness Program 1991.

A player **heads the ball** by hitting it with her head. It is not a foul if a player who jumps and heads the ball bumps into an opponent on the way down.

An **indirect free kick** is awarded for various violations (see page 200).

The **offside** rule is explained later on this page.

The ball is not **out of play** (out of bounds) until the entire ball has crossed over the touch line or goal line. A player may go out of bounds to keep the ball in play. A ball is in play once it bounces back onto the field after hitting a goal post, crossbar, or corner post, and once it hits an official who is in bounds.

A team is awarded a **penalty kick** when an opposing player commits an intentional foul. All players except the kicker and the goalkeeper must stand outside the penalty area, at least 10 yards from the ball. The goalkeeper must stand on his goal line and not move his feet until the kick is made. If the ball is stopped by the goalkeeper and rebounds into the field, play continues. If a goal is not scored and the ball goes out of bounds after being touched by the goalkeeper, the attacking team gets a corner kick.

A **shoulder charge** is the only body contact allowed. It occurs when two players press shoulders while attempting to gain possession of the ball. For a shoulder charge to be legal, players must be within playing distance of the ball and have at least one foot on the ground.

A **sliding tackle** occurs when a player slides to kick the ball away from an opponent.

A team is awarded a **throw-in** when the ball goes over the sideline, last touched by an opponent. A player throws the ball in from over her head, with both feet on the ground at the moment of release. At least part of each foot must be on or behind the sideline. If the throw-in is done incorrectly, the opposing team is awarded a throw-in.

A referee may issue a player a **warning** (yellow card) for misconduct or **eject** a player (red card) for violent conduct, a serious foul, or abusive language.

PLAYERS

Each team has up to 11 players; one is the goalkeeper. The other players are known as defenders, midfielders, and forwards, or strikers. In major competitions, a team may not use more than 3 substitutes in a game. In other competitions, up to 5 may be used. Any player, with the referee's approval and when play is stopped, may substitute for the goalkeeper.

A substitute must be summoned onto the field by the referee and must enter the field at the center line after the player she is replacing has left the field. Once a player has been replaced, she may not return to the game. (Different soccer associations have variations of this substitution rule for youth, women's, and senior competitions.)

PLAY

Some of the basic play is governed by the rules concerning offside, free kicks, and goalkeeping.

Offside

A player is offside if he is closer to the opponents' goal line than the ball is, unless the player is still in his own half of the field or at least two opponents are closer to the opponents' goal line. Offside is determined by the player's position at the moment of the pass, not at the moment he receives the pass.

A player is *not* offside when he receives a ball that bounces off a defender who had possession of the ball; that comes at him directly from a goal kick, corner kick, or throw-in; that was deflected by the goalkeeper; or that was shot at the goal and bounces off a defender. Nor is a player offside when he is in line with a defender at the moment of the pass.

A player is not called offside for merely being in an offside position. The player must be participating in the play to be ruled offside.

When a player is offside, the opposing team receives an indirect free kick at the point of the infraction.

Free Kicks

There are two types of free kicks: direct free kicks, awarded for any of nine fouls committed by the other team, and indirect free kicks, awarded for other violations made by the opposing team. Opposing players must be at least 10 yards from the ball during a free kick. Any free kick awarded to the defending team within its own goal area may be taken from any point within the goal area. An indirect free kick awarded to the attacking team within the opponents' goal area will be taken from the goal-area line nearest to the point where the infraction occurred. A goal may be scored on a direct free kick with no other player touching the ball; on an indirect free kick, another player must touch the ball first before a goal can be scored.

A *direct free kick* is awarded to a team's opponents when that team

- kicks, trips, or pushes an opponent;
- jumps into an opponent;
- violently or dangerously charges an opponent, or charges an opponent from behind;
- strikes an opponent with the hand, arm, or elbow;
- holds an opponent's body or clothing; or
- plays the ball anywhere on the arm, from the shoulder to the fingertips (except for the goalkeeper).

An *indirect free kick* is awarded the opposing team when a player

- is offside;
- obstructs an opponent by deliberately blocking his path, instead of playing the ball;
- kicks too high, thus putting an opponent in danger;
- bends low, putting himself in danger;

- conducts himself in an unsporting manner;
- charges an opponent when the ball is more than one step away; or
- charges into the goalkeeper while in the goal area, preventing the goalkeeper from playing the ball or retaining possession.

An indirect free kick is also awarded when a goalkeeper takes more than four steps before releasing the ball.

Goalkeepers are also governed by the following rules.

Goalkeeping

These rules address the use of hands and of time-delaying tactics: The goalkeeper must release the ball before taking more than four steps. She may not touch the ball again with her hands before another player touches it outside of the penalty area. A goalkeeper may use her hands to field a ball that has been deliberately headed or kneed to her by a teammate, but she may *not* use her hands to field a ball that has been intentionally kicked to her by a teammate.

A goalkeeper may not delay the game by holding the ball before punting.(Penalty: An indirect free kick is taken from the spot of the violation, or, if it occurred within the goalkeeper's area, the kick is taken from the goal-area line that runs parallel to the goal line, nearest the spot of the infraction.)

EQUIPMENT

The ball is round, is covered in leather or a leather-like material, and is between 27 and 28 inches in circumference. It must weigh 14 to 16 ounces and have 14 pounds of air pressure. Players dress in team shirts, shorts, shin guards, and socks. Shoes may have studs if they are rounded, no longer than .75 inch, and no less than .5 inch in diameter. Goalkeepers often wear elbow and knee pads and gloves. The goalkeeper wears a different-colored uniform from that of his teammates. Any equipment deemed dangerous to players may not be worn. This includes earrings, glasses, necklaces, bracelets, watches, and casts and braces that the referee considers dangerous.

OFFICIALS

One referee and two assistant referees control the game. The referee is responsible for enforcing the rules, keeping the time and score, and issuing warnings and ejecting players and coaches. The referee signals the start and end of the game.

The assistant referees indicate when and where a ball goes out of bounds and determine which team is awarded a throw-in, goal kick, or corner kick. They also call offside plays and flag other violations that the referee misses. For various officials' signals, see figure 31.2.

MODIFICATIONS

Different organizations modify the sport in different ways; in essentially all cases, younger players don't play 11 on 11, but play short-sided games ranging from 3 on 3 through 9 on 9. Following are general recommendations that can be used as is or further modified for youngsters playing soccer.

Penalty kick
(points to penalty area)

Corner kick
(points to corner area)

Goal kick
(points to goal area)

Timeout

(continued)

▶ Figure 31.2   Common soccer officials' signals.

Misconduct

Charging

Offside

Holding

Charging violently

Indirect goal kick

Striking

(continued)

▶ Figure 31.2 *(continued)*

Pushing

Handling ball

Tripping

Kicking

▶ Figure 31.2 (continued)

9 on 9

This is often played by 12-and-under leagues; a goalie is required for this level. Field size is 90 yards long by 45 yards wide. Ball size is 4. The goals are 2.7 yards high by 8 yards wide. Game length is four 15-minute periods. The basic rules of the game remain the same.

7 on 7

This is often played by 10-and-under leagues. Goalies are allowed but not required. Field size is 80 yards long by 40 yards wide. Ball size is 4. The goals are 2.3 yards high by 7 yards wide. Game length is four 12-minute periods. The basic rules are the same, except that in starting play and on free kicks and penalty kicks, opponents must be at least 8 yards away from the ball.

5 on 5

This is often played by 8-and-under leagues. Goalies are allowed but not required. Field size is 50 yards long by 25 yards wide. Ball size is 3. The goals are 2 yards high by 6 yards wide. Game length is four 10-minute periods. The basic rules are the same, except for these differences:

- On kickoffs, opponents must be at least 6 yards away from the ball.
- On fouls, players get direct free kicks, with opponents at least 6 yards away.
- Offside is not called.
- All kicks are direct free kicks.
- There are no penalty kicks.
- A player who fouls on the first throw-in gets a second chance.
- A goal kick is taken from any point within the goal area with opponents at least 6 yards away.
- Opponents must be at least 8 yards away on corner kicks.

3 on 3

This is often played by 6-and-under leagues. Goalies are not used. Field size is 30 yards long by 15 yards wide. Ball size is 3. The goals are

1.3 yards high by 2 yards wide. Game length is four 5-minute periods. The basic rules are the same as those for 5 on 5, with these exceptions:

- Play begins with a free kick with opponents at least 5 yards away.
- Direct free kicks are awarded for all fouls, with opponents 5 yards away.
- When the ball goes over a touch line, it is put back into play with a throw-in where the ball crossed the line.
- When a ball goes over the goal line (but is not a goal), it is kicked back into play where it crossed the line.

ORGANIZATIONS

American Youth Soccer Organization
12501 S. Isis Avenue
Hawthorne, CA 90250
800-872-2972
www.soccer.org

Cosmopolitan Soccer League
7800 River Road
North Bergen, NJ 07047
201-861-6606
www.newyorksoccer.com

Fédération Internationale de Football Association (FIFA)
FIFA House
Hitzigweg 11
P.O. Box 85
8030 Zurich, Switzerland
+41-1/384 9595

National Soccer Coaches Association of America
6700 Squibb Road, Suite 215
Mission, KS 66202
913-362-1747
www.nscaa.com

Soccer Association for Youth
4050 Executive Park Drive, Suite 100
Cincinnati, OH 45241
513-769-3800
www.saysoccer.org

United States Soccer Federation
www.ussoccer.com

32 Softball

oftball was first played in Chicago in 1887, indoors, with a 17-inch ball. An outdoor version of the game was played with a 12-inch ball in Minneapolis in 1895. The game was standardized in 1923, and today there are many variations, including fastpitch, slowpitch, 16-inch slowpitch, and coed play. These variations make softball a widely accessible sport, played by young and old alike. More than 4 million people play softball, 2.5 million of them in adult leagues.

The bulk of this chapter focuses on slowpitch rules. Most of these rules apply also to fastpitch and 16-inch slowpitch; for differences, see the "Modifications" section near the end of the chapter.

Objective: To score the most runs.

Scoring: A player scores a run when she safely touches first, second, third, and home before her team makes three outs.

Number of Players: 10 per team (11 if using an extra player, who bats but does not field; only 10 are on the field).

Number of Innings: Seven.

Number of Outs per Inning: Three outs for each team.

Overview: The defense fields 10 players. The extra player is optional, but if one is used, he must be in the starting lineup and be used for the entire game. Each team has a batting order it must adhere to, though substitutions may be made. Once a player is removed from the game, she can reenter the game once. The visiting team bats first, in the top half of the *inning;* the home team bats in the bottom half of the inning. The pitcher pitches and attempts to get the batter out; the batter attempts to get on base and eventually score. The most common ways to record outs are by strikeout, force out, tag out, and fly out.

FIELD

Figure 32.1 shows the dimensions of a softball field for adult slowpitch.

Home plate is five-sided, 17 inches wide across the edge facing the pitcher, 8.5 inches long on sides parallel to the batter's box, and 12 inches long on the sides of the point facing the catcher. *Bases* are 15 inches square, not more than 5 inches thick. A *double base,* 15 inches by 30 inches, can be used at first base. Half the base is in fair territory and is white; the other half is in foul territory and is orange. The *pitcher's plate* is 24 inches long by 6 inches wide; its front is 50 feet from the back point of home plate. The *outfield fence*

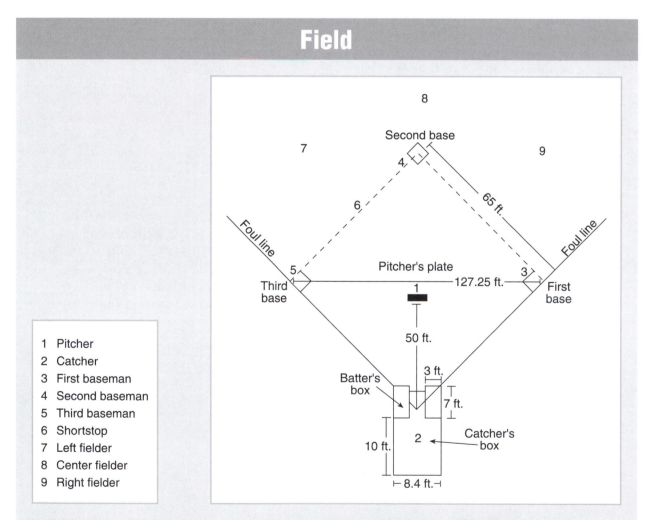

Field

1 Pitcher
2 Catcher
3 First baseman
4 Second baseman
5 Third baseman
6 Shortstop
7 Left fielder
8 Center fielder
9 Right fielder

▶ Figure 32.1   The dimensions, components, and player positions of a softball field.
Adapted from White 1990.

varies in distance, from 265 to 275 feet for women to 275 to 325 feet for men. In coed play the fences are 275 to 300 feet. A *dead ball area* is drawn with chalk outside the field of play. The line itself is in play, but if a fielder has either foot on the ground completely over the line, the ball is dead and no play can be made. If a fielder intentionally carries a live ball into the dead ball area, any runners are awarded two bases beyond the last bases they legally touched. If the act is unintentional, each runner is awarded one base.

TERMS

Note: The following list includes terms that are specific to fastpitch as well as slowpitch.

An **altered bat** is illegal. This includes inserting material inside the bat, applying more than two layers of tape to the grip, or attaching a "flare" or "cone" grip to the bat.

An **appeal play** is one in which the umpire does not have to make a decision unless requested by a coach or player. The appeal must be made before the next pitch or before the pitcher and infielders have crossed the foul line on their way to the bench.

An **assist** is credited to a fielder when her throw leads to the putout of a runner. Two or more fielders can receive assists on the same play.

A batter is credited with a **base hit** ("single") when he reaches first base safely on a hit without aid of an *error,* or by way of a fielder's choice or force play at another base.

A batter receives a **base on balls** when the umpire calls four pitches "balls" (outside the strike zone and not swung at by the batter). This allows the batter to reach first base safely. In slowpitch, the pitcher can notify the umpire if he wants to issue an intentional base on balls (also called a "walk"); the batter then may go to first base without getting any pitches.

The **base path** extends three feet on either side of a direct line between bases. A runner is out when she runs outside the base path,

except to avoid interfering with a fielder fielding a batted ball.

A **catch** means a fielder has secured the ball with his hands or glove. Regarding a catch that results in a putout—such as an outfielder catching a fly ball or a first baseman catching a throw on a force out from an infielder—the catch is good if the player has complete control of the ball but then drops it in the act of removing it from his glove or throwing it. A fly ball is not considered caught if the fielder simultaneously falls or collides with another player or the fence and the ball is dislodged.

A **chopped ball** occurs in slowpitch when the batter strikes the ball downward to bounce the ball high in the air intentionally. This is illegal and the batter is ruled out.

A **crow hop** is executed in fastpitch play by a pitcher who steps or hops off the front of the pitcher's plate, replants her pivot foot, and pushes off from this new starting point as she completes her delivery.

A **dead ball** is a ball that is not in play. A **delayed dead ball** remains live until the play is finished; at that point the proper call is made. A delayed dead ball may be called for an illegal pitch, catcher's obstruction, plate umpire interference, obstruction, or a batted or thrown ball hit with detached equipment.

A **double play** is recorded by the defense when two outs are made on the same play.

A **double** is a hit in which the batter safely reaches second base.

An **error** is charged to a fielder who misplays a ball (e.g., dropping a fly ball or throw, or fumbling a ground ball), thus prolonging an at-bat for the batter or the life of a base runner, or permitting a runner to advance one or more bases. An error may be charged even if the fielder does not touch the ball (e.g., for a ground ball that goes between the legs).

Fair territory and **foul territory** are marked by two foul lines. Each line extends from home plate. One line creates a third baseline and left field line, stopping at the left field fence; the other creates a first baseline and right field line, stopping at the right field fence. Anything on or in between the foul lines is considered fair territory; anything outside the foul lines is considered foul territory.

A **fake tag** is a form of obstruction of a runner by a fielder who neither has the ball nor is about to receive it. The umpire will award the runner the base he would have made, in the umpire's judgment, had the obstruction not occurred.

A **force play** occurs when a runner is forced to advance to the next base because the batter becomes a runner. When a batter hits a ground ball with a runner on first, the runner is forced to run to second. If a fielder touches second base with the ball in her possession before the runner reaches second, the runner is "forced out" at second. If a runner is on second when a ground ball is hit, she is not forced to advance if first base is unoccupied.

A **foul ball** is any ball hit into foul territory.

A **ground rule double** is awarded a batter when his fair ball bounces over or passes through or under the fence.

A **home run** is recorded when a batter hits a fair ball over the fence or circles the bases on an inside-the-park hit without being thrown out.

An **illegally batted ball** occurs when a ball is hit and the batter's entire foot is on the ground completely outside the lines of the batter's box, or when any part of the foot is touching home plate. It also occurs when an illegal bat is used.

The **infield** refers to that portion of the field containing the four bases. In terms of players, the infield is made up of the first, second, and third basemen and the shortstop. The pitcher and the catcher (called the "battery") also are positioned in the infield.

The **infield fly rule** prohibits an infielder from intentionally dropping a fair fly ball that can be caught with normal effort. This rule is in effect with first and second, or first, second, and third bases occupied before two are out.

When an umpire calls an infield fly rule, the batter is automatically out and runners may advance at their own risk. Any defensive player positioned in the infield at the start of the play is considered an infielder for the purpose of this rule.

Interference occurs when an offensive player impedes or confuses a defensive player as she is trying to make a play. Interference can be physical or verbal. Defensive players must be given the chance to play the ball. In fastpitch, a batter may be called for interference if he impedes the catcher in his throw on an attempted steal. A base runner may be called for interference if she is hit by a batted ball while she is not on a base and the ball has not passed an infielder, excluding the pitcher. It is not interference, however, if the batted ball was first touched by a defensive player or if no infielder had a chance to make an out on the ball.

A runner may **lead off** a base in fastpitch, once the ball has left the pitcher's hand. In slowpitch, a runner may not leave her base until the ball is batted, touches the ground, or reaches home plate, and she must return to her base if the ball is not hit.

"Leaping" is the term used in fastpitch when the pitcher goes airborne as he delivers the ball. With this delivery, the ball is released as the pitcher's feet return to the ground. This is legal in men's fastpitch, but illegal in women's fastpitch.

A **legal touch,** resulting in an out, is made by a defensive player who tags a runner with the ball while the runner is not on a base. The ball may not be juggled or dropped by the fielder, unless the runner knocks the ball from the fielder's hands or glove after the tag.

A defensive player may be called for **obstruction** if she hinders a batter from hitting the ball or impedes a base runner while the fielder does not have the ball and is not about to receive the ball.

An **out** may be recorded in a variety of ways, including strikeout, force out, tag out, and fly out.

The **outfield** is that portion of fair territory between the infield and the fence. In terms of players, the outfield consists of the left fielder, the center fielder, the right fielder, and, in slow-pitch, an extra fielder.

A batter-runner may **overslide** first base and not be put out, but a runner oversliding second or third base is in jeopardy of being tagged out.

In fastpitch, a **passed ball** is charged to the catcher when she fails to control a pitch that should have been caught or contained with normal effort and a base runner or base runners advance.

A **quick return pitch** is one made by a pitcher before the batter is set.

A batter is credited with the appropriate number of **runs batted in** (RBIs) when his hit is responsible for one or more runners' scoring. RBIs are not tallied for runs scored as a result of **errors** or if a run scores as the batter grounds into a **double play.**

A **sacrifice fly** is credited to a batter whose caught fly ball results in a runner on third base tagging up and scoring. A sacrifice fly does not count as a time at bat. A run must score for a sacrifice fly to be recorded.

In fastpitch, a runner may attempt to **steal** a base during a pitch to the batter. In slowpitch, no stealing is allowed.

A pitched ball is in a batter's **strike zone** when it is over any part of home plate between her armpits and the top of her knees in fastpitch play, or between her back shoulder and front knee in slowpitch play.

A batter is credited with a **triple** when he reaches third base safely on his hit.

A **triple play** is credited to the defense when it records three outs on the same play.

In fastpitch, a **wild pitch** occurs when a pitch eludes the catcher, allowing one or more runners to advance a base. A wild pitch is judged to be the pitcher's fault, not the catcher's. A ball that bounces in the dirt and allows any base runners to advance is automatically a wild pitch.

PLAYERS

In slowpitch, a team has 10 fielders:

- Pitcher
- Catcher
- First baseman
- Second baseman
- Third baseman
- Shortstop
- Left fielder
- Center fielder
- Right fielder
- Extra fielder

A team may also have an extra player (EP) who bats but does not field. The EP is optional, but if one is used, he must be in the starting lineup and must be used for the entire game. With an EP, all 11 players must bat, and any 10 may play defense. Defensive positions may be switched, but the batting order must remain constant.

All players, including the EP, may be replaced and may reenter the game once. The starting player and the substitute cannot be in the lineup at the same time; each player must occupy his same position in the batting order. A substitute may enter a game only once. A starting pitcher who is removed from the game may reenter the game once at any position except pitcher.

Under the *short-handed rule,* a team may start with 10 or 11 players and continue with one less player when a player leaves a game for any reason other than ejection. If the player leaving the game is a base runner, she is called out; when her turn at bat comes, an automatic out is declared. The player may not return to the lineup unless she has left for the *blood rule,* which stipulates that a player who is bleeding or who has blood on her uniform must receive appropriate treatment before continuing to play. Play may be momentarily suspended while the player receives treatment, or the player may be required to at least temporarily leave the game.

A player or coach who is ejected may stay on the bench, unless the offense is flagrant, in which case the ejected person must leave the grounds. If an ejected player continues to participate or reenters the game, the contest is forfeited to the other team.

PLAY

The basics of softball are found in the rules for pitching, batting, base running, runners advancing safely, runners being put out, and recording wins.

Pitching

The pitcher must come to a complete stop for at least one second while facing the batter and then release the ball within 10 seconds. One foot must be in contact with the pitcher's plate throughout the delivery. A pitcher may use any continuous windup but must deliver the ball on the first forward swing of the arm past the hip and toward home plate. All pitches must be thrown underhand and must reach an arc between 6 and 12 feet. The pitcher may not continue her windup after releasing the ball.

At the beginning of each half inning, and when a relief pitcher enters the game, the pitcher has one minute to complete not more than three warm-up pitches. A pitcher must be removed on the second conference in an inning. Shouting instructions from the bench is not considered a conference. A starting pitcher is credited with a win when she has pitched at least four innings and her team has a lead that it does not give up when she leaves the game. In a game shortened to five innings, the pitcher must pitch at least three innings to be credited with a victory. A pitcher is charged with a loss when he leaves the game with his team trailing, and his team fails to tie the score or gain the lead.

An umpire calls "no pitch" when play is suspended, when a runner leaves his base before the pitch reaches home or is hit, when a runner has not yet retouched her base after

a foul or dead ball, or when the ball slips from the pitcher's hand during his windup or backswing.

Batting

Players must hit in the batting order on their lineup card. The batter must stand in the batter's box (the lines are part of the box); no part of her feet may be outside the lines. The batter may not hinder the catcher from throwing while standing in the batter's box.

Batter Out

A batter is out when he swings and misses at a third strike, or fouls a third strike; when his fair or foul fly ball is caught in the air by a fielder; when, on a ground ball, a defensive player who possesses the ball touches first base before he does; or when he switches boxes after the pitcher begins to pitch.

A batter is also out when he has an entire foot on the ground out of the batter's box and he hits a fair or foul ball; when any part of his foot touches home plate and he hits a fair or foul ball; when he is caught using an illegal or altered bat; or when he bunts or chops the ball.

Other instances in which batters are out include these:

- After the batter hits the ball in fair territory, the bat strikes the ball again (unless the umpire rules this contact was unintentional).
- A batted ball in fair territory strikes the batter outside of the batter's box.
- A base runner interferes with a fielder before the batter reaches first base.
- The batter-runner runs outside the 3-foot lane after hitting a fair ball and interferes with the fielder taking the throw at first base. (The batter-runner may, however, run outside the 3-foot lane to avoid a fielder attempting to field a ball.)
- The batter-runner interferes with a fielder attempting to field the ball.
- The batter-runner rounds first base on a hit, turns toward second, and is tagged.

Base Running

A base runner must touch the bases in legal order. A runner is entitled to an unoccupied base if she reaches it before she is put out. Two runners may not occupy the same base. The runner who arrives first is entitled to the base, unless forced to advance; the other runner may be tagged out with the ball. If the first runner was forced to advance, she may be tagged out.

A run does not count if the third out is made by the batter or a runner being forced out at a base, or by a runner being tagged out before another runner touches home plate.

A runner must tag up before advancing on a caught fly ball. The runner may not leave her base until the ball is touched by the fielder. In slowpitch play, a runner may not steal. A runner hit by a batted ball is out, unless she is on a base when the ball hits her. If the closest defensive player is in front of the base the runner is on, the ball is live. If the closest defender is behind the base, the ball is dead.

Runner Advancement

A runner may advance, without the risk of being put out, when he is forced to vacate a base because the batter is walked, when a fielder is called for obstructing the runner, when the ball is overthrown (runners advance two bases from where they were when the ball left the thrower's hand), and when the ball is blocked by equipment not involved in the game (unless it is blocked by the offensive team's equipment, in which case the runner closest to home is called out).

Other situations in which runners may advance without the risk of being put out include when the batter hits an over-the-fence home run, when the batter hits a ground-rule double, when a fielder unintentionally carries a live ball into dead ball territory (one base), or when a fielder intentionally causes a live ball to go into dead ball territory (two bases).

A runner may advance, but risks being put out, when the batter hits the ball, when a fly ball is first touched, or when a fair ball strikes the umpire or another runner after having passed an infielder other than the pitcher.

A runner must return to his base when the batter hits a foul ball, when an illegal hit is declared by the umpire, when the batter or another runner is called for interference, when a pitch is not hit by the batter, or when the umpire rules that a fielder intentionally dropped a ball.

Runner Out

The runner is out when she runs out of the baseline to avoid being tagged out; when she is tagged with a live ball while not on a base; when a fielder in possession of the ball touches the base to which the runner is forced to advance; when she passes a runner ahead of her; when she leaves her base before a caught fly ball is first touched and the play is appealed; or when she misses a base and the play is appealed.

A runner is also out when she interferes with a fielder attempting to field or throw a ball; when she is hit by a batted ball while not on base; when she purposely kicks the ball or runs the bases backward to confuse the defense; or when the third-base coach runs toward home to draw a throw (the runner closest to home is out).

In addition, a runner is out when a coach or team member intentionally interferes with a thrown ball while in the coach's box; when the runner stays on her feet and deliberately crashes into a fielder who has the ball; when she leaves her base before the pitch reaches home plate, touches the ground, or is hit; or when she doesn't return immediately to her base when the pitcher receives the ball after a pitch while in the 8-foot radius of the pitcher's mound (fastpitch only).

Runner Safe

A runner is not out when he runs out of the baseline to avoid interfering with a fielder; when he is hit by a fair, untouched batted ball and the umpire rules that no fielder had a chance to make an out; when he cannot avoid contact with a fair ball that is touched by any fielder; when he is tagged with a ball that is not held securely by the fielder; and when he overruns first base and returns to the base without turning toward second.

In addition, a runner is not out when he is on base while hit by a batted ball or when he dislodges a base while sliding into it.

Recording a Win

A win may be recorded in a variety of ways:

- **Seven-inning win for the visitors:** If the visitors are ahead after seven complete innings, the game is over.

- **Seven-inning win for the home team:** If the home team is ahead after the visitors bat in the top half of the seventh inning, the game is over; if the home team scores the winning run in the bottom of the seventh, the game is over when the run scores.

- **Extra-inning victory:** A game tied at the end of seven innings goes into *extra innings* and is played until one team has scored more than the other at the end of a complete inning or until the home team scores the winning run.

- **Shortened game:** A game stopped by rain or darkness or for other reasons is considered complete if after five innings one team has scored more runs than the other team. The game is considered complete if after four and a half innings the home team has scored more runs than the visitors.

- **Forfeit:** The umpire may call a forfeit for a number of reasons, which include a team's failing to show up or refusing to begin a game, noticeably delaying or hastening the game, or willfully breaking the rules. If an ejected player does not leave within one minute, that, too, is reason to call a forfeit. The score of a forfeited game is always 7-0.

EQUIPMENT

The ball is smooth-seamed, flat-surfaced, and pebble- or dimple-textured, with concealed stitches. Its core is cork, rubber, or a polyurethane mix, covered with horsehide or cowhide. The 11-inch ball weighs between 5.9 and 6.1 ounces. The 12-inch ball weighs between 6.25 and 7 ounces.

The bat is made of hardwood, metal, graphite, or other approved material. It may not be longer than 34 inches or weigh more than 38 ounces. It may not exceed 2.25 inches in diameter. A safety grip must be between 10 and 15 inches long and not extend more than 15 inches from the bottom of the bat. Metal bats may be angular.

Gloves may be worn by any player, but only the catcher and first baseman may wear mitts, with thumb and body sections. Webbing on any glove or mitt may not exceed five inches. Pants, sliding pants, and shirts should be of the same design. Caps are optional; if they are worn, they must be of the same design. Exposed jewelry may not be worn. Shoes may have soft or hard rubber cleats or be smooth. In adult play, metal sole or heel plates may be used if the spikes do not extend more than .75 inch. Shoes with round metal spikes are illegal.

OFFICIALS

Umpires govern the game of softball. The *home plate umpire* stands behind the catcher. She controls the game and calls balls and strikes. She also calls plays involving the batter, fair and foul balls, and plays at the plate. The *base umpire* assists the home plate umpire in making calls and makes decisions at the bases. See figure 32.2 for umpires' signals.

MODIFICATIONS

The following modifications explain some of the major differences between the rules just presented and the rules for fastpitch, 16-inch slowpitch, coed, and senior play.

Fastpitch

A team has nine players, with an optional designated player (DP), who can hit for one of the nine players. If the DP plays defense for the player he's hitting for, that player is considered to have left the game. The DP can play defense for any other player, and that player can still hit.

Other differences include the following:

- **Pitching:** The pitcher's hand may go past his hip twice if there are not two com-

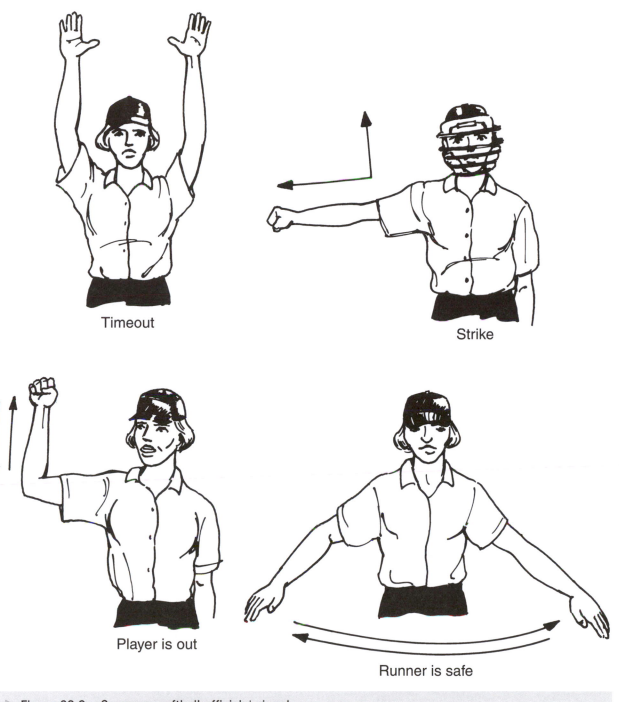

Timeout

Strike

Player is out

Runner is safe

▶ Figure 32.2 Common softball officials' signals.

plete revolutions in the windup. In men's and boys' Junior Olympic competition, the pitcher needs to have only one foot in contact with the pitcher's plate. In women's and girls' Junior Olympic competition, both feet must be in contact with the pitcher's plate.

One step must be taken forward in releasing the ball. Male adult and Junior Olympic pitchers may have both feet in the air during this step. Female adult and Junior Olympic pitchers must drag the foot or push off the pitcher's plate with the pivot foot; the leap is not legal in female competition. For both males and females, the delivery is underhanded, with the hand below the hip and the wrist not farther from the body than the elbow.

After the pitcher has taken her position, she may not throw to a base without stepping back off the pitcher's plate before throwing. Failure to step off the pitcher's plate results in a ball being called and any runners advancing one base. "No pitch" is called when the umpire judges that the pitcher is attempting to "quick pitch" a batter who is not set.

- **Ball in play:** The ball is in play when a ball or strike is called. The ball is also live during an intentional walk.

- **Batter safe:** A batter is not out on a third strike that is a foul ball, unless it is a bunt. A batter hit by a pitch—even if it bounces—that is not a strike and that he attempts to elude is awarded first base.

- **Third strike:** In Junior Olympic 10-and-under play, the batter is out on the third strike, whether the ball is caught or not.

- **Base running:** Runners must maintain contact with their bases until the ball leaves the pitcher's hand or they will be called out. Stealing is allowed at all levels except for Junior Olympic 10-and-under. In Junior Olympic 10-and-under, runners may leave base when the ball leaves the pitcher's hand but must return to the base if the ball is not hit.

A runner off her base after a pitch must advance immediately to the next base or return to her base once the pitcher has the ball within the 8-foot circle. Failure to do so results in her being called out.

Runners advance one base when the umpire calls an illegal pitch. On a wild pitch or passed ball lodged in or under the backstop, runners are entitled to advance one base.

- **Breaking ties:** In Junior Olympic girls' and women's fastpitch, if the score is tied after nine innings, the offensive team begins its half inning with the batter who had made the last out in the previous inning placed on second base.

16-Inch Slowpitch

A strike is live, but runners cannot advance. Runners may lead off their bases, but they do risk being picked off by the pitcher or catcher. They may not advance on an overthrown pick-off attempt.

Coed

The lineup consists of five males and five females, batting in alternating order. Two males and two females play in both the infield and the outfield; one male and one female split duties as pitcher and catcher. The lineups can also have two extra players (EPs), one male and one female. Any 10 players may play defense if the proper mix is kept. If a male batter is walked, whether intentionally or not, the following female batter has the option of walking also. The 11-inch ball is pitched to women; the 12-inch ball is pitched to men.

Senior

One or two EPs may be used. Unlimited *courtesy runners* are allowed; any player in the batting order may be used as a runner. A player may be used as a courtesy runner only once an inning; if it's his time at bat and he is on base, he is called out. A second home plate is placed 8 feet from the back tip of home plate, on the first base line extended. Runners must touch this second home plate. If the runner touches the original home plate, he may be called out on an appeal play. Once a runner crosses a line 20 feet from home plate, he may not return to third. He will be called out if he does so. A runner may be put out at home in a nonforce situation without being tagged; if a defensive player steps on the original home plate while holding the ball before the runner touches the second home plate, the runner is out.

ORGANIZATIONS

Amateur Softball Association/USA Softball
2801 NE 50th Street
Oklahoma City, OK 73111
www.softball.org or www.usasoftball.org

National Softball Association
P.O. Box 7
Lexington, KY 40523
859-887-4114

United States Specialty Sports Association
215 Celebration Place, Suite 180
Celebration, FL 34747
321-939-7640
www.usssa.com

© Empics

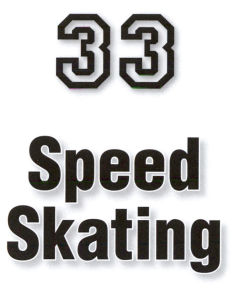

Speed Skating

Ice skates used for hunting and made of wood, bone, antlers, and leather straps first appeared in Europe in the 4th century. Iron skates were crafted in Scotland in 1572, and competitions began to take place soon after that, with racing becoming more popular across Europe in the 18th century. In 1850, the first all-steel skates were made in America, and in 1889 Netherlands hosted the first world championships. Speed skating events for men became part of the first Winter Olympics in 1924; women began Olympic competition in 1960.

Objective: To skate the fastest time.

Competitors: The number of skaters in a competition varies from two to large packs, depending on the race.

Distances: Ranges from 300 to 3,000 meters.

Overview: Skaters compete in *short-track* events, *long-track* events, *relays,* and *marathons.* They race either in packs of four to eight skaters or against one other skater. The fastest time wins in metric, or Olympic-style, racing, where no more than two skaters at a time race against the clock.

Olympic-style, long-track speed skaters reach speeds of up to 35 miles per hour; short-track speed skaters lean into the turns at a 65-degree angle to maintain speeds of up to 30 miles per hour. The world record for 10,000 meters is 27.6 miles per hour. Skaters also compete in relay and marathon competitions.

RINK

A *short-track* course is a 111.12-meter oval. A *long-track* course is a 400-meter oval. *Survey lines* (or points) define track lanes (see figure 33.1). Lines are either snowlines or blocks set on the ice for long track. The *skater's path* is considered to be .5 meter outside the survey line. This path is used in determining the distance.

The tracks have *start* and *finish lines* marked in the ice. Long-track courses also have a *fall-down mark* 10 meters beyond the starting line. Short-track courses have safety padding covering the walls around the entire ends of the rink.

TERMS

Impeding is a foul called when a skater deliberately impedes, blocks, charges, or pushes another competitor with any part of the body.

Off track is a foul called when a skater shortens the distance to be skated with one or both skates on the left side of the curve, marked by track marking blocks.

Cross track is a foul called when a skater does not stay in his or her lane and interferes with another skater.

Assistance is a foul called when a skater gives or receives assistance during a race. This does not apply to relay races.

Team skating is a foul called for any action during a race that benefits another skater. This does not apply to relay races.

Kicking out is a foul called when a skater deliberately kicks out his or her skate, thereby causing danger. This includes kicking out at the finish line and throwing the body across the finish line.

SKATERS

Skaters compete in age classes: Pony—9 years old and younger; Midget—11 and younger;

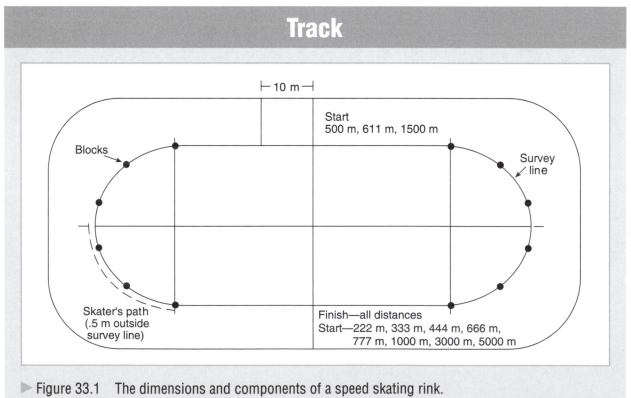

▶ Figure 33.1   The dimensions and components of a speed skating rink.
Adapted from Amateur Speedskating Union of the United States 1995.

Juvenile—13 and younger; Junior—15 and younger; Intermediate—17 and younger; Senior—18 and older; Master—30 to 39, 40 to 49, 50 to 59, and 60 to 69.

EVENTS

Speed skating events include the following:

- **Short-track:** Individual and relay events are contested on a 111.12-meter track. In individual events, four to eight skaters (the pack) start on the line; the first to cross the finish line with the leading tip of her skate blade wins. International distances for individual competitions are 500 meters, 1,000 meters, 1,500 meters, and 3,000 meters for both men and women.

- **Long-track:** Events are contested on a 400-meter oval, using one of two formats: Metric (also known as Olympic-style) or pack-style. In metric style, two skaters compete at once, in separate lanes, racing against the clock; the distances are 500 meters, 1,000 meters, 1,500 meters, 5,000 meters, and 10,000 meters for men, and 500 meters, 1,000 meters, 1,500 meters, 3,000 meters, and 5,000 meters for women. In pack-style, up to eight skaters compete at once, not confined to lanes, using drafting and race strategies.

- **Relay:** Teams of four skaters compete at varying distances; the national championship distance is 3,000 meters. Each member must take part in the race. A skater finishing a portion must touch the team member who is taking over. Relay exchanges may take place at any time except during the final two laps.

- **Marathon:** These events are contested over distances of 25 kilometers and 50 kilometers.

RACING

If a skater falls within the first 10 meters of a long-track race or the apex of the corner in a short-track race, the starter may recall the race with a second shot. If the fall was not caused by interference and does not impede other skaters, the starter won't recall the race. Falls are not called back in metric-style racing.

A skater may make one false start, after which the race will be restarted. On the second false start made by the same racer, that racer is disqualified from that event. In pack style, competitors may not cross to the inner edge of the track, except when they may do so without interfering with other skaters. Skaters must skate in a straight line once they enter the homestretch, unless they are able to change lanes without interfering with another skater.

In metric-style racing, the skater who starts on the inner track changes to the outer track at the crossing straight, and the skater starting on the outer track changes to the inner. The change in tracks occurs each time the skaters come to the crossing straight. The skater coming from the inner track may not hinder the skater coming from the outer track on the crossing straight.

In long-track races, a skater with inside or pole position must be passed on the right side, unless she leaves enough room on the left for a skater to pass. It is the responsibility of the skater who is passing to avoid collision, although the skater being passed may not act improperly and intentionally cause a collision. In short-track races, skaters may pass on the left or right side. Again, the responsibility for avoiding collision falls on the passing skater.

Skaters may be disqualified for

- impeding, blocking, charging, or pushing another skater;
- skating inside the corner markers;
- interfering with another skater by crossing to his or her path of skating;
- assisting another skater in a race or using unfair team work;
- endangering other skaters by kicking out the blade or throwing the body across the finish line;
- unsporting conduct, including foul language and fighting; and
- loafing, competing to lose, or coaching during a race.

EQUIPMENT

In short track, skaters wear safety helmets, shin guards, neck protection, gloves, and skates. There are no requirements for skates, but the boots are usually made of leather and composite materials and have steel blades of 12 to 18 inches. Long-track skates have light, low-cut boots with thin blades that are only slightly curved on the bottom. Short-track skates have sturdy, high-cut boots, with thicker, adjustable blades that have more curvature on the bottom to negotiate the sharper turns and more pronounced leans.

OFFICIALS

Large competitions include a chief referee, assistant referees, competitor stewards, starters, finish judges, timers, scorers, and a lap counter. The chief referee has overall authority, including deciding all protests.

ORGANIZATIONS

Amateur Speedskating Union of the United States
P.O. Box 450639
Westlake, OH 44145
440-889-0128
www.usspeedskating.org

34

Squash

© Empics

Variations of squash originated in England in the early 1800s, when the use of a softer ball—one that could be "squashed" by a racket—gave rise to the game's name. Squash was introduced to America in the 1880s. There are two versions of the game: one using a soft ball, and one using a harder ball and a smaller court. The international version is with the soft ball; the American version—played also in parts of Canada and Mexico—has been the hard ball version, though in the 1990s the soft ball gained in popularity in the United States, with more than 95 percent of the game in the United States being the soft ball game.

Squash's popularity has spread to numerous countries, and it is played worldwide by 15 million people, with squash courts in more than 135 countries. Recently the game has increased in popularity in South America, eastern Europe , the Far East, and the United States.

Because of the overwhelming popularity of the soft ball game, this chapter covers only the rules for the soft ball version.

Objective: To win rallies and ultimately the game by scoring more points than the opponent.

Number of Players: Two players (singles) is by far the dominant way the game is played. Doubles is occasionally played.

Scoring: In traditional play, only the server can score, and games go to 9 points. If the score reaches 8-8 the receiver may choose to call, "Set one," which means that the next player who scores wins, or "Set two," which means that the first player to reach 10 points wins. In point-a-rally (PAR) scoring, a point is scored for each rally, and games go to 15 points.

Match: A match is the best of five games.

Overview: Players hit a small rubber ball against the front wall, above the tin and within the out-of-court lines, attempting to score points by hitting the ball in such a way that the opponents cannot return it before it bounces twice. When a good serve is delivered, the opposing side attempts to return the serve. Hits continue to alternate from side to side until the rally is over. In traditional play, when the server wins rally, he scores a point; when the receiver wins a rally, she gains the serve. (In doubles and in rally play, games go to 15 points, with a point per rally.) Play is continuous throughout the game, except for equipment changes approved by the referee or for injury. There is a 90-second break between games.

COURT

The dimensions and markings of a squash court are shown in figure 34.1.

TERMS

The **board** is the lowest horizontal marking on the front wall, with the tin beneath it stretching the width of the court.

The **cut line (service line)** is a horizontal line across the front wall, 6 feet above the floor.

"Down" is the expression used when a shot strikes the tin or fails to reach the front wall.

"Game ball" means that the server needs one point to win the game.

The **half-court line** runs parallel to the side walls, dividing the court into two equal parts, intersecting the short line to form a "T."

A **hand** refers to the time during which a player has the serve.

A **handout** means that the serve is changing hands.

"Match ball" means that the server needs one point to win the match.

"Not up" is the term used when the ball has not been struck according to the rules.

The **out line** is a continuous line comprising the front wall line, both side wall lines, and the back wall line. This line marks the top boundaries of the court. Unlike in tennis, if the ball touches any part of the line, it is considered out. If there are no side wall or back wall lines, the boundaries are the tops of the walls. If a ball strikes part of the horizontal top surface of such an unlined wall, it is out, even if it rebounds into the court.

A **quarter court** is one half of the back part of the court, which is divided into two equal parts by the half-court line.

A **rally** is the play that begins with the serve and ends when the ball is no longer in play.

A **service box** is in each quarter court, bounded by the side wall, the short line, and two other lines. The server serves from this box.

The **short line** is parallel to and 18 feet from the front wall.

The **striker** is the player whose turn it is to hit the ball.

A **stroke** is gained by the player who wins a rally. A stroke results in either a point scored for the server or a change of hand.

Court

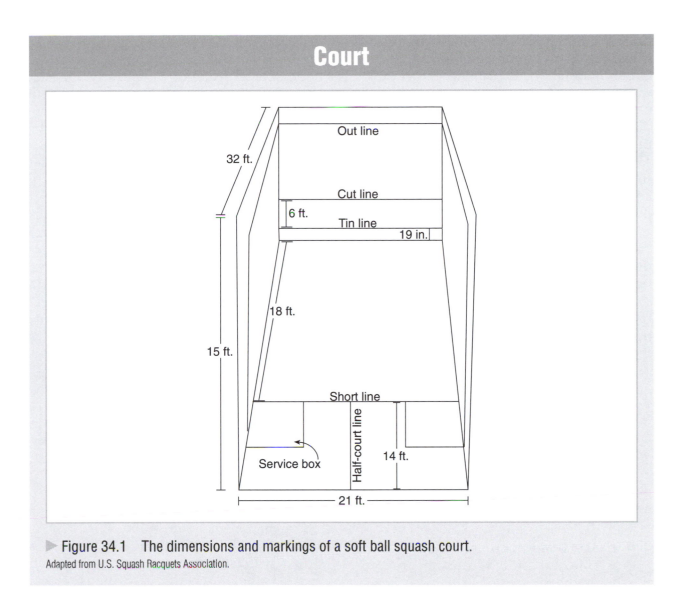

Out line

32 ft.

Cut line

6 ft.

Tin line

19 in.

18 ft.

15 ft.

Short line

Service box

Half-court line

14 ft.

21 ft.

▶ Figure 34.1   The dimensions and markings of a soft ball squash court.
Adapted from U.S. Squash Racquets Association.

The **tin** is between the board and the floor, running the length of the floor. It makes a distinctive noise when the ball hits it. It is 19 inches tall (17 inches in professional matches).

PLAYERS

Players may be coached only during intervals between games. A referee may penalize a player for a number of behaviors, including offensive or intimidating behavior, obscene language and gestures, abuse of rack)et or ball, arguing with the marker or referee, unnecessary physical contact, excessive racket swing, and dangerous play.

PLAY

The fundamental rules of squash are found in its rules for serving and for playing out rallies.

Serving

At the beginning of a game and when a receiver becomes a server, the server may choose to serve from either service box (see figure 34.1). Part of one foot must be on the floor in the service box, with no part of the foot touching the service box line, when the server strikes the ball. The server drops or throws the ball to begin the serve. The served ball may not hit any surface before striking the front wall. It must strike the front wall between the cut line and the out line so that it reaches the floor within the quarter court opposite the server's box (unless volleyed by the opponent).

A server who drops or throws the ball and then does not attempt to hit it may serve again. A server continues to serve until he loses a stroke. As long as he holds serve, he alternates boxes. If a rally ends in a let (an undecided point), he serves again from the same box.

In singles play, when a player loses the serve, the serve passes to the receiver. In doubles play, the first side to serve in a game gets only one server. Once that rally is lost, the serve switches to the opposing team. From there on, each side gets two servers; when the second server loses the serve, the serve goes to the opponents. At the beginning of the second and subsequent games, the winner of the previous game serves first. A server "serves her hand out" (loses her serve) when

- her serve first hits a side wall, floor, or ceiling;
- part of one foot is not on the floor in the server's box, with no part of that foot on the box line, when she strikes the ball; or
- the ball bounces on or outside the short or half-court line of the quarter court opposite the service box.

A serve is also lost when a server

- attempts and fails to hit a serve,
- does not strike the ball correctly (e.g., hits the ball more than once or carries the ball with the racket),
- serves the ball out,
- serves onto or below the cut line, or
- is struck by his own serve before the opponent can strike at it.

Rallies

A good serve may be returned before the ball strikes the ground or after it bounces once. It must hit the front wall above the board before touching the ground. It may not touch any part of the striker's body or clothing, or any part of the opponent's body, clothing, or racket.

If a striker hits an opponent with the ball, the striker wins the stroke if the return would have struck the front wall without first touching any other surface. The exception is if the striker has followed the ball around and turned to strike the ball to the right of his body after it has passed to his left, or vice versa—that is, the striker turns to hit the ball to the front wall after it has already passed him and struck the back wall. This is an example of "turning," and while the rules do not specifically prohibit turning, it is deemed a dangerous maneuver, because the striker loses sight of his opponent. Players are strongly encouraged to call "let" in this case. If a player does strike a ball while turning and the ball strikes the opponent, it's the opponent's point.

If a striker hits an opponent with the ball, and the ball struck another wall before striking the front wall, a let is called, unless the referee believes the return would have won the rally. In the latter case, the striker is awarded the stroke. If the return would not have been good, and it strikes an opponent, the striker loses the rally, or "no let" is awarded to the striker.

A striker may make contact only once on a return but may make any number of attempts to hit the ball before it bounces twice. If a striker swings and misses at a ball, which then hits the opponent, her clothing, or her racket, the referee will call a let if he believes the striker could have made a good return. The striker loses the stroke if the referee believes she could not have made a good return.

The outgoing striker must make every effort to allow the incoming striker a clear path to the ball. It is also the incoming striker's responsibility to make every effort to get to the ball.

To avoid interference, a player must make every effort to provide his opponent with unobstructed, direct access to the ball; a fair view of the ball; and freedom to hit the ball directly to the front wall. If interference is called, the play is a let, or a stroke is awarded to the offended player. A let is not allowed if the player would not have made a good return, if he did not make adequate effort to get to and play the ball, if he created his own interference, or if he clearly accepted the interference and played on.

A let is always allowed if one player refrains from striking the ball due to a reasonable fear of striking her opponent with the ball or with the racket. This is the case even if no interference actually occurred.

The referee will award a stroke to a player if the opponent does not make every effort to avoid interfering and the player would have made a good return. A stroke is also awarded if the player would have made a winning return, even if the opponent makes every effort to avoid interfering. The referee may also award a stroke to a player if her opponent makes unnecessary physical contact with her or endangers her with an excessive racket swing.

In addition to previous mentions of lets, rallies are replayed when

- the striker doesn't hit the ball in a manner to ensure the safety of his opponent,
- a player is distracted by an occurrence on or off the court,
- the receiver is not ready for the serve and doesn't attempt to return it,
- the ball breaks during play, or
- court conditions affect play.

A player may appeal a decision that affects the rally by saying, "Let, please." The referee stops play and decides on the appeal. Penalties that the referee may levy include a warning, and a stroke, game, or match awarded to the opponent.

EQUIPMENT

The ball has a diameter of 1.5 inches and weighs 12.7 to 13.4 ounces. It is made of rubber or butyl, or a combination; it's hollow and, appropriately enough, "squashy." Rackets are commonly made from titanium and graphite composites. They may be no longer than 27 inches; the stringed area may not be larger than 8.5 inches long by 7.25 inches wide. When the ball is not in play, another ball may be substituted for it, upon mutual consent by the players or upon an appeal by one player to the referee.

OFFICIALS

A referee controls the match, sometimes assisted by a marker. The referee makes all major calls and decisions; the marker calls the play, calls the score, and calls faults, "downs," "outs," and "handouts."

ORGANIZATIONS

United States Squash Racquets Association
P.O. Box 1216
23 Cynwyd Road
Bala Cynwyd, PA 19004
610-667-4006
www.us-squash.org

35
Swimming and Diving

The origins of swimming as a sport are not known, though swimming championships were first held in Japan in the early 1600s. For a race in London in 1844, England's Swimming Society brought over several American Indians; these Native Americans dominated the race using a style unknown to the English, a style resembling today's freestyle stroke. Swimming has been an Olympic sport since the inception of the modern Olympics in 1896.

Diving as a sport consisted of what is now known as the forward straight dive until the early 1800s, when Swedish and German gymnasts began performing acrobatic twists, turns, and jumps off the board. Diving became an Olympic sport for men in 1904 and for women in 1912. The United States has long been successful in international competition, though in the 1990s China emerged and is quite successful internationally as well. Synchronized diving made its debut at the Sydney Games in 2000.

Objective: In swimming, the objective is to record the fastest time; in diving, it is to receive the highest score from judges.

Swimming Distances: Numerous distances, ranging from 50 to 1,500 meters.

Diving Heights: Competitions are conducted from 1-meter and 3-meter springboards, as well as from 5-meter, 7.5-meter, and 10-meter platforms.

Overview: In swimming, both individual and relay races are contested over varying distances, using one stroke or a combination of strokes. Strokes used are the breaststroke, the butterfly, the backstroke, and the freestyle. In team competitions, swimmers earn points for their teams according to where they place in finishing.

In diving, several components of the dive are judged. Each dive has a degree of difficulty rating, which is multiplied by the judges' scores to obtain a total point award for the dive. Divers perform a series of dives in various body positions, with different degrees of difficulty, depending on the level of competition.

SWIMMING

Swimmers are seeded in preliminary heats according to their fastest times. The fastest swimmers in each heat are placed in center lanes of the pool. In finals heats, the slowest swimmers swim first and the fastest swimmers swim last. Swimmers who record the same time tie for that event.

To begin a race, competitors are called to their *starting blocks*. After the referee's whistle, swimmers "take their mark." When they are motionless, the starter signals the start by shooting a gun or sounding a horn. If a swimmer leaves too early, he will be disqualified at the end of the race. A swimmer is not charged with a false start if it was caused by the motion of another swimmer.

Competitors must stay in their own lanes. Swimmers may be disqualified for swimming out of their lanes or otherwise obstructing other swimmers. Grabbing lane dividers to assist forward motion is prohibited. A swim- mer is disqualified for standing on the bottom of the pool, except during a freestyle race. A swimmer may not walk or spring from the bottom of the pool or leave the pool. A swimmer who is not entered in a race but enters the pool while a race is under way is disqualified from the next event in which he was scheduled to participate. A swimmer may not compete in more than three individual events per day in a preliminaries and finals meet. In a timed finals meet, a swimmer may not compete in more than five events per day.

Pool

A long-course pool is 50 meters long; a short-course pool is 25 meters or yards long (see figure 35.1). The minimum lane width is 2.13 meters. For championship competitions the water depth is 2 meters.

Pool-bottom lane markers, 10 inches wide, mark the middle of each lane. These markers terminate in a "T" 2 meters from the pool wall. End-wall targets, in the shape of a "T," are in the center of the wall at the end of each lane, extending at least 1 meter below the surface.

Lanes are numbered from right to left as swimmers stand facing the pool. Lanes are separated by floating lane dividers with a diameter of 5 to 11 centimeters. The color of the floats from the wall to 5 meters out are different from the color for the rest of the course.

The *starting platforms* for a long-course pool are between .5 and .75 meter above the water. For a short-course pool, they're no higher than .75 meter above the water. The front edge of the platforms are flush with the wall. The top surfaces of the platforms are square, at least .5 by .5 meter, and covered with a nonslip material.

Backstroke starting grips are between 1 and 2 feet above water. The front edge of the grips is parallel with the water and flush with the face of the end wall. Three triangular *backstroke flags* are placed 5 meters from each end of the course, anywhere from 1.8 to 2.5 meters above the water.

A *recall rope* is used to recall swimmers after a false start. The rope is dropped about 11 meters from the start in a short-course pool and 15 meters in a long-course pool. Water tem-

Pool

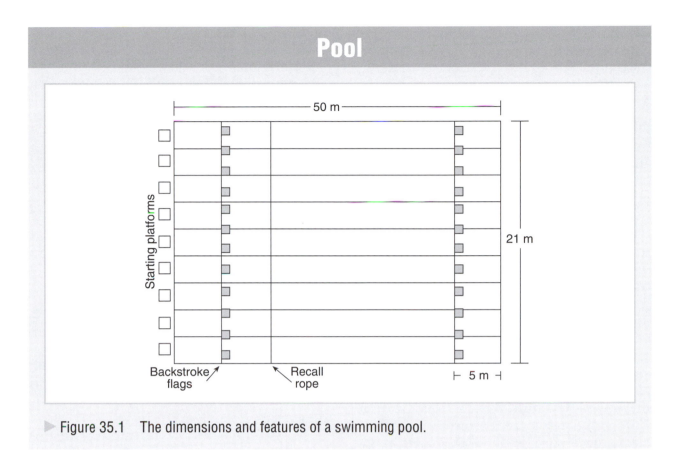

▶ Figure 35.1   The dimensions and features of a swimming pool.

perature is to be maintained at 78 to 80 degrees Fahrenheit (26 to 27 degrees Celsius).

Terms

Body refers to the torso, including the shoulders and hips.

A **forward start** is a forward entry taken facing the water.

Heats are competitions used to pare the field to a manageable number for a final event.

A **lane** is the area in which each swimmer swims. Lanes are separated by **lane lines,** which are floating markers, and are marked on the bottom of the pool by **lane markings.**

Long-course refers to events held in 50-meter pools.

Short-course refers to events held in 25-meter or 25-yard pools.

Timed finals are competitions in which heats are swum and final placements are determined by times recorded in the heats.

Breaststroke

Swimmers use a forward start from blocks. In the water, both shoulders must be in line with the water surface, and the arms must move in the same horizontal plane. The hands are pushed forward together from the breast, and brought back under the water's surface; the elbows must be underwater, except for the final stroke. The hands may not be brought beyond the hips, except during the first stroke after the start and after each turn. At least part of the swimmer's head must break the water's surface at least once on each complete stroke cycle, except after the start and turns, during which the swimmer may take one complete arm stroke and leg kick while submerged. The feet should be turned outward during the propelling part of the kick; scissors, flutters, or downward butterfly kicks are not permitted.

At turns, a swimmer must touch the wall with both hands at, above, or below the surface. Once the touch is made, a swimmer may complete the turn in any way he desires. At the finish, a swimmer must touch the wall with both hands at, above, or below the water surface.

Butterfly

The swimmer uses a forward start and keeps her shoulders in line with the water's surface and at or past the vertical toward her breast on each stroke. She may use only one arm pull underwater per stroke, but she may use two dolphin kicks. She must bring both arms forward, over the water, and pull them back together. The legs must kick in unison. A swimmer may not use a scissors or breast-stroke kick.

At turns, the body should be on the breast. Both hands must touch the wall simultaneously at, above, or below the surface. After the touch, the swimmer may complete the turn any way she wants. Her shoulders must be at or past vertical toward the breast when she leaves the wall. At the finish, she must touch the wall with both hands simultaneously at, above, or below the surface, with her shoulders in line with the surface.

Backstroke

The swimmer begins in the pool, pulling himself toward the starting block, facing the starting end. The feet must be under the water to start. The swimmer pushes off on his back. Part of the swimmer's body must break the water's surface throughout the race, except during the turns. At the start and during turns, a swimmer may be underwater for up to 15 meters.

To make a turn, some part of the swimmer's body must touch the wall. A swimmer may use a single or double arm pull to begin the turn. Upon leaving the wall, the swimmer must return to a position on his back. He finishes the race by touching the wall while on his back.

Freestyle

A swimmer uses a forward start. Any style of stroke may be used. To make a turn, a swimmer must touch the wall; to complete the race, the swimmer must touch the wall at the prescribed distance.

Individual Medley

This event consists of four equal portions, with strokes used in this order: butterfly, backstroke, breaststroke, and freestyle. Swimmers use a forward start and must complete each portion according to the rules for the appropriate strokes. When changing from one stroke to the next, the swimmer follows the turn rules for the stroke just completed, except for the backstroke, where a swimmer must touch the wall as if she were finishing a backstroke race. As with the freestyle finish, a swimmer completes this race when any part of her body touches the final wall.

Relays

In a *freestyle relay*, four swimmers each swim one-quarter of the distance, using the freestyle rules. In a *medley relay*, four swimmers each swim one-quarter of the distance, with the first swimmer using the backstroke; the second, breaststroke; the third, butterfly; and the fourth, freestyle.

No swimmer may swim more than one leg in a relay. Each swimmer must touch the touchplate or pad in his lane before his teammate begins. A team is disqualified for violating this rule.

Scoring

In *dual meets*, scoring for individual events is on a 5-3-1-0 basis; that is, the winner gets 5 points, the swimmer placing second gets 3 points, the third-place swimmer gets 1 point, and all other competitors get no points. Scoring for relays is on a 7-0 basis. For *triangular meets*, scoring for individual events is on a 6-4-3-2-1-0 basis; for relays, it's 8-4-0. Scoring for most other meets, with point values doubled for relay events, is as follows:

- 4-lane pools—5-3-2-1
- 5-lane pools—6-4-3-2-1
- 6-lane pools—7-5-4-3-2-1
- 7-lane pools—8-6-5-4-3-2-1
- 8-lane pools—9-7-6-5-4-3-2-1
- 9-lane pools—10-8-7-6-5-4-3-2-1
- 10-lane pools—11-9-8-7-6-5-4-3-2-1

In case of a tie between swimmers, the points for the tied place and the following place are added and divided in two; each swimmer is credited with the same points. For example, in a 10-lane pool, two swimmers tying for first would receive 10 points each (11 for first, 9 for second; divide that total of 20 by 2).

Equipment

Races are timed with automatic, semiautomatic, or manual timing systems. Automatic systems are activated by electric impulse and stopped when the swimmer touches the touchpad. Semiautomatic systems are activated by electric impulse and stopped by timers pushing buttons when racers finish. Manual timing is usually done with handheld stopwatches.

Officials

Officials include a referee, a starter, and a stroke or turn judge. Three timers per lane are used; they are presided over by a timing judge. Other officials, in applicable situations, include place judges and relay takeoff judges.

DIVING

The order of diving is decided by random draw. The diver's name, the dive, and its degree of difficulty are announced before each dive. After each dive, on a signal from the referee, each of the judges, without communicating with any other judge, immediately and simultaneously flashes her award.

A diver may not perform a dive other than that announced (doing so will result in a failed dive, with no score awarded) or repeat the same dive, even in a different body position.

In competitions other than national championships, a diver may elect not to perform a dive and take no points. This is to ensure the safety of the participants.

Pool

The competition *springboard* is made of flexible material and a nonskid surface. It is 20 inches wide and 16 feet long, and set at either 1 or 3 meters above the water's surface. Three-meter springboards should have guard rails extending to at least the pool's edge; boards should project at least 1.5 meters, and preferably 1.8 meters, beyond the pool's edge and over the water.

The *platform* is solid and nonflexible and has a nonslip surface. It is at least 20 feet long and 6.5 feet wide. The platform height is 10 meters; intermediate platforms can be set from 5 to 7.5 meters. For synchronized diving events, the 10-meter-high platform should be at least 8 feet wide, and preferably 10 feet. The water depth varies, depending on the height of the platform.

Terms

A **diving list** contains the dives to be performed by the diver in a competition.

A **draw** is performed by judges to select the order of the divers.

Preliminaries are the first round, or series, of dives in a contest. Some divers advance from preliminaries and some do not.

Quarterfinals are sometimes used after a preliminary round to advance divers to a semifinal round.

A diver **scratches** from the competition when he withdraws.

Semifinals are the portion of the contest between preliminaries and finals. Only a certain number of divers advance through the semifinal round to the finals.

Dives

There are six types of dives that may be performed.

1. **Forward dive:** The diver begins facing forward toward the water and rotates toward the water.
2. **Backward dive:** The diver begins standing backward on the end of the springboard or platform and rotates toward the water.
3. **Reverse dive:** The diver begins facing forward toward the water and rotates toward the springboard or platform.

4. **Inward:** The diver begins standing backward on the end of the springboard or platform and rotates toward the springboard or platform.

5. **Armstand dive:** The diver begins from a handstand on the end of the platform; this dive is performed only in platform diving.

6. **Twisting dive:** The diver includes a twist in any of the above five groups of dives; this is the largest group of dives.

Divers may execute dives in four body positions:

1. *Straight*—no bending at the knees or hips; feet together and toes pointed

2. *Pike*—bent at the hips with legs straight; feet together and toes pointed

3. *Tuck*—bent at the hips and knees; feet and knees together and toes pointed

4. *Free*—any combination of the other three positions when executing a twisting dive

Three categories of dives may be performed, and the requirements for each are specified by the level of competition:

1. **Required dives:** A specific dive or body position—or both—is designated. All divers in the contest must perform a required dive.

2. **Voluntary with limit dives:** Divers perform a number of dives from different groups. The dive choice is up to the diver, but the total degree of difficulty of all dives cannot exceed a predetermined limit.

3. **Voluntary without limit dives:** The diver performs a number of dives from different groups; there is no limit on the total degree of difficulty. These dives are commonly referred to as "optional" dives.

Scoring

A dive is judged on five parts:

1. *Approach*—the walk or run to the end of the springboard or platform; this begins

forward, reverse, and some twisting dives

2. *Takeoff*—springing and jumping from the end of the springboard or platform to begin a dive

3. *Elevation*—the amount of height in the air achieved after takeoff

4. *Execution*—the technique and grace in the air

5. *Entry*—the angle of entry, which should be vertical; the straightness of the body; and the amount of splash

Judges award points in half-point increments based on the following scale:

- Very good—8 1/2 to 10 points
- Good—6 1/2 to 8 points
- Satisfactory—5 to 6 points
- Deficient—2 1/2 to 4 1/2 points
- Unsatisfactory—1/2 to 2 points
- Completely failed—0 points

When nine judges are on hand, the two highest and two lowest scores are thrown out. When seven judges are used, the high and low scores are thrown out. In either case, the sum of the remaining scores is multiplied by the degree of difficulty and then by .6 to obtain the equivalent of a three-judge score. When five judges are used, the high and low scores are eliminated and the sum of the remaining three scores is multiplied by the dive's degree of difficulty.

Judging

The starting position for dives with an approach is assumed when the diver is ready to take the first step. For standing dives, the starting position is assumed when the diver stands still on the front end of the springboard with head erect and body and arms straight.

If the diver begins her approach or press and stops, she has committed a balk. She may move her arms preparatory to her approach or press without a balk being called. The first balk results in two points being deducted from each judge's score. A second balk on the same dive results in a failed dive. Any action before the diver takes the starting position does not count.

The forward approach should be smooth, straight, and graceful, and take not less than three steps and a hurdle. The takeoff for the "hurdle"—the jump to the end of the springboard—must be from one foot only.

In running dives, the takeoff from the springboard must be from both feet simultaneously.

Springboard dives with a forward takeoff may be performed either standing or with an approach.

In running platform dives, the diver must take at least three steps and a hop for a two-foot takeoff, and at least four steps for a one-foot takeoff. Two points will be deducted from each judge's score for violations.

On a backward or standing front dive, the diver must not bounce on the board or rock it excessively before takeoff. Doing so will result in a deduction of not more than two points from each judge, at the individual judge's discretion.

Touching the end of the board or diving to the side during the execution of the dive will result in a deduction of points, up to the discretion of each judge. While the diver is in the air, the judges look for the following: In the straight position, points are deducted if the knees or hips are bent; in the pike position, the pike should be as compact as possible (the legs must be straight).

In the tuck position, the tuck should be as compact as possible. One to two points will be deducted for opening the knees. In the free position, any combination of the three other positions must conform to the criteria of those positions. A twist dive is considered failed if the twist is greater or less than 90 degrees of the announced twist.

As described earlier, the entry into the water for all dives must be vertical, with the body straight and the toes pointed. On head-first entries, the arms should be stretched beyond the head in a line with the body, with the hands close together. If any part of the body below the waist enters the water before the hands, the dive is considered failed. On feet-first entries, the arms should be held close to the body, without bending at the elbows. (Novice divers performing certain dives are allowed to hold their arms straight overhead.)

Officials

A referee is in charge of the competition and oversees the judges (typically three for dual meets and five for regional meets). A secretary oversees the scoring table and verifies the results. The scoring table may consist of three or more recorders.

ORGANIZATIONS

United States Diving, Inc.
201 S. Capitol Avenue, Suite 430
Indianapolis, IN 46225
317-237-5252
www.usdiving.org

United States Swimming
1 Olympic Plaza
Colorado Springs, CO 80909
719-866-4578
www.usswim.org

United States Masters Swimming
800-550-SWIM
www.usms.org

36

Synchronized Swimming

© W. Lynn Seldon

Australian Annette Kellerman attracted national attention by performing water ballet at the New York Hippodrome in 1907. The sport of synchronized swimming began in Canada in the 1920s and came to the United States in the 1930s (the first collegiate competition was in 1939). Synchronized swimming was an Olympic demonstration sport from 1948 to 1968 and became a full medal Olympic sport in 1984. Canada and the United States have dominated international competitions, though Russia, Japan, China, France, and Italy have advanced significantly. Today more than 80 nations on six continents compete in the sport.

234 THE SPORTS RULES BOOK

Objective: To receive the highest score from the panel of judges.

Number of Competitors: Varies, depending on the event; synchronized swimmers compete in solo, duet, trio, and team events.

Scoring: The range is from 0 to 10, based on technical merit and artistic impression.

Overview: Synchronized swimmers perform figures and technical and free routines. *Routines* consist of any figures, strokes, swimming, and propulsion techniques. Technical routines consist of specific elements performed by all competitors at the same time; *figures* are normally performed in a relatively stationary position. Technical routines are used as preliminary events at the U.S. National and U.S. Open championships. The scores earned for figures go toward the total score, which includes the technical merit score of the routine, the artistic impression of the routine, any bonus points, and any penalty points subtracted. The highest score wins.

In larger events, preliminaries and semifinals in routine competition are held first, followed by figure competition and then the finals in routine competition.

TERMS

Note: Most of these terms refer to figure positions.

In a **back layout position,** the body extends on the back with the face, chest, thighs, and feet at the surface.

In a **ballet leg position,** the body and one leg are extended on a horizontal line either at or beneath the surface, with the other leg extended vertically, and with the water level at the ankle or as high as possible on the thigh.

In a **crane position,** the body and one leg are perpendicular to the surface with the other leg extended parallel to the surface.

In a **flamingo position,** one leg extends perpendicular to the surface and the other draws toward the chest, with the midcalf opposite the vertical leg and the foot and knee at and parallel to the surface.

In a **front layout position,** the body extends horizontally on the belly with the head, upper back, buttocks, and heels at the surface.

In a **front pike position,** the hips are bent to form a 90-degree angle, with the legs together and fully extended at the surface. The head is extended in line with the trunk toward the bottom of the pool.

In a **split position,** both legs are fully extended at the surface, evenly split forward and backward with the feet and thighs at the surface. The lower back is arched, with hips, shoulders, and head on a vertical line.

In a **tuck position,** the body is as compact as possible, heels pressed to buttocks, back rounded, knees to face, and legs together.

COMPETITORS

Competitors may compete in the following classifications: senior (14 years old and older); junior (14 to 18); and age groups (11 and under, 12-13, 14-15, 16-17, 18-19).

Competition is also conducted for designated skill levels, such as novice and intermediate. Competition is divided geographically (local, regional, zone, and national) to provide progressive opportunities for swimmers to qualify for each succeeding level. The rules for championships conducted at the local level may have minor adjustments to meet the needs of the participants.

COMPETITION

Competitions are composed of various figures and routines, with penalties figuring into the composite scores.

Figures

Figures are combinations of specific and precise movements ranging in degrees of difficulty from 1.1 to 3.5. There are four categories of figures: Ballet Leg, Dolphin, Somersault, and Diverse.

Figure competition is included in the program at all U.S. events (except nationals), but it is excluded at many international events, including the Olympic Games and the World Aquatic Championships. Figures are performed individually, without music, before panels of trained judges, and are designed to determine the swimmer's ability to control movement and demonstrate balance, coordination, flexibility, and timing.

Each swimmer is required to perform the same 4 of a possible 20 figures. Those 4 figures are drawn 18 to 48 hours prior to the figure competition. Competitors must, therefore, be able to perform all 20 figures. For some competitions the 4 figures are preselected, and particular age groups, skill levels, and special programs—such as novice, 11 and under, collegiate, and masters—have specified required figures that are known throughout the season.

Judges, seated together in panels, individually award points from 0 to 10, in one-tenth of a point increments, as follows:

- Perfect—10.0 points
- Near perfect—9.5 to 9.9 points
- Excellent—9.0 to 9.4 points
- Very good—8.0 to 8.9 points
- Good—7.0 to 7.9 points
- Competent—6.0 to 6.9 points
- Satisfactory—5.0 to 5.9 points
- Deficient—4.0 to 4.9 points
- Weak—3.0 to 3.9 points
- Very weak—2.0 to 2.9 points
- Hardly recognizable—0.1 to 1.9 points
- Completely failed—0 points

Each individual performance is measured from the standpoint of perfection in design and control, as detailed in the figure description. Design is the assessment of the swimmer's precise definition of positions, the degree of full extension of the body and limbs, and the path of movement from one position to another. Control factors include the swimmer's stability, the support of weight above the water, the water lines achieved, and how smoothly and easily the figure is performed.

To determine the figure score for each competitor, the score for each of the four figures performed is determined by first dropping the highest and lowest scores awarded, then averaging the remaining scores and multiplying the result by that figure's assigned degree of difficulty. The four figure scores are then added together, divided by the degree of difficulty of the group of figures, and multiplied by 10 to obtain the final figure score. For duet, trio, and team events, the figure scores of the competitors performing the routine are averaged to determine the figure score for that routine.

Routines

There are four routine events recognized internationally: solo, duet (two swimmers), team (four to eight swimmers), and free combination. U.S. championships usually include a trio (three swimmers) event.

Routine competition takes two different forms: the free and the technical programs. One or both may be included in a competition. The free program has no restrictions concerning music or choreography. The technical program contains at least five required elements, must be performed by all members simultaneously, and is shorter in length.

Scores are given for each routine in two categories: technical merit and artistic impression. Judges, seated at various vantage points around the pool, award points from 0 to 10.0 in one-tenth of a point increments. There are two panels of five judges, each judging one category, or one panel of five to seven judges, with each awarding scores for both categories.

The *technical merit score* is based upon execution, synchronization, and difficulty. The *artistic impression score* is based upon choreography, music interpretation, and manner of presentation. The scoring range is the same as for figures; swimmers who fail are given a 0.

The highest and lowest scores are canceled. The remaining scores are added, multiplied by 5, and divided by the number of judges to arrive at a final score.

Time requirements for free senior routines are three minutes for a solo, three-and-a-half minutes for a duet or trio, and four minutes for a team. A variation of 15 seconds over or under the requirement is allowed. Time allowances are reduced for younger and less-skilled competitors; developmental routines have no minimum time. A maximum of 10 seconds is allowed for deck movements, known as "deck work." The timing begins and ends with the accompaniment and the timing of the deck work ends when the last competitor enters the water. The competitors must perform the routine without stopping, and the routine must end in the water.

Penalties

Penalties are rarely assessed, but they may be administered by the referee for rules infractions of the particular event, and for deviation from or omission of designated movements. Penalties begin at a half point and can reach a maximum of five points for swimming out of order in a routine or in figures. Following are examples of one-point penalties:

- Failing to begin or finish with the accompaniment
- Exceeding 10 seconds for deck movements
- Exceeding the specified routine maximum or minimum time limits
- Interrupting deck movements to begin again (unless of technical nature)
- Not ending a routine in the water
- Deliberately walking on the pool bottom or using the pool bottom to assist another swimmer (one point per infraction, up to two points possible)
- Deliberately touching the pool deck (one point per infraction, up to two points possible)

Composite Score

When only two events are included in the competitive program, the figure *or* the technical routine score and the free routine score from the preliminary swim are added together to determine who will advance to the finals. The score for the preliminary free routine swim is dropped and replaced by the final free routine swim to determine the winners. The figures or technical routine are weighted 50 percent and the free routine is weighted 50 percent to determine the final score.

When three events (the figures, technical routine, and free routine) are included, the figures are weighted 25 percent, the technical routine 25 percent, and the free routine 50 percent to determine final placement.

OFFICIALS

Up to ten judges score routines. An event referee has full jurisdiction over the event.

ORGANIZATIONS

United States Synchronized Swimming
201 S. Capital, Suite 901
Indianapolis, IN 46225
317-237-5700
www.usasynchro.org

Table Tennis

© Sport the Library/SportsChrome

Table tennis, originally known as ping-pong, is believed to have been developed in England in the late 1800s or early 1900s. The sport is growing in popularity in the United States, but for decades the players from Asian and European countries have been dominant. Today the sport attracts more than 40 million competitive players worldwide and numbers many millions more who play the sport recreationally.

Objective: To score points by hitting the ball across the net and onto the opponent's side of the table without the opponent's being able to return the ball.

Number of Players: Two (singles) or four (doubles).

Length of Games and Matches: The first side to score 11 points wins—unless the score is tied at 10. Then the side that gets ahead by 2 points wins. A match is the best of any odd number of games. Most tournament matches are best of five or best of seven games. Doubles matches are normally the best of five.

Scoring: A point is awarded for good hits not returned and in other circumstances (see "Scoring" on page 240).

Overview: In singles, the server serves, the receiver returns, and the two continue to alternate hits until a point is scored. In doubles, the server serves, the receiver returns, the partner of the server returns, and the partner of the receiver returns. That sequence continues until a point is scored. In singles, after every two points, the server becomes the receiver, and the receiver becomes the server. In doubles, each player gets two serves at a time, in this repeating order:

- Player 1, team A (serving to player 1, team B)

- Player 1, team B (serving to player 2, team A)

- Player 2, team A (serving to player 2, team B)

- Player 2, team B (serving to player 1, team A)

PLAYING AREA

The *table* is 9 feet long and 5 feet wide (see figure 37.1). The playing surface is 30 inches above the floor. It may be made of any material that produces a uniform bounce. Normally the surface is dark green or blue, with a white line along each edge, forming two *side lines* and two *end lines*. For doubles, a *center line* divides each court in half; the center line is regarded as part of each right-half court.

The *playing surface* includes the top edges of the table, but not the sides below the edge. The *net* is 6 feet long and 6 inches above the playing surface, along its complete length. The *minimum playing space* should be 40 feet long, 20 feet wide, and 11.5 feet high. The *floor* should be of hard, nonslippery wood.

TERMS

A **let** is a rally that is not scored.

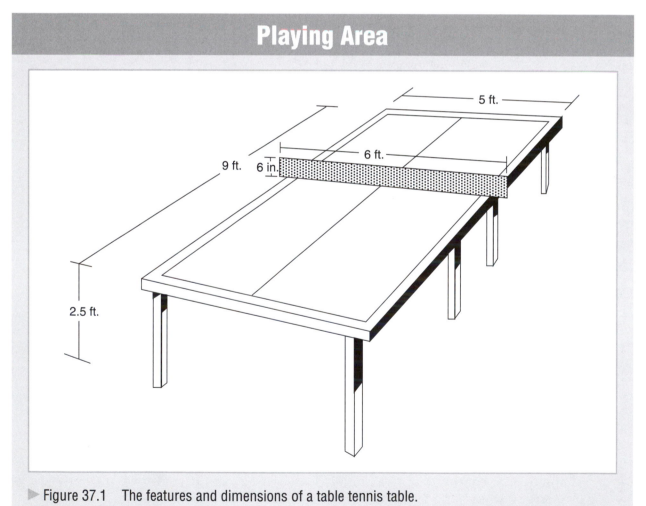

Playing Area

▶ Figure 37.1   The features and dimensions of a table tennis table.
Adapted from USA Table Tennis 1990.

The **net assembly** includes the net, the supporting cord, and the brackets and clamps.

Obstruction occurs when a player or a player's racket or clothing touches the ball in play when it is over his court or heading toward his court, and when it has not touched his court since last being struck by his opponent.

A **rally** describes the time during which the ball is in play.

The **receiver** is the player who strikes the ball second in a rally.

The **server** is the player who strikes the ball to begin the rally.

The **stroke counter** is the person who counts strokes under the expedite system.

PLAYERS

Players typically wear a short-sleeved shirt, shorts or skirt, socks, and soft-soled shoes. Clothing may be of any color, but the main color must be different from that of the ball in use.

PLAY

Play is continuous, although a player may ask for a one-minute break between games. The referee may stop play for up to 10 minutes for an incapacitated player if the delay does not disadvantage the opposing player or team. Brief pauses at the end of every six points may be taken to towel off or for similar purposes.

Players or teams change ends at the end of every game. In the final game, sides change ends when the first side scores 5 points. At this same point in a doubles match, the receiving team switches receiving order. The player or pair who served first in the preceding game receives first in the next game.

A ball is in play until it touches something other than the table, the net assembly, the racket, or the racket hand below the wrist, unless the ball is a let (a rally in which no point is scored).

A let occurs when a serve touches the net assembly and otherwise is a good serve, when a serve is made before the receiving team is ready, or when a disturbance outside the receiver's control occurs. A let is also called when an error in the playing order or ends occurs or when a player changes rackets without notifying the umpire and opponent (the second time this occurs, the player is disqualified).

The expedite system is put into effect if a game exceeds 10 minutes, unless both sides have scored at least 9 points. In this system, the serve alternates after each point. If the receiver makes 13 good returns including the serve, the receiver wins a point. Once the expedite system is put into play, it stays in effect for the rest of the match, with the sides alternating serves after every point.

Serving

The server holds the ball on the open palm of his free hand. The ball must be stationary, above the table, and behind the serving end line. The server tosses the ball nearly vertically upward at least 6 inches, without spinning it. The server strikes the ball on the descent with the racket behind the serving end line. The ball must touch the server's court first, pass over or around the net, and touch the receiver's court.

From the start of service until it is struck, the ball must be above the level of the playing surface and behind the server's end line, and it cannot be hidden from the receiver by any part of the body or clothing of the server or his doubles partner. In doubles, the served ball must hit on the server's right-half court and then the receiver's right-half court. If a player misses the ball while attempting to serve, he loses a point.

Returns

A return is good when it passes over or around the net or its supports and strikes the opponent's court. A return may touch the net or its supports, as long as it lands in the opponent's court. The ball may not bounce twice on the same side, or be hit twice on the same side, before its return.

SCORING

A player scores a point when the opponent

- fails to make a good serve,
- fails to make a good return,
- obstructs the ball,
- allows the ball to bounce twice in her court,
- strikes the ball twice in making one return,
- moves the table while the ball is in play,
- touches the playing surface with the free hand,
- touches the net or its supports while the ball is in play,
- strikes the ball out of sequence in doubles play, or
- fails to return the serve and 12 successive returns under the expedite system.

EQUIPMENT

The ball is spherical, weighs 2.7 grams, and has a diameter of 40 millimeters. It is made of celluloid or similar plastic and may be white or orange and matte. The racket may be of any size, shape, and weight. The blade must be continuous, of even thickness, flat, and rigid. At least 85 percent of the blade's thickness must consist of natural wood. The color of the blade must be uniformly dark and matte. The sides of the blade used to strike the ball are covered with rubber. The blade should be black on one side and bright red on the other.

OFFICIALS

If available, an umpire or assistant umpire makes calls during the match.

MODIFICATIONS

Wheelchair competition follows the rules listed elsewhere in this chapter, except for the following modifications:

The table must not have any physical barrier that might hinder the normal and legal movements of a wheelchair. If the receiver does not strike a serve, and the served ball bounces twice on the receiver's court, the serve is a let. Players classified as IA, IB, or IC may toss the ball up with either hand, and they may touch the playing surface with the free hand while the ball is in play, but they may not use the free hand for support while hitting the ball.

Competitors' feet may not touch the floor during play, and competitors may not rise noticeably off their cushions during play. Their cushions may be of any size. Wheelchairs are not required to have back support.

ORGANIZATIONS

USA Table Tennis
1 Olympic Plaza
Colorado Springs, CO 80909-5769
719-866-4583
www.usatt.org

38

Taekwondo

Taekwondo originated in Korea more than 20 centuries ago and is one of the most popular modern martial arts today. *Tae* means "to strike with the foot;" *kwon* means "fist" or "to strike with the hand;" *do* means "the way of," or "art of." Thus, *taekwondo* stands for "the art of kicking and punching."

Taekwondo was introduced to the United States in the 1950s and was officially recognized as a means of self-defense when many Korean martial artists unified their techniques under the style now known as taekwondo. There are now about 5 million practitioners of taekwondo in the United States, and the sport made its premier as a medal sport in the 2000 Olympics.

Objective: To score the most points.

Scoring: Each scoring technique (see "Scoring" on page 243) is worth one point.

Number of Competitors: Two per contest; only same-sex competitions are allowed.

Length of Contest: Three rounds lasting three minutes each, with one minute's rest in between, for both males and females.

Overview: Competitors use fast, spinning kicks to score points by connecting in legal scoring areas on their opponents. They use no weapons, only their bare hands and feet. The competitor who scores the most valid points wins.

Individuals compete in weight divisions and must weigh in one hour before the competition. The contest begins with the referee's call of "shijak," which means "start." Each opponent then attempts to score points in legal scoring areas of his opponent's trunk and face, and to prevent his opponent from scoring. At the end of the contest, the competitors bow to each other and then turn and bow to the head of court. The referee then raises the hand of the winner.

COMPETITION AREA

The competition area measures 12 meters square. It is covered with an elastic mat and may be on a platform raised 50 to 60 centimeters. The inner part of the competition area, measuring 8 meters square, is called the *contest area;* the surrounding area up to the boundary lines is called the *alert area.* See figure 38.1.

TERMS

The **alert area** is the area between the outer boundary line and the **contest area** (the inner part of the competition area measuring 8 meters square). The total competition area measures 12 meters on each side.

A **gam-jeom** penalty is a deduction penalty. It is a more serious penalty than a kyong-go

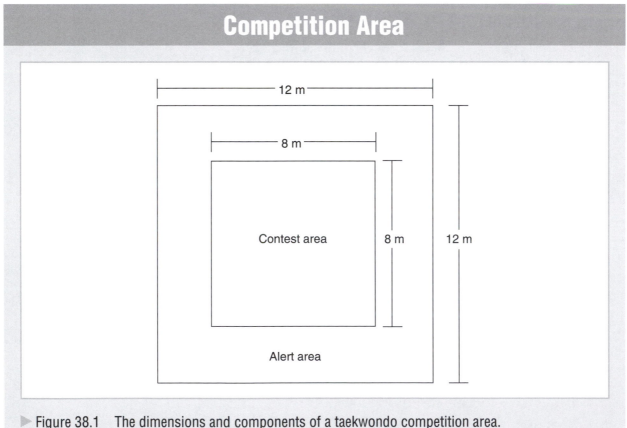

► Figure 38.1   The dimensions and components of a taekwondo competition area.
Adapted from International Judo Federation 1997.

penalty. A contestant who commits a gam-jeom penalty has one point deducted.

Kalyeo means "break." The referee will call "kalyeo" to keep an attacker from a downed opponent.

Keuman means "stop." The referee calls this to end each round.

Keysok means "continue." The referee calls "keysok" when a downed contestant is ready to resume.

A **kyong-go** penalty is a warning penalty. It is less severe than a gam-jeom penalty. Two kyong-go penalties equal one deduction point.

The **permitted area** on a contestant, where attacks using permitted techniques may be delivered, are the trunk and the face.

Permitted techniques include using the fist and the foot to deliver blows.

Shijak means "start." The referee uses this term to begin a contest.

A **valid point** is scored when a permitted technique is scored to a legal scoring area on the trunk or face.

COMPETITORS

Each competitor wears a uniform with protective gear, including a trunk protector, head protector, groin guard, and forearm and shin guards. Women also wear breast guards. Men and women compete in weight divisions. In the United States, those divisions are as follows:

Female, Junior Divisions (through age 17)

- Fin: under 92.5 lb
- Fly: 92.5 – 97 lb
- Bantam: 97.1 – 101.4 lb
- Feather: 101.5 – 108 lb
- Light: 108.1 – 114.6 lb
- Welter: 114.7 – 121.2 lb
- Light Middle: 121.3 – 130 lb
- Middle: 130.1 – 138.9 lb

- Light Heavy: 139 – 149.9 lb
- Heavy: over 149.9 lb

Male, Junior Division (through age 17)

- Fin: under 99 lb
- Fly: 99 – 105.8 lb
- Bantam: 105.9 – 112.4 lb
- Feather: 112.5 – 121.2 lb
- Light: 121.3 – 130 lb
- Welter: 130.1 – 138.9 lb
- Light Middle: 139 – 149.9 lb
- Middle: 150 – 160.9 lb
- Light Heavy: 161 – 172 lb
- Heavy: over 172 lb

Female, Adult Division

- Fin: under 103.4 lb
- Fly: 103.4 – 112.2 lb
- Bantam: 112.3 – 121 lb
- Feather: 121.1 – 129.8 lb
- Light: 129.9 – 138.6 lb
- Welter: 138.7 – 147.4 lb
- Middle: 147.5 – 158.4 lb
- Heavy: over 158.4 lb

Male, Adult Division

- Fin: under 118.8 lb
- Fly: 118.8 – 127.6 lb
- Bantam: 127.7 – 136.4 lb
- Feather: 136.5 – 147.4 lb
- Light: 147.5 – 158.4 lb
- Welter: 158.5 – 171.6 lb
- Middle: 171.7 – 184.8 lb
- Heavy: over 184.8 lb

SCORING

A contestant may use the front parts of the forefinger and middle finger of her clenched fist to deliver a *fist technique*. She may deliver a *foot technique* by using her foot.

Legal scoring areas include the midsection of the trunk (the abdomen and both sides of the flank) and the front of the face. A contestant may attack an opponent's trunk with feet or hands but may attack the face only with feet. A closed fist is required to make contact with the hands; opponents cannot push each other with open palms.

A contestant scores a point each time he accurately and powerfully delivers a permitted technique in a legal scoring area. Each scoring technique is worth one point, with the exception of a kick to the head, for which two points are awarded. If a contestant knocks down her opponent by delivering an attack to the trunk protector, which covers the back, she earns a point. A point is not valid if, after delivering a legitimate technique, the contestant intentionally falls or commits an illegal act. A point is also not valid if the contestant used any prohibited act in delivering the attack.

Knockdowns

A knockdown occurs when any part of the body other than the sole of the foot touches the floor, due to an opponent's delivered technique. A contestant is also judged to be knocked down if she is staggering and unable to continue the match.

When a knockdown occurs, the referee calls for a break and counts from 1 to 10 at one-second intervals. If the downed contestant rises, the referee will count up to 8 and, if he believes the contestant is able to continue, he calls for the match to resume. If the contestant does not rise or does not appear able to continue by the count of 8, the referee will declare the opponent the victor.

Decisions

If the score is tied at the end of three rounds and one contestant has had more points deducted than the other, the contestant who was awarded the most total points wins. If the score is tied and the point deduction totals are also the same, the referee decides the winner, based on superiority and initiative shown. A contestant may register a win by

knockout, by the referee stopping the contest, by score or superiority, by withdrawal or disqualification, or by the referee's punitive declaration.

The referee may suspend a contest for injury to one or both contestants. The injured contestant may be treated for one minute. If a contestant does not demonstrate the will to continue after such an injury, then he loses the contest, unless the injury was caused by a "gam-jeom" prohibited act (see "Penalties and Prohibited Acts"). If the prohibited act was a "kyong-go" (one of less severity), then the winner is the one with the most points at the time the contest was suspended.

PENALTIES AND PROHIBITED ACTS

There are two types of penalties for prohibited acts: kyong-go (a warning penalty) and gam-jeom (a one-point deduction penalty). Two kyong-go penalties result in a one-point deduction. If a contestant has three points deducted from her score, she loses the contest. If a contestant accumulates an odd number of kyong-go penalties, the last penalty does not result in any point deduction. Examples of each type of prohibited act are listed in table 38.1.

OFFICIALS

The referee controls the match. Judges mark valid points scored by contestants. The head of court has overall control of the competition area and confirms the match decision. A recorder times the match and records the points scored.

ORGANIZATIONS

United States Taekwondo Union
1 Olympic Plaza
Colorado Springs, CO 80909
719-866-4632
www.ustu.com

Table 38.1   Prohibited Acts

Penalty	Called for . . .
Kyong-go	Grabbing, pushing, or holding an opponent
	Intentionally crossing the alert line
	Evading an opponent by turning the back
	Intentionally falling down
	Feigning injury
	Attacking with the knee
	Intentionally attacking the groin
	Intentionally stomping or kicking the leg or foot
	Hitting the opponent's face with hands or fist
	Gesturing to indicate a scoring or deduction
	Using offensive language
	Displaying misconduct
Gam-jeom	Attacking a fallen opponent
	Intentionally attacking after the referee calls for a break
	Intentionally attacking the back of the head
	Severely attacking the opponent's face with hands or fists
	Butting
	Crossing the boundary line
	Throwing an opponent
	Expressing violent or extreme remarks or behavior

39
Team Handball

Team handball originated in Europe in the 1920s and was introduced to the United States in the late 1920s and early 1930s. The United States formed a team for the 1936 Olympics, at which team handball was a demonstration sport. Interest lagged in the United States until the late 1950s, when the United States Team Handball Federation was formed from a group of clubs in New York and New Jersey. Team handball became an official Olympic sport for men in 1972; women's competition was added in 1976. The sport is now played in more than 150 nations, with more than 8 million players affiliated with the International Handball Federation.

Objective: To score the most goals.

Number of Players: Seven players per side may be on the court at once.

Length of Game: A game consists of two 30-minute halves, with a 10-minute intermission. The playing clock normally runs continuously but is on occasion stopped (see "Keeping Time" on page 250).

Scoring: A goal is scored when the entire ball crosses the goal line.

Overview: A coin toss determines which team first gets possession of the ball. The game begins with a throw-off at center court. All players must be on their own half of the court when the throw is made, with the opponents at least 3 meters from the thrower. The throw-off to begin the second half is taken by the team that defended the first throw-off.

Team handball is a fast-moving, exciting game that combines running, jumping, catching, and throwing. Elements of soccer, basketball, water polo, and hockey can be seen as players attempt to maneuver past opponents and throw the ball past the goalkeeper and into the goal to score.

COURT

The court is 40 meters long and 20 meters wide (see figure 39.1). It has two goal areas and a playing area. The lines marking the boundaries on the sides of the field are called sidelines; the shorter boundary lines are called goal lines for the portion between the goal posts, and outer goal lines for the portions on either side of the goal.

Each goal is netted and is 3 meters wide and 2 meters high. The goal area is marked by a goal area line that fans in a semicircle 6 meters away from the goal post. The free-throw line, or 9-meter line, is a broken line fanning in a semicircle 9 meters from the goal post. The 7-meter line is 1 meter long. It is parallel to, and 7 meters from, the rear edge of the goal line, and it is directly in front of the goal. The goalkeeper's restraining line (the 4-meter line) is 15 centimeters long and 4 meters from the rear edge of the goal line, directly in front of the goal. The center line runs the width of the

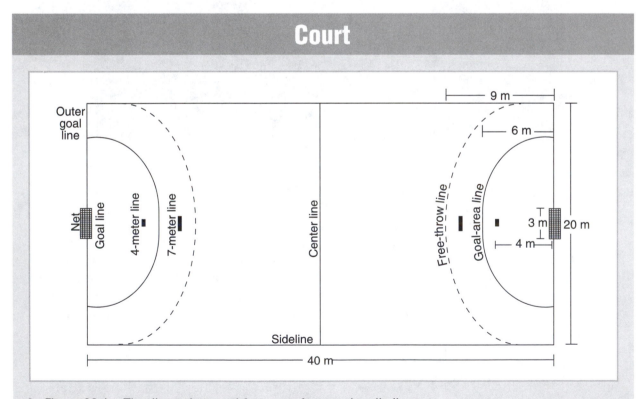

Court

▶ Figure 39.1   The dimensions and features of a team handball court.
Adapted from International Handball Federation 1993.

court at midcourt, dividing the court into equal halves.

TERMS

The **center line** runs the width of the court, dividing the court into equal halves.

A **free throw** is awarded for goalkeeper infractions and other violations (see "Throws"); the player taking the free throw takes it from the point of infraction or, if the violation occurred between the 9-meter line and the goal-area line, from the nearest point outside the 9-meter, or free-throw, line.

The **free-throw line** is also known as the *9-meter line*. It is a broken, nearly semicircular line, drawn three meters from, and parallel to, the goal-area line.

The **goal area** is defined by the goal-area line, which is drawn 6 meters in front of the goal line in front of the goal and 6 meters from the goal post on each side of the goal. The line is a semicircle, with each end touching the goal line on either side of the goal.

The **goalkeeper's restraining line** is also known as the 4-meter line. It is 4 meters from the rear edge of the goal line, directly in front of the goal.

A **goalkeeper's throw** is awarded to the goalkeeper when the ball crosses the outer goal line. The goalkeeper must throw the ball from the goal area and beyond the goal-area line.

The **7-meter line** is 1 meter long. It is directly in front of the goal, 7 meters away from the rear edge of the goal line.

A **7-meter throw** is awarded in various situations (see "Throws") and is taken by a player who may not step on or beyond the 7-meter line before he throws the ball.

A **throw-in** is taken to put the ball back into play after it has gone out of bounds. It is taken where the ball went out of bounds, or, if it crossed the outer goal line, from the intersection of the goal line and the sideline nearest where it went out of bounds.

A **throw-off** is used to begin each half and to resume play after a team has scored a goal. The team in possession of the ball must be on its own side during a throw-off, which takes place at center court.

PLAYERS

A team consists of 14 players, 7 of whom may be on the field at one time. A team must have at least 5 players to begin a game, but the game may continue if a team is later reduced to fewer than 5 players on the court. Each team must use a goalkeeper at all times.

Substitutes may enter the game at any time and for an unlimited number of times. They don't need to notify the timekeeper, but the players they are replacing must be off the field before they enter. Substitutes must enter a game at the substitute line, which is near midcourt. A faulty substitution results in a two-minute suspension for the offending player and a free throw for the opponents. The goalkeeper wears colors distinct from all other players on the court.

Teams use different offensive sets and have different names for positions, but one basic offensive set is to have three players—left backcourt, center, and right backcourt—just beyond the free-throw line, and three others—left wing, circle runner, and right wing—between the free-throw line and the goal-area line. Wing players tend to be smaller and quicker players who can shoot from difficult angles. Circle runners, or pivots, who are often directly in front of the goal, are larger and aggressive and may set picks and screens for the backcourt players. Centers are like quarterbacks, directing the offense. The other backcourt players tend to be taller, with the ability to jump and shoot over the defense from the backcourt.

PLAY

Most of the rules of play are understood through the regulations for keeping time, advancing the ball, approaching an opponent, goalkeeping, and throws.

Keeping Time

The clock is always stopped when a referee disqualifies or excludes a player or calls a referee-throw (see "Throws"). Each team also may use a one-minute timeout per half. The clock may also be stopped for extraordinary incidents (spectators or objects on the court, goal damaged, and so on), consultations between the referees and the timekeeper or scorekeeper, injuries, and delays in executing a formal throw. In addition, the clock stops for warnings or suspensions, goalkeeper substitutions during a 7-meter throw, and a player's not giving up the ball or throwing it away.

Advancing the Ball

Players may throw, catch, stop, push, or hit the ball, using their open or closed hands, arms, heads, torsos, thighs, and knees. A player may hold a ball for a maximum of three seconds. A player may

- take a maximum of three steps with the ball;
- bounce the ball once and catch it while standing or running; and
- dribble the ball and then catch it.

If a player is holding the ball, she must dribble, pass, or shoot it within three seconds or after taking three steps. She may dribble it continuously an unlimited number of times, but once she has picked up her dribble she may not begin dribbling again unless another player touches the ball. She may take three steps, and then dribble, and then take three more steps; at this point she must pass or shoot the ball within three seconds.

Offensive players are not allowed to touch the ball with any part of the body below the knee (unless the ball has been thrown at the player by an opponent); dive for the ball (except for the goalkeeper); play the ball intentionally out of bounds (except for the goalkeeper, in blocking a shot); or "stall" without trying to score (this is "passive play" and the defensive team is awarded a free throw at the point where the ball was when play was interrupted).

Approaching an Opponent

A player may use his arms and hands to try to gain possession of the ball, and he may use his torso to obstruct an opponent either with or without the ball. But he may not

- obstruct an opponent by using his arms, hands, or legs;
- pull or hit the ball with one or both hands out of the hands of an opponent (flipping the ball is allowed);
- use his fist to hit the ball from an opponent;
- endanger an opponent with the ball, or endanger the goalkeeper; or
- hold, trip, run into, hit, or jump onto an opponent.

Less serious infractions merit first a warning and then a suspension (in which the offending player sits out two minutes). More serious infractions result in disqualification.

Goalkeeping

Only the goalkeeper may be in the goal area. A court player may not play the ball when it is stationary or rolling in the goal area. A court player may, however, play the ball when it is in the air above the goal area if she is not in the goal area herself. A free throw is awarded to the opposing team when a court player enters the goal area in possession of the ball; a free throw is also awarded when a court player enters the goal area without the ball but gains an advantage in doing so.

A 7-meter throw is given when a defending court player enters the goal area and gains an advantage over a player with the ball. No throw is awarded if a player enters the goal area without the ball and gains no advantage. If a defending player intentionally plays the ball into his own goal area and the goalkeeper touches it, the opponents are awarded a free throw. If the goalkeeper doesn't touch it and the ball stops in the goal area or goes out of bounds, the opponents are awarded a free throw.

The goalkeeper may

- touch the ball with any part of her body while inside the goal area;
- move with the ball inside the goal area, with no restrictions;
- leave the goal area without the ball, at which time she becomes subject to the rules applying to all players in the playing area; and
- leave the goal area with the ball and play it in the playing area, if she has not been able to control it.

A goalkeeper may not endanger an opponent; intentionally play the ball out over the goal line, after gaining control of the ball; leave the goal area while in control of the ball; or touch the ball outside the goal area after making a goalkeeper throw, unless another player has since touched the ball.

In addition, a goalkeeper may not touch the ball in contact with the floor outside the goal area when he is inside the goal area; pick up the ball outside the goal area and bring it inside the goal area; touch the ball with any part of his body below his knee, if he's not in the act of defending goal; or cross the 4-meter line before the thrower has thrown the ball in taking a 7-meter throw.

Throws

The following throws may be made during a game.

- A **throw-off** is used to begin a half and to resume play after a goal from center court. Each team is on its own side of the court (except after a goal). Opponents must be at least 3 meters from the thrower. The referee whistles; the thrower has three seconds to throw.
- A **throw-in** is used when the ball has gone out of bounds. The referee doesn't whistle; a player on the team awarded the ball throws the ball in with one foot on the sideline until the ball leaves his hand. He may not play the ball in to himself. Opponents must stand at least 3 meters away, though they may stand outside their goal line, even if it's less than 3 meters away.

- A **goalkeeper's throw** is used when the ball crosses the outer goal line. It is thrown from the goal area. The goalkeeper throws the ball over the goal-area line; the referee does not whistle. The goalkeeper may not touch the ball again until another player has touched it.
- A **free throw** is used for numerous violations, including goalkeeper infractions, court player infractions in the goal area, infractions when playing the ball, passive play, and infractions connected with other throws. It is thrown either where the infraction occurred, or, if the violation occurred between the 9-meter line and the goal-area line, then from the nearest point immediately outside the 9-meter line. Without a whistle, the player takes the throw with opponents at least 3 meters away. Teammates may not be on the 9-meter line or between it and the goal line before the player takes the throw.
- A **7-meter throw** is used when a clear chance of scoring is destroyed by a defensive player's illegal action or a referee's inadvertent whistle, when a goalkeeper enters her goal area with the ball, when a court player enters her own goal area while playing defense, or when a player plays the ball to her goalkeeper in the goal area. It is thrown at the 7-meter line. A referee blows her whistle, and the player has three seconds to take a shot on goal from behind the 7-meter line. The player must not touch on or beyond the line before the ball leaves her hand. Just the goalkeeper and the thrower are initially involved; the ball is not played again until it has touched the goalkeeper or goal. All other players must be beyond the 9-meter line or 3 meters or farther away from the player when she takes the throw. The throw is retaken if a defensive player violates this positioning (unless the player scored a goal); the player may also throw again if the goalkeeper moves beyond the 4-meter line before she releases the ball.

SCORING

A team scores a goal when the entire ball crosses the entire width of the goal line and enters the goal, and the scoring team has not committed an infraction on the play. If the game is tied at the end of regulation and a winner must be determined, teams play an overtime period: two halves of five minutes each. A coin toss determines who throws in.

If the score is still tied at the end of the first overtime, the teams play a second overtime period. If a tie exists at the end of the second overtime period, a penalty shootout occurs. Each team selects five shooters who alternate shooting from the penalty line. If a tie still exists at the end of each team's five penalty shots, individual penalty shots continue until a winner is determined.

PENALTIES

A referee may warn, suspend, disqualify, or exclude a player. *Warnings* result from less serious infractions, such as were noted in "Approaching an Opponent" (page 250). They also may result from violations occurring when a player is executing a formal throw and from unsporting conduct. The referee indicates a warning by holding up a yellow card.

Suspensions occur for repeated infractions, for faulty substitutions, and for failure to put the ball on the floor when the referee makes a decision. Suspensions last two minutes and are indicated by the referee's holding up her hand with two fingers extended. The team may not replace the player during the suspension. A player can receive another two-minute suspension (four minutes total) if the player immediately repeated an infraction (e.g., kept arguing with the referee).

Disqualifications occur when a player not entitled to participate enters the court; when there are serious infractions and repeated events of unsporting conduct; or when a player receives his third suspension. The team may not replace the disqualified player for two minutes. A referee indicates a disqualification by holding up a red card.

Exclusions result from an assault either on or outside the court, against another player, a referee, any other official, or anyone in the area. Spitting is regarded as assault. The referee indicates an exclusion by crossing his arms in front of his face. The team may not replace the excluded player. If the excluded player is a goalkeeper, another player may assume goalkeeper duties, but the team must play the remainder of the game short one player.

EQUIPMENT

The ball is spherical, is made of leather or synthetic material, and has an inflated rubber bladder. It has the following dimensions:

Men's—58 to 60 centimeters in circumference, weighing 425 to 475 grams

Women's—54 to 56 centimeters in circumference, weighing 325 to 400 grams

OFFICIALS

Two referees, with equal authority, are in charge of the game. A timekeeper and a scorekeeper assist the referees.

ORGANIZATIONS

USA Team Handball
1 Olympic Plaza
Colorado Springs, CO 80909
719-866-4036

40 Tennis

Tennis' roots trace back to 13th-century France, where players hit a ball over a net with their hands. The game was brought to Wales, where it evolved into lawn tennis, with players using rackets. The game became popular in 19th-century England; the first Wimbledon championships were held in 1877.

Tennis was also introduced in America in the 19th century but didn't catch on as a major sport, either professionally or recreationally, until the 1960s. Recreational play in the United States peaked in the mid-1970s, with 34 million playing at least once per year; now about 21 million play at least once a year. The number of those who play regularly in the United States is on the rise, from 7.3 million in 1995 to nearly 10.5 million now.

Objective: To hit the ball over the net into the opponent's court either out of the opponent's reach or so that the opponent is unable to return the ball.

Number of Players: Either two (singles) or four (doubles).

Scoring: A point is scored in a variety of ways; see "Scoring" on page 256.

Length of Games, Sets, and Matches: The first player to have a two-point advantage and to have scored at least four points wins the *game*. The first player or side to win six games and lead by two games wins the *set*. A *match* is composed of the best two of three sets or the best three of five.

Overview: Each game begins at 0-0, or *love*. The first point scored is 15, the second is 30, the third is 40, and the fourth is game point. Game point wins the game unless the score is a *deuce* (40-40). If the server scores in deuce, she gains the *advantage,* or *ad;* if she scores the next point, she wins. If her opponent scores the next point, it is again deuce. A player must win by two points. When the server has the advantage, it is called *ad-in;* when the receiver has the advantage, it is called *ad-out.*

If a set is 6-6, a *tiebreaker* is often used to determine the winner. Players play 12 points; the first player to reach at least 7 points and be ahead by 2 points wins the tiebreaker and the set. If the score is 6-6 after 12 points, the players change ends and resume play until one is ahead by 2 points.

COURT

A court is 78 feet long by 27 feet wide for singles play, or 36 feet wide for doubles play (see figure 40.1). It is divided in half by a net, made of cord, 36 inches high in the center and 42 inches high at the two supporting side-posts. Service lines are parallel to and 21 feet from the net. They are 18 feet in front of the baselines, which are also parallel to the net and mark the outer boundary of each side of the court.

A center service line, parallel to the side-line, intersects the net and divides the service courts into two sections on both sides of the net. The center service line connects the two service lines. There are two service courts on each side of the net, covering the area between the net, the service line, the center service line, and the sideline. Each service court is 21 feet long by 13.5 feet wide. This area is also called the *forecourt.*

The *backcourt* is the area between the service line and the baseline. It is 18 feet long by 27 feet wide for singles play, or 36 feet wide for doubles play. The court surface is clay, grass, or a composition.

TERMS

An **ace** (one point) is scored by a server whose good serve is not touched.

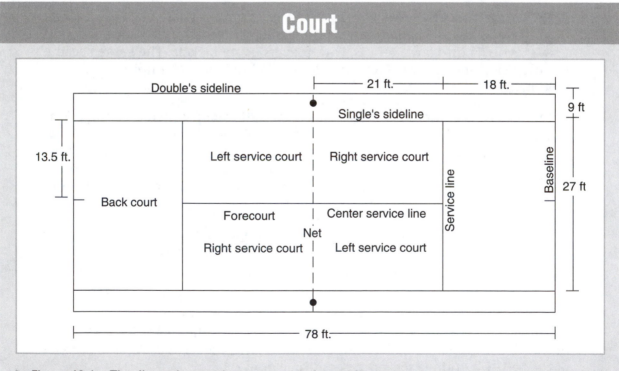

▶ Figure 40.1   The dimensions and components of a tennis court.
Adapted from United States Tennis Association, Inc. 1995.

A server commits a **fault** when she hits the ball into the net or outside her opponent's court (service fault) or when she steps on or over the baseline before she hits her serve.

A **game** is won by the first player to score four points and be ahead by two.

Game point is the point that can decide the game.

Hindrance may be called when a player is hindered by either his opponent or a spectator. Depending on the situation, hindrance results in a let, a playover, or a point awarded to the player hindered.

A **let** occurs on a serve, when the ball strikes the net and lands in the opponent's proper service court, or when play is interrupted. A let requires that the point be replayed.

A **match** is won by the player who wins the best two of three or three of five sets.

Match point is the point that can decide the match.

A **rally** is a series of hits between players.

The **serve** is the play (the stroke or shot) that begins each point.

A **set** is won by the player who wins six games and is ahead by two games, or who wins a tiebreaker.

Set point is the point that can decide the set.

A **volley** is a hit before the ball strikes the ground.

PLAYERS

Tennis is played in singles matches (two players) or doubles matches (four players). The following rules apply to doubles matches:

- Doubles use the widest portion of the court (36 feet).
- For serving, the same size service courts are used as in singles.
- Teams alternate serves after each game, as in singles play; team A serves the first game, team B the second, and so on.

- Each team's players alternate serving complete games. Player 1 on team A would serve game 1; player 2 on team A would serve game 3, and so on.
- Players also alternate receiving serves.
- If a player is discovered to have served out of turn, his partner will serve the next point, but all prior points count. If a game is completed before the error is discovered, the play stands as is and the order of service remains as altered.
- If a team is discovered to have changed its receiving order, this order will remain until the end of the game, at which time the team will resume its normal receiving order.
- Doubles partners do not have to alternate hits.
- If both partners hit a ball, either simultaneously or consecutively, the hit is illegal. If, however, one partner's racket touches the other partner's racket but does not hit the ball, this is legal.

PLAY

The basics of tennis are understood through its rules for serving, returning serve, and playing.

Serving

Players alternate serves: player A serves the first game, player B the second, and so on. They also alternate the sides of the court they serve from, beginning each game on the right side. The serve is made into the service court diagonally opposite the side the server is standing on. Players switch ends of the court at the end of the first, third, fifth, and subsequent alternate games.

Play is continuous; the receiver must play to the reasonable pace of the server and must be ready to receive serve when the server is ready to serve. When changing ends, a maximum of 1 minute, 30 seconds may elapse from the time the ball went out of play to end the previous game to the time the first serve begins the next game.

The server must stand with both her feet behind the baseline (see figure 40.1 on page 254) and within the imaginary continuations of the center line and sideline. When the receiver is ready, the server tosses the ball in the air and hits it with her racket before it hits the ground. The ball must pass over the net and hit within the receiver's proper service court.

If the ball strikes the net and lands inside the proper service court, the play is called a let and does not count. A let may also be called for an interruption of play. A service fault occurs when the server swings and misses, or hits the ball into the net, or hits the ball outside the opponent's proper service court.

A foot fault occurs when the server steps on or beyond the baseline, or over the imaginary extensions of the center line or sideline, while serving. Once the racket strikes the ball, the server may step on or over the baseline, center line, or sideline.

A server is allowed one fault (either service or foot). The player serves from behind the same half of the court on the second serve. If the player faults on his second serve, this is called a double fault and he loses a point.

In a tiebreaker, the player whose turn it is to serve serves first. His opponent serves the next two serves. It continues with each player serving twice until the set has been decided. Players change ends every 6 points. An alternative to using a tiebreaker is to continue the set until one player has a two-game lead; which system is used is up to the tournament officials. The points that decide the result of a game, set, or match are called game point, set point, and match point, respectively.

The server's score is always given first.

Returning Serve and Playing

The receiver must return the serve on the first bounce, hitting it over the net and into his opponent's court. A ball striking a boundary line is in play. During a rally, or series of hits by the players, the ball may hit the net if the ball crosses and lands inbounds in the opponent's court. A let occurs only during the serve (or when a point is inadvertently interrupted).

After the serve is returned, players may volley by hitting the ball before it bounces on their side or use ground strokes to return the ball after one bounce. A player's racket may cross over the net after she has returned (made contact with) the ball.

If a player intentionally hinders an opponent from making a stroke, the hindered player receives a point. If the action is unintentional, the point is replayed.

SCORING

The server scores a point if he hits an *ace* (a serve that the receiver cannot return), or if his serve hits his opponent. The receiver scores a point if the server double-faults. A player loses a point if she

- cannot return a ball before it bounces twice on her side,
- returns the ball out of bounds,
- hits the ball into the net,
- carries or catches the ball on her racket or deliberately touches the ball with her racket more than once,
- touches the net or posts,
- hits the ball by throwing her racket, or
- hits the ball before it has crossed the net.

EQUIPMENT

The ball is hollow rubber, either white or yellow. It is between 2.5 and 2.63 inches in diameter and weighs between 2 and 2.1 ounces. The racket may be up to 32 inches long and 12.5 inches wide. The strung surface, a pattern of crossed strings, may not be more than 15.5 inches long and 11.5 inches wide. Rackets are made of various materials; they may be of any weight.

OFFICIALS

Matches are typically officiated by an umpire, whose decision is final; by net-cord judges, who place their fingers on the net to detect lets on serves; by linesmen, who make boundary decisions; and by foot-fault judges, who call foot faults. In many tournaments where umpires and linesmen are not available, however, players call their own lines.

MODIFICATIONS

Wheelchair tennis is played the same as regular tennis, except that wheelchair players are allowed two bounces of the ball. The first bounce must be within the court, but the second bounce may be outside the court boundaries and still be in play.

The server may not roll or spin his chair while serving nor have any wheel touching on or beyond the baseline or imaginary extensions of the center line and sideline. A server may not use any part of his lower extremities to brake or stabilize himself while serving. Doing so results in a fault.

If a player is physically unable to serve in a conventional manner, another person may drop the ball to begin the player's serve. The wheelchair is considered part of the body. As such, if the ball touches a chair, that player loses a point. A player also loses a point if

- she hits her own partner with a ball;
- she uses any part of her feet or lower extremities to brake or stabilize while serving, stroking a ball, turning, or stopping; or
- she fails to keep one buttock in contact with her chair while hitting a ball.

ORGANIZATIONS

Peter Burwash International Special Tennis Programs
2203 Timberloch Place, Suite 126
The Woodlands, TX 77380
281-363-4707

United States Professional Tennis Association
1 USPTA Center
3535 Briarpark Drive, Suite 1
Houston, TX 77042
800-USPTA-4U

United States Tennis Association
70 W. Red Oak Lane
White Plains, NY 10604
www.usta.com

41
Track and Field

© Empics

Competition in track and field events dates back to the 7th century B.C. Modern track and field (or "athletics," as it is known internationally) sprang from university events in England in the 19th century. Today the sport is popular worldwide and is one of the headline sports at the Olympic Games. In the United States it is very popular at the youth and high school levels.

Objective: Depending on the event, to run the fastest, throw the farthest, or jump the highest or farthest.

Events: Running events (sprints, hurdles, middle distances, distances, and relays); throwing events (discus, hammer, javelin, shot put, and weight throw); and jumping events (high jump, long jump, triple jump, and pole vault).

Overview: In some competitions, team scores are kept; others are geared to individual (non-team) competition. The rules in the main body of this chapter pertain to the senior classification (16 years old and older). The sport is modified widely for groups of various ages and abilities; toward the end of the chapter some of these modifications are highlighted.

COMPETITION AREA

Outdoor competition takes place on and around a 400-meter oval track (see figure 41.1). A track has six to nine lanes, measuring between 1.22 meters and 1.25 meters in width. The surface is usually a synthetic composition.

Running events take place on the track; field events take place on the field inside the track or in a field away from the track. Indoor tracks vary in size; many are 200 meters in length. They usually have banked turns and a board surface.

TERMS

A **false start** occurs when a runner begins a race before the starting pistol is fired. A competitor is disqualified for two false starts.

Some competitions have **heats,** or qualifying rounds, to narrow the field and advance runners to the finals.

A **photo finish** is the term used when a finish is so close that the winner must be determined by a photographic device at the finish line.

A **wind-aided effort** refers to running events up to and including the 200-meter race, as well as the long jump and triple jump, where the velocity of the wind exceeds 2 meters per second in the direction of the competition. Records set on a wind-aided effort are not allowed.

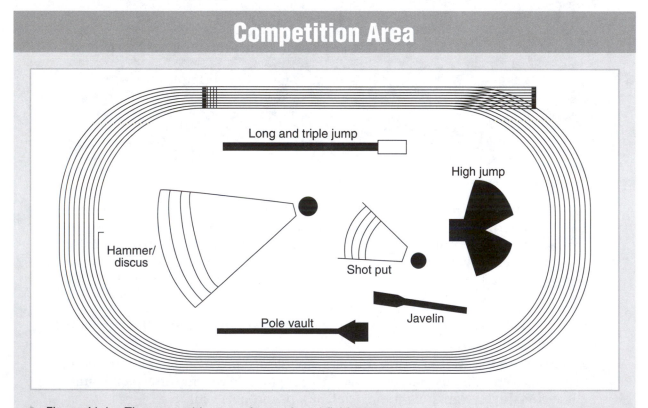

 Figure 41.1   The competition area for track and field events.

Adapted from Athletic Congress's Development Committees with Gambetta 1981.

SPRINTS

Running events include the sprints (60-meter, indoor only; 100-, 200-, and 400-meter); the hurdles (60-meter, indoor only; 100-meter for women, 110-meter for men, and 400-meter for both); and the middle distances and distance events (from 800 to 10,000 meters). Walking events are also contested at 3K, 5K, 10K, and 20K.

Runners in events up to and including the 400-meter dash use starting blocks to protect the track. Both of a runner's feet must be in contact with the blocks, which often are equipped with a device that helps starters detect false starts. Many races are recorded by electronic timers, which register times to a hundredth of a second. Most events allow athletes to wear spiked footwear, with up to 11 spikes.

A runner's left hand is always toward the inside of the track; races are run counterclockwise. Many meets have heats, or qualifying rounds, through which runners must advance to get to the finals. Runners are randomly assigned lanes in the first round; after that, their performance determines in which lane they will run.

Sprinters (competitors in races of 400 meters or less) run in the same lane the whole race. In the 200-meter and 400-meter events, where sprinters must race around curves, the starting places are staggered so that each runner runs the same distance.

In 800-meter events, runners run in lanes until after the first turn, when they can cut to the inside lane. Races beyond 800 meters are not run in lanes.

Start

All competitors must be completely behind the starting line, with no parts of their bodies touching it or extending beyond it. For races of 400 meters or less, the commands are "on your marks" and "set." When all competitors are set, the starter fires a starting pistol. For races beyond 400 meters, the command is "on your marks," and when runners are ready, the gun is fired. All competitors must immediately follow the commands; delaying in getting set, or resetting once a runner is set, will result in a false start.

A runner is allowed two false starts. No false start may be assessed generally to the field; each one must be charged to an individual. In the event a race has to be recalled because of a false start, the starter fires his pistol again. In races where starting blocks are used (up to and including the 400-meter), false-start detection apparatus may be hooked up to the blocks.

Race

Any runner who jostles or impedes another runner may be disqualified. In races run entirely in lanes, competitors must stay in their lanes or be disqualified. In races begun in lanes, runners must remain in their lanes until the break-line mark. A runner who leaves the track (crossing over the inside boundary line of the first lane without being pushed off) is out of the race. An exception to this rule is in races of 20,000 meters, in which a runner may temporarily leave the track if in returning he doesn't shorten his distance. After entering the straightaway of a race with two or more turns, runners are to run in a straight line to the finish, except to avoid other runners.

Finish

A runner officially ends her race when her torso reaches the finish line. The head, neck, arms, hand, legs, and feet do not count. In case of a tie, one of three things may happen:

- Both runners advance to the next round, if practical.
- If not, the two runners compete again, if practical.
- If not, lots are drawn to determine who advances to the next round.

In a first-place tie, if it's practical, the runners compete again; if not, the tie stands.

HURDLES

Hurdle events include the 60-meter (indoors only), 100-meter, 110-meter, and 400-meter.

Hurdles races are run entirely in lanes. A runner must clear the hurdle with both legs. He is disqualified if his trailing leg dips lower than the height of the hurdle, if he runs around a hurdle, or if he intentionally knocks over a hurdle. Hurdlers are not disqualified, however, for unintentionally knocking over hurdles.

The top bar of the hurdle is made of wood or plastic. The hurdle is durable enough that it is not easily broken by a competitor hitting it. Heights of hurdles and distances between hurdles are shown in table 41.1.

STEEPLECHASE

The 3,000-meter steeplechase has 28 hurdle jumps and 7 water jumps (5 jumps per lap, with the water jump as the fourth jump). Runners run the first 200 meters without taking a hurdle; from there on they take 5 hurdles per lap.

The 2,000-meter steeplechase, run in some women's and junior events, has 18 hurdle jumps and 5 water jumps.

The height of the men's hurdles is 36 inches; women's hurdles are 30 inches. The hurdles are 13 feet wide and the bar on top of each hurdle is 5 inches square. The water jump is 12 feet long. The water is 27.5 inches deep at the beginning of the jump, nearest the hurdle; it slopes to the level of the field at the end of the jump.

A runner is disqualified if he doesn't fully take a hurdle. He may not trail a leg or foot lower than the horizontal plane of the top of the hurdle. Runners may clear a hurdle by jumping over it without touching it or by placing a foot on the hurdle and vaulting over it.

RELAYS

Relay events include the 400-, 800-, 1600-, and 3200-meter. A relay race is made up of teams of four runners each. Each runner runs a set distance before passing a baton to a teammate. A baton is a hollow tube, usually made of metal, not longer than 30 centimeters and weighing no less than 50 grams.

The baton handoff must take place in a 20-meter takeover zone, with the starting line in the middle of this zone. If the handoff occurs outside of this zone, the team is disqualified. It is the baton's position, and not that of the runners, that determines whether the handoff was legal or not.

For races where lanes cease to be used, waiting runners move to an inside position to receive the handoff as their incoming teammates arrive. For races where lanes are used, runners who have finished their leg must remain in their lanes after handing off, to avoid interfering with other runners.

In outdoor relays up to and including the 4 × 200 meters and the 800-meter medley,

Table 41.1 Hurdle Specifications, Senior Competition			
Hurdle event	No. of hurdles	Height of hurdles (in)	Distance between hurdles (m)
Women's 60-meter	5	33	8.50
Men's 60-meter	5	42	9.14
Women's 100-meter	10	33	8.50
Men's 110-meter	10	42	9.14
Women's 400-meter	10	30	35.0
Men's 400-meter	10	36	35.0

Adapted from USA Track & Field 1995.

runners about to receive handoffs may use an acceleration zone, which is 10 meters outside the exchange zone. In indoor relays, such an acceleration zone is not used.

In the 4 × 100 and 4 × 200 relays, the race is run entirely in lanes. In the 800-medley relay, the first, second, and third runners run in lanes, with the fourth runner moving to the inside. In the 4 × 400 relay, the first runner runs entirely in her lane, while the second runner runs the curve to a break line before moving to the inside. In the 4 × 800 relay, the first runner runs the curve in her lane to a break line before moving to the inside.

JUMPING EVENTS

Jumping events include

- the high jump, where competitors attempt to jump over a crossbar;
- the pole vault, where competitors use a flexible pole in attempting to vault over a crossbar;
- the long jump, where competitors sprint to a takeoff board and attempt to leap the farthest into a sand pit; and
- the triple jump, where competitors sprint to a takeoff board and take a hop, step, and jump into a sand pit.

High Jump

The apron surrounding the high jump pit is a 15-meter semicircle. In championship events, a 20-meter runway is suggested. The high jump standards (the uprights and posts) are rigid. The crossbar may be wood, metal, or another approved material; its cross-section is circular and may be up to three centimeters in diameter. The bar may sag a maximum of two centimeters.

The landing pit of cushioned foam rubber is 5 meters long by 4 meters wide. The height of a jump is measured from the ground to the lowest portion of the crossbar. Jumpers may use one or two markers to assist in their runup and takeoff.

Jumpers compete in the order drawn. A competitor may choose to pass at any height, but he may not later attempt a jump at that height, except in a jump-off to break a first-place tie. When more than two or three jumpers are still in the competition, each has about one and a half minutes to take her jump. When only two or three competitors remain, each jumper may take up to three minutes.

If the jumper knocks the bar off the standards, or if she touches an area beyond the uprights before going over the bar, the jump is a failure. After three consecutive missed jumps at any height, the competitor is finished. A jumper may fail at one height and then pass on his next turn, waiting for the next height.

At the end of each round the bar is raised at least 2 centimeters. Rounds continue until only one competitor remains in the competition. That jumper may attempt greater heights. If two jumpers are tied, the jumper with the fewest attempts at the winning height wins. If the jumpers are still tied, the competitor with the fewest overall misses wins.

Pole Vault

The suggested runway for the pole vault is 40 to 45 meters. The takeoff box, where the vaulter plants his pole after his runup, is about 24 inches wide by 39 inches long, sinking into the ground in front of the standard's uprights, which are rigid. The crossbar is similar to that for the high jump but slightly heavier.

The landing area is cushioned foam rubber, 5 meters square. The pole may be of any material, length, and diameter, but its basic surface must be smooth. A vaulter may use one or two layers of adhesive tape on the pole and may use resin or an adhesive substance on his hands for a better grip. A vaulter may use one or two markers alongside the runway to assist in his runup and may have the standards moved back toward the landing area by up to 31.5 inches. As with the high jump, the measurement is from the ground to the lowest portion of the crossbar.

The procedure is similar to that for the high jump: A vaulter may pass at any height, and he is out of the competition after three consecutive misses. The bar is moved up at least 2 inches after each round. Competition continues until only one vaulter remains. Ties are broken as in the high jump. A jump is a miss if the vaulter knocks the bar off the standards; if the athlete or the pole touches an area beyond the uprights before he clears the bar; or if the competitor, while in the air, moves his lower hand above his upper hand or moves his upper hand off the pole. Each vaulter has two minutes to attempt his vault. When only two or three vaulters remain, this extends to four minutes. If a pole is broken during an attempt, the attempt does not count against the competitor.

Long Jump

There is no maximum limit on the runup; a competitor is only limited by the actual length of the runway. Competitors may place one or two markers along the runway to assist in their steps on the runup. On the runup the jumper approaches the takeoff board, made of wood and about eight inches wide by four feet long. The jumper's foot must not mark beyond the takeoff line at the far end of the board. Beyond this board is a plasticine board, about four inches wide, on which athletes' footprints may be spotted.

A windsock is placed near the takeoff board so that jumpers can determine the approximate direction and strength of the wind. The landing area is a sand pit, 3 meters wide by 9 meters long, beginning at least 1 meter beyond the takeoff line. The sand must be level with the takeoff board.

In competitions with more than eight jumpers, each competitor takes three jumps, in rotating order. Each competitor counts his best jump. The eight best marks advance; these eight athletes get three more jumps. The longest legal jump wins.

In competitions with eight or fewer athletes, each jumper gets six jumps and counts her best legal jump. Each jumper has one and a half minutes to take a jump. The measurement is taken from the takeoff line to the nearest sand broken by the competitor. A jump is a foul when the athlete

- touches the ground beyond the takeoff line,
- takes off beyond either side of the takeoff board (whether behind the line or not),
- touches the ground outside the landing area closer to the takeoff line than to the nearest mark made in the pit, or
- walks back through the landing area.

Triple Jump

The jumping area is the same as for the long jump. The placement of the takeoff board depends on the caliber of competition. In major competition for men, the distance between the board and the landing area should be at least 13 meters; for women, 10 meters. The recommended distance between the takeoff board and the end of the landing area is 21 meters.

The competitor sprints down the runway, takes off on either foot from the takeoff board, lands on that same foot, takes a long step and lands on the opposite foot, and jumps into the landing area. It is not a foul if the jumper touches the "off" leg or foot on the ground during the jump. All other rules and procedures for the triple jump are the same as for the long jump.

THROWING EVENTS

Athletes compete against each other to record the longest throw of various implements in the discus throw, the hammer throw, the javelin throw, the shot put, and the weight throw. These general rules apply to all throwing events: In throws from a circle, the athlete must begin from a stationary position. The competitor may touch the inside of the band or stopboard, but not the top. Failing to start from a stationary position and touching the top of the stopboard are fouls.

Other fouls include touching any surface outside the circle, improperly releasing the implement, failing to leave the circle from the back, and leaving the circle before the implement lands.

Except in the hammer and weight throws, or to cover an open cut, athletes may not tape their fingers. They may use a substance on their hands to improve their grip, and they may wear belts to protect their backs from injury. Competitors have a minute and a half to begin their trial, once their name is called by the event official.

Except for the hammer and weight throws, no gloves are allowed. No flags or markers may be placed in the landing sector, which fans out in two lines from the throwing circle at a 40-degree angle. A throw is not valid if it does not land within the landing sector marked on the ground.

If a competitor misses his turn, that turn is lost, but he may still use any subsequent turns he has coming to him. In a field of nine or more competitors, each athlete gets three attempts, and the eight individuals with the best attempts advance. In a field of eight or less, all competitors get six throws. The best legal throw for each competitor is used to determine final standings.

For the discus, hammer, shot put, and weight throw, the measurement is made from the inside of the circle's circumference along a line to the nearest point of the mark made by the implement. For the javelin, the measurement is made from the inside edge of the throwing arc on a line to the point where the ground was broken by the tip of the javelin.

Discus

The discus is a smooth implement, usually wood with a metal rim. It is thrown from a circle that is 2.5 meters in diameter. Men throw a discus weighing two kilograms; women throw a disc weighing one kilogram. Contestants may not wear spiked shoes. A cage surrounds the throwing area to protect spectators.

Javelin

The javelin is a slender metal shaft thrown from behind a curved arc at the end of a runway, which is between 30 and 36.5 meters long and 4 meters wide. The arc is white board or metal and has a radius of 8 meters. The men's javelin is 8.8 feet long and weighs 1.8 pounds; the women's javelin is 7.5 feet long and weighs 1.3 pounds. Tape may not be used on the jave-

lin. The surface and finish must be smooth. A nonslip grip is placed in the middle of the shaft. Competitors may wear spiked shoes.

The javelin is thrown into a landing sector, which begins 8 meters behind the arc and extends out in a 29-degree angle. The javelin must be held with one hand and thrown over the shoulder. The tip of the javelin must strike the ground first for the throw to be valid. Other fouls are recorded when

- the competitor turns her back to the throwing area after preparing to throw;
- the throw does not land completely in the landing sector;
- the competitor touches the arc, the ground beyond the arc, or the boundary lines; or
- the competitor leaves the runway before the javelin touches the ground.

Javelin throwers may place one or two marks along the runway to assist in the runup.

Hammer

The hammer consists of three parts: a solid metal head, a wire about 4 feet long, and a single- or double-loop grip. The senior men's hammer weighs 16 pounds; the women's hammer weighs 8.8 pounds. The hammer thrower may wear gloves. He may rest the head of the hammer either inside or outside the throwing circle. He grips the hammer with both hands.

It is not a foul if the hammer touches the ground or the top of the iron band in the throwing circle as the competitor is making his turns in preparing to throw. It is a foul, however, if the hammer touches the ground or iron band and the hammer thrower stops his throw. If the hammer breaks during the throw or while in the air, it is not considered an attempt. The competitor may throw another hammer.

Shot Put

The shot put is a solid metal ball. The men's shot weighs 16 pounds; the women's weighs 8.8 pounds. Contestants "put" (throw) the shot from a circle with a 7-foot diameter. The shot is put from the shoulder, with one hand. The hand holds the shot close to the chin; it may not be dropped from its position during the put. The shot may not be brought behind the line of the shoulders.

Weight Throw

The weight consists of three parts: a solid metal head, a handle of round metal, and a steel link connection. Men throw a 35-pound weight; women throw a 20-pound weight. In making the throw, a competitor uses both hands, holding the weight by the handle, assuming any position she chooses.

COMBINED EVENTS

Men and women have several combined events to compete in, both indoors and out. The most common combined event for men is the decathlon, which consists of 10 events over two days. On day 1, men compete in the 100-meter dash, the long jump, the shot put, the high jump, and the 400-meter dash. On day 2, they compete in the 110-meter hurdles, the discus throw, the pole vault, the javelin throw, and the 1,500-meter run.

The most common women's combined event is the heptathlon, which consists of seven events over two days. On day 1, women compete in the 100-meter hurdles, the high jump, the shot put, and the 200-meter dash. On day 2, they compete in the long jump, the javelin throw, and the 800-meter run.

Rules for combined events generally are the same as for the individual events, with the following exceptions:

- Competitors get three trials each in the long jump, shot put, discus throw, and javelin throw.
- A competitor is disqualified in the hurdles or running events after three false starts.
- An athlete who does not take part in one event is disqualified from the competition.

- Points are awarded for times and distances recorded for each event. Highest score wins.

MODIFICATIONS

This section contains some of the basic rules that modify the sport for youth, masters, and race walking.

Youth

Youth track is divided into these divisions:

- Bantam (10-and-under)
- Midget (11-12)
- Youth (13-14)
- Intermediate (15-16)
- Young men/women (17-18)

Important modifications of rules for these classifications include the following:

- In bantam, midget, and youth competition, starting blocks are not necessary, though runners may choose to use them. In races of 800 meters or more, qualifying rounds are run. In one-day events, all races of 200 meters or more are run as finals.
- Hurdle distances and heights are as shown in table 41.2. Intermediate boys and young men run a 2,000-meter steeplechase. In field events, in lieu of three attempts in a preliminary round and three attempts in a final round, competitors may have one round with four attempts. Implement weights are as shown in table 41.3.

In the javelin, the measurement is made from the center of the circle to the first point of contact the javelin makes with the ground in the landing sector. The contact may be with any part of the javelin. In the high jump and pole vault, competitors may use more than two marks to assist in their runup, and if they pass on three consecutive heights, they are allowed one warm-up jump without the crossbar in place.

Table 41.2   Hurdle Specifications, up to Age 18

Division	Distance	Hurdles	Height (in)
Midgets (boys and girls)	80	8	30
Youth girls	100	10	30
Youth boys	100	10	33
Youth (boys and girls)	200	5	30
Intermediate and young women	100	10	33
Intermediate and young men	110	10	39
Intermediate and young women	400	10	30
Intermediate and young men	400	10	36

Adapted from USA Track & Field 1995.

Table 41.3   Implement Specifications, up to Age 18

Division	Shot	Discus	Javelin
Bantam (10 and under)	6 lb	---	---
Midgets (11 to 12)	6 lb	---	---
Youth girls (13 to 14)	6 lb	---	---
Youth boys (13 to 14)	4 kg (8.8 lb)	---	---
Intermediate girls (15 to 16)	4 kg (8.8 lb)	1 kg (2.2 lb)	600 g (21.2 oz)
Intermediate boys (15 to 16)	12 lb	1.6 kg (3.5 lb)	800 g (28.2 oz)
Young women (17 to 18)	4 kg (8.8 lb)	1 kg (2.2 lb)	600 g (21.2 oz)
Young men (17 to 18)	12 lb	1.6 kg (3.5 lb)	800 g (28.2 oz)

Adapted from USA Track & Field 1995.

Masters

Masters competition is split into 5-year age groups, beginning with 30-34 (submasters). No starting blocks are necessary, but competitors may use them. Competitors are disqualified after one false start.

In the high jump and pole vault, athletes who pass on three consecutive heights are allowed one warm-up jump without the crossbar in place. Hurdle heights are increasingly lowered as competitors reach older age groups. Implement weights (for the shot put, discus, javelin, and so on) are lowered as well.

Race Walking

Race walking may take place on either road or track. The main rules include the following:

- Unbroken contact must be maintained with the ground (the lead foot must touch the ground before the back foot leaves the ground).

- The support leg must be straightened for at least a moment.

One warning is given for a violation; a second occurrence means disqualification.

ORGANIZATIONS

New York Road Runners
9 East 89th Street
New York, NY 10128
212-423-2249
www.nyrrc.org

Road Runners Club of America
510 North Washington Street
Alexandria, VA 22314
703-836-0558
www.rrca.org

USA Track & Field
One RCA Dome, Suite 140
Indianapolis, IN 46225
317-261-0500
www.usatf.org

Triathlon

The first known triathlon, comprised of a three-part swimming-cycling-running event, was held in 1974 in San Diego, California. John Collins, a U.S. naval officer who competed in this first informal triathlon, brought the sport to Hawaii, helping to create the "Ironman Triathlon" from three separate endurance events already in existence there. The first Ironman was held in 1978, with 12 men finishing; the next year, 13 men and 1 woman finished.

The sport began to take off in the early 1980s; now more than a thousand compete in the Ironman event, with thousands more turned away. Triathlons of varying distances are held throughout the United States and internationally. There are somewhere between 150,000 and 200,000 active triathletes in the United States. The sport made its Olympic debut at the 2000 Olympics in Sydney, Australia.

Objective: To complete the course in the fastest time while keeping within the rules.

Overview: Although the most common events in a triathlon are swimming, bicycling, and running, in that order, USA Triathlon recognizes other forms of the sport, including a different order of events, or even different events. The rules in this chapter, however, pertain to swimming, biking, and running.

Depending on the size of the field, a triathlon begins with either a *mass start,* in which all athletes begin at once, or a *wave start,* in which triathletes are grouped and begin at different times. After completing the swim, triathletes enter the transition area, where they don helmets and shoes, get on their bikes, and begin the cycling course. Upon finishing the cycling phase, they again enter a transition area, place their bikes in a designated corral, and begin the running phase. Once they complete the run, the race is over.

DISTANCES

USA Triathlon recognizes four distance categories. The distances may vary somewhat, but the basic categories are shown in table 42.1.

TERMS

Banned substances include stimulants, narcotics, anabolic steroids, beta-blockers, diuretics, and peptide hormones and analogues.

A **mass start** is one in which all athletes begin at once.

Obstruction is the act of intentionally or accidentally blocking, charging, obstructing, or interfering with the forward progress of another athlete. Such a violation results in a variable time penalty.

The **transition area** is set up for the transitions between the swim and the bike and between the bike and the run.

A triathlete may not gain **unfair advantage** by using her body to push, pull, hold, strike, or force her way through other triathletes. Violation results in a variable time penalty.

A **variable time penalty** is assessed for fouls such as obstruction and unfair advantage. The time penalized depends on the race distance:

- Sprint—30 seconds
- International—1 minute
- Long—2 minutes
- Ultra—4 minutes

A **wave start** is one in which groups of athletes begin at different times.

TRIATHLETES

Triathletes must compete in appropriate age groups. They are assessed variable time penalties for receiving unauthorized assistance, including food, drink, equipment, support, pacing, a replacement bicycle, or bicycle parts. They may exit a course, but they must reenter at the point they exited or be assessed a variable time penalty.

SWIMMING

Swimmers may use any stroke; they may tread water, float, or stand on the bottom to rest. They may also hold on to buoys, boats, ropes, or other objects to rest, but they may not make forward progress while holding onto an object. They may make forward progress while standing on the bottom.

Swimmers may wear *wetsuits* in water temperatures up to and including 78 degrees Fahrenheit (25.6 degrees Celsius). They may wear wetsuits when the water temperature is

Table 42.1 Triathlon Distances

Type	Swim (mi)	Bike (mi)	Run (mi)
Sprint	.5	12.4	3.1
International	.93	24.8	6.2
Long	1.2	56.0	13.1
Ultra	2.4	112.0	26.2

between 78 and 84 degrees Fahrenheit, but they are not eligible for prizes or awards. When the water temperature is 84 degrees Fahrenheit (28.9 degrees Celsius) or greater, they may not wear wetsuits.

CYCLING

Cyclists must obey all traffic laws, unless directed to do otherwise by a race official. Cyclists must use only their own force in propelling their bikes. They may not use their hands to push or carry their bikes unless their bikes are disabled. Cyclists assume sole responsibility for knowing the course. Officials will not adjust race times if cyclists get off course.

Cyclists who endanger themselves or others will be disqualified. They may not wear or carry headsets, radios, or other items deemed dangerous by race officials. They must wear approved helmets with fastened chinstraps (see "Equipment").

Cyclists may not work together to improve performance or team position. No cyclist may be in the *drafting zone* of another cyclist or of a motor vehicle, except if he is passing. A cyclist's drafting zone is 7 meters long and 2 meters wide, with the length beginning at the front of the front wheel. A motor vehicle's drafting zone is 15 meters wide and 30 meters long. Cyclists must keep to the right of the course unless passing. They may not attempt to pass unless they have adequate space to do so.

A cyclist is generally entitled to a position on the course if he gained it without touching another cyclist. Although cyclists who have established the right of way may not obstruct the progress of other cyclists, a cyclist who is overtaking another cyclist bears the primary responsibility for avoiding a positioning foul, even if the cyclist ahead decreases speed. A cyclist overtakes another cyclist when his front wheel goes beyond the front wheel of the other cyclist.

When a cyclist overtakes another cyclist, the overtaken cyclist bears primary responsibility for avoiding a positioning foul. An overtaken cyclist must move completely out of the drafting zone of the cyclist who has just passed her before she attempts to pass that cyclist. A cyclist may be in the drafting zone of another cyclist only

- when it takes 15 seconds or less to overtake the cyclist;
- for safety reasons, course blockage, in transition areas, or when making a turn of 90 degrees or greater; or
- when race officials allow it because of narrow lanes.

No cyclist may be directly behind another cyclist, even if she is out of the other cyclist's drafting zone. A cyclist who violates a position foul rule is assessed a variable time penalty for the first violation and is disqualified for the second violation.

RUNNING

Triathletes must run or walk the run course; anyone who crawls forward will be disqualified by USA Triathlon rules (though Ironman North America permits crawling). Contestants are responsible for knowing and following the course. They may not wear or carry headsets, radios, or similar equipment. They may carry nonbreakable containers of liquid.

EQUIPMENT

Swimmers must wear either the official race cap or a brightly-colored swim cap. They may wear goggles or face masks, but these are not required. They may not wear fins, paddles, gloves, floating devices, or any artificial propulsion device.

Cyclists must wear helmets that meet or exceed the specifications of the American National Standard Institute (ANSI) or the Snell Memorial Foundation. They must fasten their chinstraps before they mount their bikes and not unfasten them until after they dismount.

Bicycles may not exceed 2 meters in length or 75 centimeters in width. The distance between the center of the chain wheel axle and the ground must be at least 24 centimeters. Bikes may not have any wind resistance shields or devices attached anywhere. The front wheel of the bike must be of spoke construction; the rear wheel may be either spoke or solid. The two wheels may have a different diameter if race officials determine they are safe. Each wheel must have one working brake.

OFFICIALS

Race officials consist of a head referee, marshals, judges, and a head timer. The head referee has complete charge of the event, except for decisions made by a protest committee.

ORGANIZATIONS

USA Triathlon
616 W. Monument Street
Colorado Springs, CO 80905
719-597-9090
www.usatriathlon.org

Ultimate

© Scobel Wiggins

Objective: To score the most goals.

Scoring: A goal is scored when any player catches any legal pass in the end zone of attack; the player's first point of contact with the ground must be completely in the end zone.

Number of Players: Seven per team.

Size of Field: 40 yards wide by 70 yards long, with 25-yard end zones on either end.

Disc: Any flying disc that is acceptable to both team captains.

Length of Game: Until one team reaches or exceeds 15 goals and is ahead by 2 or more goals.

Overview: Ultimate is a noncontact disc sport. Players are not allowed to run while holding the disc; the disc is advanced by passing it to other players. The disc may be passed in any direction. Any time a pass is incomplete, intercepted, or knocked down or contacts an out-of-bounds area, a turnover occurs, resulting in a change of disc possession.

FIELD

The standard field of play is a rectangular area with dimensions as shown in figure 43.1. The *brick mark* is 18 meters from each end zone, midway between the sidelines. The *playing field proper* is the playing field excluding the end zones. The corners of the playing field proper and the end zones are marked by cones.

TERMS

The **best perspective** is the most complete viewpoint available to a player. This perspective includes the relative positions of the disc, ground, players, and line markers involved in the play.

A **brick** is any pull that initially lands out-of-bounds untouched by the receiving team.

Legitimate position is the stationary position established by a player's body, excluding extended arms and legs, that can be avoided by all opposing players when time and distance are taken into account.

The **pivot** is the part of the body in continuous contact with a single spot on the field during a thrower's possession.

To be in **possession** of the disc, a player must have sustained contact with, and control of, a nonspinning disc.

A **pull** is the throw from one team to the other that starts play at the beginning of a half or after a goal.

Field

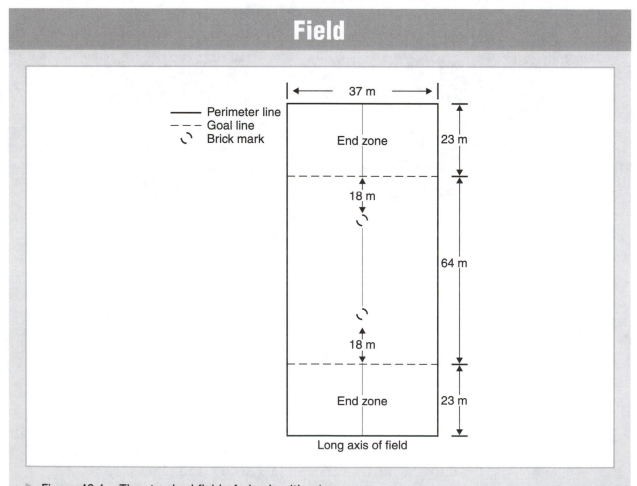

▶ Figure 43.1   The standard field of play in ultimate.
Provided by the Ultimate Players Association (www.upa.org).

PLAYERS

Ultimate arose from a game invented by students at Columbia High School in Maplewood, New Jersey in 1967. It is now played worldwide, with as many as 100,000 people estimated to play in the U.S. and Canada alone, and is the largest flying-disc sport. It is a fast-growing sport played in more than 30 countries at club, college, high school, community, and corporate levels. It holds competitions for coed, men's, women's, junior's, and master's play.

Thrower

The thrower is the offensive player with the disc, or the player who has just released the disc. Once an offensive player has picked up the disc, that player is required to put the disc into play. If the disc is on the playing field proper, an offensive player must put the disc in play within ten seconds. If the disc is not on the playing field proper, an offensive player must put the disc in play within twenty seconds. The thrower can pivot in any direction, but once the marker has established a legitimate stationary position, the thrower may not pivot into the marker's body. The thrower cannot change the pivot until the throw is released.

Marker

Only one defensive player may guard the thrower at any one time; that player is the marker. No other defensive player can establish a position within three meters of the thrower's pivot unless that defender is guarding another offensive player in that area. There must be at least one disc diameter between the upper bodies of the thrower and the marker at all times. The marker's extended arms and legs may not be positioned to restrict the thrower from pivoting or throwing.

Generally, the thrower is allowed ten seconds to throw. This possession may be timed by the marker's stall count. The marker loudly announces "stalling" and counts from one to ten loudly enough for the thrower to hear. Only a marker within three meters of the thrower's point of ground contact may initiate or continue a stall count.

If the defense switches markers, the new marker must reinitiate the stall count. A marker leaving the three-meter radius and returning is considered a new marker.

The marker may not straddle (place one foot on either side of) the thrower's pivot or deliberately block the thrower's vision.

Receiver

The receiver is any offensive player either in the act of catching the disc, or not in possession of the disc. If a receiver speeds up, changes direction, or obviously takes more steps than are required to stop after catching a pass and before establishing a pivot, that player has traveled. If a receiver catches a pass on the run and then releases a pass after the third ground contact before coming to a complete stop, that player has traveled. Bobbling to gain control of the disc is permitted, but purposeful, controlled bobbling to oneself to advance the disc in any direction is considered traveling. If the disc is caught simultaneously by offensive and defensive players, the offense retains possession. If an airborne player catches the disc and is contacted by an opposing player before landing, and that contact causes the receiver to land out of bounds, the receiver may call a foul and retain possession at the spot of the foul.

PLAY

Much of the basics of ultimate can be understood through its rules regarding the length of game, pulls, inbounds and out of bounds, and end zone possession.

Length of Game

A standard game is played until one team reaches or exceeds 15 goals with a margin of at least 2 goals over its opponent. (Halftime occurs when one team first reaches or exceeds half the game total needed to win.) There are variations on that length, however, including

- a soft cap, which is a maximum score limit imposed before the event;

- a time cap, which is a maximum score limit imposed during a game once a predetermined time of play has elapsed and after the current scoring attempt is completed; and
- a hard cap, which can be imposed once a predetermined time of play has elapsed and after the current scoring attempt is completed. If the score is tied, the teams play until one additional goal is scored.

Note: A time cap creates a new cap to the game score that didn't exist at the start of the game. For example, suppose a game score is 11-10 and the time slot for a particular round of play is expiring. A reduced winning score can be set to ensure completion of the game. In general it is the higher score plus 2. A hard cap ensures the end of the game because the time slot for a particular round of play has expired. This cap means that whoever is ahead at the completion of the current scoring attempt has won the game. If the game is tied, it is now sudden death. These caps are used to control the logistics of tournament play to ensure games are played.

Pulls

Play starts at the beginning of each half and after each goal with a pull, where a player on the pulling team throws the disc to the opposing team. The players on the pulling team are free to move anywhere in their end zone, but they may not cross the goal line until the disc is released. The players on the receiving team must stand with one foot on the goal line they are defending without changing position relative to one another. As soon as the disc is released, it is in play and all players may move in any direction. Other rules governing pulling and restarting play include:

- If a pull hits and remains inbounds, it is put into play at the spot where it came to rest.
- If a pull hits ground inbounds and rolls out of bounds before being touched by the receiving team, or if a pull goes out of bounds after being touched by the receiv-

ing team, the disc is put into play nearest to where it last crossed the perimeter line before going out of bounds.

- If a pull initially hits the ground out of bounds, the receiving team has the option of putting the disc into play nearest to where the disc last crossed the perimeter line in flight or, after signaling for a brick/middle, before gaining possession of the disc.
- If the pull is caught, the disc is put into play on the playing field nearest to where the disc was caught. If the pull is dropped by the receiving team, it is a turnover.
- Each time a goal is scored, the teams switch the direction of their attack and the team that scored pulls to the opposing team.
- All offensive players must establish a stationary position by the end of a timeout, and the defense has up to twenty seconds to check the disc into play.
- When any call or event stops play, all players must come to a stop as quickly as possible and remain in their respective positions until play is restarted.
- When play is to be restarted with a check, but no marker is near enough to touch the disc in the thrower's hand, play is restarted using an offensive self-check. When play is to be restarted with a check but no offensive player is near enough to take possession of the disc at the appropriate spot, play is restarted using a defensive self-check.

Inbounds and Out of Bounds

The entire playing field is inbounds. The perimeter lines are not part of the playing field and are out of bounds. For a player to be considered inbounds after gaining possession of the disc, that player's first point of ground contact with any area must be completely inbounds.

An airborne player whose last ground contact was with an out-of-bounds area is out of bounds. Exceptions include the following:

- When momentum carries a player out of bounds after that player has gained possession of an inbounds disc and landed inbounds, the player is considered inbounds. The disc is put into play at the spot on the perimeter line where the player went out of bounds.

- The thrower may contact an out-of-bounds area while pivoting, provided that the pivot remains in contact with the playing field.

- Contact between players does not confer the state of being inbounds or out of bounds from one to the other.

End Zone Possession

If a team gains possession in the end zone that it is defending following a turnover, the player taking possession must immediately decide to put the disc into play at that spot or to carry the disc to the closest point on the goal line and put it into play there.

If a player catches a pass from a teammate in the end zone that they are defending, that player does not have a choice of advancing the disc to the goal line.

If a team gains possession other than by interception of a pass in the end zone that it is attacking (which is a goal), the player taking possession must carry the disc directly to the closest spot on the goal line and put the disc into play from there.

VIOLATIONS AND FOULS

A foul is the result of physical contact between opposing players that affects the outcome of the play. It is the responsibility of all players to avoid contact in every way possible. In general, the player initiating contact is guilty of a foul. A foul can only be called by the player who has been fouled and must be announced by loudly calling out "foul!" immediately after the foul has occurred.

Whenever a call is made, play continues until the thrower in possession acknowledges the call. If the disc is in the air or the thrower is in the act of throwing at the time of the call,

© Scobel Wiggins

Contact between players should be avoided at all times.

play continues until the outcome of that pass is determined.

In general, when a foul or violation stops play, players must resume their respective positions at the time the foul or violation was called. If a dispute arises concerning a foul, violation, or the outcome of a play, and the teams cannot come to a satisfactory resolution, the disc is returned to the thrower and put into play with a check, with the count the same or at six if over five. (That is, if the count was at eight, it begins again at six.)

If offsetting infractions are called by offensive and defensive players on the same play, the disc reverts to the thrower with the count the same, or at six if over five, and play restarts with a check. A throwing foul may be called when there is contact between the thrower and the marker. The disc in a thrower's possession is considered part of the thrower. Although it should be avoided whenever possible, incidental contact occurring during the follow-through (after the disc has been released) is not sufficient grounds for a foul, unless the contact constitutes harmful endangerment.

A *receiving foul* may be called when there is contact between opposing players in the process of attempting a catch, interception, or knockdown. A certain amount of incidental contact before, during, or immediately after the catching attempt is often unavoidable and is not a foul. When the disc is in the air, players must play the disc, not the opponent. A player may not move in a manner solely to prevent an opponent from taking an unoccupied position via an unoccupied path; doing so is a *blocking foul*. No defensive player may touch the disc while it is in the possession of an offensive player. If a defensive player initiates contact with the disc, and the offensive player loses possession as a result, it is a *stripping foul*. No offensive player may move to obstruct a defensive player guarding a receiver; doing so is a violation called a *pick*.

EQUIPMENT

Any flying disc may be used as long as it is acceptable to both team captains. If the captains cannot agree, the current official disc of the Ultimate Players Association should be used. Cleats with any dangerous parts are not allowed.

OBSERVERS AND OFFICIALS

Ultimate relies upon a spirit of sporting behavior that places the responsibility for fair play on the players. Typically no referees or officials are used; it is up to the players to adhere to the rules and to make the appropriate calls.

Observers may be used if desired by the captains or tournament organizers, however. Observers are nonplayers whose role is to watch the action of the game carefully.

ORGANIZATIONS

Ultimate Players Association
741 Pearl Street, Side Suite
Boulder, CO 80302
303-447-3472
www.upa.org

44 Volleyball

Volleyball is a popular and diverse sport with many variations, including indoor, outdoor, and beach volleyball; 2-, 3-, 4-, or 6-player teams; Mixed-Six (coed); games to 11 points, to 15 points, or by the clock; and the rally-point system. Volleyball is played by about 46 million Americans and about 800 million worldwide and has been an Olympic sport since 1964. It originally was developed as an alternative to basketball by William G. Morgan of the YMCA in Holyoke, Massachusetts, in 1895.

Objective: To score more points than the other team by hitting the ball over the net so that the opponents cannot return the ball or prevent it from hitting the ground in their court.

Number of Players: 2, 3, 4, or 6 players, depending on the type of play.

Scoring: Rally scoring is used exclusively in USA Volleyball and NCAA action and is being phased in at the high school level; in this system, a point is scored on every play.

Games and Matches: A match is the best of three or five games. Each nondeciding game is played to 25 points using rally scoring (30 points in college). A game must be won by at least 2 points; there is no scoring cap. The deciding game is played to 15. Again, a team must win by at least 2 points and there is no scoring cap.

Overview: The referee blows her whistle for the first serve, which begins play. After the serve, players may move around on their sides of the court, but they may not step completely over the center line. (In college, rules allow the hand and foot to completely cross the center line and give some latitude with other body parts, such as the knee or forearm, to cross partially over the center line.)

Players may hit the ball with any part of their bodies. They may clasp their hands together and strike the ball underhand or overhand, with either an open hand or a closed fist. A point is scored on every play; the team that scores serves the next ball.

The main body of this chapter refers to indoor, six-player rules. Modifications are noted near the end of the chapter.

COURT

The court includes the *playing area* and the *free zone* (see figure 44.1). It is divided into two equal parts by the *center line,* which runs the width of the court under the net. *Attack*

lines are on both sides of the net. The *net* itself is made of mesh and is a minimum of 32 feet long and 39 inches wide with a 2-inch canvas band at the top. For men, the top of the net is 2.4 meters high; for women, it is 2.2 meters high. The top and the bottom of the net are fastened to the posts to remain taut.

Two white side bands, if used, are fastened vertically to the net; they are considered part of the net. An antenna is fastened at the outer edge of each side band and placed on opposite ends of the net.

TERMS

An **attack-hit** is a hit aimed into the opponent's court. All actions directing the ball toward the opponent, except a serve or block, are attack-hits.

Attack lines separate each side of the court into a front zone and a back zone. Players in

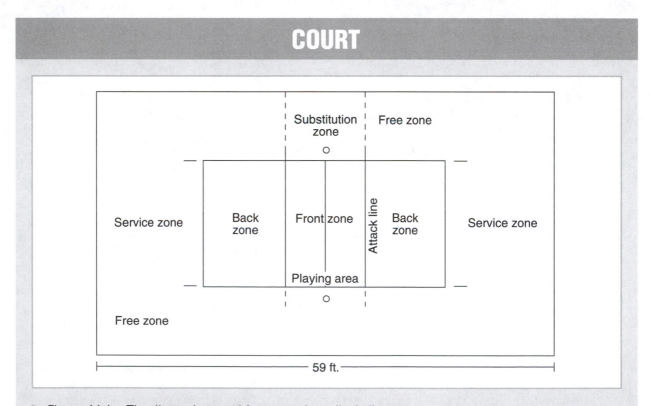

▶ Figure 44.1   The dimensions and features of a volleyball court.
Adapted from Federation Internationale de Volleyball 1997.

the back row may attempt an attack hit when they are behind the attack line, or when they are in front of the line when the ball is lower than the top of the net.

Back-row players are the three who are situated in the back zone when the serve is made.

A **block** occurs when one or more players at the net deflect the ball coming from the opponent.

A **delay** may be called by a referee when a team takes too long to substitute or otherwise delays play. The first delay results in a warning; the second results in a loss of a rally.

A **dig** is made by a player who first contacts the ball over the net (unless this player is making a block).

A **fault** results in a lost serve and a point awarded to the opposition. For more on faults, see page 282.

A **front-row** player is one who is positioned in the front zone, between the attack line and the net.

A **held ball,** which is a fault, may be called when a player does not contact the ball cleanly.

A **hit** is any contact by a player with the ball. A player may hit the ball once during a play, although if it is the team's first hit and is not a block, the ball may contact the same player on various parts of the body consecutively, provided that the contacts occur in one action.

A **match** is won by the team that wins the most games in the match.

A **playing fault** is any breach of the rules by a player. A fault results in loss of the rally.

A **rally** is the exchange of hits between the teams. The team that wins the rally gets a point and the serve.

A team's **rotation order** must be kept when it gains the serve. Each time it gains a serve, players rotate one position clockwise. Failure to do so is a fault.

Sanctions are given for various penalties. In the NCAA, a *yellow card* signifies a warning; a *red card* is a penalty for a more serious offense that results either in the serving team losing the serve or in the receiving team losing a point. When the referee holds up both a red card and a yellow card in one hand, the offending player is expelled from the game. When the referee holds up a red card in one hand and a yellow card in the other, the offending player is expelled for the match. USA Volleyball rules allow for a verbal warning. The yellow card indicates a penalty (loss of rally), the red card indicates expulsion from the game, and the red and yellow card together indicate expulsion from the match.

Players of the serving team may not **screen** the opponents from seeing the server or the path of the ball. Screening includes arm waving, jumping, and moving sideways as the serve is being made. It also occurs when the server is hidden behind two or more players.

A **serve** puts the ball into play. The server may move freely behind the end line when serving. See page 282 for more on serving.

A **set** is a contact that sets up a spike. The typical order of contacts is dig, set, spike.

A **sideout** occurs when the serving team does not score, and the serve goes over to the other team.

A **spike** is a hard-driven ball that is hit in an attempt to score.

A player may **tip** a ball with her fingers if she does not throw or hold the ball and the contact is brief.

PLAYERS

Each team has six players on the court: three in the front row and three in the back row (left, center, and right in both rows). Each front-row player must have at least part of one foot closer to the center line than both feet of the corresponding back-row player. Outside players in each row must have at least part of one foot closer to their side line than both feet of the center player in the same row. Player position is determined by the position of the foot last in contact with the floor at the time the ball is served.

Once the ball is served, players may move to any position within their side of the court. When a team gains the serve, its players rotate one position clockwise. In USA Volleyball Open play, a team is allowed a maximum of six substitutions per game. A starting player may leave the game and reenter once. A substitute player may not reenter a game after he is replaced, and he may be replaced only by the player he replaced. In all other USA Volleyball play, a team may substitute 12 times per game; a starting player may reenter a game twice; and a substitute player may enter a game three times.

Each team has an option to register a "Libero" player. The Libero player is restricted to playing in the back row and cannot serve, block, or attack-hit when the ball is above the height of the top of the net. The Libero wears a different-colored shirt from the other team members and does not take part in normal substitutions; rather, the Libero enters or leaves a game on her own, while the ball is out of play and before the whistle for service. Replacements involving the Libero do not count as regular substitutions.

PLAY

Most of the basics of volleyball can be understood through its rules for serving, ball in play, net play, attacking, and blocking.

Serving

Players must follow the service order recorded on the lineup sheet. A player retains the serve until the other team wins the right to serve. A player has eight seconds to serve once the referee whistles for service. If a player serves before the whistle, the play is canceled and the serve is repeated.

The server may serve from anywhere behind the end line. After completing the serve, the player may step or land inside the court. If the server tosses the ball and it touches the ground without touching the player, this is a service error. A service fault occurs if the ball

- touches a player of the serving team;
- fails to pass through the crossing space over the net;
- touches the net, antenna, or any other object;
- lands out of bounds; or
- passes over a "screen" of one or more players.

Ball in Play

The ball is inbounds when it touches any portion of the court, including the boundary lines. The ball is out of bounds when it touches the floor completely outside the boundary lines. It is also out when it touches an object outside the boundary lines, when it crosses the net outside the crossing space, or when it touches the net, rope, antenna, or post outside the antenna or side band. (Note: If a player, in pursuing an opponent's serve, goes out of bounds before hitting the ball, the ball is still in play.)

NCAA rules allow for the pursuit rule (pursuit of a ball that crosses outside the crossing space after the first contact).

Each team has three hits, in addition to blocking, to return the ball. A hit is any contact with the ball, whether intentional or not. A player may not contact the ball twice during a rally, unless the first contact is a block or unless two players contact the ball simultaneously. In this case it is counted as one contact, and any player may hit the ball next. A player may not receive assistance from a teammate in trying to hit a ball, but a teammate may hold back a player who is about to cross the center line or touch the net.

Net Play

If a ball outside the crossing space has not fully crossed the vertical plane of the net, it may be played back to a teammate. A ball is "out" when it completely crosses under the net. A ball may touch the net and still be in play. If a ball is driven into the net, it may be recovered if the team hasn't used its three hits.

- A serve that contacts the net and continues into the opponent's court remains in play.
- A blocker may contact the ball beyond the plane of the net but may not interfere with an opponent's play. A hitter's hands or arms may cross the net if the contact was made on his side of the net or within the net's plane. If any part of a player touching the floor (such as hands, knees, or feet) crosses completely over the center line into the opponent's court, however, a fault is called regardless of whether it interfered with the opponent's play.

NCAA rules allow the hand and foot to completely cross the center line and allow some latitude with other body parts (e.g., a knee or forearm) to cross partially over the center line. A fault is called when there are interference or safety concerns.

USA Volleyball allows penetration into the opponent's court beyond the center line to touch the opponent's court with one or both hands or feet, provided some part of the penetrating hands and feet remains either in contact with or directly above the center line.

A player may not touch the net. The only exceptions are incidental contact by a player's hair or an insignificant contact by a player not involved in the play. If a driven ball causes the net to touch a player, this is not a fault.

Attacking-Hitting

An attack-hit is any action directing the ball toward the opponent's court, except for serves and blocks. Front-row players may make an attack-hit when the ball is at any height. Back-row players may make an attack-hit at any height as long as they are behind the attack line at takeoff; they may land beyond the line. A back-row player may also make an attack-hit from the front zone if the ball is below the top of the net.

Blocking

A block occurs at the net as a player or players attempt to block the ball from entering their side of the court. At least one blocker must have a portion of his body above the net at some point during the block. A block is not counted as one of the team's three hits.

A player who blocks the ball may be the first to contact the ball after the block. A player may place her hands and arms beyond the net in an attempt to block if she does not interfere with her opponents' play. An example of interference is when an offensive player is setting a pass and a defensive player touches the ball with her hands or arms over the net. It is not interference if the defensive player touches the ball beyond the net when the offensive team is attacking.

Consecutive contacts with the ball are permitted in blocking if the contacts are quick and continuous and made during one action. A serve cannot be blocked.

SCORING

A point is scored when

- the ball lands in bounds on the opponents' court,
- the opponents are unable to return the ball within three hits,
- the opponents hit the ball out of bounds, or
- the opponents commit a fault, or foul.

If one team is penalized, the other team receives the serve and a point. If the receiving team faults, the serving team gets a point. If the serving team faults, the receiving team gets a point and the serve.

MISCONDUCT

Misconduct is classified as unsporting conduct, rude conduct, offensive conduct, or aggression. It may be directed at officials, players, coaches, or fans. Depending on the degree of the misconduct, a player may be warned, penalized, expelled for the game, or expelled for the match.

EQUIPMENT

The ball is spherical and bound in leather or approved synthetic materials. Its circumference is 25.5 to 27 inches; its weight is 9 to 10 ounces. It has 4.5 to 6 pounds of air pressure per square inch. Players wear jerseys and shorts, or one-piece outfits; no jewelry may be worn. Players wear soft- or rubber-soled shoes.

OFFICIALS

The officials include the first referee, the second referee, the scorekeeper, and two or four line judges. The first referee stands at one end of the net and has final authority over all decisions. He may overrule other officials. The second referee stands near the post outside the playing court, opposite the first referee. He signals faults, including net, center-line, and back faults, and assists the first referee. The second referee authorizes game interruptions, substitutions, and timeouts.

The scorekeeper sits facing the first referee; he records points and timeouts and checks that substitutions are legal. Line judges stand at opposite corners of the court, opposite the service zones (if two judges are used), or at each corner (if four judges are used). They stand at the intersection of the end line and side line and rule whether balls are in or out, signal when a ball crosses the net outside the crossing space, and indicate when a server foot-faults. Officials' signals are shown in figure 44.2.

MODIFICATIONS

The two main variations of the sport allow for coed play and for outdoor play. The net heights suggested by USA Volleyball are indicated in table 44.1.

A re-serve is no longer allowed in NCAA and USA Volleyball rules. An exception that may be used for 14-and-under play (USAV rules) allows one service tossing error for each service (within 5 seconds for the re-serve).

Twelve-and-under competition may be conducted using a lighter ball (7 to 8 ounces instead of 9 to 10 ounces).

Mixed-Six Play

The rules for Mixed-Six (coed) play are the same as for indoor play, except for the following:

- Males and females alternate serves and court positions.

Table 44.1 Net Heights		
Age groups	Females/reverse mixed six (ft/in)	Males/mixed-six (ft/in)
55 and above	—	7, 9⅝
45 and above	7, 4⅛	—
18 and under	7, 4⅛	7, 11⅝
16 and under	7, 4⅛	7, 11⅝
14 and under	7, 4⅛	7, 4⅛
12 and under	7, 0	7, 0
10 and under	6, 6	7, 0

Adapted from USA Volleyball 1995.

Sideout

Ball in bounds or line violation

Ball out

Ball contacted by a player when going out-of-bounds

Four hits

Crossing center line

Carried ball, thrown ball, held ball, or lifted ball

(continued)

▶ Figure 44.2   Common volleyball officials' signals.

Double hit

Ball contacted below the waist

Substitution

Ball served into net or player touching net

Over the net

Double fault or play over

Illegal block or screen

Point

▶ Figure 44.2 *(continued)*

- When the ball is played more than once by a team, at least one hit must be made by a female. A block does not count as a hit. Females may make all three hits; a male is not required to hit.

- An illegally hit ball by an illegal blocker becomes a double fault, and the opponent is awarded the point or serve.

- When only one male is in the front row, one back-row male may, after beginning in the back row, come forward of the attack line in order to block.

- No female back-row player may block.

- The net height is 2.4 meters (the same as in men's play).

Reverse Mixed-Six Play

The rules for Reverse Mixed-Six play are the same as for Mixed-Six play, with the following exceptions: When only one female is in the front row, one female in the back row may be in the attack zone in order to block. No male may block or spike. Male players may contact the ball above the net and send it into the opponent's court, but the trajectory of the ball upon contact must be upward. The net height is 2.2 meters (the same as for women's play). When the ball is played more than once on a side, it must be contacted at least once by a male.

Outdoor Play

The popularity of volleyball is evidenced by outdoor participation on beaches or grass. The rules for outdoor play are the same as for indoor play, with these exceptions:

- Brightly-colored boundary lines (flat bands or tape) mark the boundaries; if they move during play, play continues. If it can't be determined whether the ball was in or out, the rally is replayed. It is the players' responsibility to correct the boundary lines if they are moved.

- Attack lines are marked, but the center line is not.

- Teams may consist of 2, 3, 4, or 6 players, either of the same sex or coed.

- In doubles competition, no substitutions are allowed. Rosters are as follows for other play: triples competition—5 players; 4-player competition—6 players; 6-player competition—12 players. Unlimited substitution is allowed in triples, 4-player competition, and 6-player competition, as long as each player plays within her serving position during a single game.

- Players may wear jewelry, caps, visors, casts, eyewear, and so on, at their own risk. Rubber-soled shoes may be worn on grass, but nonflexible cleats or spikes are not allowed.

- The deciding game of a best-of-three games match may be a game to 15, played by rally-point rules, or a game to 7 played by scoring rules in which only the serving team can score.

- In doubles, triples, and 4-player competition, players may position themselves anywhere on the court, and the server may serve from anywhere beyond the end line.

- In doubles and triples play, the first contact after a hard-driven ball (a spike or block) can be a lift or push, as long as the motion is continuous and does not change directions.

- In doubles and triples play, if a ball is intentionally set into the opponent's court, the shoulders of the player setting the ball must be square to the direction of the ball.

- In doubles play, if a player serves out of turn, the play is allowed and that player holds serve until the opponents gain the serve. When the out-of-turn player's team regains the serve, her teammate will serve.

- In doubles, triples, and 4-player competition, players may not "dink," or tip, an attack-hit with the fingers.

- In doubles and triples competition, a player may not make an attack-hit using an overhand set that puts the ball on a sideways trajectory with the player's shoulders.

- In 6-player competition, a back-row player may not participate in a block.
- In 15-point games, teams switch sides each time the total score reaches a multiple of 5. In 11-point games, teams switch sides each time the total score reaches a multiple of 4. In 7-point games, switches occur on multiples of 2.

ORGANIZATIONS

USA Volleyball
715 S. Circle Drive
Colorado Springs, CO 80910
719-228-6800
www.usavolleyball.org

© Mary Messenger

Water Polo

Water polo originally drew its rules from rugby, and in the 1860s it was being played in rivers and lakes. By 1870 the sport had moved indoors, and by the late 1880s water polo was introduced to America. By that time the game had become more similar to soccer with its passing and its caged goals. Water polo became an Olympic sport in 1900.

Objective: To score points by putting the ball into the opponent's goal.

Number of Players: Each team has seven players in the water, a goalkeeper and six field players.

Scoring: A player scores a goal when the entire ball passes fully over the goal line and into the goal (between the posts and under the crossbar).

Length of Game: A game consists of four seven-minute periods; time stops when the ball is out of play.

Overview: To begin a game, players line up on their goal lines at least one meter apart and at least one meter from the goal posts. No more than two players may be between the goal posts, and no part of a player's body at water level may be beyond the goal line. A referee blows a whistle to begin play and tosses the ball on the half-distance line, near the edge of the field of play. The clock begins when a player touches the ball. Each team attempts to advance the ball by passing and dribbling it to get into position to score. A team has 35 seconds to shoot at its opponent's goal.

If the score is tied at the end of four periods, *extra time* goes into effect if the game requires a definite result. The teams play two three-minute periods with a one-minute break in between. If the score is still tied, a penalty shootout takes place. If the game does not require a definite result (e.g., a preliminary round game), the tie stands.

FIELD OF PLAY

The pool has a *half-distance line,* dividing the width of the pool in half. It also has *seven-meter, four-meter,* and *two-meter lines,* which are seven meters, four meters, and two meters from each goal line, respectively. *Goal lines* run the width of the pool. A *reentry area* is marked at each end of the pool, two meters from the corner, on the side opposite the official table (see figure 45.1).

Each *goal* consists of white, rigid goal posts, a crossbar, and a net. Goals are rectangular; they are three meters wide and centered between the sides of the pool.

TERMS

The **advantage rule** allows referees to not declare a foul if, in their opinion, calling the foul would be an advantage to the offending player's team.

A **corner throw** is taken by the attacking team from the two-meter mark on the side nearest where the ball crossed the goal line.

An **exclusion foul** results in a free throw for the team fouled and in the temporary or permanent exclusion of the offending player.

Extra time is used to break a tie score at the end of regulation. Extra time consists of two three-minute periods; if the score is still tied, a third period is played in "sudden death" style: The first team to score wins.

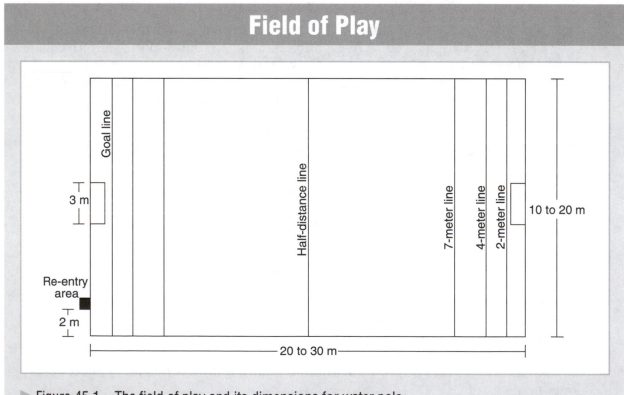

▶ Figure 45.1   The field of play and its dimensions for water polo.
Adapted from White 1990.

A **free throw** is awarded for ordinary and exclusion fouls.

A **goal throw** is a free throw awarded to the goalkeeper and taken within the two-meter area.

A **neutral throw** is made by the referee to put the ball back into play after players from each team have committed simultaneous fouls, or when the ball hits an overhead obstruction and rebounds into the field of play.

An **ordinary foul** results in a free throw for the offended team.

A **penalty foul** results in a penalty throw for the offended team.

A **penalty shootout** results if the score is still tied after two periods of extra time. Each team selects five shooters; these shooters take penalty throws, alternating by team. If the score is still even after all five shooters on each team have taken a penalty throw, then pairs of shooters (one from each team) shoot until one team scores and the other does not.

A **penalty throw** may be taken by any player of the team awarded the throw, except for the goalkeeper. The throw is made from the opponent's four-meter line as a direct shot on goal.

A **personal foul** is assessed against a player who commits an exclusion or penalty foul. A player who commits three personal fouls is excluded from the game.

PLAYERS

A team consists of seven players in the pool and no more than six reserves. Substitutes may enter freely between periods, before extra time, after a goal has been scored, or during a time-out. During play, a substitute may enter from the re-entry area after the exiting player has entered the re-entry area. If a player is bleeding, he must immediately leave the water. The game is not stopped; a substitute may immediately replace the injured player, who may return after the bleeding has stopped.

Age classifications for competition include 13-and-under, 15-and-under, 16-17, 18-20, open, and masters.

PLAY

After a goal, once the players are in their respective halves of the pool, the referee whistles the ball into play. A player of the team just scored upon puts the ball into play by passing to a teammate; the teammate may be forward, backward, or to the side of the passer. The clock begins when the player releases the ball.

SCORING

A team may score a goal from anywhere within the field of play, although a goalkeeper may not touch the ball beyond the half-distance line or go beyond that line herself.

A field player may score a goal with any part of his body except a clenched fist. (A goalkeeper may score a goal with a clenched fist.) At least two players, excluding the defending goalkeeper, must have intentionally touched the ball on the play for a goal to count. A player may score a goal by obtaining a goal throw or free throw from the goalkeeper and throwing the ball into the goal; it doesn't have to touch another player first.

A player may score a goal by immediately shooting from outside the seven-meter line after her team has been awarded a free throw outside seven meters. The player may not score after putting the ball into play unless the ball has been touched intentionally by another player other than the defending goalkeeper.

A goal is legal if the 35-second clock or the period clock expires after the ball has left a player's hand but before the ball enters the goal. If the ball floats over the goal line in this circumstance, the goal is good if the ball floated over the goal due to its own momentum.

FOULS

There are three types of fouls: ordinary and exclusion fouls, which result in free throws, and penalty fouls, which result in penalty throws. (Personal fouls are charged for exclusion and penalty fouls but not for ordinary fouls.) A player committing three personal fouls is excluded for the remainder of the game. Free throws and penalty throws are described in "Penalty Fouls."

Ordinary Fouls

An ordinary foul is called for

- advancing beyond the goal line at the start of a period, before the referee gives the signal to start;
- assisting a player;
- holding onto or pushing off from the goal posts or sides or ends of the pool;
- standing on the floor of the pool while taking an active part in the game;
- holding the ball underwater while being tackled;
- striking the ball with a clenched fist (except the goalkeeper, within the four-meter area);
- touching the ball with two hands at once (except the goalkeeper);
- impeding the movement of an opponent who is not holding the ball;
- pushing, or pushing off from, an opponent;
- being within two meters of the opponent's goal, except when in possession of the ball or behind the line of the ball;
- unduly delaying a free throw, corner throw, or goal throw;
- the goalkeeper's going beyond the half-distance line, or touching a ball beyond that line;
- maintaining possession of the ball for more than 35 seconds without shooting at the opponent's goal; or
- sending the ball out of the pool.

Exclusion Fouls

An exclusion foul results in a free throw for the team offended and in the exclusion of the player who committed the foul. This player can reenter the game at the earliest of these occurrences: 20 seconds of playing time has elapsed; a goal has been scored; the excluded player's team has regained possession of the ball; or play has stopped and then restarted, with possession in favor of the excluded player's team. An exclusion foul is called in a number of instances, including leaving the water or sitting or standing on the steps or side of the pool during play, except for injury or illness (this exception must be allowed by the referee); intentionally splashing water in an opponent's face; holding, sinking, or pulling back an opponent who does not have the ball; intentionally kicking or hitting an opponent, or attempting to do so; interfering with a free throw, corner throw, or goal throw; and goalkeeper's failing to take position for a penalty throw after being told to do so by the referee.

In addition, players are excluded for the remainder of the game for using foul language or violent or persistent foul play; for interfering with a free throw, corner throw, or goal throw; for the goalkeeper's failing to take position for a penalty throw after being told to do so by the referee; for interfering with a penalty throw (exclusion from game); for committing an act of brutality (exclusion from game); or for refusing to obey, or disrespecting, an official (exclusion from game).

When players from both teams simultaneously commit personal fouls, both players are excluded and a neutral throw is made.

Penalty Fouls

A penalty foul, resulting in a penalty throw for the team offended, is called for

- a player's committing any defensive foul within the four-meter area when a goal probably would have resulted;
- a defending player's kicking or striking an opponent within the four-meter area;
- an excluded player's intentionally interfering with the goal alignment or other aspects of play; or
- any player's pulling over the goal to prevent a likely score.

One of these throws may be awarded, according to the foul: goal, corner, neutral, free, or penalty.

- **Goal throw:** A goal throw is awarded when the entire ball has passed the goal line, outside of the goal posts (i.e., it hasn't scored), and was last touched by an attacking team player. The throw is taken by the defending goalkeeper within the two-meter area. If the goalkeeper is out of the water, it is taken by another defender.

- **Corner throw:** A corner throw is awarded when the ball has passed the goal line but has not gone between the goal posts and was last touched by a defender. The throw is taken by an attacking team player from the two-meter mark on the side where the ball crossed the goal line. The throw may be taken by any attacking player if undue delay does not occur.

- **Neutral throw:** A neutral throw is awarded when players from each team commit a foul at the same time or when, at the start of a period, the ball falls into a position of definite advantage for one team. The referee throws the ball into the water or up into the air at the same lateral position where the event occurred, so that players of both teams have an equal chance to gain possession. Players may touch the ball before it touches the water. The goalkeeper is excluded from taking a neutral throw.

- **Free throw:** A free throw is awarded for ordinary and exclusion fouls. The throw must be made so that the other players can see the ball leave the thrower's hand. The thrower may carry or dribble the ball before throwing. The ball is in play when it leaves the hand of the player passing it to another player. The throw must be taken at or behind the line of the foul.

- **Penalty throw:** A penalty throw is awarded for a penalty foul and may be taken by any player except the goalkeeper, from any point on the opponent's four-meter line. No player other than the defending goalkeeper may be in the four-meter area, and no player may be within two meters of the player taking the penalty throw. On the referee's signal, the player must immediately throw, with an uninterrupted motion, toward the goal. If the ball rebounds off the goal or the goalkeeper, it is in play, and another player does not need to touch it before a goal can be scored.

TIMEOUTS

Each team is entitled to two timeouts of a minute each during a game. The timeout must be called by the coach of the team in possession of the ball. After a timeout has been called, the players must go to their half of the field of play until 45 seconds of the timeout has concluded and been signaled by the officials' table or by the referee. Play is resumed by a free throw at the half-way line or at the corner, if the timeout was taken immediately before taking a corner throw. If the game extends into extra time, each team is permitted an additional time-out. Timeouts may be taken at any time. For example, if a team has not used any timeouts during regular time, it may use all three of its timeouts during extra time.

EQUIPMENT

The ball is round, weighs between 400 and 450 grams, and has a circumference between 68 and 71 centimeters for men and between 65 and 67 centimeters for women. The two teams wear caps of contrasting colors (other than solid red or the color of the ball). Goal-keepers wear red caps. The goalkeeper's cap is numbered 1; the rest of the caps are numbered 2 through 13.

OFFICIALS

Games are controlled by up to eight officials: referees, goal judges, timekeepers, and secretaries. The referee is in absolute control of the game. Goal judges make calls and signals on goals and corner and goal throws. Timekeepers keep the time and keep track of excluded players and reentries. Secretaries maintain records of the game.

MODIFICATIONS

The following modifications are made for Junior Olympic competition (18-and-under) and for Masters competition (30-and-over).

- **Junior Olympics:** A game lasts four five-minute periods. Each team is allowed one two-minute timeout per half. Substitutes may be made during a timeout. The maximum size of the field of play is 25 meters from goal line to goal line and 20 meters in width.

- **Masters:** Age groups are in five-year intervals, starting with 30 years old (30+, 35+, and so on). A team is placed in the age group of its youngest player; there are no age limits for older players playing in younger age groups. The distance between goal lines is 23.5 meters minimum, and the minimum width of the field of play is 17 meters. A game lasts four five-minute periods. Each team receives two one-minute timeouts.

ORGANIZATIONS

United States Water Polo, Inc.
1685 W. Unitah
Colorado Springs, CO 80904
www.usawaterpolo.com

© Sport the Library/SportsChrome

46

Water Skiing

Water skiing got its beginnings in the United States in 1922 when Ralph Samuelson, an 18-year-old Minnesotan, figured that if he could ski on snow, he could ski on water as well.

Competitions are held in various divisions, beginning with boys' and girls' divisions for 9 years old and younger, and ending with men's and women's divisions for 75 years old and older. Within each division, skiers are rated and compete according to their performance levels; there are six performance levels in each division.

Objective: To receive the highest score.

Scoring: Each contestant receives points in proportion to a national standard (see "Scoring" on page 299).

Overview: Water skiing is a sport that combines strength, dexterity, grace, and precision at high speeds. Skiers perform in three events: jumping, slalom, and tricks. Places are determined in each event, based on scores, with highest being best. Boys I and Girls I divisions (nine years old and younger) are the only divisions that do not complete all three events. These divisions do not take part in the jump competition.

Competitions may be held for individuals and for teams. At national tournaments, skiing order is based on seedings, with the highest-rated skier going last. At other tournaments, order may be based either on seedings or on a draw.

COURSES

Courses for the jump, slalom, and trick events are marked with buoys and have the following specifications:

A *jump course* has a 15-meter runup to the ramp, which must be parallel to the course. The ramp is 3.7 to 4.3 meters wide and 6.4 to 6.7 meters long out of the water. It has an apron that extends to 8 inches below the water (see figure 46.1a).

A *slalom course* is 259 meters long, with buoys set up throughout (see figure 46.1b).

A *trick course* measures between 157.5 and 192.5 meters long by 12 to 18 meters wide, with an additional 13.5 to 16.5 meters at each end of the course. Buoys set approximately 200 meters apart mark the course.

TERMS

A **balk** occurs when a skier refuses to take a ramp in a jumping event.

A **fall** occurs when a skier loses possession of the tow line, does not have at least one ski on, or does not have his weight primarily supported by one or both skis and is not able to regain skiing position.

A **handle throw** occurs when a skier refuses to enter a jump, slalom, or trick course by throwing her handle in the air before reach-

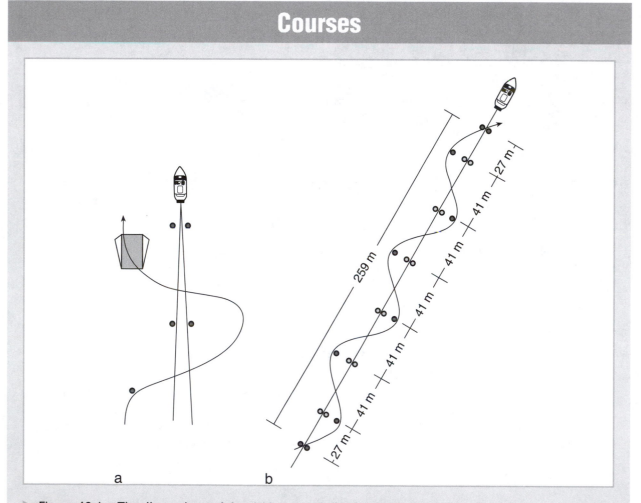

Courses

▶ Figure 46.1   The dimensions of the *(a)* jump and *(b)* slalom courses.

Adapted from Kistler 1988.

ing the entry point. She is not penalized for this if the majority of judges agree that she had reason to refuse to enter the course.

A **pass** is registered if a skier in skiing position passes the 180-meter buoy mark on the jump course and does not make a jump, if he falls, or if his handle throw is not acceptable to the judges. Once the boat moves past the ramp, the skier must jump or pass.

A **reride** request may be made by the contestant or by a judge. A reride is allowed for unfair conditions or for faulty equipment. The reride must be taken before the next contestant starts.

A skier has **skiing position** when she has possession of the tow line; is riding on the water with a ski or skis on her feet; and, supported by her ski or skis, is able to regain control.

A judgment of **unfair conditions** can result in a reride for a competitor. Unfair conditions include malfunctioning equipment, fast slalom times, slow jump times, and short trick times.

A **wake** is the area of water disturbed by the towboat, lying at the rope's length, with the crest of the wave as the wake's nominal boundary.

COMPETITORS

Skiers compete in the following age divisions:

- Boys I/Girls I: 9 years old and under
- Boys II/Girls II: 12 and under
- Boys III/Girls III: 13-16
- Men I/Women I: 17-24
- Men II/Women II: 25-34
- Men III/Women III: 35-44
- Men IV/Women IV: 45-54
- Men V/Women V: 55-64
- Men VI/Women VI: 65-74
- Men VII/Women VII: 75 and over
- Open Men/Open Women: any age

Boys I/Girls I divisions do not compete in jumps. Skiers are rated according to ability as follows: second class, first class, expert, master, exceptional performance, and open. Ratings standards are available from the American Water Ski Association.

JUMPING

Each contestant gets three passes through the jump course. The course begins with a 180-meter buoy and ends with 100-meter buoys.

If the towboat passes the ramp, the skier must pass or jump. If the skier passes because of hazard or interference, he is allowed another pass. A skier is considered to have passed a jump if he falls within or outside the course, or if his handle throw is not acceptable to the judges. He is considered to have made a jump when he passes over the ramp, lands, and skis to the ride-out buoys without falling. The skier must regain skiing position to be credited with a scoring jump. A skier must be on his skis within three minutes of a fall, or he passes his remaining jumps.

The jumper may tell the boat driver what speed to use; the maximum speed ranges from 28 miles per hour for Boys II, Girls II, and Women VI and VII divisions to 35 miles per hour for Open Men, Men I, and Men II divisions. The jumper may tell the boat driver at what distance to pass the ramp. The driver must drive straight and parallel to the right side of the ramp.

A jumper may petition for a reride due to unfair conditions or for the boat going either too fast or too slow. The boat is timed in two segments to ascertain accurate speeds. A jumper may refuse to enter the course by throwing her handle before she reaches the course entry buoy. If the judges agree with her decision not to enter the course, she is not penalized. If they don't agree, the jumper is charged with a pass. If the jumper's handle is damaged after a throw, she is granted three minutes to repair or change the handle. If she is not ready to ski after three minutes, she may not continue that round.

Jump distances are measured from the end of the jump ramp to the point where the skier's heels reach their maximum depression in the water (usually where the plume of water rises upon landing). Distances are calculated to the nearest whole foot; a half foot or more is rounded up.

A jumper's single longest jump is her official score for the event. If two jumpers tie, then the one with the longest second jump places higher. If all three of their jumps are equal, then each tied contestant gets two more passes through the course.

SLALOM

The skier skis through the entrance gate of the slalom course and must pass around the outside of the six buoys and proceed through the far-end gate. If she has not missed any buoys or end gates, she may continue making runs through the course until she falls or misses a buoy or gate. The sponsoring club may choose to make rules exceptions or format changes if approved by the AWSA.

A *miss* is defined as riding inside a buoy or outside an end gate, or riding over, straddling, or grazing a buoy. A skier is not penalized for grazing a buoy. A fall inside or outside the course ends the run at that point.

Boat speeds range from a minimum and maximum of 16 and 30 miles per hour, respectively, for Boys I and Girls I divisions, to 30 and 36 miles per hour, respectively, for Open Men. Speed increases by 2 miles per hour on each pass, until the maximum speed for that division is reached. A skier may select his starting speed and rope length, which ranges from 10.25 to 18.25 meters. Once maximum speed is attained, the rope length is shortened on each subsequent pass, anywhere from 2.25 meters when the rope is between 18.25 and 16 meters long, to.5 meter, beginning when the rope is 11.25 meters long.

The boat is driven in a straight line through the center of the course. A reride may be granted for unfair conditions or when the boat speed is either too slow or too fast. A skier may refuse to enter the course by throwing her handle before she reaches the entry gate. If the judges agree with her decision not to enter the course, she is not penalized. If they don't agree, the skier is scored "0." Once she enters the course, she may not refuse to enter the course on subsequent passes.

If the skier's handle is damaged after a throw, she is granted three minutes to repair or change the handle. If she is not ready to ski after three minutes, she may not continue that round.

Judges mark scores for each pass. Any disagreement is decided by the majority of judges before the next pass. Skiers earn full, half-, or quarter-points for not missing a buoy or gate. In case of a tie, the skier with the most consecutive points scored wins. If skiers are still tied after this, the skier with the fastest boat speed at the shortest rope length where the miss occurred is the winner.

TRICKS

Each contestant gets two 20-second passes through the trick course. He may perform as many tricks as he can during each pass. A trick is any activity that occurs between two hesitations. To receive credit for tricks, a skier must perform tricks listed in the rules and return to skiing position. At larger tournaments the skiers must turn in their declared trick lists before they compete and perform tricks in the order listed to earn points.

A pass begins when the skier makes his first move to do a surface trick after reaching the entrance buoy, when the skier crosses a wake to attempt a wake trick, or when the skier makes no movement to do a trick as he passes the second entrance buoy. A pass ends when 20 seconds have elapsed, when the skier falls, when three minutes have elapsed while the skier is repairing or replacing equipment, or when the skier falls twice while practicing. If the skier falls at the end of the first pass and the 20 seconds have already elapsed, it is not considered a fall.

The skier may choose her boat speed, which must be maintained within one-half mile per hour. She may request a speed change by hand signal in the 50 meters before she enters the course, but if she does this she must accept whatever speed the boat attains and not ask for a reride, assuming that the speed is constant in the course.

The boat path is specified by the judges before the event; the second path is in the opposite direction of the first. The path is reasonably straight throughout the course. A skier may request a reride for unfair conditions, for boat speed that varies beyond the limit allowed, for a boat that does not follow the path, and for timing device malfunctions.

A skier may throw the handle before entering the course. He is not penalized for this if the judges agree with his reasoning for not entering. If the judges do not agree, he is charged with a fall while practicing. If a skier's handle is damaged after a throw, he may be given three minutes to repair or fix it. If he is not ready after that time, he may not continue that round. Trick skiers may use only one line; they may not use a helper line.

When a skier executes a *toe turn trick,* where she is towed by one foot, the towing foot may not touch water.

Judges score each trick; if five judges are scoring, at least three must credit a skier for a trick for the skier to receive points. The American Water Ski Association recognizes 55 tricks, with point values ranging from 20 for a sideslide on two skis to 1,000 for a wake double-flip.

If two trick skiers are tied, the skier with the highest-scoring single pass wins. If they are still tied, they get one more pass through the trick course to break the tie.

SCORING

Each event has a standard of 1,000 National Overall Performance Standards (NOPS) points. (The American Water Skiing Association provides formulas for each event.) Each contestant receives points in proportion to the standard. For example, a trick skier with 1,130 points compared to a 2,560 NOPS would get 441 overall points: $1,130/2,560 \times 1,000 = 441$.

A jumper receives points in proportion to the square of his distance to the square of the NOPS distance. For example, if the NOPS standard is 150 feet, and the jumper jumps 130 feet, he scores 751 points: $[(130 \times 130)/(150 \times 150)] \times 1,000 = 751$.

Points are carried to the first decimal (one-tenth of a point), if necessary, to break a tie. If a tie still exists, the winner is the one with the highest single-event NOPS score.

EQUIPMENT

Towboats must be able to maintain required speeds. Each is equipped with a towing pylon that has an area integrated in its design for a trick release mechanism. Tow lines are .24 inch thick and 23 meters long. An event also should have one or two safety boats in use.

Skiers must wear approved flotation devices or suits or vests designed to provide flotation. Maximum ski width must not be greater than 30 percent of the length; skiers may use any type of foot binding and fixed fins.

Boat-guide buoys may be spherical, cylindrical, rectangular, or bullet-shaped. Skier buoys are usually spherical, 22 to 28 centimeters in diameter, with 7 to 11 centimeters showing out of the water. Buoys are fastened to anchor lines.

OFFICIALS

Officials include a chief judge, an assistant chief judge, and a qualifications judge, as well as appointed judges, boat drivers, and scorers. In case of disagreement among judges, the majority rules. An issue is settled before the next contestant begins. Judges are separated, when possible, to ensure independent opinions.

ORGANIZATIONS

American Water Ski Association
www.usawaterski.org

Wrestling

Wrestling is recognized as the world's oldest sport, with records of it dating back to the 5th century B.C. It was part of the ancient Olympic Games, which began in 776 B.C., and it was part of the modern Games, which began in 1896.

The two main styles of international wrestling are *Greco-Roman* and *freestyle.* In Greco-Roman, wrestlers may not attack their opponent's legs or use their own legs to trip, lift, or execute any holds. In freestyle, wrestlers may use their legs to execute holds and to defend against attacks.

While the styles differ, the requirements for scoring points and for winning are the same. Near the end of the chapter is a section on NCAA (National Collegiate Athletic Association) rules.

Objective: To win by pinning the opponent's shoulders to the mat (a *fall*), or to win by scoring more points.

Length of Bout: International bouts are two three-minute periods with a 30-second break. Collegiate bouts are seven minutes (3-2-2). High school bouts are six minutes (2-2-2).

Scoring: Wrestlers score points in a number of ways; see "Scoring" on page 304.

Overview: Wrestlers weigh in before the competition to ensure that they are not over their weight limit and to match athletes according to size.

The referee calls the wrestlers to the center of the mat and makes sure that the wrestlers' bodies have no greasy or sticky substances on them, that they are not perspiring, and that their fingernails are cut short. The wrestlers shake hands, and when the referee blows a whistle, the bout begins. Both wrestlers start the bout standing, in a neutral position. A bout may be stopped for injury, but if the wrestler cannot continue within two minutes, the bout is over and the opponent wins.

The referee may warn one or both wrestlers regarding *passivity,* which is against the aims and spirit of all-out wrestling. After a verbal warning, if a wrestler is still passive, the referee may stop the bout and give the wrestler a formal warning. The referee then gives the more active wrestler the choice of resuming the action standing or in the *par terre* position (on the mat).

COMPETITION AREA

The *mat* is cushioned canvas or synthetic material with a diameter of 9 meters (see figure 47.1). The center circle is in the center of the mat, 1 meter in diameter. It has a thin red border. The central wrestling area is 7 meters in diameter.

The *passivity zone* is red and encircles the central wrestling area. It is 1 meter wide. The protection area surrounds the passivity zone and is 1.2 to 1.5 meters wide.

For greater visibility, the mat can be set on a platform not more than 1.1 meters high. No ropes or posts are allowed. Diagonally opposite corners of the mat are marked in red and blue.

TERMS

Most organizations have a **blood rule** that guides the course of action when a participant is bleeding.

A **bout** is the competition, or match, between two wrestlers.

A wrestler creates a **bridge** to support himself on his head, elbows, and feet, to keep from touching his shoulders to the mat.

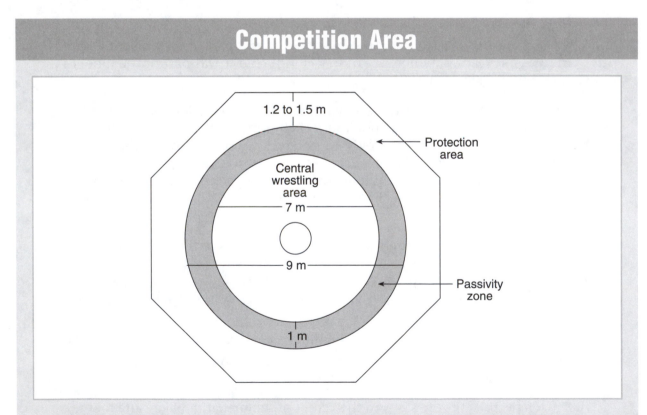

► Figure 47.1   The dimensions and features of the competition area of a wrestling match.
Adapted from USA Wrestling 1994.

Brutality is unnecessary roughness with intent to injure the opponent. A wrestler may be disqualified for such an act.

A wrestler receives a **bye** in tournament action when she has no opponent in a given round.

A **caution** may be issued for using an illegal hold, for fleeing a hold or the mat, or for refusing to take the proper starting position. A wrestler is disqualified after three cautions.

The **center circle** is 1 meter in diameter in the center of the mat. It is the starting area.

The **central wrestling area** is the middle of the mat, 7 meters across, where most of the action should take place.

A **correct hold** refers to a well-executed throw that doesn't result in a *takedown* or in putting the opponent in danger.

A **counter move** is one that stops or blocks an opponent's attack. A wrestler may score on a counter move.

A wrestler is in the **danger position** when the line of his shoulders or back forms an angle with the mat that's less than 90 degrees, and when he resists with the upper body to avoid a fall.

A **decision** refers to a victory on points, with a margin of one to nine points.

A **default** occurs when a bout is determined by injury.

A wrestler is **disqualified** after three cautions, or for misconduct.

A wrestler is awarded an **escape point** when she escapes from the bottom position and rises to a standing position to face her opponent.

A **fall** is scored when a wrestler pins his opponent's shoulders to the mat.

A wrestler **flees a hold** when she refuses contact to prevent the opponent from executing a hold. This may result in a caution, a penalty point, and choice of position for the opponent.

Fleeing the mat to elude an opponent's attack may result in a caution, a penalty point,

and choice of position for the opponent. If the fleeing occurred from a danger position, two penalty points are awarded to the opponent.

A **forfeit** occurs when a wrestler fails to show for his bout.

A **grand amplitude** hold is a high, sweeping throw during which the opponent is lifted off the mat.

A **gut wrench** is a hold applied to a wrestler's torso to turn her to score points. Two points are awarded for a gut wrench when executed in the *danger position,* one point when not in the danger position. A wrestler must score at least one technical point after scoring a gut wrench, however, before she can score on another gut wrench.

An **illegal hold** is one prohibited by the rules (see "Illegal Actions and Holds," page 305). A wrestler is cautioned for an illegal hold, and the opponent may be awarded one or two points.

Par terre position is a starting position in which one wrestler begins with hands and knees on the ground and the other wrestler begins with his hands on the back of the wrestler on the ground.

The **passivity zone** is the outermost part of the mat that is in bounds. When wrestlers reach the passivity zone, the referee calls "Zone!" and they must attempt to return to the center of the mat while not interrupting their action.

Positive points are the classification points awarded to a wrestler to determine her position in her group (see "Scoring" on page 304).

The **protection area** of the mat borders the *passivity zone* (see figure 47.1 on page 302). It is out of bounds.

A **reversal** (one point) is executed by a wrestler who comes out from underneath the other wrestler and gains control of his opponent.

A **slam** occurs when a wrestler throws an opponent down with unnecessary force without accompanying her to the mat. A slam is illegal in youth competition.

A **slip throw** is an unsuccessful attempt at a throw from either a standing position or the par terre position.

A **takedown** (one point) occurs when a wrestler takes his opponent to the mat in a position not in danger.

A **technical fall** occurs when a wrestler wins by 10 or more points (15 or more points in high school and college).

Technical points refer to points scored for holds and moves. Penalty points may also count as technical points.

WRESTLERS

Wrestlers compete in age divisions categorized by weight, as follows:

- Bantam (7 to 8): 9 weight classes from 40 to 75 pounds, plus heavyweight
- Midget (9 to 10): 15 classes from 50 to 130 pounds, plus heavyweight
- Novice (11 to 12): 17 classes from 60 to 165 pounds, plus heavyweight
- Schoolboy/girl (13 to 14): 19 classes from 70 to 175 pounds, plus heavyweight
- Cadet (15 to 16): 13 classes from 83.5 to 242 pounds
- Junior (17 to 18): 12 classes from 98 to 275 pounds
- Junior FILA (19 to 20), university (18 to 24), and senior (19 and up): 10 classes from 105 to 286 pounds

COMPETITION

Overtime happens when neither wrestler has scored three points or when the score is tied at the end of regulation. The overtime period is not longer than one regulation period. Wrestlers begin in the standing position.

The *minimum victory rule*—where a wrestler must score at least three technical points—is still in effect in overtime. The bout is over when a wrestler achieves a fall or when one competitor scores a technical point that raises his total to at least three technical points.

If neither wrestler has scored three or more technical points at the end of overtime, the wrestler with the most points wins. If the score is tied, the wrestler with the least cautions and warnings for passivity wins. If a winner can't be determined this way, officials choose a winner.

SCORING

Various moves and holds are given point values of 1, 2, 3, or 5. Following are examples of how wrestlers may score points. Wrestlers score one point when they execute a takedown (bring the opponent to the mat but do not put him in danger of a fall), execute a reversal (move out from underneath an opponent and gain control), force the opponent down on one or two outstretched arms or on his back, or compete against an opponent who flees a hold or the mat.

They also score a point when they hold the opponent in a position of danger for five seconds or longer and when they escape by breaking free while in the par terre position and rise to a standing position to face the opponent.

Wrestlers score two points when they place the opponent in a position of danger or in an instantaneous fall situation (when both the opponent's shoulders touch the mat at the same time), when they roll the opponent onto her shoulders, when they face an opponent who flees a hold while in danger, when they face an opponent who goes into an instantaneous fall or rolls onto his shoulders while executing a hold, and when they block the opponent's execution of a hold while in the standing position and in a danger position.

Wrestlers score three points when they execute a hold (a short-amplitude move), while standing, that brings the opponent to a position of danger on the mat; when they raise the opponent off the ground and place him in danger (this can happen with one or both of the attacking wrestler's knees on the ground and even if the defending wrestler maintains contact with the ground with a hand); and when they execute a grand amplitude hold that does not place the opponent in immediate danger.

Wrestlers score five points when they execute a grand amplitude hold from a standing position that places the opponent in immediate danger, and when they lift the opponent off the ground in executing a grand amplitude hold that places him in immediate danger.

The classification points awarded at the end of a bout are as follows:

- Four points for victory by fall, technical fall, injury default, withdrawal, forfeit, or disqualification

- Three points for victory by points

- One point in a loss where at least one technical point is scored by the losing wrestler

A wrestler may win a bout in a number of ways:

- She may score more points than the opponent.

- She may score a *fall* (pin her opponent's shoulders to the mat long enough for the referee to say "tombé"). Both shoulders must be simultaneously pinned against the mat long enough for the referee to observe total control. When the fall takes place at the edge of the mat, both shoulders must be completely in contact with the passivity zone; the head may not be touching the protection area. A fall in the protection area is not valid. The fall is valid when the judge or mat chairman agrees with the referee's decision. The referee strikes the mat and blows a whistle to signify a fall.

- She may score a *technical fall* (a 10-point difference; the bout is stopped when any immediate attack or counterattack is finished).

- The opponent may forfeit, withdraw, be disqualified, or be unable to continue because of injury.

ILLEGAL ACTIONS AND HOLDS

Wrestlers are not allowed to pull hair, ears, or genitals; to pinch, bite, kick, or head-butt; to strangle; to twist fingers; to use a hold that may fracture or dislocate a limb; or to act in any way to injure an opponent intentionally.

Wrestlers may not cling to the mat, talk during the bout, or grab the sole of the opponent's foot. (Grabbing the upper part of the foot or the heel is allowed.) Wrestlers may not flee a hold or flee the mat. Illegal holds include

- holding the throat;

- twisting an arm more than 90 degrees, including behind the back;

- applying a forearm lock;

- executing a three-quarter nelson or double nelson (unless executed from the side, without using the legs on any part of the opponent's body);

- stretching the opponent's spinal column;

- using two arms on an opponent's head or neck (one arm may be used);

- breaking a "bridge" by pushing in the direction of the opponent's head;

- lifting an opponent in a bridge position and throwing her to the mat; and

- holding an opponent upside down and then falling on top of her (a "header").

If a wrestler uses any of these holds, the action is void, and the wrestler is either warned or cautioned. If a defending wrestler executes an illegal hold in an attempt to prevent the attacking wrestler from executing his hold, he will be cautioned, and his opponent will be given two points.

EQUIPMENT

Wrestlers wear singlets (tight-fitting, one-piece uniforms), either red or blue, corresponding to each one's corner of the mat. Headgear to protect the ears is prohibited in international competition but is allowed in the United States at the junior and younger levels. Knee pads are permissible. Wrestlers must wear shoes with soft, pliable soles. Except in case of injury, bandages on wrists, arms, and ankles are not allowed.

OFFICIALS

Three officials work competitions: a referee, a mat chairman, and a judge. Referees work the mat and are in charge of the bout. Each referee wears a red cuff on the left arm and a blue cuff on the right arm and raises the appropriate arm and fingers to indicate points for the wrestlers.

The mat chairman is the head official and settles any disagreements between the referee and the judge. The judge marks points on a score sheet, consults with the referee, and verifies and signals a fall. He may indicate a passive wrestler. Doctors and other medical attendants may declare a wrestler unfit to continue. Officials' signals are shown in figure 47.2.

MODIFICATIONS

Modifications for National Collegiate Athletic Association rules are categorized in the following sections: mat, weight classifications and rules, match length and procedures, and scoring.

Mat

The wrestling area is circular (no less than 32 feet and no greater than 42 feet in diameter). A mat area, or apron, at least 5 feet wide, encompasses the wrestling area.

At the center of the mat is a circle, 10 feet in diameter. Inside this circle are two 1-inch starting lines; they are 3 feet long and 10 inches apart. One starting line is green and located closest to the home team; the other is red, and nearest the visitors.

Weight Classifications and Rules

Wrestlers are divided into 10 weight classifications, including

- 125 pounds,
- 133 pounds,
- 141 pounds,
- 149 pounds,
- 157 pounds,
- 165 pounds,
- 174 pounds,
- 184 pounds,
- 197 pounds, and
- heavyweight (198 pounds to 286 pounds).

For dual, triangular, and quadrangular meets, wrestlers *weigh in* 30 minutes before the meet. For tournaments, wrestlers weigh in each day.

In all tournaments, wrestlers may weigh one pound more each day, above the weight limit of the previous day (up to two pounds more). Wrestlers may not forfeit in one weight class and wrestle in another, or compete in more than one weight class in any meet. A wrestler may, however, weigh in at one weight and then shift to a higher weight class.

Match Length and Procedures

Matches last seven minutes, split into periods of three, two, and two minutes. Multiple dual meet matches and tournament matches may last less than seven minutes. Each match is begun with both wrestlers standing. A premeet coin toss determines which team has the choice of position (top, bottom, neutral) at the start of the second period. The winner may choose the odd- or even-numbered weight classes.

The wrestler with the choice of position may either make his choice or defer until the third period. If he defers, his opponent chooses the position to begin the second period. In a tournament, choice of position is determined for each match by a coin toss by the referee at the beginning of the second period. The other wrestler has the choice for the third period.

An injured or ill wrestler has up to one and a half minutes of injury timeout throughout the match. This time is cumulative, and only the referee may call such timeouts. Timeout for excessive bleeding does not count against the wrestler's one and a half minutes of injury timeout.

If the match score is tied at the end of regulation, one sudden-death overtime period, with a two-minute maximum, immediately follows. Wrestlers begin in the neutral position; the first to score wins.

Scoring

As mentioned earlier, wrestlers may score by takedown, escape, and reversal. They may also score a near fall, where a wrestler has her opponent in a controlled pinning situation for at least two seconds (two points) or at least

Indicating no control

Awarding points

Reversal

Near fall

Stalling

Unsportsmanlike conduct

(continued)

► Figure 47.2 Common wrestling officials' signals.

Stopping the match

Start the injury clock

Stop the injury clock

Out of bounds

Technical violation

Illegal hold or unnecessary roughness

(continued)

▶ Figure 47.2 *(continued)*

Indicating wrestler in control

Stalemate

Timeout

Neutral position

Potentially dangerous

▶ Figure 47.2 *(continued)*

five seconds (three points). Points may also be awarded for an imminent score, when a wrestler is injured and action is stopped just before successful completion of a scoring move that appeared imminent.

If a wrestler accumulates one minute or more of time advantage, she receives one point. Both shoulders of a wrestler must be pinned to the mat for one second for a fall to occur. Part of both shoulders must be inbounds. A technical fall occurs when a wrestler gains a 15-point advantage. (A time advantage cannot be counted toward a technical fall until regulation time expires.)

A major decision occurs when the margin of victory is between 8 and 14 points, inclusively. A decision is a victory with the margin less than 8 points. Individual and team scoring are as follows:

- Individual points: near fall, 2 or 3; takedown, 2; reversal, 2; escape, 1; time advantage, 1

- Team points, dual: fall, forfeit, default, or disqualification, 6; technical fall, 5; major decision, 4; decision, 3

- Team points, tournament: fall, forfeit, default, or disqualification, 1; bye followed by a win, championship bracket, 1; technical fall, 3/4; major decision, 1/2; bye followed by a win, consolation bracket, 1/2

ORGANIZATIONS

National Wrestling Coaches Association
P.O. Box 254
Mayheim, PA 17545
717-653-8009

USA Wrestling
6155 Lehman Drive
Colorado Springs, CO 80918
719-598-9440
www.usawrestling.org

CREDITS

Table 1.2: Adapted from International Ski Federation, 1992, *The international ski competition rules* (Switzerland: Author), 22.

Figure 2.1, Table 2.1: Adapted, by permission, from Fédération Internationale de Tir à l'Arc, 1994, *F.I.T.A. constitution and rules* (Milan, Italy: Author) 76, 77.

Figures 3.1 and 3.2: Adapted, by permission, from T.D. Jacques, 1994, *Australian football: Steps to success* (Champaign, IL: Human Kinetics), 2-3.

Figure 4.1: Adapted, by permission, from The International Badminton Federation, 1990, Badminton. In *Sports rules encyclopedia*, 2d ed., edited by J.R. White (Champaign, IL: Leisure Press), 17.

Figure 5.1: Adapted, by permission, from J.R. White, 1990, *Sports rules encyclopedia*, 2d ed. (Champaign, IL: Leisure Press), 27.

Figure 6.1: Adapted, by permission, from J.R. White, 1990, *Sports rules encyclopedia*, 2d ed. (Champaign, IL: Leisure Press), 38.

Figure 7.2: Adapted, courtesy of American Bowling Congress/Women's International Bowling Congress/ Young American Bowling Congress, 1995, *1995-96 playing rules book* (Greendale, WI: American Bowling Congress), 6.

Table 8.1: Adapted, by permission, from United States Amateur Boxing, Inc., 1995, *USA boxing: official rules 1995-1997* (Colorado Springs: Author), 57, 59.

Figure 10.1: Adapted, by permission, from T. Melville, 1993, *Cricket for Americans: Playing and understanding the game* (Bowling Green, OH: Bowling Green State University Popular Press), 5.

Table 11.1: Adapted, by permission, from United States Ski and Snowboard Association, 1993, *Cross country rulebook* (Park City, UT: Author), 64-65.

Figure 12.1: Adapted, courtesy of, USA Curling ™, 1995, *U.S. Curling Association rules for play 1995/ 96* (Stevens Point, WI: Author), 2.

Figure 13.1: Adapted, by permission, from The Diagram Group, 1983, *The rulebook* (New York, NY: St. Martin's Press), 74.

Figures 15.1 and 15.2: Adapted, by permission, from United States Fencing Association, 1994, *United States Fencing Association rulebook* (Colorado Springs: author), 4.

Figure 18.1: Adapted, by permission, from National Football League, 1994, *Official rules of the NFL* (Chicago, IL: Triumph Books).

Tables 19.1 and 19.2 Adapted, by permission, from United States Golf Association, 2002, *USGA Handicap System Manual*.

Figures 20.1 and 20.2 Adapted, by permission, from USA Gymnastics.

Figure 21.1: Adapted, by permission, from U.S. Handball Association, 1991, *The new and official United States Handball Association rulebook* (Tucson, AZ: Author), 38.

Figure 22.1: Adapted, by permission, from USA Hockey, 1990, Ice hockey. In *Sports rules encyclopedia*, 2d ed., edited by J.R. White (Champaign, IL: Leisure Press), 343.

Table 22.2: Adapted, by permission, from USA Hockey, 1993, *Official playing rules 1993-95* (Colorado Springs: Author), 12.

Figure 23.1: Adapted, by permission, from International Judo Federation. *Home page.* [Online]. Available WWW (World Wide Web): http://www.ijf.org/24.gif (2002).

Figure 24.1: Adapted, by permission, from USA Karate Federation, 1995, *USA Karate rules and regulations for competitions including the World Karate Federation rules for competition* (Akron, OH: Author), 2.

Figure 25.1: Adapted, by permission, from U.S. Women's Lacrosse Association, 1996, *Official rules for women's lacrosse* (Chevy Chase, MD: Author), 11, 15.

Figure 25.2: Adapted, by permission, from National Collegiate Athletic Association, 1996, *NCAA lacrosse men's rules* (Overland Park, KS: Author), 10.

Figure 26.1: Adapted, by permission, from Wilma Shakespear, 1997, *Netball: Steps to success* (Champaign, IL: Human Kinetics), 3.

Figure 28.1: Adapted, by permission, from USA Roller Skating, *USA roller hockey rules*, 2d ed. (Lincoln, NE: Author), 7.

Figure 28.2: Adapted, by permission, from USA Roller Skating.

Table 29.1: Adapted, by permission, from U.S. Rowing Association, 1996, *1996 rules of rowing* (Indianapolis, IN: Author), 36.

Figure 30.1: Adapted, by permission from J.T. Powell, 1976, *Inside rugby: the team game* (Washington, D.C.: Regnery Publishing, Inc.), 7.

Figure 31.1: Adapted, by permission, from American Coaching Effectiveness Program, 1991, *Rookie coaches soccer guide* (Champaign, IL: Human Kinetics), 39.

Figure 32.1: Adapted, by permission, from J.R. White, 1990, *Sports rules encyclopedia*, 2d ed. (Champaign, IL: Leisure Press), 27.

Figure 33.1: Adapted, by permission, from Amateur Speedskating Union of the United States, 1988, *1988-1989 Amateur Skating Union handbook* (Glen Ellyn, IL: Author), 70.

Figure 34.1: Adapted, by permission, from U.S. Squash Racquets Association, *International rules of squash* (Bala-Cynwyd, PA: Author), 23.

Figure 37.1: Adapted, by permission, from United States Table Tennis Association, 1990, Table tennis. In *Sports rules encyclopedia* 2d ed., edited by J.R. White (Champaign, IL: Leisure Press), 543.

Figure 38.1: Adapted, by permission, from International Judo Federation. *Home page*. [Online]. Available WWW (World Wide Web): http://www.ijf.org/24.gif (April 1997).

Figure 39.1: Adapted, by permission, from International Handball Federation,1993, *International handball federation: rules of the game* (Switzerland: Author), 7.

Figure 40.1: Adapted, by permission, from United States Tennis Association, Inc., 1995, *1995 rules of tennis and cases and decisions* (White Plains, NY: Author), 2.

Figure 41.1: Adapted, by permission, from The Athletics Congress's Development Committees and V. Gambetta, 1981, *The Athletic Congress's track and field coaching manual* (Champaign, IL: Leisure Press), 1.

Tables 42.1, 42.2, 42.3: Adapted, by permission, from USA Track and Field, 1995, *Competition rules 1995* (Indianapolis, IN: Author), 97, 154, 152.

Table 44.1: Adapted, by permission, from USA Volleyball, 1995, *United States Volleyball official rules* (Lynn, MA: H.O. Zimman, Inc.), 13.

Figure 44.1: Adapted, by permission, from Federation Internationale de Volleyball, 1997, *Official 1995 United States Volleyball rules as approved by USA Volleyball*, edited by J.B. Blue (France: Author), 81.

Figure 45.1: Adapted, by permission, from United States Water Polo, Inc., 1990, Water polo abridgment of official water polo rules. In *Sports rules encyclopedia*, 2d ed., edited by J.R. White (Champaign, IL: Human Kinetics), 659.

Figure 46.1: Adapted, by permission, from B. Kistler, 1988, *Hit it: your complete guide to water skiing* (Champaign, IL: Leisure Press), 124.

Figure 47.1: Adapted, by permission, from USA Wrestling, 1997, *International rulebook and guide to wrestling 1997 edition* (Colorado Springs, CO: Author), 15.

REFERENCES

Amateur Softball Association/USA Softball (1993). *'94 ASA guide & playing rules.* Oklahoma City: Author.

Amateur Speedskating Union of the United States (1995). *Speedskating handbook.* Author.

American Amateur Racquetball Association (1995). *1995-96 official rules of racquetball.* Colorado Springs: Author.

American Horse Shows Association (1995). *The American Horse Shows Association rule book 1996-1997.* New York City, NY: Author.

American Water Ski Association (1996). *Official tournament rules.* Winter Haven, FL: Author.

Babe Ruth Baseball (1995). *Bambino division rules and regulations.* Trenton, NJ: Author.

Broido, B. (1992). *Spalding book of rules and 1993 sports almanac.* Indianapolis: Masters Press.

East, A. *Frequently asked questions (FAQ) for rec.sport. football.australian.* [Online]. Available WWW (World Wide Web): www.ozsports.com.au/Football/FAQ.html (April 30, 1977).

Fédération Internationale de Football Association (1994). *Official rules of soccer.* Chicago: Triumph Books.

Gullion, L. (1993). *Nordic skiing: Steps to success.* Champaign, IL: Human Kinetics.

Jacques, Trevor D. (1994). *Australian football: Steps to success.* Champaign, IL: Human Kinetics.

International Archery Federation (1994). *Constitution and rules: FITA.* Milan, Italy: Author.

International Biathlon Union (1994). *Event & competition rules.* Wals-Himmelreich, Austria: Author.

International Canoe Federation (1993). *Flatwater racing competition rules.* Budapest: Author.

International Canoe Federation (1993). *Slalom and wildwater racing competition rules.* Budapest: Author.

International Federation of Netball Associations (1991). *Official rules.* Mosman, Australia: Author.

International Gymnastics Federation (1989). *Code of points: Artistic gymnastic for men.* Switzerland: Author.

International Gymnastics Federation (1989). *Code of points: Artistic gymnastic for women.* Switzerland: Author.

International Handball Federation (1993). *Rules of the game.* Basel, Switzerland: Author.

International Hockey Federation (1995). *Rules of hockey 1995.* Surrey, England: Author.

International Rugby Football Board. *The laws of the game of rugby football.* [Online]. Available WWW (World Wide Web): http://rugby.phys.uidaho.edu/rugby/Rules/LawBook/contents.html (April 30, 1997).

International Ski Federation (1992). *The international ski competition rules.* Berne, Switzerland: Author.

Magnay, J. (1991). *8th world netball championship—Sydney 1991.* Hornsby, Australia: Chevron Publishing Group.

Major League Baseball (1994). *Official baseball rules (1994 edition).* St. Louis: The Sporting News.

Melville, T. (1993). *Cricket for Americans: Playing and understanding the game.* Bowling Green, OH: Bowling Green State University Popular Press.

National Collegiate Athletic Association (1996). *1996 NCAA men's lacrosse rules.* Overland Park, KS: Author.

The National Collegiate Athletic Association (1995). *1995 offical rules of basketball.* Chicago: Triumph Books.

The National Collegiate Athletic Association (1992). *1993 NCAA wrestling: Rules and interpretations.* Overland Park, KS: Author.

National Federation of State High Schools (1995). *High school soccer rules book.* Kansas City, MO: Author.

National Football League (1994). *Official rules of the NFL.* Chicago: Triumph Books.

National Hockey League (1994). *1995 official rules of the NHL.* Chicago: Triumph Books.

National Off-Road Bicycle Association (1995). *1995 competition guide: National off-road bicycle association.* Colorado Springs: Author.

NBA Properties (1994). *1994-95 official NBA rules.* St. Louis: The Sporting News.

PONY Baseball (1995). *Pony baseball 1994-95 rules and regulations.* Washington, PA: Author.

Pop Warner Football (1994). *The complete set of official rules: 1994, 1995, 1996.* Langhorne, PA: Author.

Professional Publications, Inc. (1994). *Soccer: Do you know the rules?* Belmont, CA: Blue Moose Press.

Soccer Association for Youth (1995). *SAY soccer rules.* Cincinnati: Author.

Thomas, M. (1994). *Know the game: Netball.* London: Black.

Ultimate Players Association: *10th Edition Rules* [Online]. Available WWW (World Wide Web): www.upa.org (April 14, 2003).

United States Amateur Confederation of Roller Skating (no date). *USA roller hockey rules.* Lincoln, NE: Author.

United States Badminton Association (1995). *Official rules of play & court officials handbook.* Colorado Springs: Author.

United States Curling Association (1995). *Rules of play 1995-96: Club and bonspiel use.* Stevens Point, WI: Author.

United States Diving (1995). *United States diving rules & regulations 95-96.* Indianapolis: Author.

United States Fencing Association (1994). *United States Fencing Association rule book.* Colorado Springs: Author.

United States Figure Skating Association (1995). *The 1996 official USFSA rulebook.* Colorado Springs: Author.

United States Flag & Touch Football League (1994). *1994-95 official rule book & constitution: United States flag & touch football league.* Mentor, OH: Author.

The United States Golf Association and the Royal and Ancient Golf Club of St. Andrews, Scotland (1994). *1995 official rules of golf.* Chicago: Triumph Books.

United States Handball Association (1991). *The new and official United States Handball Association rulebook.* Tucson: Author.

United States Judo Association (1994). *1994 contest rules of the international judo federation.* Colorado Springs: Author.

The United States Rowing Association (1996). *1996 rules of rowing.* Indianapolis: Author.

United States Ski Association (1993). *Cross country rulebook.* Park City, UT: Author.

United States Squash Racquets Association (1993). *The international rules of squash.* Bala Cynwyd, PA: Author.

United States Squash Racquets Association (1987). *The rules of squash.* Bala Cynwyd, PA: Author.

United States Swimming (1996). *United States Swimming 1996 rules and regulations.* Colorado Springs: Author.

United States Synchronized Swimming (1995). *1995-1996 United States Synchronized Swimming official rules.* Indianapolis: Author.

United States Taekwondo Union (1993). *United States Taekwondo Union: School/club handbook.* Colorado Springs: Author.

United States Team Handball Federation (1996). *Basic rules of team handball.* Colorado Springs: Author.

United States Tennis Association (1995). *1995 rules of tennis & cases and decisions.* White Plains, NY: H.O. Zimman.

United States Water Polo, Inc. (1996). *1996 water polo playing rules.* Colorado Springs: Author.

United States Women's Lacrosse Association (1995). *Official rules for women's lacrosse: 1995.* Hamilton, NY: Author.

U.S. Cycling Federation (1995). *1995 rules of bicycle racing.* Colorado Springs: Author.

U.S. Youth Soccer (1995). *The official U.S. youth soccer 8 v 8 program under ten.* Richardson, TX: Author.

U.S. Youth Soccer (1995). *The small sided game: The official U.S. youth soccer 3 v 3 program under six.* Richardson, TX: Author.

U.S. Youth Soccer (1995). *The small sided game: The official U.S. youth soccer 4 v 4 program under eight.* Richardson, TX: Author.

USA Boxing (1995). *USA boxing: Official rules 1995-1997.* Colorado Springs: Author.

USA Hockey (1993). *Official playing rules 1993-95.* Colorado Springs: Author.

USA Karate Federation (1995). *USA karate rules and regulations for competitions.* Akron: Author.

USA Table Tennis (1994). *The law of table tennis.* Colorado Springs: Author.

USA Track & Field (1995). *Competition rules 1995.* Indianapolis: Author.

USA Triathlon (1996). *Tri-Fed/USA competitive rules.* Colorado Springs: Author.

USA Volleyball (1995). *1996 United States volleyball official rules.* Lynn, MA: H.O. Zimman.

USA Wrestling (1995). *International rule book & guide to wrestling: Freestyle and Greco-Roman, 1995 edition.* Colorado Springs: Author.

White, J.R. (1990). *Sports rules encyclopedia (second edition).* Champaign, IL: Human Kinetics.

Women's International Bowling Congress and American Bowling Congress (1994). *Playing rules 1994-95: ABC/WIBC.* Greendale, WI: Authors.

Yacenda, J. (1992). *Alpine skiing: Steps to success.* Champaign, IL: Human Kinetics.

ABOUT THE AUTHORS

Human Kinetics began in 1974 in the basement of Rainer Martens' home in Champaign, Illinois, when Martens—then a professor at the University of Illinois—decided to publish the proceedings of a sport psychology conference he had organized.

Human Kinetics has grown to be the world's largest producer of information in the physical activity field and is the premier publisher in sports and fitness. The company is also committed to developing quality resources in such areas as sport and exercise science, physical education, and coaching.

Their world headquarters is based in Champaign, Illinois, where they employ more than 270 people in more than 130,000 square feet of office and warehouse facilities. HK's offices in England, Canada, Australia, and New Zealand bolster international efforts.

To learn more about the products developed within the many divisions of Human Kinetics, please visit www.HumanKinetics.com.

Thomas Hanlon has written 22 books, mostly for Human Kinetics. He also acted as a ghostwriter for *Teens Can Make It Happen* for Stedman Graham, which made the *New York Times* Bestseller List in 2000. Hanlon, an avid runner and sports enthusiast, lives in Champaign, Illinois, with his wife, Janet, and their two children.